D0282809

THE COMPLETE SPELLERS' DICTIONARY

DAVID DOWNING

ILLUSTRATIONS BY **MARIO RISSO**

Gramercy Books
New York

This combined edition includes the full text of the two volumes published separately as:

SPELL IT RIGHT DICTIONARY Copyright ©1992 by NTC Publishing Group
303 DUMB SPELLING MISTAKES... and what you can do about them
Copyright ©1990 by NTC/Contemporary Publishing Group

This 2001 edition is published by Gramercy Books™, an imprint of
Random House Value Publishing, Inc., 280 Park Avenue, New York, NY 10017,
by arrangement with NTC/Contemporary Publishing Group.

Gramercy Books™ and design are trademarks of
Random House Value Publishing, Inc.

Printed in the United States of America

Random House
New York • Toronto • London • Sydney • Auckland
http://www.randomhouse.com/

(Originally published as: *Spell It Right Dictionary* and *303 Dumb Spelling Mistakes...and what you can do about them*)

Library of Congress Cataloging-in-Publication Data

Downing, David C.
  The complete spellers' dictionary / David Downing ; illustrations by Mario Risso.
      p. cm.
  "This combined edition includes the full text of two volumes published separately as:
Spell it right dictionary ... [and] 303 dumb spelling mistakes ... and what you can do
about them"—T.p. verso.
  ISBN 0-517-16381-0
    1. English language—Orthography and spelling—Dictionaries. 2. Spellers. I. Risso,
Mario, 1926- II. Downing, David C. NTC's spell it right dictionary. III. Downing, David
C. 303 dumb spelling misstakes—and what you can do about them. IV. Title.

PE1146 .D834 2001
423'.1—dc21

                              00-066286

8 7 6 5 4 3 2

To the User

If you don't know how to spell a word, you are supposed to look it up in a dictionary. But how can you look it up if you don't know how to spell it?

For example, if you are not sure how to spell the word for a compulsive thief, you might try looking up "cleptomaniac." In a regular dictionary all your searching in the *c*'s would be in vain, because the word you need begins with a *k*: *kleptomaniac*. And if you gave up on the fancy word and started looking for "theif," you would have just as little success: *Thief* is one of those "*i* before *e*" words.

NTC's Spell It Right Dictionary is designed to help you discover the correct spelling of a word quickly and easily. It includes over 7,000 commonly misspelled words and over 17,000 ways in which those words are most likely to be misspelled. It also includes many words that are commonly confused.

The *Dictionary* is easy to use. Simply look up a word under your best guess at its correct spelling. In the alphabetical word list, you will find an entry that

- identifies the spelling as correct;
- identifies the spelling as incorrect and provides the correct spelling; or
- distinguishes between two or more words commonly confused.

English spelling can be quite illogical. Some of the irregularities can be traced to the language's checkered (or is it *chequered*?) past, especially its many borrowings from other languages. Differences between American and British usage add a bit of craziness. The few "rules" that do help make sense of American English spelling are listed in the Appendix at the end of the *Dictionary*.

How to Use This Dictionary

NTC's Spell It Right Dictionary is designed to help you quickly resolve questions of spelling and usage. Here's how it works:

1. Correct spellings are printed in **boldface type** and syllabified. For example:

   pre·scrip·tion

2. Incorrect spellings appear in lightface type without syllabication. They are followed by a colon and the correct spelling printed in **boldface type** and syllabified. For example:

   perscription : **pre·scrip·tion**

3. Spellings that are acceptable British variants appear in lightface type without syllabication. They are followed by the designation *Brit.* in parentheses, then by the preferred American spelling printed in **boldface type** and syllabified. For example:

   acknowledgement (*Brit.*) : **ac·knowl·edg·ment**

4. Entries for easily confused words provide additional information so that you can readily identify the word you need. Entries for easily confused words include brief definitions or synonyms and parts of speech in parentheses. If an incorrect spelling might lend itself to more than one correct spelling, all possible words (and their definitions) are offered. For example:

   ad·vice (*noun*); **ad·vise** (*verb*)
   dear (precious); **deer** (animal)
   it's (it is); **its** (belonging to it)
   per·ish (to cease to exist); **par·ish** (church community)
   exept : **ac·cept** (to receive) *or* **ex·cept** (to exclude)

5. Because English spelling is so arbitrary, often more than one form (or variant) of a word is in current usage. Variants of a word that are used with essentially the same frequency are listed in alphabetical order in the word list. However, an incorrect spelling refers only to the variant that comes first alphabetically or that is in slightly more frequent use in American English. Less commonly used variants are listed as incorrect spellings. For example:

levaled : **lev·eled**
lev·eled *or* **lev·elled**
lev·elled *or* **lev·eled**
Ju·go·sla·via *or* **Yu·go·sla·via**
Yugaslovia : **Yu·go·sla·via**
Yu·go·sla·via *or* **Ju·go·sla·via**

A Note on Syllabication

The words listed in this *Dictionary* have dots (·) to indicate where each word may be hyphenated if it is divided at the end of a line. In general, you should follow these guidelines when hyphenating words:

1. Do not divide one-syllable words. If a one-syllable word will not fit at the end of a line, type the whole word on the next line.

2. Do not leave only one letter at the end of one line (*o·ver, i·dea*) or at the beginning of the next (*word·y, Ohi·o*).

3. Avoid hyphenating the last word on a page.

4. If a word already contains a hyphen, divide it at the hyphen (*self-· esteem,* not *self-es·teem*).

5. In general, words with double consonants may be divided between the consonants (*ar·rogant, fal·lible*). However, when a suffix is added to a root word ending in double consonants, the hyphen comes after both consonants (*kiss·ing, stroll·ing*).

Terms and Abbreviations

adj.	adjective	*noun*	
adv.	adverb	*past of*	past tense of verb
Brit.	British variant spelling	*plur.*	plural form of noun
fem.	feminine form of word	*sing.*	singular form of noun
masc.	masculine form of word	*verb*	

A

abait : **abate**
abalish : **abol·ish**
ab·a·lo·ne
abaloney : **ab·a·lo·ne**
abanden : **aban·don**
aban·don
abarigine : **ab·o·rig·i·ne**
abarrance : **ab·er·rance**
abate
abayance : **abey·ance**
abbandon : **aban·don**
abbate : **abate**
abberance : **ab·er·rance**
ab·bess (head of convent);
   abyss (bottomless pit)
abbet : **ab·bot**
ab·bey
abblaze : **ablaze**
abboard : **aboard**
ab·bot
ab·bre·vi·ate
abbrieviate : **ab·bre·vi·ate**
abbuse : **abuse**
abby : **ab·bey**
abcess : **ab·scess**
   (inflammation) *or* **ob·sess** (to
   preoccupy)
abdecate : **ab·di·cate**
ab·di·cate
ab·do·men
abdomenal : **ab·dom·i·nal**
abdomin : **ab·do·men**
ab·dom·i·nal
abducion : **ab·duc·tion**
ab·duc·tion
aberence : **ab·er·rance**
ab·er·rance
ab·er·rant
aberrent : **ab·er·rance**
abey·ance

abeyence : **abey·ance**
abhominable : **abom·i·na·ble**
ab·hor
abhorance : **ab·hor·ence**
ab·hor·ence
abil·i·ty
abillity : **abil·i·ty**
abismal : **abys·mal**
abiss : **abyss**
ab·jure (to renounce); **ad·jure**
   (to ask)
ablaize : **ablaze**
ablaze
abley : **ably**
ablivion : **obliv·i·on**
ably
abnagate : **ab·ne·gate**
ab·ne·gate
abnigate : **ab·ne·gate**
ab·nor·mal
abnormel : **ab·nor·mal**
abnoxious : **ob·nox·ious**
aboard
abol·ish
abolission : **ab·o·li·tion**
ab·o·li·tion
abollish : **abol·ish**
abolone : **ab·a·lo·ne**
abomanable : **abom·i·na·ble**
abom·i·na·ble
abor : **ab·hor**
abord : **aboard**
aborence : **ab·hor·ence**
ab·o·rig·i·ne
aboriginnie : **ab·o·rig·i·ne**
aboriginy : **ab·o·rig·i·ne**
abracive : **abra·sive**
abrade
abraid : **abrade**
abra·sive

1

abreast
abregate : **ab•ro•gate**
abrest : **abreast**
abreviate : **ab•bre•vi•ate**
abridgement (*Brit.*) :
   abridg•ment
abridg•ment
abrieviate : **ab•bre•vi•ate**
ab•ro•gate
abrubt : **abrupt**
abrupt
absalute : **ab•so•lute**
absalutely : **ab•so•lute•ly**
abscence : **ab•sence**
ab•scess (inflammation) *or*
   ob•sess (to preoccupy)
ab•sence
absensce : **ab•sence**
absense : **ab•sence**
ab•sen•tee
absentie : **ab•sen•tee**
absenty : **ab•sen•tee**
abserd : **ab•surd**
absess : **ab•scess**
   (inflammation) *or* **ob•sess** (to
   preoccupy)
ab•so•lute
ab•so•lute•ly
absolutly : **ab•so•lute•ly**
ab•sorb
absorbant : **ab•sorb•ent**
ab•sorb•ent
absorbtion : **ab•sorp•tion**
ab•sorp•tion
abstainence : **ab•sti•nence**
abstanence : **ab•sti•nence**
abstinance : **ab•sti•nence**
ab•sti•nence
ab•surd
abun•dance
abun•dant
abundence : **abun•dance**

abundent : **abun•dant**
abuse
abut•ment
abuttment : **abut•ment**
abuze : **abuse**
abys•mal
abyss (bottomless pit); **ab•bess**
   (head of convent)
abyssmal : **abys•mal**
abzerd : **ab•surd**
aca•cia
ac•a•dem•ic
ac•a•dem•i•cal•ly
academicly : **ac•a•dem•i•cal•ly**
acasha : **aca•cia**
accademy : **acad•em•y**
accasion : **oc•ca•sion**
ac•cede (to agree reluctantly);
   ex•ceed (to go beyond)
acceed : **ac•cede**
accelarate : **ac•cel•er•ate**
ac•cel•er•ate
accelerater : **ac•cel•er•a•tor**
ac•cel•er•a•tor
ac•cent
ac•cept (to receive); **ex•cept** (to
   exclude)
ac•cept•able
ac•cept•ance
acceptible : **ac•cept•able**
accesory : **ac•ces•so•ry**
ac•cess
accessable : **ac•ces•si•ble**
accessery : **ac•ces•so•ry**
ac•ces•si•ble
ac•ces•sion
ac•ces•so•ry
accidant : **ac•ci•dent**
ac•ci•dent
ac•ci•den•tal•ly
accidently : **ac•ci•den•tal•ly**
ac•claim

ac·cli·ma·tize
accommadate :
　ac·com·mo·date
ac·com·mo·date
accomodate : ac·com·mo·date
ac·com·pa·ni·ment
accompanyment :
　ac·com·pa·ni·ment
ac·com·plice
accomplis : ac·com·plice
ac·com·plish
ac·cord
accordien : ac·cor·di·on
ac·cor·di·on
ac·count·able
ac·count·ant
accountent : ac·count·ant
ac·cou·ter·ment or
　ac·cou·tre·ment
accoutrament : ac·cou·tre·ment
ac·cou·tre·ment or
　ac·cou·ter·ment
accross : across
accummulate : ac·cu·mu·late
ac·cu·mu·late
ac·cu·mu·la·tion
ac·cu·ra·cy
ac·cu·rate
accurisy : ac·cu·ra·cy
accurite : ac·cu·rate
ac·cu·sa·tion
ac·cuse
ac·cus·tom
ac·cus·tomed
accustommed : ac·cus·tomed
accutrement : ac·cou·tre·ment
acedemic : aca·dem·ic
acelerate : ac·cel·er·ate
acent : ac·cent
acept : ac·cept
acer·bic
acertain : as·cer·tain

acess : ac·cess
acessible : ac·ces·si·ble
acession : ac·ces·sion
acessory : ac·ces·so·ry
acetic : as·cet·ic
acheive : achieve
achieve
achieve·ment
acident : ac·ci·dent
acknowledgement (*Brit.*) :
　ac·knowl·edg·ment
ac·knowl·edg·ment
acknowlege : ac·knowl·edge
ackumen : acu·men
aclaim : ac·claim
aclimatize : ac·cli·ma·tize
acommodate : ac·com·mo·date
acompaniment :
　ac·com·pa·ni·ment
acomplice : ac·com·plice
acomplish : ac·com·plish
acord : ac·cord
acordion : ac·cor·di·on
acountent : ac·count·ant
acousticks : acous·tics
acous·tics
acoutrement : ac·cou·tre·ment
ac·quain·tance
acquaintence : ac·quain·tance
acquaintense : ac·quain·tance
acquatic : aqua·tic
ac·qui·esce
acquiese : ac·qui·esce
acquiesse : ac·qui·esce
ac·quire
ac·qui·si·tion
ac·quit
acquited : ac·quit·ted
ac·quit·tal
ac·quit·ted
acquittel : ac·quit·tal
acrage : acre·age

acre
acre•age
acrebat : acro•bat
acrige : acre•age
across
actavate : ac•ti•vate
acter : ac•tor
acteress : ac•tress
ac•ti•vate
ac•tor
actoress : ac•tress
ac•tress
ac•tu•al
ac•tu•al•ly
actule : ac•tu•al
actully : ac•tu•al•ly
acu•men
acumin : acu•men
acummulation :
  ac•cu•mu•la•tion
acumulate : ac•cu•mu•late
acumulation : ac•cu•mu•la•tion
acuracy : ac•cu•ra•cy
acurate : ac•cu•rate
acusation : ac•cu•sa•tion
acuse : ac•cuse
acustics : acous•tics
acustom : ac•cus•tom
ad (advertisement); add (to
  combine)
ad•age
ad•a•mant
adament : ad•a•mant
adapt (to modify); adept
  (skilled); adopt (to accept)
adapt•able
adapt•er
adaptible : adapt•able
adaptor : adapt•er
adaquacy : ade•qua•cy
adaquate : ade•quate

add (to combine); ad
  (advertisement)
add hoc : ad hoc
add lib : ad lib
addage : ad•age
addative : ad•di•tive
ad•den•da (plur.); ad•den•dum
  (sing.)
ad•den•dum (sing.); ad•den•da
  (plur.)
addept : ad•ept
addick : ad•dict
ad•dict
ad•dic•tion
ad•di•tion (adding); e•di•tion
  (book)
ad•di•tive
addopt : adopt
addrenalin : ad•ren•a•line
ad•dress
addulation : ad•u•la•tion
addult : adult
addulterer : adul•ter•er
addulteress : adul•ter•ess
addultery : adul•ter•y
adeau : adieu
adeiu : adieu
adelescence : ad•o•les•cence
adendum : ad•den•dum
adept (skilled); adapt (to
  modify); adopt (to accept)
adequasy : ade•qua•cy
ade•quate
adequit : ade•quate
adhear : ad•here
adherance : ad•her•ence
ad•her•ence (quality of
  adhering); ad•her•ents
  (followers)
ad hoc
adhoc : ad hoc
adhock : ad hoc

adict : **ad•dict**
adiction : **ad•dic•tion**
adieu (good-bye); **ado** (fuss)
adige : **adage**
ad•ja•cent
adjasent : **ad•ja•cent**
ad•jec•tive
ad•join
ad•journ
ad•ju•di•cate
ad•jure (to ask); **ab•jure** (to renounce)
adjurn : **ad•journ**
ad•just
ad•just•able
adjustible : **ad•just•able**
ad•ju•tant
adjutent : **ad•ju•tant**
ad-lib
admaral : **ad•mir•al**
admendment : **amend•ment**
admeration : **ad•mi•ra•tion**
adminester : **ad•min•is•ter**
ad•min•is•ter
administerate : **ad•min•is•trate**
ad•min•is•trate
administrater : **ad•min•is•tra•tor**
adminition : **ad•mo•ni•tion**
adminster : **ad•min•is•ter**
ad•mi•ral
ad•mir•er
admirerer : **ad•mir•er**
admiror : **ad•mir•er**
admision : **ad•mis•sion**
admissable : **ad•mis•si•ble**
ad•mis•si•ble
admitance : **ad•mit•tance**
admited : **ad•mit•ted**
ad•mit•tance
ad•mit•ted
admittence : **ad•mit•tance**

admittense : **ad•mit•tance**
ad•mo•ni•tion
ado (fuss); **adieu** (good-bye)
ado•be
adobie : **ado•be**
adoby : **ado•be**
adolecense : **ado•les•cence**
adolecent : **ado•les•cent**
ado•les•cence
ado•les•cent
adolesence : **ado•les•cence**
adolesense : **ado•les•cence**
adolesent : **ado•les•cent**
adom : **atom**
adoo : **adieu** (good-bye) *or* **ado** (fuss)
adopt (to accept); **adapt** (to modify); **adept** (skilled)
ador•able
adorible : **ador•able**
adorn
adorn•ment
adourn : **adorn**
adournment : **adorn•ment**
adrenalin : **ad•ren•a•line**
ad•ren•a•line
adrenlin : **ad•ren•a•line**
adrenolin : **ad•ren•a•line**
adres : **ad•dress**
adress : **ad•dress**
adrinalin : **ad•ren•a•line**
adsorb : **ab•sorb**
adsorption (*Brit.*) : **ab•sorp•tion**
adu•la•tion
adult
adultarate : **adul•ter•ate**
adul•ter•er
adul•ter•ess
adulteror : **adul•ter•er**
adul•ter•y
adultrer : **adul•ter•er**

adultress : **adul·ter·ess**
adultry : **adul·ter·y**
advacate : **ad·vo·cate**
advacator : **ad·vo·ca·tor**
ad·vance
advanse : **ad·vance**
ad·van·tage
ad·van·ta·geous
advantagious : **ad·van·ta·geous**
advantige : **ad·van·tage**
advenchure : **ad·ven·ture**
ad·ven·ture
ad·ven·tur·er
adventuror : **ad·ven·tur·er**
adventurur : **ad·ven·tur·er**
adversarry : **ad·ver·sary**
ad·ver·sary
ad·verse (unfavorable); **averse**
   (disinclined)
ad·ver·tise·ment
ad·ver·tis·er
advertisor : **ad·ver·tis·er**
advertize (*Brit.*) : **ad·ver·tise**
advertizer (*Brit.*) : **ad·ver·tis·er**
advertizing (*Brit.*) :
   ad·ver·tis·ing
ad·vice (*noun*); **ad·vise** (*verb*)
ad·vis·able
ad·vise (*verb*); **ad·vice** (*noun*)
ad·vis·ed·ly
ad·vis·er *or* **ad·vis·or**
advisible : **ad·vis·able**
advisidly : **ad·vis·ed·ly**
ad·vis·or *or* **ad·vis·er**
advizable : **ad·vis·able**
advizer : **ad·vis·er**
ad·vo·cate
advocater : **ad·vo·ca·tor**
ad·vo·ca·tor
aeleron : **ai·le·ron**
aer·ate
aer·i·al

ae·rie (nest); **airy** (relating to
   air); **ee·rie** (weird)
aero·dy·na·mic
aerodynamick : **aero·dy·nam·ic**
aeronatic : **aero·nau·tic**
aero·nau·tic
aeronawtic : **aero·nau·tic**
aeronotic : **aero·nau·tic**
aeronottic : **aero·nau·tic**
aero·sol
aes·thet·ic *or* **es·thet·ic**
afability : **af·fa·bil·i·ty**
afable : **af·fa·ble**
afadavit : **af·fi·da·vit**
afair : **af·fair**
afare : **af·fair**
afect : **af·fect**
afection : **af·fec·tion**
af·fa·bil·i·ty
affabillity : **af·fa·bil·i·ty**
af·fa·ble
affadavet : **af·fi·da·vit**
affadavid : **af·fi·da·vit**
affadavit : **af·fi·da·vit**
af·fair
affare : **af·fair**
af·fect (to influence); **ef·fect**
   (result; to bring about
   results)
affense : **of·fense**
affibility : **af·fa·bil·i·ty**
affible : **af·fa·ble**
af·fi·da·vit
af·fil·i·ate
affilliate : **af·fil·i·ate**
af·fin·i·ty
af·fir·ma·tive
affirmitive : **af·fir·ma·tive**
affluance : **af·flu·ence**
affluant : **af·flu·ent**
af·flu·ence

af•flu•ent (prosperous);
  ef•flu•ent (flowing out)
affraid : **afraid**
Afgan : **Af•ghan**
Afganistan : **Af•ghan•i•stan**
Af•ghan
Afghanastan : **Af•ghan•i•stan**
Af•ghan•i•stan
afiliate : **af•fil•i•ate**
afinity : **af•fin•i•ty**
afirm : **af•firm**
afirmative : **af•fir•ma•tive**
afluent : **af•flu•ent**
afore•said
aforism : **aph•o•rism**
aforsaid : **afore•said**
afrade : **afraid**
afraid
against
aganize : **ag•o•nize**
agany : **ag•o•ny**
agast : **aghast**
agate
agatt : **agate**
aged
ageing : **aging**
agen•cy
agensy : **agen•cy**
agetate : **ag•i•tate**
agete : **agate**
aggile : **ag•ile**
aggility : **agil•i•ty**
aggitate : **ag•i•tate**
aggnostic : **ag•nos•tic**
aggnosticism : **ag•nos•ti•cism**
aggonize : **ag•o•nize**
aggony : **ag•o•ny**
aggragate : **ag•gre•gate**
aggrandise (*Brit.*) :
  ag•gran•dize
ag•gran•dize
ag•gra•vate

ag•gra•vat•ed
aggreave : **ag•grieve**
aggreeable : **agree•able**
ag•gre•gate
ag•gre•ga•tion
ag•gress (to attack); **egress**
  (exit)
aggresser : **ag•gres•sor**
ag•gres•sion
ag•gres•sor
aggrevate : **ag•gra•vate**
aggreve : **ag•grieve**
aggriculture : **ag•ri•cul•ture**
ag•grieve
agground : **aground**
aghast
agid : **aged**
agile
agilety : **agil•i•ty**
agil•i•ty
agill : **ag•ile**
agillity : **agil•i•ty**
agincy : **agen•cy**
aging
aginst : **against**
agi•tate
agnastic : **ag•nos•tic**
agnasticism : **ag•nos•ti•cism**
agnaustic : **ag•nos•tic**
agnausticism : **ag•nos•ti•cism**
ag•nos•tic
agnostick : **ag•nos•tic**
agnosticysm : **ag•nos•ti•cism**
agnostischism : **ag•nos•ti•cism**
agnostisism : **ag•nos•ti•cism**
agoanize : **ag•o•nize**
agoany : **ag•o•ny**
agonie : **ag•o•ny**
agonise (*Brit.*) : **ag•o•nize**
ag•o•nize
agonnize : **ag•o•nize**
agonny : **ag•o•ny**

agraculture : **ag·ri·cul·ture**
agrandize : **ag·gran·dize**
agravate : **ag·gra·vate**
agreable : **agree·able**
agreave : **ag·grieve**
agreculture : **ag·ri·cul·ture**
agreeabal : **agree·able**
agreeabel : **agree·able**
agree·able
agreeible : **agree·able**
agregate : **ag·gre·gate**
agress : **ag·gress** (to attack) *or*
  egress (exit)
agression : **ag·gres·sion**
agriculchure : **ag·ri·cul·ture**
agricullture : **ag·ri·cul·ture**
ag·ri·cul·ture
agrieve : **ag·grieve**
agrikulture : **ag·ri·cul·ture**
aground
agrownd : **aground**
aid (to help); **aide** (helper)
aid-de-camp : **aide-de-camp**
aide (helper); **aid** (to help)
aide-de-camp
ailaron : **ai·ler·on**
ai·ler·on
ailerron : **ai·ler·on**
aim·less
aimliss : **aim·less**
airasol : **aero·sol**
airboarn : **air·borne**
airborn : **air·borne**
air·borne
aireate : **aer·ate**
aireborne : **air·borne**
airial : **ae·ri·al**
airiate : **aer·ate**
airodinamic : **aero·dy·nam·ic**
airodynamic : **aero·dy·nam·ic**
airodynammic : **aero·dy·nam·ic**
aironautic : **aero·nau·tic**

aironawtic : **aero·nau·tic**
airosol : **aero·sol**
airplain : **air·plane**
air·plane
airy (relating to air); **ae·rie**
  (nest)
ais·le (walkway); **is·le** (small
  island)
ajacent : **ad·ja·cent**
ajective : **ad·jec·tive**
ajile : **ag·ile**
ajitate : **ag·i·tate**
ajoin : **ad·join**
ajourn : **ad·journ**
ajudicate : **ad·ju·di·cate**
ajust : **ad·just**
akacia : **aca·cia**
aknowledge : **ac·knowl·edge**
aknowledgment :
  ac·knowl·edg·ment
akre : **acre**
akrobat : **ac·ro·bat**
Al·a·ba·ma
Alabamma : **Al·a·ba·ma**
alabasster : **al·a·bas·ter**
al·a·bas·ter
alabi : **al·i·bi**
alacritty : **alac·ri·ty**
alac·ri·ty
alakrity : **alac·ri·ty**
alamony : **al·i·mo·ny**
Alasca : **Alas·ka**
Alas·ka
alay : **al·lay**
albam : **al·bum**
Albanea : **Al·ba·ni·a**
Al·ba·ni·a
Albaquerque : **Al·bu·quer·que**
albatros : **al·ba·tross**
al·ba·tross
albeat : **al·be·it**
al·be·it

albem : **al•bum**
albetross : **al•ba•tross**
albiet : **al•be•it**
albim : **al•bum**
al•bi•no
albinoes : **al•bi•nos**
al•bi•nos
albinow : **al•bi•no**
Albiquerque : **Al•bu•quer•que**
albitross : **al•ba•tross**
alblum : **al•bum**
al•bum
Al•bu•quer•que
Albuquirque : **Al•bu•quer•que**
alcahol : **al•co•hol**
alcali : **al•ka•li**
alcemy : **al•che•my**
al•che•my
alchohol : **al•co•hol**
alcohal : **al•co•hol**
al•co•hol
alebasster : **al•a•bas•ter**
alebaster : **al•a•bas•ter**
alebi : **al•i•bi**
aledge : **al•lege**
alegation : **al•le•ga•tion**
alege : **al•lege**
Aleghenies : **Al•le•ghe•nies**
alegiance : **al•le•giance**
alegory : **al•le•go•ry**
alegro : **al•le•gro**
alein : **alien**
alergy : **al•ler•gy**
aleron : **ai•ler•on**
aleus : **ali•as**
Aleu•tians
aleviate : **al•le•vi•ate**
alfabet: **al•pha•bet**
al•fal•fa
alfallfa : **al•fal•fa**
alfalpha : **al•fal•fa**
al•ga (*sing.*); **al•gae** (*plur.*)

algabra : **al•ge•bra**
al•gae (*plur.*); **al•ga** (*sing.*)
algaebra : **al•ge•bra**
al•ge•bra
algibra : **al•ge•bra**
aliance : **al•li•ance**
alias
Alibama : **Al•a•ba•ma**
al•i•bi
aliby : **al•i•bi**
alien
aliess : **alias**
aligator : **al•li•ga•tor**
align *or* **aline**
alimmony : **al•i•mo•ny**
alimoney : **al•i•mo•ny**
al•i•mo•ny
aline *or* **align**
aliteration : **al•lit•er•a•tion**
alitteration : **al•lit•er•a•tion**
alkahol : **al•co•hol**
al•ka•li
alkalie : **al•ka•li**
alkeli : **al•ka•li**
alkemy : **al•che•my**
alkohol : **al•co•hol**
Allabama : **Al•a•ba•ma**
allabaster : **al•a•bas•ter**
allacate : **al•lo•cate**
allacrity : **alac•ri•ty**
allagation : **al•le•ga•tion**
allagator : **al•li•ga•tor**
Allaghenies : **Al•le•ghe•nies**
allagorry : **al•le•go•ry**
allagory : **al•le•go•ry**
allagro : **al•le•gro**
allamony : **al•i•mo•ny**
Allaska : **Alas•ka**
al•lay
allaygro : **al•le•gro**
Allbania : **Al•ba•ni•a**
allbatross : **al•ba•tross**

allbeit : **al·be·it**
allbino : **al·bi·no**
allbum : **al·bum**
Allbuquerque : **Al·bu·quer·que**
allchemy : **al·che·my**
allcohol : **al·co·hol**
alleaviate : **al·le·vi·ate**
alledge : **al·lege**
alledgedly : **al·leg·ed·ly**
allegance : **al·le·giance**
al·le·ga·tion
allegator : **al·li·ga·tor**
al·lege
allegence : **al·le·giance**
Al·le·ghe·nies
al·le·giance
allegorey : **al·le·go·ry**
allegorry : **al·le·go·ry**
al·le·go·ry
al·le·gro
allegroe : **al·le·gro**
alleiviate : **al·le·vi·ate**
allergie : **al·ler·gy**
al·ler·gy
allerjy : **al·ler·gy**
alleron : **ai·ler·on**
Alleutians : **Aleu·tians**
al·le·vi·ate
al·ley (road); **al·ly** (friend)
allfalfa : **al·fal·fa**
allgebra : **al·ge·bra**
al·li·ance
allias : **alias**
allibi : **al·i·bi**
allience : **al·li·ance**
alligater : **al·li·ga·tor**
alligation : **al·le·ga·tion**
al·li·ga·tor
alligattor : **al·li·ga·tor**
Allighenies : **Al·le·ghe·nies**
allimony : **al·i·mo·ny**
allirgy : **al·ler·gy**

al·lit·er·a·tion
alliterration : **al·lit·er·a·tion**
allitiration : **al·lit·er·a·tion**
allitteration : **al·lit·er·a·tion**
allkali : **al·ka·li**
allmanac : **al·ma·nac**
allmighty : **al·mighty**
allmond : **al·mond**
allmost : **al·most**
al·lo·cate
alloha : **alo·ha**
al·lot (to assign a portion) **a lot** (many)
al·lot·ment
al·lot·ted
al·low
al·low·able
al·low·ance
allowence : **al·low·ance**
allowible : **al·low·able**
allpaca : **al·pa·ca**
allphabet : **al·pha·bet**
all ready *or* **already**
allready : **all ready** *or* **al·ready**
all right
alltercation : **al·ter·ca·tion**
allthough : **al·though**
alltimeter : **al·tim·e·ter**
allto : **al·to**
all to·geth·er (all in one place); **al·to·geth·er** (totally, wholly)
alltruism : **al·tru·ism**
al·lude (to refer); **e·lude** (to escape)
alluminum : **alu·min·um**
allurgy : **al·ler·gy**
al·lu·sion (reference); **elu·sion** (evasion); **il·lu·sion** (false idea or image)
al·lu·sive (making references); **elu·sive** (avoiding); **il·lu·sive** (deceptive)

allways : **al•ways**
al•ly (friend); **al•ley** (road)
al•ma•nac
almanack : **al•ma•nac**
almenac : **al•ma•nac**
almend : **al•mond**
al•mighty
alminac : **al•ma•nac**
almity : **al•mighty**
al•mond
al•most
almund : **al•mond**
alocate : **al•lo•cate**
alo•ha
aloominum : **alu•min•um**
a lot (many); **al•lot** (to assign a portion)
alot : **al•lot** (to assign a portion) *or* **a lot** (many)
alotment : **al•lot•ment**
alottment : **al•lot•ment**
aloud
alow : **al•low**
alowable : **al•low•able**
alowd : **aloud**
alowha : **alo•ha**
al•pa•ca
alpacka : **al•pa•ca**
al•pha•bet
alphalfa : **al•fal•fa**
alphebet : **al•pha•bet**
alphibet : **al•pha•bet**
al•ready *or* **all ready**
alright : **all right**
al•tar (table used in worship); **al•ter** (to change)
altarcation : **al•ter•ca•tion**
al•ter (to change); **al•tar** (table used in worship)
al•ter•ca•tion
alterkation : **al•ter•ca•tion**
alternater : **al•ter•na•tor**

al•ter•na•tor
altho : **al•though**
al•though
al•tim•e•ter
altimiter : **al•tim•e•ter**
al•to
altoes : **al•tos**
al•to•geth•er (totally); **all to•geth•er** (all in one place)
al•tos
altrueism: **al•tru•ism**
altruesm : al•tru•ism
al•tru•ism
alude : **al•lude** (to refer) *or* **elude** (to escape)
Aluetians : **Aleu•tians**
alumanum : **alu•min•um**
alumenem : **alu•min•um**
alumenum : **alu•min•um**
alu•min•um
alusion : **al•lu•sion** (reference) *or* **elu•sion** (evasion) *or* **il•lu•sion** (false idea or image)
alusive : **al•lu•sive** (making references) *or* **elu•sive** (avoiding) *or* **il•lu•sive** (deceptive)
al•ways
amal•gam
amalgem : **amal•gam**
amallgam : **amal•gam**
amarous : **amor•ous**
amass
am•a•teur
amathist : **ame•thyst**
amatoor : **am•a•teur**
amatuer : **am•a•teur**
amature : **am•a•teur**
amaze•ment
amazemint : **amaze•ment**
amazment : **amaze•ment**

ambaguity : **am·bi·gu·i·ty**
ambasador : **am·bas·sa·dor**
ambassader : **am·bas·sa·dor**
am·bas·sa·dor
ambassator : **am·bas·sa·dor**
ambedextrous : **am·bi·dex·trous**
ambeguity : **am·bi·gu·i·ty**
ambent : **am·bi·ent**
ambersand : **am·per·sand**
ambiant : **am·bi·ent**
ambideckstrous :
   am·bi·dex·trous
ambidexterous :
   am·bi·dex·trous
am·bi·dex·trous
ambidextrus : **am·bi·dex·trous**
am·bi·ent
ambigooity : **am·bi·gu·i·ty**
ambiguety : **am·bi·gu·i·ty**
am·bi·gu·i·ty
ambint : **am·bi·ent**
ambivalant : **am·biv·a·lent**
am·biv·a·lent
ambivelent : **am·biv·a·lent**
ambivilent : **am·biv·a·lent**
ambroasia : **am·bro·sia**
ambrosa : **am·bro·sia**
ambrosha : **am·bro·sia**
am·bro·sia
am·bu·lance
ambulence : **am·bu·lance**
ambyent : **am·bi·ent**
ameable : **ami·a·ble**
ameago : **ami·go**
amealiorate : **ame·lio·rate**
ameanable : **ame·na·ble**
ameba : **amoe·ba**
ameeba : **amoe·ba**
ameeliorate : **ame·lio·rate**
amego : **ami·go**
ameleorate : **ame·lio·rate**
ameliarate : **ame·lio·rate**

amelierate : **ame·lio·rate**
ameliorait : **ame·lio·rate**
ame·lio·rate
ame·na·ble
amenaty : **amen·i·ty**
amend (to change or add to);
   emend (to correct)
amend·ment
ameneble : **ame·na·ble**
amenety : **amen·i·ty**
amenible : **ame·na·ble**
ame·ni·ty
amennable : **ame·na·ble**
ameoba : **amoe·ba**
amerous : **amor·ous**
ameteur : **am·a·teur**
amethist : **ame·thyst**
ame·thyst
amfibian : **am·phib·ian**
amfitheater : **am·phi·the·a·ter**
amiabal : **ami·a·ble**
amiabel : **ami·a·ble**
ami·a·ble
amicabal : **am·i·ca·ble**
am·i·ca·ble
amiceble : **am·i·ca·ble**
amicible : **am·i·ca·ble**
amickable : **am·i·ca·ble**
amieble : **ami·a·ble**
amiggo : **ami·go**
ami·go
aminable : **ame·na·ble**
Amish
amithyst : **ame·thyst**
ammass : **amass**
ammeba : **amoe·ba**
ammendment : **amend·ment**
ammenity : **amen·i·ty**
ammethyst : **ame·thyst**
ammigo : **ami·go**
Ammish : **Amish**
ammliorate : **ame·lio·rate**

ammonea : **am•mo•nia**
am•mo•nia
ammonition : **am•mu•ni•tion**
ammonnia : **am•mo•nia**
ammonya : **am•mo•nia**
ammoral : **amor•al**
ammorphus : **amor•phous**
ammortize : **amor•tize**
ammount : **amount**
ammulet : **amu•let**
ammulit : **amu•let**
ammunishin : **am•mu•ni•tion**
am•mu•ni•tion
ammusement : **amuse•ment**
amnasty : **am•nes•ty**
amneasia : **am•ne•sia**
amneesia : **am•ne•sia**
amnesha : **am•ne•sia**
am•ne•sia
amnessty : **am•nes•ty**
amnestie : **am•nes•ty**
am•nes•ty
amoarous : **am•o•rous**
amoartize : **amor•tize**
amoe•ba
among
amonia : **am•mon•ia**
amonya : **am•mo•nia**
amoorous : **amor•ous**
amor•al
amorale : **amor•al**
amorfous : **amor•phous**
amorfus : **amor•phous**
amorish : **am•o•rous**
am•o•rous
amorphis : **amor•phous**
amor•phous
amortise (*Brit.*) : **amor•tize**
amor•tize
amorus : **am•o•rous**
amoung : **among**
amount

amourous : **am•o•rous**
amourphous : **amor•phous**
amourtize : **amor•tize**
ampasand : **am•per•sand**
ampeer : **am•pere**
ampeir : **am•pere**
ampeire : **am•pere**
amper : **am•pere**
am•pere
am•per•sand
ampesand : **am•per•sand**
ampezand : **am•per•sand**
amphatheater :
   am•phi•the•a•ter
amphebian : **am•phib•i•an**
amphetheater :
   am•phi•the•a•ter
am•phib•i•an
amphibien : **am•phib•i•an**
amphibyan : **am•phib•i•an**
am•phi•the•a•ter
amphitheatre (*Brit.*) :
   am•phi•the•a•ter
amphithiater : **am•phi•the•a•ter**
amplefy : **am•pli•fy**
am•pli•fy
am•pu•tee
amputiy : **am•pu•tee**
amputy : **am•pu•tee**
am•u•let
amulette : **am•u•let**
amund : **al•mond**
amunition : **am•mu•ni•tion**
amuse•ment
amusemint : **amuse•ment**
amuzement : **amuse•ment**
amyable : **ami•a•ble**
amythist : **ame•thyst**
anach•ro•nism
anachronnism : **anach•ro•nism**
anachronysm : **anach•ro•nism**
anackronism : **anach•ro•nism**

anacronism : **anach·ro·nism**
anagesic : **an·al·ge·sic**
anagraham : **ana·gram**
ana·gram
anagramm : **ana·gram**
analegy : **anal·o·gy**
analgeasic : **an·al·ge·sic**
analgeesic : **an·al·ge·sic**
analgeezic : **an·al·ge·sic**
an·al·ge·sic
analgesick : **an·al·ge·sic**
analgezic : **an·al·ge·sic**
analigy : **anal·o·gy**
analisees : **anal·y·ses**
analises : **anal·y·ses**
analisis : **anal·y·sis**
analisiss : **anal·y·sis**
analisys : **anal·y·sis**
analitic : **an·a·lyt·ic**
analitick : **an·a·lyt·ic**
analityc : **an·a·lyt·ic**
analize : **an·a·lyze**
analjesic : **an·al·ge·sic**
anallogy : **anal·o·gy**
anallyses : **anal·y·ses**
anallysis : **anal·y·sis**
anallytic : **an·a·lyt·ic**
analoge : **anal·o·gy**
analogee : **anal·o·gy**
analoggy : **anal·o·gy**
analogie : **anal·o·gy**
anal·o·gy
analoje : **anal·o·gy**
analyse (*Brit.*) : **an·a·lyze**
anal·y·ses (*plur.*); **anal·y·sis**
   (*sing.*)
anal·y·sis (*sing.*); **anal·y·ses**
   (*plur.*)
an·a·lyt·ic
an·a·lyze
anamosity : **an·i·mos·i·ty**
ananymity : **an·o·nym·i·ty**

Anapolis : **An·nap·o·lis**
anarchie : **an·ar·chy**
an·ar·chy
anarcky : **an·ar·chy**
anasthesia : **an·es·the·sia**
anatamy : **anat·o·my**
anatome : **anat·o·my**
anatomie : **anat·o·my**
anat·o·my
ancer : **an·chor**
ancerage : **an·chor·age**
ancesstor : **an·ces·tor**
ancester : **an·ces·tor**
ancesteral : **an·ces·tral**
ancestir : **an·ces·tor**
an·ces·tor
ancestoral : **an·ces·tral**
an·ces·tral
ancestrall : **an·ces·tral**
ancestree : **an·ces·try**
ancestrel : **an·ces·tral**
ancestrie : **an·ces·try**
an·ces·try
anchant : **an·cient**
anchar : **an·chor**
ancharage : **an·chor·age**
anchent : **an·cient**
ancher : **an·chor**
ancherage : **an·chor·age**
anchint : **an·cient**
an·chor
an·chor·age
anchoredge : **an·chor·age**
anchorege : **an·chor·age**
anchorige : **an·chor·age**
an·cient
anciety : **an·xi·ety**
ancilary : **an·cil·lary**
an·cil·lary
ancillery : **an·cil·lary**
ancilliary : **an·cil·lary**
ancilliery : **an·cil·lary**

anckor : **an•chor**
anckorage : **an•chor•age**
andiran : **and•iron**
andiren : **and•iron**
andirn : **and•iron**
and•iron
anecdoat : **an•ec•dote**
an•ec•dote (story); **an•ti•dote**
  (remedy)
aneckdote : **an•ec•dote**
aneemia : **ane•mia**
anegesic : **an•al•ge•sic**
anegram : **ana•gram**
anekdote : **an•ec•dote**
anelgesic : **an•al•ge•sic**
anemea : **ane•mia**
ane•mia
anem•o•ne
anemoney : **anem•o•ne**
anemonne : **anem•o•ne**
anemony : **anem•o•ne**
anemosity : **an•i•mos•i•ty**
an•es•the•sia
anesthessia : **an•es•the•sia**
anesthisia : **an•es•the•sia**
anesthsya : **an•es•the•sia**
an•gel (spiritual being); **an•gle**
  (figure in geometry)
an•gel•ic
angelick : **an•gel•ic**
angellic : **an•gel•ic**
an•gle (figure in geometry);
  an•gel (spiritual being)
An•go•ra
Angorra : **An•go•ra**
angxiety : **an•xi•ety**
anhemia : **ane•mia**
anihilate : **an•ni•hi•late**
an•i•mal
animall : **an•i•mal**
animel : **an•i•mal**
animocity : **an•i•mos•i•ty**

animone : **anem•o•ne**
animony : **anem•o•ne**
animositty : **an•i•mos•i•ty**
an•i•mos•i•ty
animossity : **an•i•mos•i•ty**
animul : **an•i•mal**
aniversary : **an•ni•ver•sa•ry**
aniversery : **an•ni•ver•sa•ry**
anjelic : **an•gel•ic**
ankel : **an•kle**
anker : **an•chor**
ankerage : **an•chor•age**
an•kle
annachronism : **anach•ro•nism**
annagram : **ana•gram**
annalogy : **anal•o•gy**
annalyses : **anal•y•ses**
annalysis : **anal•y•sis**
annalytic : **an•a•lyt•ic**
annalyze : **an•a•lyze**
An•nap•o•lis
annarchy : **an•ar•chy**
annatation : **an•no•ta•tion**
annatomy : **anat•o•my**
annaversary : **an•ni•ver•sa•ry**
annaversery : **an•ni•ver•sa•ry**
annesthesia : **an•es•the•sia**
anneversary : **an•ni•ver•sa•ry**
annihalate : **an•ni•hi•late**
an•ni•hi•late
annilate : **an•ni•hi•late**
an•ni•ver•sa•ry
anniversery : **an•ni•ver•sa•ry**
annivursery : **an•ni•ver•sa•ry**
annoint : **anoint**
annomaly : **anom•a•ly**
an•no•ta•tion
announser : **an•nounc•er**
an•noy•ance
annoyence : **an•noy•ance**
an•nu•al
anoint

anomale : **anom·a·ly**

anomally : **anom·a·ly**

anom·a·ly

anommaly : **anom·a·ly**

anonimity : **an·o·nym·i·ty**

anonimous : **anon·y·mous**

an·o·nym·i·ty

anon·y·mous

anonymus : **anon·y·mous**

anotation : **an·no·ta·tion**

anounce : **an·nounce**

anouncer : **an·nounc·er**

anounse : **an·nounce**

anoyance : **an·noy·ance**

anser : **an·swer**

ansestor : **an·ces·tor**

ansestral : **an·ces·tral**

ansestry : **an·ces·try**

anshent : **an·cient**

ansiety : **an·xi·ety**

ansilary : **an·cil·lary**

ansillary : **an·cil·lary**

ansor : **an·swer**

an·swer

ant (insect); **aunt** (female relative)

antaganist : **an·tag·o·nist**

antaggonist : **an·tag·o·nist**

antaginist : **an·tag·o·nist**

an·tag·o·nist

antamology : **en·to·mol·o·gy** (study of insects) *or* **et·y·mol·o·gy** (study of words)

ant·arc·tic

antartic : **ant·arc·tic**

antecedant : **an·te·ced·ent**

an·te·ced·ent

anteceedent : **an·te·ced·ent**

antemology : **en·to·mol·o·gy** (study of insects) *or*

et·y·mol·o·gy (study of words)

antena : **an·ten·na**

an·ten·na

antesedent : **an·te·ced·ent**

antham : **an·them**

an·them

anthim : **an·them**

antholagy : **an·thol·o·gy**

anthollogy : **an·thol·o·gy**

an·thol·o·gy

anthum : **an·them**

antic (clownish); **an·tique** (old)

anticedent : **an·te·ced·ent**

anticepate : **an·ti·ci·pate**

anticipait : **an·ti·ci·pate**

an·ti·ci·pate

an·ti·dote (remedy); **an·ec·dote** (story)

an·tique (old); **an·tic** (clownish)

antisipate : **an·ti·ci·pate**

antissipate : **an·ti·ci·pate**

antomology : **en·to·mol·o·gy** (study of insects) *or* **et·y·mol·o·gy** (study of words)

anual : **an·nu·al**

anxiaty : **an·xi·ety**

an·xi·ety

anxioty : **an·xi·ety**

any·body (any person); **any body** (any body at all)

any·one (any person); **any one** (any item)

Apache

Apachee : **Apache**

apachure : **ap·er·ture**

Apalachian : **Ap·pa·la·chian**

apalogize : **apol·o·gize**

Apamattox : **Ap·po·mat·tox**

aparatus : **ap·pa·ra·tus**

aparel : **ap·par·el**

aparent : **ap•par•ent**
aparint : **ap•par•ent**
apart
aparteid : **apart•heid**
apart•heid
aparthide : **apart•heid**
aparthied : **apart•heid**
apartide : **apart•heid**
apastasy : **apos•ta•sy**
Apatche : **Apache**
ap•a•thet•ic
apathetick : **ap•a•thet•ic**
apa•thy
apatite : **ap•pe•tite**
apature : **ap•er•ture**
apeace : **apiece**
apeal : **ap•peal**
apease : **ap•pease**
apeice : **apiece**
Apelachian : **Ap•pa•la•chian**
apendage : **ap•pend•age**
apendectomy :
    ap•pen•dec•to•my
apendege : **ap•pend•age**
apera : **op•era**
aperchure : **ap•er•ture**
ap•er•ture
apethetic : **ap•a•thet•ic**
apethy : **apa•thy**
apetite : **ap•pe•tite**
apeture : **ap•er•ture**
aphasea : **apha•sia**
aphasha : **apha•sia**
apha•sia
apherism : **aph•o•rism**
aphirism : **aph•o•rism**
aph•o•rism
apiece
apindectomy :
    ap•pen•dec•to•my
apithy : **apa•thy**
apitite : **ap•pe•tite**

aplaud : **ap•plaud**
apliance : **ap•pli•ance**
apocalips : **apoc•a•lypse**
apocalipse : **apoc•a•lypse**
apoc•a•lypse
apocelypse : **apoc•a•lypse**
apockalypse : **apoc•a•lypse**
apockriphal : **apoc•ry•phal**
apockryphal : **apoc•ry•phal**
apocrifal : **apoc•ry•phal**
apocriphal : **apoc•ry•phal**
apocryfal : **apoc•ry•phal**
apoc•ry•phal
apointe : **ap•poin•tee**
apolagise : **apol•o•gize**
apolagize : **apol•o•gize**
apolegize : **apol•o•gize**
apologise (*Brit.*) : **apol•o•gize**
apol•o•gize
apolojize : **apol•o•gize**
Apomattox : **Ap•po•mat•tox**
aposle : **apos•tle**
apossel : **apos•tle**
apossle : **apos•tle**
aposstasy : **apos•ta•sy**
aposstle : **apos•tle**
apostacy : **apos•ta•sy**
apos•ta•sy
aposticy : **apos•ta•sy**
apostisy : **apos•ta•sy**
apos•tle
apos•tro•phe
appairel : **ap•par•el**
appairent : **ap•par•ent**
Appalachan : **Ap•pa•la•chian**
Appalachen : **Ap•pa•la•chian**
Ap•pa•la•chian
Appalachin : **Ap•pa•la•chian**
Appamattox : **Ap•po•mattox**
apparal : **ap•par•el**
apparant : **ap•par•ent**
apparatis : **ap•pa•ra•tus**

ap·pa·ra·tus
ap·par·el
ap·par·ent
apparil : **ap·par·el**
appart : **apart**
appartheid : **apart·heid**
appathetic : **ap·a·thet·ic**
appatite : **ap·pe·tite**
appatizing : **ap·pe·tiz·ing**
appeace : **ap·pease**
ap·peal
ap·pear·ance
appearanse : **ap·pear·ance**
appearant : **ap·par·ent**
appearence : **ap·pear·ance**
appearense : **ap·pear·ance**
ap·pease
appeerance : **ap·pear·ance**
appeil : **ap·peal**
appeirance : **ap·pear·ance**
appele : **ap·peal**
ap·pend·age
appendecktomy :
  ap·pen·dec·to·my
appendectome :
  ap·pen·dec·to·my
ap·pen·dec·to·my
appendege : **ap·pend·age**
appendidge : **ap·pend·age**
appendige : **ap·pend·age**
apperture : **ap·er·ture**
appetight : **ap·pe·tite**
appetising (*Brit.*) : **ap·pe·tiz·ing**
ap·pe·tite
ap·pe·tiz·ing
appettite : **ap·pe·tite**
appettizing : **ap·pe·tiz·ing**
appiece : **apiece**
appiese : **ap·pease**
appindage : **ap·pend·age**
appindectomie :
  ap·pen·dec·to·my

appindige : **ap·pend·age**
appitite : **ap·pe·tite**
appitizing : **ap·pe·tiz·ing**
ap·plaud
applawd : **ap·plaud**
ap·pli·ance
applianse : **ap·pli·ance**
applicabel : **ap·pli·ca·ble**
ap·pli·ca·ble
applicabul : **ap·pli·ca·ble**
appliceble : **ap·pli·ca·ble**
applicible : **ap·pli·ca·ble**
applickable : **ap·pli·ca·ble**
applience : **ap·pli·ance**
appliense : **ap·pli·ance**
applod : **ap·plaud**
applodd : **ap·plaud**
applyance : **ap·pli·ance**
appocryphal : **apoc·ry·phal**
ap·point·ee
appointie : **ap·poin·tee**
appointy : **ap·poin·tee**
appologize : **apol·o·gize**
Appomatox : **Ap·po·mat·tox**
Ap·po·mat·tox
appostasy : **apos·ta·sy**
appostrophe : **apos·tro·phe**
ap·praise (to assess); **ap·prise**
  (to inform); **ap·prize** (to
  value)
appreceate : **ap·pre·ci·ate**
ap·pre·ci·ate
ap·pre·ci·a·tion
appreeciate : **ap·pre·ci·ate**
apprentace : **ap·pren·tice**
apprentece : **ap·pren·tice**
ap·pren·tice
apprentiss : **ap·pren·tice**
appreshiate : **ap·pre·ci·ate**
appresiate : **ap·pre·ci·ate**
appricot : **apri·cot**
Appril : **April**

apprintice : **ap•pren•tice**
apprintiss : **ap•pren•tice**
ap•prise (to inform); **ap•praise** (to assess); **ap•prize** (to value)
ap•prize (to value); **ap•praise** (to assess); **ap•prise** (to inform)
ap•proach•able
approachibal : **ap•proach•able**
approachible : **ap•proach•able**
approachibul : **ap•proach•able**
approapriate : **ap•pro•pri•ate**
approchabal : **ap•proach•able**
approchable : **ap•proach•able**
approoval : **ap•prov•al**
appropiate : **ap•pro•pri•ate**
appropreate : **ap•pro•pri•ate**
appropreit : **ap•pro•pri•ate**
ap•pro•pri•ate
ap•prov•al
approvel : **ap•prov•al**
approvil : **ap•prov•al**
approxamate : **ap•prox•i•mate**
approxemate : **ap•prox•i•mate**
approximant : **ap•prox•i•mate**
approximat : **ap•prox•i•mate**
ap•prox•i•mate
approximent : **ap•prox•i•mate**
approximet : **ap•prox•i•mate**
apracot : **apri•cot**
apraise : **ap•praise** (to assess) *or* **ap•prise** (to inform) *or* **ap•prize** (to value)
apreciate : **ap•pre•ci•ate**
aprecot : **apri•cot**
aprentice : **ap•pren•tice**
apri•cot
apricott : **apri•cot**
April
Aprill : **April**

aprise : **ap•prise** (to inform) *or* **ap•prize** (to value)
aproachable : **ap•proach•able**
aprochable : **ap•proach•able**
aprooval : **ap•prov•al**
apropriate : **ap•pro•pri•ate**
aproval : **ap•prov•al**
aproxamate : **ap•prox•i•mate**
aproximate : **ap•prox•i•mate**
apsorb : **ab•sorb**
aptatude : **ap•ti•tude**
aptetude : **ap•ti•tude**
ap•ti•tude
aptutood : **ap•ti•tude**
apurture : **ap•er•ture**
aquaduct : **aq•ue•duct**
aquariam : **aquar•i•um**
aquariem : **aquar•i•um**
aquar•i•um
aquarrium : **aquar•i•um**
aqua•tic
aqueduck : **aq•ue•duct**
aq•ue•duct
aquerium : **aquar•i•um**
aquiduct : **aq•ue•duct**
aquiesce : **ac•qui•esce**
aquire : **ac•quire**
aquisition : **ac•qui•si•tion**
aquit : **ac•quit**
aquittel : **ac•quit•tal**
arabesk : **ar•a•besque**
ar•a•besque
araign : **ar•raign**
arange : **ar•range**
arangement : **ar•range•ment**
arber : **ar•bor**
ar•bor
ar•bo•re•al
arborial : **ar•bo•re•al**
arborreal : **ar•bo•re•al**
arborrial : **ar•bo•re•al**

arc (part of a circle); ark (boat or box)
arcaic : **ar•cha•ic**
arcangel : **arch•an•gel**
Arcansas : **Ar•kan•sas**
arceology : **ar•chae•ol•o•gy**
ar•chae•ol•o•gy or
  ar•che•ol•o•gy
ar•cha•ic
archake : **ar•cha•ic**
arch•an•gel
archangil : **arch•an•gel**
archangle : **arch•an•gel**
archanjel : **arch•an•gel**
archaque : **ar•cha•ic**
archatect : **ar•chi•tect**
archealogy : **ar•chae•ol•o•gy**
archeologgy : **ar•chae•ol•o•gy**
ar•che•ol•o•gy or
  ar•chae•ol•o•gy
archepelago : **ar•chi•pel•a•go**
archetect : **ar•chi•tect**
archiology : **ar•chae•ol•o•gy**
ar•chi•pel•a•go
archipelego : **ar•chi•pel•a•go**
archipellago : **ar•chi•pel•a•go**
ar•chi•tect
arcipelago : **ar•chi•pel•a•go**
arcitect : **ar•chi•tect**
arckaic : **ar•cha•ic**
arc•tic
arder : **ar•dor**
ar•dor
areal : **ae•ri•al**
areate : **aer•ate**
arebesk : **ar•a•besque**
arebesque : **ar•a•besque**
are•na
arenna : **are•na**
arest : **ar•rest**
arestocracy : **ar•is•toc•ra•cy**
Arezona : **Ar•i•zo•na**

argasy : **ar•go•sy**
argesy : **ar•go•sy**
argossy : **ar•go•sy**
ar•go•sy
arguement : **ar•gu•ment**
ar•gu•ment
arial : **ae•ri•al**
arid
arie : **ae•rie** (nest) or **airy**
  (relating to air)
arina : **are•na**
arise
aristockracy : **ar•is•toc•ra•cy**
ar•is•toc•ra•cy
aristocrasy : **ar•is•toc•ra•cy**
aristocricy : **ar•is•toc•ra•cy**
aristocrisy : **ar•is•toc•ra•cy**
arithmatic : **arith•me•tic**
arith•me•tic
arival : **ar•riv•al**
arive : **ar•rive**
Ar•i•zo•na
ark (boat or box); arc (part of a circle)
arkaic : **ar•cha•ic**
Arkansah : **Ar•kan•sas**
Ar•kan•sas
Arkansaw : **Ar•kan•sas**
arkeology : **ar•chae•ol•o•gy**
arkitect : **ar•chi•tect**
ar•ma•da
armadda : **ar•ma•da**
ar•ma•dil•lo
armadilo : **ar•ma•dil•lo**
armastice : **ar•mi•stice**
Armeania : **Ar•me•nia**
armedillo : **ar•ma•dil•lo**
Armenea : **Ar•me•nia**
Ar•me•nia
armer : **ar•mor**
armestice : **ar•mi•stice**
armidillo : **ar•ma•dil•lo**

Arminia : **Ar·me·nia**
ar·mi·stice
armistise : **ar·mi·stice**
armistiss : **ar·mi·stice**
ar·mor
armorda : **ar·ma·da**
armordillo : **ar·ma·dil·lo**
armour (*Brit.*) : **ar·mor**
arodinamic : **aero·dy·nam·ic**
arodynamic : **aero·dy·nam·ic**
arogant : **ar·ro·gant**
aro·ma
aronautic : **aero·nau·tic**
arose
arosol : **aero·sol**
around
arouse
aroyo : **ar·royo**
arragant : **ar·ro·gant**
arraighn : **ar·raign**
ar·raign
arrain : **ar·raign**
arraingement : **ar·range·ment**
ar·range
ar·range·ment
arrangemint : **ar·range·ment**
arrangment : **ar·range·ment**
arrena : **are·na**
ar·rest
arrid : **arid**
arrie : **ae·rie** (nest) *or* **airy**
  (relating to air)
arrina : **are·na**
arrise : **arise**
ar·ri·val
ar·rive
arrivel : **ar·riv·al**
arrivil : **ar·riv·al**
arrivle : **ar·riv·al**
arrodinamic : **aero·dy·nam·ic**
arrodynamic : **aero·dy·nam·ic**
ar·ro·gant

arrogent : **ar·ro·gant**
arroio : **ar·royo**
arroma : **aro·ma**
arronautic : **aero·nau·tic**
arrose : **arose**
arrosol : **aero·sol**
arround : **around**
arrouse : **arouse**
ar·royo
arsen : **ar·son**
ar·se·nal
arsenel : **ar·se·nal**
arsenle : **ar·se·nal**
arsin : **ar·son**
arsinal : **ar·se·nal**
arsinel : **ar·se·nal**
ar·son
artachoke : **ar·ti·choke**
artacle : **ar·ti·cle**
artafice : **ar·ti·fice**
artaficial : **ar·ti·fi·cial**
artechoke : **ar·ti·choke**
artefice : **ar·ti·fice**
arteficial : **ar·ti·fi·cial**
arterry : **ar·tery**
ar·tery
artharitis : **ar·thri·tis**
arthiritis : **ar·thri·tis**
arthritas : **ar·thri·tis**
ar·thri·tis
arthritus : **ar·thri·tis**
Ar·thur (name); **au·thor**
  (writer)
artic : **arc·tic**
artical : **ar·ti·cle**
articel : **ar·ti·cle**
artichoak : **ar·ti·choke**
ar·ti·choke
ar·ti·cle
ar·ti·fice
ar·ti·fi·cial
artifise : **ar·ti·fice**

artifishal : **ar•ti•fi•cial**
artifisial : **ar•ti•fi•cial**
artifrice : **ar•ti•fice**
artifricial : **ar•ti•fi•cial**
artilary : **ar•til•lery**
artilery : **ar•til•lery**
artillarry : **ar•til•lery**
artillary : **ar•til•lery**
ar•til•lery
artiry : **ar•tery**
ar•tis•ti•cal•ly
artisticly : **ar•tis•ti•cal•ly**
artory : **ar•tery**
asail : **as•sail**
asailant : **as•sail•ant**
asassin : **as•sas•sin**
asault : **as•sault**
as•cend
as•cen•sion
as•cent (act of going upward);
    as•sent (to agree; agreement)
ascerbic : **acer•bic**
ascert : **as•sert**
as•cer•tain
ascertane : **as•cer•tain**
as•cet•ic
asemble : **as•sem•ble**
asend : **as•cend**
aserbic : **acer•bic**
asert : **as•sert**
asertain : **as•cer•tain**
asess : **as•sess**
asessor : **as•ses•sor**
asetic : **as•cet•ic**
asfalt : **as•phalt**
asfault : **as•phalt**
asfixiate : **as•phyx•i•ate**
ashure : **azure**
asign : **as•sign**
asilim : **asy•lum**
asilum : **asy•lum**
asimilate : **as•sim•i•late**

asist : **as•sist**
asistance : **as•sis•tance**
asistant : **as•sis•tant**
asma : **asth•ma**
asociate : **as•so•ciate**
asparagis : **as•par•a•gus**
as•par•a•gus
asparegus : **as•par•a•gus**
asperagus : **as•par•a•gus**
asperin : **as•pi•rin**
asphallt : **as•phalt**
as•phalt
asphault : **as•phalt**
asphixeate : **as•phyx•i•ate**
asphixiate : **as•phyx•i•ate**
asphyxeate : **as•phyx•i•ate**
as•phyx•i•ate
aspicious : **aus•pi•cious**
aspiren : **as•pi•rin**
as•pi•rin
aspren : **as•pi•rin**
asprin : **as•pi•rin**
as•sail
as•sail•ant
assailent : **as•sail•ant**
assalant : **as•sail•ant**
assalent : **as•sail•ant**
assalt : **as•sault**
assasin : **as•sas•sin**
as•sas•sin
as•sas•sin•a•tion
as•sault
as•sem•ble
assend : **as•cend**
as•sent (to agree; agreement);
    as•cent (act of going upward)
as•sert
as•sess
assesser : **as•ses•sor**
assession : **ac•ces•sion**
as•sess•ment
as•ses•sor

as·sign
assimalate : as·sim·i·late
as·sim·i·late
assimmilate : as·sim·i·late
assine : as·sign
as·sist
as·sis·tance
as·sis·tant
assistence : as·sis·tance
assistense : as·sis·tance
assistent : as·sis·tant
assoceate : as·so·ciate
as·so·ciate
assosheate : as·so·ciate
assoshiate : as·so·ciate
asspirin : as·pi·rin
assteroid : as·ter·oid
asstrma : asth·ma
asstrology : as·trol·o·gy
asstronomer : as·tron·o·mer
as·sume
as·sump·tion
assumtion : as·sump·tion
as·sur·ance
assurence : as·sur·ance
assylum : asy·lum
astaroid : as·ter·oid
astere : aus·tere
asteresk : as·ter·isk
as·ter·isk
asterix : as·ter·isk
as·ter·oid
asthema : asth·ma
asthetic : aes·thet·ic
asth·ma
Astralia : Aus·tral·ia
astralogy : as·trol·o·gy
astranaut : as·tro·naut
astranomer : as·tron·o·mer
Astria : Aus·tria
astrisk : as·ter·isk
astroid : as·ter·oid

astroknot : as·tro·naut
astrollogy : as·trol·o·gy
astrologgy : as·trol·o·gy
as·trol·o·gy
astronamer : as·tron·o·mer
as·tro·naut
astronemer : as·tron·o·mer
astronnomer : as·tron·o·mer
as·tron·o·mer
astronot : as·tro·naut
astronought : as·tro·naut
asume : as·sume
asumption : as·sump·tion
asurance : as·sur·ance
asylam : asy·lum
asylim : asy·lum
asy·lum
atainable : at·tain·able
atem : at·om
atemology : en·to·mol·o·gy
   (study of insects) or
   et·y·mol·o·gy (study of
   words)
atend : at·tend
athalete : ath·lete
athaletic : ath·let·ic
athelete : ath·lete
atheletic : ath·let·ic
athleet : ath·lete
ath·lete
ath·let·ic
athlettic : ath·let·ic
athority : au·thor·i·ty
atitude : at·ti·tude
atmasphere : at·mo·sphere
atmesphere : at·mo·sphere
atmosfere : at·mo·sphere
atmospere : at·mo·sphere
atmosphear : at·mo·sphere
atmospheer : at·mo·sphere
at·mo·sphere
at·om

atonomy : **au•ton•o•my**
atorney : **at•tor•ney**
atrocety : **atroc•i•ty**
atrochious : **atro•cious**
atro•cious
atrocitty : **atroc•i•ty**
atroc•i•ty
atrocius : **atro•cious**
atroshious : **atro•cious**
atrosity : **atroc•i•ty**
attainabal : **at•tain•able**
attainabel : **at•tain•able**
at•tain•able
attaineble : **at•tain•able**
attainible : **at•tain•able**
attanable : **at•tain•able**
attatude : **at•ti•tude**
at•tend
at•tend•ance
at•tend•ant
attendence : **at•tend•ance**
attendent : **at•tend•ant**
atterney : **at•tor•ney**
atterneys : **at•tor•neys**
atternies : **at•tor•neys**
attierney : **at•tor•ney**
at•ti•tude
attom : **at•om**
attornees : **at•tor•neys**
at•tor•ney
at•tor•neys
attornies : **at•tor•neys**
attorny : **at•tor•ney**
atymology : **en•to•mol•o•gy**
   (study of insects) *or*
   et•y•mol•o•gy (study of
   words)
auc•tion•eer
auctioneir : **auc•tion•eer**
auctionier : **auc•tion•eer**
audable : **au•di•ble**
audacety : **au•dac•i•ty**

au•da•cious
audacitty : **au•dac•i•ty**
au•dac•i•ty
audashious : **au•da•cious**
audasious : **au•da•cious**
audasity : **au•dac•i•ty**
audassity : **au•dac•i•ty**
audatious : **au•da•cious**
audiance : **au•di•ence**
aud•i•ble
au•di•ence
auditer : **au•di•tor**
au•di•tor
au•ger (drilling tool); **au•gur**
   (to predict)
au•gur (to predict); **au•ger**
   (drilling tool)
auktioneer : **auc•tion•eer**
aunt (female relative); **ant**
   (insect)
aurthor : **au•thor**
auspichious : **aus•pi•cious**
aus•pi•cious
auspicius : **aus•pi•cious**
auspisious : **aus•pi•cious**
auspitious : **aus•pi•cious**
Ausstralia : **Aus•tral•ia**
Ausstria : **Aus•tria**
austair : **aus•tere**
austare : **aus•tere**
austeer : **aus•tere**
austeir : **aus•tere**
aus•tere
austier : **aus•tere**
Aus•tral•ia (continent);
   Aus•tria (European nation)
Aus•tria (European nation);
   Aus•tral•ia (continent)
autharize : **au•thor•ize**
authenic : **au•then•tic**
au•then•tic
auther : **au•thor**

autherize : **au•thor•ize**
au•thor (writer); **Ar•thur** (name)
authoraty : **au•thor•i•ty**
authorety : **au•thor•i•ty**
authorise (*Brit.*) : **au•thor•ize**
authoritty : **au•thor•i•ty**
au•thor•i•ty
au•thor•ize
autioneer : **auc•tion•eer**
au•to•mat•i•cal•ly
automaticly : **au•to•mat•i•cal•ly**
automn : **au•tumn**
autonnomy : **au•ton•o•my**
autonome : **au•ton•o•my**
autonomie : **au•ton•o•my**
au•ton•o•my
autum : **au•tumn**
autumm : **au•tumn**
au•tumn
auxilary : **aux•il•ia•ry**
aux•il•ia•ry
auxilliary : **aux•il•ia•ry**
avacado : **av•o•ca•do**
availabal : **avail•able**
avail•able
availible : **avail•able**
avalable : **avail•able**
avalanch : **av•a•lanche**
av•a•lanche
avaleable : **avail•able**
avant-garde
avant-guard : **avant-garde**
avanue : **av•e•nue**
av•a•rice
avarise : **av•a•rice**
avariss : **av•a•rice**
avaunt-garde : **avant-garde**
aveator : **avi•a•tor**
avecado : **av•o•ca•do**
avelanche : **av•a•lanche**
avenoo : **av•e•nue**

aventurer : **ad•ven•tur•er**
av•e•nue
av•er•age
averedge : **av•er•age**
averege : **av•er•age**
averice : **av•a•rice**
averige : **av•er•age**
averise : **av•a•rice**
averse (disinclined); **ad•verse** (unfavorable)
avertise : **ad•ver•tise**
avertising : **ad•ver•tis•ing**
aviater : **avi•a•tor**
aviatir : **avi•a•tor**
avi•a•tor
avid
avilanche : **av•a•lanche**
avinue : **av•e•nue**
avirage : **av•er•age**
avocaddo : **av•o•ca•do**
av•o•ca•do
avoidabel : **avoid•able**
avoid•able
avoid•ance
avoidanse : **avoid•ance**
avoidence : **avoid•ance**
avoidense : **avoid•ance**
avoidible : **avoid•able**
avrage : **av•er•age**
avvid : **avid**
awaikening : **awak•en•ing**
awairness : **aware•ness**
await
awak•en•ing
awakining : **awak•en•ing**
awakning : **awak•en•ing**
aware•ness
awareniss : **aware•ness**
awarness : **aware•ness**
awate : **await**
awesom : **awe•some**
awe•some

awesume : **awe•some**

awsome : **awe•some**

axcel : **ax•le** (wheel shaft) *or* **ex•cel** (to be superior)

axel : **ax•le** (wheel shaft) *or* **ex•cel** (to be superior)

axelerate : **ac•cel•erate**

ax•le (wheel shaft); **ex•cel** (to be superior)

azailea : **aza•lea**

aza•lea

azalia : **aza•lea**

azhure : **azure**

azma : **asth•ma**

azthetic : **aes•thet•ic**

azthma : **asth•ma**

azure

B

Babalon : **Bab•y•lon**
babbies : **ba•bies**
babboon : **ba•boon**
babby : **ba•by**
Babbylon : **Bab•y•lon**
Babelon : **Bab•y•lon**
Babillon : **Bab•y•lon**
ba•boon
babtise : **bap•tize**
babtism : **bap•tism**
Babtist : **Bap•tist**
ba•by
Bab•y•lon
babys : **ba•bies**
bacalaureate : **bac•ca•lau•re•ate**
bacan : **ba•con**
bac•ca•lau•re•ate
baccalaureit : **bac•ca•lau•re•ate**
baccalauriate : **bac•ca•lau•re•ate**
baccaloreate : **bac•ca•lau•re•ate**
baccelaureate :
   bac•ca•lau•re•ate
bacchelor : **bach•el•or**
baccilli : **ba•cil•li**
baccilly : **ba•cil•li**
baccon : **ba•con**
baceball : **base•ball**
baceless : **base•less**
bacement : **base•ment**
bacen : **ba•con**
bachalor : **bach•e•lor**
bacheler : **bach•e•lor**
bachelir : **bach•e•lor**
bach•e•lor
bachelore : **bach•e•lor**
bachteria : **bac•te•ri•a**
bachterium : **bac•te•ri•um**
bacically : **ba•si•cal•ly**
bacili : **ba•cil•li**
bacilica : **ba•sil•i•ca**

ba•cil•li (*plur.*); **ba•cil•lus** (*sing.*)
ba•cil•lus (*sing.*); **ba•cil•li** (*plur.*)
bacilus : **ba•cil•lus**
bacin : **ba•sin**
bacinet : **bas•si•net**
bacis : **ba•sis**
backalaureate :
   bac•ca•lau•re•ate
backen : **ba•con**
backfeild : **back•field**
back•field
backgamen : **back•gam•mon**
backgamman : **back•gam•mon**
backgammen : **back•gam•mon**
backgammin : **back•gam•mon**
back•gam•mon
back•ground
backround : **back•ground**
backterea : **bac•te•ri•a**
backteria : **bac•te•ri•a**
backteriem : **bac•te•ri•um**
backterium : **bac•te•ri•um**
back•ward
backwerd : **back•ward**
backword : **back•ward**
backwurd : **back•ward**
ba•con
bactearia : **bac•te•ria**
bactearium : **bac•te•ri•um**
bacterea : **bac•te•ria**
bactereum : **bac•te•ri•um**
bac•te•ria (*plur.*); **bac•te•ri•um**
   (*sing.*)
bac•te•ri•um (*sing.*); **bac•te•ria**
   (*plur.*)
bacterrea : **bac•te•ria**
bacterreum : **bac•te•ri•um**
bacterrium : **bac•te•ri•um**
bactiria : **bac•te•ria**
bactirium : **bac•te•ri•um**

baddinage : **ba•di•nage**
baddly : **bad•ly**
baddminton : **bad•min•ton**
badely : **bad•ly**
badenage : **ba•di•nage**
badenoge : **ba•di•nage**
badge
badinadge : **ba•di•nage**
ba•di•nage
badinoge : **ba•di•nage**
badlly : **bad•ly**
bad•ly
bad•min•ton
badmiton : **bad•min•ton**
badmitten : **bad•min•ton**
badmitton : **bad•min•ton**
bafel : **baf•fle**
baffel : **baf•fle**
baf•fle
bafful : **baf•fle**
bafle : **baf•fle**
bagage : **bag•gage**
bagaje : **bag•gage**
bage : **badge**
bagege : **bag•gage**
bager : **bad•ger**
baggadge : **bag•gage**
bag•gage
baggaje : **bag•gage**
baggege : **bag•gage**
baggie : **bag•gy**
bag•gy
bagy : **bag•gy**
bail (to get out of jail; to
   remove water); **bale** (hay)
bailef : **bai•liff**
baileff : **bai•liff**
bailif : **bai•liff**
bai•liff
baist : **baste**
bait (lure); **bate** (to subside)
baje : **badge**

bajer : **bad•ger**
bakary : **bak•ery**
bakeing : **bak•ing**
baken : **ba•con**
bak•er
bakerry : **bak•ery**
bak•ing
bakker : **bak•er**
balad : **bal•lad**
bal•ance
balanse : **bal•ance**
balast : **bal•last**
balck : **balk**
bal•co•nies
balconnies : **bal•co•nies**
balconny : **bal•co•ny**
bal•co•ny
baldnes : **bald•ness**
bald•ness
baldnis : **bald•ness**
baldniss : **bald•ness**
bale (hay); **bail** (to get out of
   jail; to remove water)
baled : **bal•lad**
balence : **bal•ance**
balerena : **bal•le•ri•na**
balerina : **bal•le•ri•na**
balet : **bal•let**
balif : **bai•liff**
baliff : **bai•liff**
balist : **bal•last**
balit : **bal•lot**
balk
balkonies : **bal•co•nies**
balkonnies : **bal•co•nies**
balkonny : **bal•co•ny**
balkony : **bal•co•ny**
balkonys : **bal•co•nies**
bal•lad
ballance : **bal•ance**
ballarena : **bal•le•ri•na**
ballarina : **bal•le•ri•na**

bal•last
ballat : bal•let
ballay : bal•let
balled : bal•lad
ballence : bal•ance
ballerena : bal•le•ri•na
bal•le•ri•na
ballest : bal•last
bal•let (dance); bal•lot (vote)
balley : bal•let
ballid : bal•lad
ballist : bal•last
ballit : bal•lot
bal•loon
bal•lot (vote); bal•let (dance)
ballote : bal•lot
ballsa : bal•sa
ballsah : bal•sa
ballsam : bal•sam
ballsum : bal•sam
Balltimore : Bal•ti•more
ballud : bal•lad
ballune : bal•loon
ballust : bal•last
balmy
baloon : bal•loon
baloone : bal•loon
balot : ball•let (dance) or
   bal•lot (vote)
bal•sa
balsah : bal•sa
bal•sam
balsum : bal•sam
Baltemore : Bal•ti•more
Bal•ti•more
bam•boo
bambu : bam•boo
bambue : bam•boo
bammboo : bam•boo
bammy : balmy
ba•nal
ba•nana

bananah : ba•nana
bananna : ba•nana
banche : ban•shee
banchee : ban•shee
bandadge : ban•dage
ban•dage
bandaje : ban•dage
ban•dana or ban•dan•na
ban•dan•na or ban•dana
bandedge : ban•dage
bandege : ban•dage
bandeje : ban•dage
bandet : ban•dit
bandetry : ban•dit•ry
bandidge : ban•dage
bandige : ban•dage
ban•dit
banditery : ban•dit•ry
banditt : ban•dit
bandittry : ban•dit•ry
bandwagen : band•wag•on
bandwaggen : band•wag•on
bandwaggon : band•wag•on
band•wag•on
banel : ba•nal
baner : ban•ner
banesh : ban•ish
bangel : ban•gle
ban•gle
bangul : ban•gle
ban•ish
bankrubt : bank•rupt
bankrupcy : bank•rupt•cy
bank•rupt
bank•rupt•cy
bankwet : ban•quet
bankwit : ban•quet
bannal : ba•nal
bannana : ba•nana
bannanna : ba•nana
bannar : ban•ner
bannditry : ban•dit•ry

ban·ner
banngle : **ban·gle**
bannir : **ban·ner**
bannish : **ban·ish**
ban·quet (feast); **ban·quette** (bench)
ban·quette (bench); **ban·quet** (feast)
banquit : **ban·quet**
banqwit : **ban·quet**
banshe : **ban·shee**
ban·shee
banshie : **ban·shee**
banshy : **ban·shee**
ban·tam
bantem : **ban·tam**
bantim : **ban·tam**
bantum : **ban·tam**
ban·zai (cheer); **bon·sai** (dwarf tree)
banzi : **ban·zai** (cheer) *or* **bon·sai** (dwarf tree)
banzie : **ban·zai** (cheer) *or* **bon·sai** (dwarf tree)
baonet : **bay·o·net**
Baptest : **Bap·tist**
baptise (*Brit.*) : **bap·tize**
baptisim : **bap·tism**
bap·tism
Bap·tist
baptysm : **bap·tism**
baracade : **bar·ri·cade**
baracks : **bar·racks**
baracuda : **bar·ra·cu·da**
barage : **bar·rage**
baratone : **bar·i·tone**
barbacue : **bar·be·cue**
barbaque : **bar·be·cue**
barbarean : **bar·bar·i·an**
bar·bar·i·an
barbearian : **bar·bar·i·an**
bar·be·cue

barbequ : **bar·be·cue**
barbeque : **bar·be·cue**
barberian : **bar·bar·i·an**
barbicue : **bar·be·cue**
barbique : **bar·be·cue**
bare (uncovered); **bear** (animal); **bear** (to carry)
bare·back
bare·faced
barefased : **bare·faced**
bare·foot
bare·hand·ed
barel : **bar·rel**
bare·ly (just enough); **bar·ley** (grain)
baren : **bar·on**
bareness : **bar·on·ess** (noblewoman) *or* **bar·ren·ness** (emptiness)
baretone : **bar·i·tone**
barette : **bar·rette**
bar·gain
bargan : **bar·gain**
barge
bargen : **bar·gain**
bargin : **bar·gain**
bargun : **bar·gain**
barier : **bar·ri·er**
baritoan : **bar·i·tone**
bar·i·tone
barje : **barge**
bar·ley (grain); **bare·ly** (just enough)
barnacel : **bar·na·cle**
bar·na·cle
barnakel : **bar·na·cle**
barnakle : **bar·na·cle**
barnuckle : **bar·na·cle**
barnukle : **bar·na·cle**
baroak : **ba·roque**
baroke : **ba·roque**
ba·rom·e·ter

baromiter : **ba·rom·e·ter**
bar·on (nobleman); **bar·ren**
 (unproductive)
bar·on·ess (noblewoman);
 bar·ren·ness (emptiness)
baronness : **bar·on·ess**
 (noblewoman) *or*
 bar·ren·ness (emptiness)
baroom : **bar·room**
baroqe : **ba·roque**
ba·roque
barracade : **bar·ri·cade**
barracaid : **bar·ri·cade**
bar·racks
barracooda : **bar·ra·cu·da**
bar·ra·cu·da
bar·rage
barrahge : **bar·rage**
barraks : **bar·racks**
barrakuda : **bar·ra·cu·da**
barratone : **bar·i·tone**
barrbarian : **bar·bar·i·an**
barrecade : **bar·ri·cade**
barrecks : **bar·racks**
barreir : **bar·ri·er**
bar·rel
bar·ren (unproductive); **bar·on**
 (nobleman)
barreness : **bar·on·ess**
 (noblewoman) *or*
 bar·ren·ness (emptiness)
bar·ren·ness (emptiness);
 bar·on·ess (noblewoman)
barret : **bar·rette**
barrete : **bar·rette**
barrett : **bar·rette**
bar·rette
bar·ri·cade
barricaid : **bar·ri·cade**
barricks : **bar·racks**
bar·ri·er
barrikade : **bar·ri·cade**

barril : **bar·rel**
barritone : **bar·i·tone**
barrometer : **ba·rom·e·ter**
barroness : **bar·on·ess**
 (noblewoman) *or*
 bar·ren·ness (emptiness)
barronness : **bar·on·ess**
barron : **bar·on**
bar·room
barry : **ber·ry** (fruit) *or* **bury**
 (to cover with earth)
bary : **ber·ry** (fruit) *or* **bury** (to
 cover with earth)
baryl : **ber·yl**
barytone : **bar·i·tone**
ba·salt
basault : **ba·salt**
basball : **base·ball**
base·ball
base·less
baselica : **ba·sil·i·ca**
baseliss : **base·less**
base·ment
basemint : **base·ment**
basen : **ba·sin**
ba·ses (*plur.*); **ba·sis** (*sing.*)
bash·ful
bashfull : **bash·ful**
ba·si·cal·ly
basicaly : **ba·si·cal·ly**
basicly : **ba·si·cal·ly**
basikally : **ba·si·cal·ly**
basileca : **ba·sil·i·ca**
basili : **ba·cil·li**
ba·sil·i·ca
basilika : **ba·sil·i·ca**
basilli : **ba·cil·li**
basillica : **ba·sil·i·ca**
basillus : **ba·cil·lus**
basilus : **ba·cil·lus**
ba·sin
basinet : **bas·si·net**

ba•sis (*sing.*); ba•ses (*plur.*)
Bask : **Basque**
baskette : **bas•ket**
baskit : **bas•ket**
baskitball : **bas•ket•ball**
basless : **base•less**
basment : **base•ment**
basoon : **bas•soon**
Basque
bassalt : **ba•salt**
bassenet : **bas•si•net**
bassili : **ba•cil•li**
bassilus : **ba•cil•lus**
bassin : **ba•sin**
bas•si•net
bassinette : **bas•si•net**
bassis : **ba•sis**
bassket : **bas•ket**
bassketball : **bas•ket•ball**
bas•soon
basstard : **bas•tard**
Basstille : **Bas•tille**
bast : **baste**
bast•ard
baste
Basteel : **Bas•tille**
Bastele : **Bas•tille**
basterd : **bas•tard**
Bas•tille
bastird : **bas•tard**
basune : **bas•soon**
bata : **be•ta**
bataleon : **bat•tal•ion**
batalion : **bat•tal•ion**
batary : **bat•tery**
batchelor : **bach•el•or**
bate (to subside); **bait** (lure)
Baten Rouge : **Ba•ton Rouge**
baten : **ba•ton**
bater : **bat•ter**
batery : **bat•tery**
bath (*noun*); **bathe** (*verb*)

bathe (*verb*); **bath** (*noun*)
Ba•ton Rouge
Baton Ruge : **Ba•ton Rouge**
ba•ton
battal : **bat•tle**
bat•tal•ion
battallion : **bat•tal•ion**
battary : **bat•tery**
battel : **bat•tle**
battelion : **bat•tal•ion**
bat•ter
batterry : **bat•tery**
bat•tery
bat•tle
battleon : **bat•tal•ion**
Batton Rouge : **Ba•ton Rouge**
batton : **ba•ton**
bauball : **bau•ble**
baubble : **bau•ble**
baubel : **bau•ble**
bau•ble
baucite : **baux•ite**
baudy : **bawdy**
bauk : **balk**
bauxcite : **baux•ite**
baux•ite
bawdie : **bawdy**
bawdy
bayenette : **bay•o•net**
bayinet : **bay•o•net**
bay•o•net
bayonnet : **bay•o•net**
bayoo : **bay•ou**
bay•ou
Bayrut : **Bei•rut**
ba•zaar (a fair); **bi•zarre** (strange)
bazar : **ba•zaar** (a fair) *or* **bi•zarre** (strange)
ba•zoo•ka
bazuka : **ba•zoo•ka**
bazzooka : **ba•zoo•ka**

beacan : **bea·con**
beach (shore); **beech** (tree)
beachead : **beach·head**
beach·head
beachnut : **beech·nut**
beacin : **bea·con**
beacker : **beak·er**
bea·con
beaditude : **be·at·i·tude**
beaf : **beef**
beagel : **bea·gle**
bea·gle
beagul : **bea·gle**
bea·ker
beakon : **bea·con**
beam
bear (animal); **bear** (to carry);
    bare (uncovered)
bearacade : **bar·ri·cade**
bearacuda : **bar·ra·cu·da**
bearback : **bare·back**
beard
bearfaced : **bare·faced**
bearfoot : **barefoot**
bearhanded : **bare·hand·ed**
bearly : **bare·ly**
bearometer : **ba·rom·e·ter**
bearrel : **bar·rel**
bearrier : **bar·ri·er**
beast
beastial : **bes·tial**
beat (to strike or to defeat);
    beet (plant)
beatatude : **be·at·i·tude**
beatician : **beau·ti·cian**
beatitood : **be·at·i·tude**
be·at·i·tude
beatle : **bee·tle**
beattitude : **be·at·i·tude**
beau·ti·cian
beautition : **beau·ti·cian**
beautty : **beau·ty**

beautycian : **beau·ti·cian**
bea·ver
becase : **be·cause**
becauze : **be·cause**
becawse : **be·cause**
becuz : **be·cause**
beddlam : **bed·lam**
Beddouin : **Bed·ou·in**
beddspread : **bedspread**
beddstead : **bed·stead**
bed·lam
bedlem : **bed·lam**
bedlum : **bed·lam**
Bedoin : **Bed·ou·in**
Bed·ou·in
Bedowin : **Bed·ou·in**
bed·spread
bedspred : **bed·spread**
bedsted : **bed·stead**
beech (tree); **beach** (shore)
beechhead : **beach·head**
beech·nut
beecon : **bea·con**
beef
beefs or **beeves**
beegle : **bea·gle**
beeker : **beak·er**
beekon : **bea·con**
beem : **beam**
beer (brewed drink); **bier**
    (funeral stand)
beerd : **beard**
beest : **beast**
beestial : **bes·tial**
beet (plant); **beat** (to strike or
    to defeat)
beetel : **bee·tle**
beet·le
beever : **bea·ver**
beeves or **beefs**
befoar : **be·fore**
befor : **be·fore**

be·foul
befour : **be·fore**
befowl : **be·foul**
beger : **beg·gar**
beg·gar
begger : **beg·gar**
beggin : **be·gin**
begginner : **be·gin·ner**
begginning : **be·gin·ning**
beggotten : **be·got·ten**
begguile : **be·guile**
begial : **be·guile**
begile : **be·guile**
be·gin
beginer : **be·gin·ner**
begining : **be·gin·ning**
beginn : **be·gin**
be·go·nia
begonnia : **be·go·nia**
begonya : **be·go·nia**
begoten : **be·got·ten**
begottin : **be·got·ten**
be·grudge
begrudje : **be·grudge**
begruge : **be·grudge**
be·guile
be·hav·ior
behaviour (*Brit.*) : **be·hav·ior**
beheemoth : **be·he·moth**
be·he·moth
behemuth : **be·he·moth**
beig : **beige**
beige
beighe : **beige**
beije : **beige**
beird : **beard**
Beiroot : **Bei·rut**
Bei·rut
beish : **beige**
beknighted : **be·night·ed**
bekweath : **be·queath**
beleaf : **be·lief**

beleager : **be·lea·guer**
be·lea·guer
beleagur : **be·lea·guer**
beleavable : **be·liev·able**
beleave : **be·lieve**
beleef : **be·lief**
beleeger : **be·lea·guer**
beleevable : **be·liev·able**
beleeve : **be·lieve**
beleif : **be·lief**
beleivable : **be·liev·able**
beleive : **be·lieve**
Belgem : **Bel·gium**
Belgim : **Bel·gium**
Bel·gium
Belgum : **Bel·gium**
belicose : **bel·li·cose**
believabel : **be·liev·able**
be·liev·able
believeble : **be·liev·able**
beligerent : **bel·lig·er·ent**
Beljim : **Bel·gium**
Beljum : **Bel·gium**
belkonies : **bal·co·nies**
belkony : **bal·co·ny**
belleaguer : **be·lea·guer**
bellegerent : **bel·lig·er·ent**
Bellgium : **Bel·gium**
bellicoce : **bel·li·cose**
bel·li·cose
belligerant : **bel·lig·er·ent**
bel·lig·er·ent
belligerint : **bel·lig·er·ent**
bellijerent : **bel·lig·er·ent**
bellikose : **bel·li·cose**
bellweather : **bell·weth·er**
bell·weth·er
beloe : **be·low**
be·low
belweather : **bell·weth·er**
belwether : **bell·weth·er**
bemewsed : **be·mused**

bemoosed : **be•mused**
be•mused
bemussed : **be•mused**
bemuzed : **be•mused**
benadiction : **ben•e•dic•tion**
benafactor : **ben•e•fac•tor**
benafit : **ben•e•fit**
benal : **ba•nal**
benall : **ba•nal**
benana : **ba•nana**
be•neath
beneathe : **be•neath**
benedicktion : **ben•e•dic•tion**
ben•e•dic•tion
beneeth : **be•neath**
benefacent : **be•nef•i•cent**
ben•e•fac•tor
benefaktor : **ben•e•fac•tor**
benefet : **ben•e•fit**
be•nef•i•cent
benefiscent : **be•nef•i•cent**
benefisent : **be•nef•i•cent**
ben•e•fit
benevolant : **be•nev•o•lent**
be•nev•o•lent
benidiction : **ben•e•dic•tion**
benificent : **be•nef•i•cent**
benifit : **ben•e•fit**
be•night•ed
benightid : **be•night•ed**
benited : **be•night•ed**
bennediction : **ben•e•dic•tion**
bennefactor : **ben•e•fac•tor**
benneficent : **be•nef•i•cent**
bennefit : **ben•e•fit**
bennzene : **ben•zene**
benzean : **ben•zene**
benzeen : **ben•zene**
ben•zene
benzine : **ben•zene**
beqeath : **be•queath**
be•queath

bequeathe : **be•queath**
bequeeth : **be•queath**
beracuda : **bar•ra•cu•da**
beray : **be•ret**
be•reaved
bereeved : **be•reaved**
bereived : **be•reaved**
be•ret
berey : **be•ret**
berieved : **be•reaved**
beril : **ber•yl**
beroque : **ba•roque**
berrage : **bar•rage**
berrel : **bar•rel**
berrier : **bar•ri•er**
berril : **ber•yl**
ber•ry (fruit); **bury** (to cover
with earth)
ber•serk
bersirk : **ber•serk**
bersurk : **ber•serk**
berth (bed); **birth** (to be born)
Berut : **Bei•rut**
bery : **ber•ry**
ber•yl
beryll : **ber•yl**
berzerk : **ber•serk**
besalt : **ba•salt**
beseach : **be•seech**
be•seech
beseege : **be•siege**
beseich : **be•seech**
beseige : **be•siege**
beserk : **ber•serk**
besiech : **be•seech**
be•siege
besmearch : **be•smirch**
besmerch : **be•smirch**
be•smirch
besmurch : **be•smirch**
bestal : **bes•tial**
bes•tial

bestoe : **be•stow**
be•stow
bestowe : **be•stow**
be•ta
beter : **bet•ter**
Bethlahem : **Beth•le•hem**
Beth•le•hem
Bethlihem : **Beth•le•hem**
betta : **be•ta**
bet•ter
betwean : **be•tween**
be•tween
betwein : **be•tween**
beuaty : **beau•ty**
beutician : **beau•ti•cian**
beuty : **beau•ty**
beval : **bev•el**
bevarage : **bev•er•age**
bev•el
bevelle : **bev•el**
bev•er•age
beveredge : **bev•er•age**
beverege : **bev•er•age**
bevirage : **bev•er•age**
bevvel : **bev•el**
bevvy : **bevy**
bevy
be•wail
bewair : **be•ware**
bewale : **be•wail**
be•ware
bewear : **be•ware**
bewhale : **be•wail**
bewhich : **be•witch**
bewich : **be•witch**
be•witch
bezooka : **ba•zoo•ka**
bi•as
bi•ased
biassed : **bi•ased**
Bibble : **Bi•ble**
bibbliography : **bib•li•og•ra•phy**

Bibel : **Bi•ble**
Bi•ble
bibleography : **bib•li•og•ra•phy**
bibliografy : **bib•li•og•ra•phy**
bib•li•og•ra•phy
bibliogrephy : **bib•li•og•ra•phy**
bibliogrify : **bib•li•og•ra•phy**
bibliogriphy : **bib•li•og•ra•phy**
bi•cy•cle
bi•cy•clist
biege : **beige**
bier (funeral stand); **beer**
  (brewed drink)
Bierut : **Bei•rut**
bieuty : **beau•ty**
bigonia : **be•go•nia**
bi•o•chem•ist
bious : **bi•as**
bioused : **bi•ased**
birth (to be born); **berth** (bed)
bius : **bi•as**
biused : **bi•ased**
biwitch : **be•witch**
Bizantine : **Byz•an•tine**
boalder : **boul•der**
boar (male pig); **boor**
  (ill-mannered person); **bore**
  (to drill a hole; to cause
  boredom; one who bores)
board
Boardeaux : **Bor•deaux**
board•er (renter); **bor•der**
  (boundary)
boarderline : **bor•der•line**
boardom : **bore•dom**
boast
boatanical : **bo•tan•i•cal**
bobble : **bau•ble**
boddy : **bawdy** (lewd) *or* **body**
  (corpus)
body
boemian : **bo•he•mi•an**

bogis : **bo·gus**
bo·gus
boheemian : **bo·he·mi·an**
bo·he·mi·an
boicott : **boy·cott**
Boi·se
Boisee : **Boi·se**
boisenbery : **boy·sen·ber·ry**
boiserus : **bois·ter·ous**
Boisie : **Boi·se**
boisonberry : **boy·sen·ber·ry**
bois·ter·ous
boistrous : **bois·ter·ous**
bokay : **bou·quet**
bol·der (more fearless);
   boul·der (rock)
bollsa : **bal·sa**
bollsam : **bal·sam**
bolsa : **bal·sa**
bolsa : **bal·sam**
bombadeer : **bom·bar·dier**
bombadier : **bom·bar·dier**
bombardeer : **bom·bar·dier**
bombardeir : **bom·bar·dier**
bom·bar·dier
bomb·er
bomberdier : **bom·bar·dier**
bomboo : **bam·boo**
bommer : **bomb·er**
bonannza : **bo·nan·za**
bo·nan·za
bon·dage
bondaje : **bond·age**
bondedge : **bond·age**
bondege : **bond·age**
bondige : **bond·age**
bonet : **bon·net**
boney : **bony**
bonis : **bo·nus**
bonnanza : **bo·nan·za**
bon·net
bonnit : **bon·net**

bonnus : **bo·nus**
bon·sai (dwarf tree); **ban·zai**
   (cheer)
bo·nus
bony
bonzai : **ban·zai** (cheer) *or*
   bon·sai (dwarf tree)
bonzi : **ban·zai** (cheer) *or*
   bon·sai (dwarf tree)
boobonic : **bu·bon·ic**
bookeeper : **book·keep·er**
book·keep·er
boomarang : **boom·er·ang**
boom·er·ang
boor (ill-mannered person);
   boar (male pig); **bore** (to
   drill a hole; to cause
   boredom; one who bores)
boor·ish
boo·tee *or* **boo·tie** (baby shoe);
   boo·ty (spoils of war)
boo·ty (spoils of war); **boo·tee**
   (baby shoe)
booz : **booze**
booze
boquay : **bou·quet**
boquet : **bou·quet**
borbon : **bour·bon**
bord : **board**
borde : **board**
Bor·deaux
bor·der (boundary); **board·er**
   (renter)
bor·der·line
Bordeux : **Bor·deaux**
Bordieux : **Bor·deaux**
Bordoe : **Bor·deaux**
bordom : **bore·dom**
bore (to drill a hole; to cause
   boredom; one who bores);
   boar (male pig); **boor**
   (ill-mannered person)

boredem : **bore·dom**
bore·dom
boredum : **bore·dom**
borgeois : **bour·geois** (*adj.*)
borgeoisie : **bour·geoisie** (*noun*)
borish : **boor·ish**
bor·ough (town); **bur·ro** (pack animal); **bur·row** (animal hole)
borow : **bor·row**
borro : **bor·row**
bor·row
bos·om
bosoom : **bos·om**
bossom : **bos·om**
botaney : **bot·a·ny**
bo·tan·i·cal
botanicle : **bo·tan·i·cal**
botanikal : **bo·tan·i·cal**
botannical : **bo·tan·i·cal**
botanny : **bot·a·ny**
bot·a·ny
boteny : **bot·a·ny**
botiny : **bot·a·ny**
botle : **bot·tle**
botom : **bot·tom**
bottal : **bot·tle**
bottanical : **bo·tan·i·cal**
bottel : **bot·tle**
bottem : **bot·tom**
bot·tle
bottocks : **but·tocks**
bot·tom
bottoneer : **bou·ton·niere**
bottum : **bot·tom**
bought
bougt : **bought**
bouil·lon (soup); **bul·lion** (gold blocks)
boukay : **bou·quet**
boulavard : **boul·e·vard**
boul·der

boul·e·vard
boulevarde : **boul·e·vard**
bounce
bound·ary
boundery : **bound·ary**
boundiry : **bound·ary**
boundry : **bound·ary**
bounse : **bounce**
boun·te·ous
boun·ti·ful
bountifull : **boun·ti·ful**
bountious : **boun·te·ous**
bountius : **boun·te·ous**
bountyful : **boun·ti·ful**
bouquay : **bou·quet**
bou·quet
bourben : **bour·bon**
bour·bon
bourgeis : **bour·geois** (*adj.*)
bourgeisie : **bour·geoisie** (*noun*)
bour·geois (*adj.*); **bour·geoi·sie** (*noun*)
bourgeoisee : **bour·geoisie** (*noun*)
bour·geoisie (*noun*); **bour·geois** (*adj.*)
bourgois : **bour·geois** (*adj.*)
bourgoisie : **bour·geoisie** (*noun*)
bourshois : **bour·geois** (*adj.*)
bourshoisie : **bour·geoisie** (*noun*)
bourshwa : **bour·geois** (*adj.*)
bourshwasie : **bour·geoisie** (*noun*)
boutoniere : **bou·ton·niere**
bou·ton·niere
bouttoniere : **bou·ton·niere**
bouyancy : **buoy·an·cy**
bouyant : **buoy·ant**
bouyency : **buoy·an·cy**
bouyensy : **buoy·an·cy**

bouyent : **buoy•ant**
bouyint : **buoy•ant**
bownce : **bounce**
bownteous : **boun•te•ous**
boxite : **baux•ite**
boy (lad); **buoy** (sea marker)
boyancy : **buoy•an•cy**
boyant : **buoy•ant**
boycot : **boy•cott**
boy•cott
boyency : **buoy•an•cy**
boyent : **buoy•ant**
boykott : **boy•cott**
Boyse : **Boi•se**
boy•sen•ber•ry
boysonberry : **boy•sen•ber•ry**
boysterous : **bois•ter•ous**
brace•let
bracelett : **brace•let**
bracelit : **brace•let**
bragart : **brag•gart**
brag•gart
braggert : **brag•gart**
braik : **brake** (to slow or stop)
  or **break** (to shatter)
Brail : **Braille**
Braille
brain
brakable : **break•able**
brake (to slow or stop); **break**
  (to shatter)
brakethrough : **break•through**
Brale : **Braille**
Bralle : **Braille**
brane : **brain**
braselet : **brace•let**
braselit : **brace•let**
Brasil : **Bra•zil**
brauny : **brawn•y**
bra•va•do
bravadoe : **bra•va•do**
bravary : **brav•ery**

braverry : **brav•ery**
brav•ery
bravodo : **bra•va•do**
bravry : **brav•ery**
brawny
Bra•zil
Brazill : **Bra•zil**
breach (to break); **breech**
  (hinder or lower part)
breachcloth : **breech•cloth**
breaches (breaks); **breech•es**
  (trousers)
bread (food); **bred** (raised)
breadth
break (to shatter); **brake** (to
  slow or stop)
breakabel : **break•able**
break•able
break•fast
breakfest : **break•fast**
breakfist : **break•fast**
breakible : **break•able**
break•through
breakthru : **break•through**
breakthrugh : **break•through**
breast
breath (*noun*); **breathe** (*verb*)
breathe (*verb*); **breath** (*noun*)
breathren : **breth•ren**
breath•er
breaze : **breeze**
breazily : **breez•i•ly**
breckfast : **break•fast**
bred (raised); **bread** (food)
bredth : **breadth**
breech (hinder or lower part);
  breach (to break)
breech•cloth
breechclothe : **breech•cloth**
breech•es (trousers); **breaches**
  (breaks)
breef : **brief**

breethe : **breathe**
breether : **breath•er**
breezaly : **breez•i•ly**
breeze
breez•i•ly
bregade : **bri•gade**
breif : **brief**
breivity : **brev•i•ty**
brekfast : **break•fast**
brekfest : **break•fast**
brest : **breast**
breth : **breath**
bretheren : **breth•ren**
breth•ren
brevado : **bra•va•do**
brevety : **brev•i•ty**
brev•i•ty
brewary : **brew•ery**
brewerry : **brew•ery**
brew•ery
brewry : **brew•ery**
bribary : **brib•ery**
brib•ery
bribry : **brib•ery**
brid•al (marriage); **brid•le**
  (harness)
bridge
bridje : **bridge**
brid•le (harness); **brid•al**
  (marriage)
brief
brievity : **brev•i•ty**
bri•gade
brigadeer : **brig•a•dier**
brigadeir : **brig•a•dier**
brig•a•dier
brigaid : **bri•gade**
brige : **bridge**
brigedier : **brig•a•dier**
briggade : **bri•gade**
briggadier : **brig•a•dier**
bright•en

brightin : **bright•en**
briliance : **bril•liance**
briliant : **bril•liant**
brillance : **bril•liance**
bril•liance
brillianse : **bril•liance**
bril•liant
brillience : **bril•liance**
brilliense : **bril•liance**
brillient : **bril•liant**
brissle : **bris•tle**
brisstle : **bris•tle**
bristel : **bris•tle**
bris•tle
Brit•ain (nation); **Brit•on**
  (person)
Britan : **Brit•ain** (nation) *or*
  Brit•on (person)
Britania : **Bri•tan•ni•a**
Bri•tan•ni•a
Britany : **Brit•ta•ny**
Briten : **Brit•ain** (nation) *or*
  Brit•on (person)
briten : **bright•en**
Britesh : **Brit•ish**
Britian : **Brit•ain** (nation) *or*
  Brit•on (person)
Brit•ish
britle : **brit•tle**
Britny : **Brit•ta•ny**
Brit•on (person); **Brit•ain**
  (nation)
Brit•ta•ny
brittel : **brit•tle**
Brittish : **Brit•ish**
brit•tle
Britton : **Brit•ain** (nation) *or*
  Brit•on (person)
broach (to open); **brooch**
  (ornamental pin)
bro•chure
bronny : **brawny**

brooch (ornamental pin);
  broach (to open)
Brooklin : **Brook·lyn**
Brook·lyn
Brooklynn : **Brook·lyn**
broose : **bruise**
broshure : **bro·chure**
brosure : **bro·chure**
broth·er
brouse : **browse**
browse
browze : **browse**
bruise
bruize : **bruise**
bru·net *or* **bru·nette**
bru·nette *or* **bru·net**
brunnette : **bru·net**
bruse : **bruise**
Brusels : **Brus·sels**
brusk : **brusque**
brusqe : **brusque**
brusque
Brussells : **Brus·sels**
Brussels
Brussles : **Brus·sels**
bru·tal
brutel : **bru·tal**
bruther : **broth·er**
brutil : **bru·tal**
brutle : **bru·tal**
Buanos Aires : **Bue·nos Ai·res**
bubbel : **bub·ble**
bub·ble
buble : **bub·ble**
bu·bon·ic
bubonick : **bu·bon·ic**
bubonnic : **bu·bon·ic**
bucanneer : **buc·ca·neer**
buc·ca·neer
buccaneir : **buc·ca·neer**
buccanier : **buc·ca·neer**
buccanneer : **buc·ca·neer**

bucher : **butch·er**
bucholic : **bu·col·ic**
buckaneer : **buc·ca·neer**
buckel : **buc·kle**
buckeneer : **buc·ca·neer**
buc·ket
buckit : **buc·ket**
buc·kle
bucksom : **bux·om**
bu·col·ic
bucolick : **bu·col·ic**
Buda : **Bud·dha**
Budda : **Bud·dha**
Bud·dha
Budd·hist
Buddist : **Budd·hist**
bud·get
budgetarry : **bud·get·ary**
bud·get·ary
budgetery : **bud·get·ary**
budgit : **bud·get**
budgitary : **bud·get·ary**
Budha : **Bud·dha**
Budist : **Budd·hist**
Buenas Aires : **Bue·nos Ai·res**
Bue·nos Ai·res
Buenos Airres : **Bue·nos Ai·res**
Buenos Ires : **Bue·nos Ai·res**
bufalo : **buf·fa·lo**
bufelo : **buf·fa·lo**
bufet : **buf·fet**
buffallo : **buf·fa·lo**
buf·fa·lo
buffat : **buf·fet**
buffay : **buf·fet**
buffelo : **buf·fa·lo**
buf·fet
buffey : **buf·fet**
buf·foon
buffoonary : **buf·foon·ery**
buf·foon·ery
buffune : **buf·foon**

buffunery : **buf•foon•ery**
bufoon : **buf•foon**
bufoonery : **buf•foon•ery**
bugal : **bu•gle**
bugel : **bu•gle**
buget : **bud•get**
bugetary : **bud•get•ary**
buggler : **bu•gler**
buglar : **bu•gler**
bu•gle
bu•gler
build
bukle : **buc•kle**
bukolic : **bu•col•ic**
bulet : **bul•let**
buletin : **bul•le•tin**
bulevard : **boul•e•vard**
bulk•i•er
bulkyer : **bulk•i•er**
bullack : **bul•lock**
bullavard : **boul•e•vard**
bulldoser : **bull•doz•er**
bull•doz•er
bulleck : **bul•lock**
bul•let
bulleten : **bul•le•tin**
bullevard : **boul•e•vard**
bul•le•tin
bul•lion (gold blocks);
   bouil•lon (soup)
bullit : **bul•let**
bullitin : **bul•le•tin**
bul•lock
bullrush : **bul•rush**
bullwark : **bul•wark**
bullwerk : **bul•wark**
bullwork : **bul•wark**
bulock : **bul•lock**
bul•rush
bul•wark
bulwerk : **bul•wark**
bulwork : **bul•wark**

bundal : **bun•dle**
bundel : **bun•dle**
bun•dle
bungaloe : **bun•ga•low**
bun•ga•low
bungelow : **bun•ga•low**
bungolow : **bun•ga•low**
bun•ion
bunnion : **bun•ion**
bunyan : **bun•ion**
bunyen : **bun•ion**
bunyon : **bun•ion**
buoy (sea marker); **boy** (lad)
buoy•an•cy
buoyansy : **buoy•an•cy**
buoy•ant
buquet : **bou•quet**
buray : **be•ret**
burben : **bour•bon**
burbon : **bour•bon**
burch : **birch**
burdansom : **bur•den•some**
bur•den
bur•den•some
burdensum : **bur•den•some**
burdonsome : **bur•den•some**
bureacrisy : **bu•reau•cra•cy**
bu•reau
bu•reau•cra•cy
bureaucrasy : **bu•reau•cra•cy**
burgen : **bur•geon**
burgeois : **bour•geois**
burgeoisie : **bour•geoisie**
bur•geon
bur•glar
bur•glary
burgler : **bur•glar**
burglery : **bur•glary**
burglir : **bur•glar**
burglury : **bur•glary**
buri•al
buriel : **buri•al**

burieu : **bu•reau**
burieucracy : **bu•reau•cra•cy**
bur•lap
burlesk : **bur•lesque**
bur•lesque
bur•ley (tobacco); **bur•ly**
  (muscular)
bur•ly
burreau : **bu•reau**
burreaucracy : **bu•reau•cra•cy**
burret : **bar•rette**
burrette : **bar•rette**
burrey : **bury**
bur•ro (pack animal);
  bor•ough (town); **bur•row**
  (animal hole)
bur•row (animal hole);
  bor•ough (town); **bur•ro**
  (pack animal)
bur•sar
burser : **bur•sar**
burserk : **ber•serk**
bur•si•tis
bursitus : **bur•si•tis**
burthday : **birth•day**
burthmark : **birth•mark**
burthplace : **birth•place**
bury (to cover with earth);
  ber•ry (fruit)
buryal : **buri•al**
bus•es *or* **bus•ses**
bushal : **bush•el**
bush•el
bushell : **bush•el**
busi•er
busi•ness (economic activity);
  busy•ness (being busy)
busom : **bos•om**
bus•ses *or* **bus•es**
bussier : **busi•er**

bussle : **bus•tle**
busstle : **bus•tle**
bustel : **bus•tle**
bus•tle
busyier : **busi•er**
busy•ness (being busy);
  busi•ness (economic activity)
butain : **bu•tane**
bu•tane
butchary : **butch•ery**
butch•er
butch•ery
bute : **butte**
buter : **but•ter**
butition : **beau•ti•cian**
butlar : **but•ler**
butocks : **but•tocks**
butress : **but•tress**
butte
but•ter
buttler : **but•ler**
but•tocks
buttonier : **bou•ton•niere**
buttox : **but•tocks**
but•tress
buttriss : **but•tress**
buty : **beau•ty**
bux•om
buxum : **bux•om**
buzard : **buz•zard**
buze : **booze**
buz•zard
buzzerd : **buz•zard**
bycicle : **bi•cy•cle**
byciclist : **bi•cy•clist**
byochemist : **bi•o•chem•ist**
byou : **bay•ou**
Byzanteen : **Byz•an•tine**
Byz•an•tine
Byzentine : **Byz•an•tine**

C

cabage : **cab•bage**
ca•bana
cabanna : **ca•bana**
cabaray : **cab•a•ret**
cab•a•ret
cab•bage
cabbana : **ca•bana**
cabbedge : **cab•bage**
cabbege : **cab•bage**
cabbin : **cab•in**
caben : **cab•in**
cabenet : **cab•i•net**
caberet : **cab•a•ret**
cab•in
cab•i•net
cabinnet : **cab•i•net**
cabnet : **cab•i•net**
cacafony : **ca•coph•o•ny**
cacaphony : **ca•coph•o•ny**
cacheir : **cash•ier**
cachew : **cash•ew**
cachoo : **cash•ew**
cack•le
cacktus : **cac•tus**
cacle : **cack•le**
cacofony : **ca•coph•o•ny**
ca•coph•o•ny
cactos : **cac•tus**
cac•tus
cacus : **cau•cus**
cadance : **ca•dence**
cadanse : **ca•dence**
ca•dav•er
cadavir : **ca•dav•er**
cadavver : **ca•dav•er**
caddet : **ca•det**
ca•dence
cadense : **ca•dence**
ca•det
cadett : **ca•det**

cadette : **ca•det**
cae•sar•e•an
caesarian : **cae•sar•e•an**
cafaterea : **caf•e•te•ria**
cafateria : **caf•e•te•ria**
cafaterria : **caf•e•te•ria**
cafee : **cof•fee**
cafeen : **caf•feine**
cafeine : **caf•feine**
cafene : **caf•feine**
cafetearia : **caf•e•te•ria**
cafeterea : **caf•e•te•ria**
caf•e•te•ria
cafeterria : **caf•e•te•ria**
caff : **cough**
caffateria : **caf•e•te•ria**
caffee : **cof•fee**
caffeen : **caf•feine**
caf•feine
caffene : **caf•feine**
caffeteria : **caf•e•te•ria**
caffiene : **caf•feine**
caffine : **caf•feine**
cagole : **ca•jole**
caidence : **ca•dence**
cainine : **ca•nine**
cairamel : **car•a•mel**
cairful : **care•ful**
cairless : **care•less**
Cai•ro
cairopractor : **chi•ro•prac•tor**
Cairro : **Cai•ro**
cajoal : **ca•jole**
ca•jole
cajolle : **ca•jole**
cakophony : **ca•coph•o•ny**
caktos : **cac•tus**
caktus : **cac•tus**
calaber : **cal•i•ber**
calacko : **cal•i•co**

Calafornia : **Cal·i·for·nia**
calamety : **ca·lam·i·ty**
calamitty : **ca·lam·i·ty**
ca·lam·i·ty
calammity : **ca·lam·i·ty**
calamny : **cal·um·ny**
calander : **cal·en·dar** (chart of
  dates) *or* **cal·en·der** (pressing
  machine) *or* **col·an·der**
  (drainer)
calaper : **cal·i·per**
calarie : **cal·o·rie** (energy unit)
  or **cel·ery** (vegetable)
calary : **cal·o·rie** (energy unit)
  or **cel·ery** (vegetable)
calasthenics : **cal·is·then·ics**
calceim : **cal·ci·um**
calceum : **cal·ci·um**
cal·ci·um
calcuelate : **cal·cu·late**
cal·cu·late
calculis : **cal·cu·lus**
calcullate : **cal·cu·late**
calcullus : **cal·cu·lus**
calculous : **cal·cu·lus**
cal·cu·lus
caleber : **cal·i·ber**
caleco : **cal·i·co**
Calefornia : **Cal·i·for·nia**
caleidascope : **ka·lei·do·scope**
caleko : **cal·i·co**
cal·en·dar (chart of dates);
  cal·en·der (pressing
  machine);**col·an·der** (drainer)
cal·en·der (pressing machine);
  cal·en·dar (chart of dates);
  col·an·der (drainer)
calenndar : **cal·en·dar** (chart of
  dates) *or* **cal·en·der** (pressing
  machine) *or* **col·an·der**
  (drainer)
caleper : **cal·i·per**

calepso : **ca·lyp·so**
calery : **cal·o·rie** (energy unit)
  or **cel·ery** (vegetable)
cal·i·ber
calibir : **cal·i·ber**
calibre (*Brit.*) : **cal·i·ber**
calicco : **cal·i·co**
calicko : **cal·i·co**
cal·i·co
caliedoscope : **ka·lei·do·scope**
Californea : **Cal·i·for·nia**
Cal·i·for·nia
caliko : **cal·i·co**
calindar : **cal·en·dar** (chart of
  dates) *or* **cal·en·der** (pressing
  machine) *or* **col·an·der**
  (drainer)
calinder : **cal·en·dar** (chart of
  dates) *or* **cal·en·der** (pressing
  machine) *or* **col·an·der**
  (drainer)
cal·i·per
calipper : **cal·i·per**
calipso : **ca·lyp·so**
calis : **cal·lous** (lack of feeling)
  or **cal·lus** (hardened skin)
calissthenics : **cal·is·then·ics**
calissthintics : **cal·is·then·ics**
cal·is·then·ics
calisthinics : **cal·is·then·ics**
callaflower : **cau·li·flow·er**
callamity : **ca·lam·i·ty**
callasthenics : **cal·is·then·ics**
callcium : **cal·ci·um**
callculate : **cal·cu·late**
callculus : **cal·cu·lus**
calldran : **caul·dron**
calldren : **caul·dron**
calldron : **caul·dron**
callendar : **cal·en·dar** (chart of
  dates) *or* **cal·en·der** (pressing

machine) *or* col•an•der
(drainer)
callery : cal•o•rie (energy unit)
or cel•ery (vegetable)
callesthenics : cal•is•then•ics
calliber : cal•i•ber
callico : cal•i•co
callidoscope : ka•lei•do•scope
calliflour : cau•li•flow•er
calliflower : cau•li•flow•er
Callifornia : Cal•i•for•nia
calliper : cal•i•per
callipso : ca•lyp•so
callis : cal•lous (lack of feeling)
or cal•lus (hardened skin)
calliss : cal•lous (lack of
feeling) *or* cal•lus (hardened
skin)
callisthenics : cal•is•then•ics
callisthinicks : cal•is•then•ics
callisthinics : cal•is•then•ics
callorie : cal•o•rie
callory : cal•o•rie
cal•lous (lack of feeling);
cal•lus (hardened skin)
callumny : cal•um•ny
cal•lus (hardened skin);
cal•lous (lack of feeling)
callvary : Cal•va•ry (site of the
Crucifixion) *or* cav•al•ry
(horse troops)
Callvinist : Cal•vin•ist
callypso : ca•lyp•so
calocko : cal•i•co
caloco : cal•i•co
calomny : cal•um•ny
calorey : cal•o•rie
cal•o•rie
calorrey : cal•o•rie
calorrie : cal•o•rie
calory : cal•o•rie

calous : cal•lous (lack of
feeling) *or* cal•lus (hardened
skin)
calqulate : cal•cu•late
calqulus : cal•cu•lus
calseum : cal•ci•um
calsium : cal•ci•um
caluclate : cal•cu•late
calummny : cal•um•ny
calumney : cal•um•ny
calumnie : cal•um•ny
cal•um•ny
calus : cal•lous (lack of feeling)
or cal•lus (hardened skin)
Cal•va•ry (site of the
Crucifixion); cav•al•ry (horse
troops)
calvelry : Cal•va•ry (site of the
Crucifixion) *or* cav•al•ry
(horse troops)
Calvenist : Cal•vin•ist
calvery : Cal•va•ry (site of the
Crucifixion) *or* cav•al•ry
(horse troops)
Cal•vin•ist
Calvinnist : Cal•vin•ist
ca•lyp•so
calypsoe : ca•lyp•so
camal : cam•el
camara : cam•era
ca•ma•ra•de•rie *or* com•rad•ery
camarodery : ca•ma•ra•de•rie
camealia : ca•mel•lia
cameilia : ca•mel•lia
cam•el
camelia : ca•mel•lia
ca•mel•lia
camelya : ca•mel•lia
cam•eo
cam•era
cameraderie : ca•ma•ra•de•rie
camerra : cam•era

camfor : **cam•phor**
camielia : **ca•mel•lia**
camil : **cam•el**
camill : **cam•el**
camillia : **ca•mel•lia**
camio : **cam•eo**
camioe : **cam•eo**
camira : **cam•era**
cammal : **cam•el**
cammara : **cam•era**
cammel : **cam•el**
cammelia : **ca•mel•lia**
cammeo : **cam•eo**
cammera : **cam•era**
cammerra : **cam•era**
cammillia : **ca•mel•lia**
cammio : **cam•eo**
cammira : **cam•era**
cammirra : **cam•era**
cammouflage : **cam•ou•flage**
cammuflauge : **cam•ou•flage**
camoflage : **cam•ou•flage**
camoflauge : **cam•ou•flage**
camofloge : **cam•ou•flage**
cam•ou•flage
campagne : **cam•paign**
cam•paign
campaigne : **cam•paign**
campain : **cam•paign**
campane : **cam•paign**
campes : **cam•pus**
campfor : **cam•phor**
campher : **cam•phor**
cam•phor
camphur : **cam•phor**
campis : **cam•pus**
camppus : **cam•pus**
cam•pus
campuss : **cam•pus**
camra : **cam•era**
camraderie : **ca•ma•ra•de•rie**
camuflague : **cam•ou•flage**

camuflauge : **cam•ou•flage**
camufloge : **cam•ou•flage**
canabal : **can•ni•bal**
canabel : **can•ni•bal**
canable : **can•ni•bal**
Can•a•da
Canadean : **Ca•na•di•an**
Ca•na•di•an
Canadien : **Ca•na•di•an**
Canaidian : **Ca•na•di•an**
canarry : **ca•nary** (bird) *or*
  can•nery (factory)
ca•nary (bird); **can•nery**
  (factory)
canaster : **can•is•ter**
can•cel
cancelation : **can•cel•la•tion**
can•celed *or* **can•celled**
cancell : **can•cel**
cancellaition : **can•cel•la•tion**
can•cel•la•tion
can•celled *or* **can•celed**
can•cer
cancil : **can•cel**
cancillation : **can•cel•la•tion**
cancilled : **can•celed**
cancor : **can•cer**
cancur : **can•cer**
candal : **can•dle**
candalabra : **can•de•la•bra**
candalstick : **can•dle•stick**
canded : **can•did**
candedacy : **can•di•da•cy**
candedasy : **can•di•da•cy**
candel : **can•dle**
can•de•la•bra
candellabra : **can•de•la•bra**
candelstick : **can•dle•stick**
cander : **can•dor**
can•did
can•di•da•cy
candidasy : **can•di•da•cy**

candidcy : **can·di·da·cy**
candidecy : **can·di·da·cy**
candidicy : **can·di·da·cy**
candidisy : **can·di·da·cy**
candil : **can·dle**
candilabra : **can·de·la·bra**
candilstick : **can·dle·stick**
can·dle
candleabra : **can·de·la·bra**
can·dle·stick
can·dor
candur : **can·dor**
Canecticut : **Con·nect·i·cut**
Caneda : **Can·a·da**
canen : **can·non** (artillery) *or* **can·on** (list of books; clergy; church law)
canery : **ca·nary** (bird) *or* **can·nery** (factory)
canester : **can·is·ter**
canibal : **can·ni·bal**
Canida : **Can·a·da**
canien : **ca·nine**
canin : **can·non** (artillery) *or* **can·on** (list of books; clergy; church law)
ca·nine
canion : **can·yon**
can·is·ter
cannabal : **can·ni·bal**
cannabel : **can·ni·bal**
cannable : **can·ni·bal**
Cannada : **Can·a·da**
Cannadian : **Ca·na·di·an**
cannary : **ca·nary** (bird) *or* **can·nery** (factory)
cannaster : **can·is·ter**
cannebal : **can·ni·bal**
canneble : **can·ni·bal**
cannen : **can·non** (artillery) *or* **can·on** (list of books; clergy; church law)

can·nery (factory); **ca·nary** (bird)
cannester : **can·is·ter**
Canneticut : **Con·nect·i·cut**
can·ni·bal
cannibel : **can·ni·bal**
cannible : **can·ni·bal**
cannin : **can·non** (artillery) *or* **can·on** (list of books; clergy; church law)
cannine : **ca·nine**
cannister : **can·is·ter**
cannoe : **ca·noe**
can·non (artillery); **can·on** (list of books; clergy; church law)
cannu : **ca·noe**
cannue : **ca·noe**
cannun : **can·non** (artillery) *or* **can·on** (list of books; clergy; church law)
cannuster : **can·is·ter**
cannyon : **can·yon**
ca·noe
can·on (list of books; clergy; church law); **can·non** (artillery)
canoo : **ca·noe**
Cansas : **Kan·sas**
cansel : **can·cel**
cansellation : **can·cel·la·tion**
canselled : **can·celed**
canser : **can·cer**
cansillation : **can·cel·la·tion**
cant (slope; hypocrisy); **can't** (cannot)
can't (cannot); **cant** (slope; hypocrisy)
cantakerous : **can·tan·ker·ous**
cantaloape : **can·ta·loupe**
cantalope : **can·ta·loupe**
can·ta·loupe
cantankarous : **can·tan·ker·ous**

can•tan•ker•ous
cantankerus : **can•tan•ker•ous**
can•ta•ta
cantatta : **can•ta•ta**
cantean : **can•teen**
can•teen
canteloape : **can•ta•loupe**
cantelope : **can•ta•loupe**
canteloupe : **can•ta•loupe**
cantene : **can•teen**
can•ter (horse trot); **can•tor**
  (chanter)
cantilope : **can•ta•loupe**
cantiloupe : **can•ta•loupe**
cantine : **can•teen**
can•tor (chanter); **can•ter** (horse
  trot)
cantota : **can•ta•ta**
cantotta : **can•ta•ta**
canue : **ca•noe**
canun : **can•non** (artillery) *or*
  can•on (list of books; clergy;
  church law)
canuster : **can•is•ter**
can•vas (cloth); **can•vass** (to
  survey)
can•vass (to survey); **can•vas**
  (cloth)
canves : **can•vas** (cloth) *or*
  can•vass (to survey)
canvess : **can•vas** (cloth) *or*
  can•vass (to survey)
canvis : **can•vas** (cloth) *or*
  can•vass (to survey)
canviss : **can•vas** (cloth) *or*
  can•vass (to survey)
canvus : **can•vas** (cloth) *or*
  can•vass (to survey)
canvuss : **can•vas** (cloth) *or*
  can•vass (to survey)
canyen : **can•yon**
canyin : **can•yon**

can•yon
capabal : **ca•pa•ble**
capabel : **ca•pa•ble**
ca•pa•bil•i•ty
capabillity : **ca•pa•bil•i•ty**
ca•pa•ble
capablety : **ca•pa•bil•i•ty**
capaccity : **ca•pac•i•ty**
capacety : **ca•pac•i•ty**
capachious : **ca•pa•cious**
ca•pa•cious
capacitty : **ca•pac•i•ty**
ca•pac•i•ty
capallary : **cap•il•lary**
capashious : **ca•pa•cious**
capasious : **ca•pa•cious**
capasitty : **ca•pac•i•ty**
capasity : **ca•pac•i•ty**
capatious : **ca•pa•cious**
capchure : **cap•ture**
capcion : **cap•tion**
capcise : **cap•size**
capcize : **cap•size**
capebility : **ca•pa•bil•i•ty**
capeble : **ca•pa•ble**
capellary : **cap•il•lary**
capibility : **ca•pa•bil•i•ty**
capible : **ca•pa•ble**
capilary : **cap•il•lary**
cap•il•lary
capillerry : **cap•il•lary**
capillery : **cap•il•lary**
cap•i•tal (city; property);
  cap•i•tol (statehouse)
cap•i•tal•ism
capitel : **cap•i•tal** (city;
  property) *or* **cap•i•tol**
  (statehouse)
capitelism : **cap•i•tal•ism**
capitle: **cap•i•tal** (city;
  property) *or* **cap•i•tol**
  (statehouse)

cap·i·tol (statehouse); **cap·i·tal**
(city; property)
capitolism : **cap·i·tal·ism**
capittal : **cap·i·tal** (city;
property) *or* **cap·i·tol**
(statehouse)
capitul: **cap·i·tal** (city;
property) *or* **cap·i·tol**
(statehouse)
cappellary : **cap·il·lary**
cappillary : **cap·il·lary**
cappital : **cap·i·tal** (city;
property) *or* **cap·i·tol**
(statehouse)
cappitalism : **cap·i·tal·ism**
capsel : **cap·sule**
capsell : **cap·sule**
capshen : **cap·tion**
capshun : **cap·tion**
capshure : **cap·ture**
capsil : **cap·sule**
capsill : **cap·sule**
capsise : **cap·size**
cap·size
capsool : **cap·sule**
capsul : **cap·sule**
cap·sule
cap·tain
captan : **cap·tain**
capten : **cap·tain**
capter : **cap·tor**
captian : **cap·tain**
captin : **cap·tain**
cap·tion
captoin : **cap·tion**
cap·tor (*noun*); **cap·ture** (*verb*)
captur : **cap·tor** (*noun*) *or*
cap·ture (*verb*)
cap·ture (*verb*); **cap·tor** (*noun*)
Carabean : **Car·ib·be·an**
caraboo : **car·i·bou**
carabou : **car·i·bou**

ca·rafe
caraffe : **ca·rafe**
caramal : **car·a·mel**
car·a·mel
caramul : **car·a·mel**
car·at *or* **kar·at** (weight of
gems); **car·et** (^); **car·rot**
(vegetable)
carature : **car·i·ca·ture**
car·a·van
carbahydrate : **car·bo·hy·drate**
carban : **car·bon**
carbean : **car·bine**
carbeen : **car·bine**
carbehidrate : **car·bo·hy·drate**
carbehydrate : **car·bo·hy·drate**
carben : **car·bon**
carbene : **car·bine**
carberater : **car·bu·re·tor**
carberator : **car·bu·re·tor**
carberetor : **car·bu·re·tor**
carbihydrate : **car·bo·hy·drate**
carbin : **car·bon**
car·bine
carbohidrait : **car·bo·hy·drate**
carbohidrate : **car·bo·hy·drate**
car·bo·hy·drate
car·bon
carborater : **car·bu·re·tor**
carborator : **car·bu·re·tor**
carboretor : **car·bu·re·tor**
carburator : **car·bu·re·tor**
carbureter : **car·bu·re·tor**
car·bu·re·tor
car·cass
carcus : **car·cass**
carcuss : **car·cass**
cardanal : **car·di·nal**
cardeac : **car·di·ac**
cardegan : **car·di·gan**
cardenal : **car·di·nal**
cardenel : **car·di·nal**

car•di•ac
cardiack : **car•di•ac**
cardiak : **car•di•ac**
car•di•gan
cardiggan : **car•di•gan**
cardiggin : **car•di•gan**
cardigin : **car•di•gan**
car•di•nal
cardinall : **car•di•nal**
cardinel : **car•di•nal**
cardinnal : **car•di•nal**
carear : **ca•reer**
carebou : **car•i•bou**
carecature : **car•i•ca•ture**
ca•reer
care•ful (cautious); **car•ful** (full
  car)
carefull : **care•ful**
carel : **car•ol** (song) *or* **car•rel**
  (study table)
care•less
careliss : **care•less**
caremel : **car•a•mel**
carere : **ca•reer**
ca•ress
car•et (^); **car•rot** (vegetable);
  kar•at (weight of gems)
carevan : **car•a•van**
car•ful (full car); **care•ful**
  (cautious)
cariage : **car•riage**
Ca•rib•be•an
Caribean : **Ca•rib•be•an**
Caribian : **Ca•rib•be•an**
cariboo : **car•i•bou**
car•i•bou
car•i•ca•ture
caricture : **car•i•ca•ture**
carisma : **char•is•ma**
cariture : **car•i•ca•ture**
carkas : **car•cass**
carkass : **car•cass**

carkess : **car•cass**
carmel : **car•a•mel**
carnadge : **car•nage**
car•nage
car•nal
carnavore : **car•ni•vore**
carnedge : **car•nage**
carnege : **car•nage**
carnel : **car•nal**
carnevore : **car•ni•vore**
carnidge : **car•nage**
carnige : **car•nage**
carnil : **car•nal**
carnivor : **car•ni•vore**
car•ni•vore
car•ol (song); **car•rel** (study
  table)
carosell : **car•ou•sel**
ca•rouse
car•ou•sel
carpat : **car•pet**
car•pen•ter
car•pet
carpinter : **car•pen•ter**
carpit : **car•pet**
Carrabean : **Ca•rib•be•an**
Carrabian : **Ca•rib•be•an**
carradge : **car•riage**
carrafe : **ca•rafe**
carrage : **car•riage**
carramel : **car•a•mel**
carrasel : **car•ou•sel**
carravan : **car•a•van**
carreer : **ca•reer**
car•rel (study table); **car•ol**
  (song)
carremel : **car•a•mel**
carresel : **car•ou•sel**
carress : **ca•ress**
carrevan : **car•a•van**
car•riage
Carribean : **Ca•rib•be•an**

Carribian : **Ca•rib•be•an**
carribou : **car•i•bou**
carridge : **car•riage**
carrige : **car•riage**
carrivan : **car•a•van**
carrol : **car•rel** (study table) *or*
  car•ol (song)
carrosel : **car•ou•sel**
car•rot (vegetable); **car•et** (^);
  kar•at (weight of gems)
carrouse : **ca•rouse**
carrousel : **car•ou•sel**
carryvan : **car•a•van**
cartalage : **car•ti•lage**
cartalege : **car•ti•lage**
cartalige : **car•ti•lage**
cartan : **car•ton**
cartelage : **car•ti•lage**
cartelige : **car•ti•lage**
carten : **car•ton**
car•ti•lage
cartilege : **car•ti•lage**
cartin : **car•ton**
car•ton
car•toon
cartradge : **car•tridge**
cartrage : **car•tridge**
cartredge : **car•tridge**
car•tridge
cartrige : **car•tridge**
cartune : **car•toon**
caseeno : **ca•si•no**
casel : **cas•tle**
caseno : **ca•si•no**
caserole : **cas•se•role**
casheer : **cash•ier**
casheir : **cash•ier**
cashere : **cash•ier**
cash•ew
cash•ier
cashmear : **cash•mere**
cashmeer : **cash•mere**

cashmeir : **cash•mere**
cash•mere
cashmier : **cash•mere**
cashoo : **cash•ew**
cashou : **cash•ew**
ca•si•no
casock : **cas•sock** (robe) *or*
  cos•sack (Russian cavalry)
cassack : **cas•sock** (robe) *or*
  cos•sack (Russian cavalry)
cassarole : **cas•se•role**
cassaroll : **cas•se•role**
cassel : **cas•tle**
casseno : **ca•si•no**
cas•se•role
casseroll : **cas•se•role**
cassick : **cas•sock** (robe) *or*
  cos•sack (Russian cavalry)
cassino : **ca•si•no**
cassirole : **cas•se•role**
cassoc : **cas•sock** (robe) *or*
  cos•sack (Russian cavalry)
cas•sock (robe); **cos•sack**
  (Russian cavalry)
casstle : **cas•tle**
cast (to throw off); **caste** (social
  system)
cas•ta•net
castanette : **cas•ta•net**
caste (social system); **cast** (to
  throw off)
castel : **cas•tle**
castenette : **cas•ta•net**
castinet : **cas•ta•net**
castinette : **cas•ta•net**
cas•tle
catachism : **cat•e•chism**
cataclism : **cat•a•clysm**
cat•a•clysm
cat•a•comb
catacome : **cat•a•comb**
catagory : **cat•e•go•ry**

catakism : **cat•e•chism**
catalist : **cat•a•lyst**
cat•a•log *or* **cat•a•logue**
cat•a•logue *or* **cat•a•log**
cat•a•lyst
catarpillar : **cat•er•pil•lar**
catasstrophe : **ca•tas•tro•phe**
catastrofe : **ca•tas•tro•phe**
ca•tas•tro•phe
catastrophy : **ca•tas•tro•phe**
catchup : **cat•sup**
cat•e•chism
catechysm : **cat•e•chism**
cateclism : **cat•a•clysm**
cateclysm : **cat•a•clysm**
catecomb : **cat•a•comb**
categorey : **cat•e•go•ry**
cat•e•go•ry
catekism : **cat•e•chism**
catelist : **cat•a•lyst**
catelog : **cat•a•log**
caterpilar : **cat•er•pil•lar**
caterpiler : **cat•er•pil•lar**
cat•er•pil•lar
caterpiller : **cat•er•pil•lar**
cathalic : **cath•o•lic**
cathelic : **cath•o•lic**
cathilic : **cath•o•lic**
catholec : **cath•o•lic**
cath•o•lic
Ca•thol•i•cism
Catholisism : **Ca•thol•i•cism**
Cathollicism : **Ca•thol•i•cism**
catilog : **cat•a•log**
catle : **cat•tle**
catsap : **cat•sup**
catsep : **cat•sup**
catshup : **cat•sup**
catsip : **cat•sup**
cat•sup *or* **ketch•up**
cattagory : **cat•e•go•ry**

cattal : **cat•tle**
cattalist : **cat•a•lyst**
cattalog : **cat•a•log**
cattalyst : **cat•a•lyst**
cattasrophe : **ca•tas•tro•phe**
cattegory : **cat•e•go•ry**
cattel : **cat•tle**
catterpillar : **cat•er•pil•lar**
cat•tle
caucas : **cau•cus**
cauchious : **cau•tious**
cau•cus
cauldran : **caul•dron**
cauldren : **caul•dron**
cauldrin : **caul•dron**
caul•dron
cau•li•flow•er
causalitty : **cau•sal•i•ty**
cau•sal•i•ty
causallety : **cau•sal•i•ty**
causallity : **cau•sal•i•ty**
causeous : **cau•tious**
caushion : **cau•tion**
caushious : **cau•tious**
causion : **cau•tion**
causstic : **caus•tic**
caus•tic
caustick : **caus•tic**
cau•tion
cau•tious
cav•al•cade
cavalcaid : **cav•al•cade**
cavaleer : **cav•a•lier**
cavaleir : **cav•a•lier**
cavalere : **cav•a•lier**
cavalery : **Cal•va•ry** (site of the
    Crucifixion) *or* **cav•al•ry**
    (horse troops)
cav•a•lier
cavalkade : **cav•al•cade**
cavallcade : **cav•al•cade**

cav•al•ry (horse troops);
   Cal•va•ry (site of the
   Crucifixion)
cavelcade : cav•al•cade
cavelier : cav•a•lier
cavellry : Cal•va•ry (site of the
   Crucifixion) or cav•al•ry
   (horse troops)
cavelry : Cal•va•ry (site of the
   Crucifixion) or cav•al•ry
   (horse troops)
cavernis : cav•ern•ous
cav•ern•ous
cavernus : cav•ern•ous
cavilcade : cav•al•cade
cavilere : cav•a•lier
cavilier : cav•a•lier
cavilry : Cal•va•ry (site of the
   Crucifixion) or cav•al•ry
   (horse troops)
cavurnous : cav•ern•ous
cawcus : cau•cus
cawldren : caul•dron
cawldron : caul•dron
cawtion : cau•tion
ceadar : ce•dar (tree) or se•der
   (Passover meal)
ce•dar (tree); se•der (Passover
   meal)
cedaver : ca•dav•er
ceder : ce•dar (tree) or se•der
   (Passover meal)
cedir : ce•dar (tree) or se•der
   (Passover meal)
ceesarean : cae•sar•e•an
cegar : ci•gar
cegarette : cig•a•rette
ceil•ing
cejole : ca•jole
celabate : cel•i•bate
celabrant : cel•e•brant
celabration : cel•e•brate

celabrent : cel•e•brant
celabrity : ce•leb•ri•ty
celar : cel•lar
celary : cel•ery (vegetable) or
   sal•a•ry (wages)
celebet : cel•i•bate
celebit : cel•i•bate
celebrait : cel•e•brate
cel•e•brant
cel•e•brate
celebrent : cel•e•brant
celebrety : ce•leb•ri•ty
celebritty : ce•leb•ri•ty
ce•leb•ri•ty
celerry : cel•ery (vegetable) or
   sal•a•ry (wages)
cel•ery (vegetable); sal•a•ry
   (wages)
celesteal : ce•les•tial
ce•les•tial
cel•i•bate
cellabrate : cel•e•brate
cel•lar (basement); sell•er (one
   who sells)
cellary : cel•ery (vegetable) or
   sal•a•ry (wages)
cellebrant : cel•e•brant
cellebrity : ce•leb•ri•ty
celler : cel•lar (basement) or
   sell•er (one who sells)
cellery : cel•ery (vegetable) or
   sal•a•ry (wages)
cellestial : ce•les•tial
cellibate : cel•i•bate
cel•lo
cellouloid : cel•lu•loid
Celltic : Cel•tic
cel•lu•loid
celo : cel•lo
Celon : Cey•lon
Cel•tic
celuloid : cel•lu•loid

cematary : **cem·e·tery**
cematery : **cem·e·tery**
cemeleon : **cha·me·leon**
cemelion : **cha·me·leon**
cemetarry : **cem·e·tery**
cemetary : **cem·e·tery**
cemeterry : **cem·e·tery**
cem·e·tery
cemettery : **cem·e·tery**
cemical : **chem·i·cal**
cemistry : **chem·is·try**
cencership : **cen·sor·ship**
cenchurion : **cen·tu·ri·on**
cenchury : **cen·tu·ry**
cencus : **cen·sus**
cenema : **cin·e·ma**
cen·ser (incense container);
  cen·sor (to remove
  objectionable material);
  cen·sure (to condemn);
  sen·sor (that which senses)
censership : **cen·sor·ship**
censes : **cen·sus**
cen·sor (to remove
  objectionable material);
  cen·ser (incense container);
  censure (to condemn);
  sen·sor (that which senses)
cen·sor·ship
cen·sure (to condemn); **cen·ser**
  (incense container); **cen·sor**
  (to remove objectionable
  material); **sen·sor** (that
  which senses)
cen·sus
censuss : **cen·sus**
centar : **cen·taur**
cen·taur
centerian : **cen·tu·ri·on**
centerion : **cen·tu·ri·on**
centeripetal : **cen·trip·e·tal**
centermeter : **cen·ti·me·ter**

centerpeace : **cen·ter·piece**
centerpece : **cen·ter·piece**
centerpeice : **cen·ter·piece**
cen·ter·piece
centery : **cen·tu·ry**
cen·ti·me·ter
centimetre (*Brit.*) :
  cen·ti·me·ter
centoorion : **cen·tu·ri·on**
centor : **cen·taur**
centour : **cen·taur**
centrepetal : **cen·trip·e·tal**
centrifecal : **cen·trif·u·gal**
centrifegal : **cen·trif·u·gal**
centriffugal : **cen·trif·u·gal**
centrifical : **cen·trif·u·gal**
centrifigal : **cen·trif·u·gal**
centrifucal : **cen·trif·u·gal**
cen·trif·u·gal
centrifugle : **cen·trif·u·gal**
centrimeter : **cen·ti·me·ter**
cen·trip·e·tal
centripetle : **cen·trip·e·tal**
centripidal : **cen·trip·e·tal**
centripital : **cen·trip·e·tal**
centripittal : **cen·trip·e·tal**
cents (money); **sense**
  (intelligence)
centur : **cen·taur**
centurian : **cen·tu·ri·on**
centurien : **cen·tu·ri·on**
cen·tu·ri·on
centurry : **cen·tu·ry**
cen·tu·ry
cerabellum : **cer·e·bel·lum**
ceramec : **ce·ram·ic**
ce·ram·ic
cerammic : **ce·ram·ic**
ceramony : **cer·e·mo·ny**
cerca : **cir·ca**
cerculate : **cir·cu·late**
cercus : **cir·cus**

ce•re•al (grain); se•ri•al (in a
  series)
cerebellam : cer•e•bel•lum
cerebellem : cer•e•bel•lum
cer•e•bel•lum
cerebelum : cer•e•bel•lum
ce•re•bral
cerebrel : ce•re•bral
ce•re•brum
cereebral : ce•re•bral
ceremoney : cer•e•mo•ny
cer•e•mo•ny
cerial : ce•re•al (grain) or
  se•ri•al (in a series)
ceribral : ce•re•bral
ceribrum : ce•re•brum
cerimony : cer•e•mo•ny
cerramic : ce•ram•ic
cerrebellum : cer•e•bel•lum
cerremony : cer•e•mo•ny
cerrhosis : cir•rho•sis
cerrosis : cir•rho•sis
cer•tain
certan : cer•tain
certian : cer•tain
certifecate : cer•tif•i•cate
certifficate : cer•tif•i•cate
certificant : cer•tif•i•cate
certificat : cer•tif•i•cate
cer•tif•i•cate
certin : cer•tain
cesairean : cae•sar•e•an
cesarean : cae•sar•e•an
cesarian : cae•sar•e•an
cessarian : cae•sar•e•an
cess•pool
cestern : cis•tern
Cey•lon
chafeur : chauf•feur
chaffer : chauf•feur
chaffuer : chauf•feur
chaffure : chauf•feur

chafure : chauf•feur
chaimberlain : cham•ber•lain
chaimberlin : cham•ber•lain
chairopractor : chi•ro•prac•tor
chaist : chaste
chalera : chol•era
chal•ice
chalise : chal•ice
chaliss : chal•ice
challice : chal•ice
challise : chal•ice
cham•ber•lain
chamberlan : cham•ber•lain
chamberlin : cham•ber•lain
chamealeon : cha•me•leon
chamealion : cha•me•leon
chameeleon : cha•me•leon
chameelion : cha•me•leon
cha•me•leon
chamise : che•mise
cham•pagne
champaigne : cham•pagne
champain : cham•pagne
champaine : cham•pagne
champane : cham•pagne
chanceller : chan•cel•lor
chan•cel•lor
chancelor : chan•cel•lor
chancillor : chan•cel•lor
chandaleer : chan•de•lier
chandalier : chan•de•lier
chandelear : chan•de•lier
chandeleer : chan•de•lier
chandelere : chan•de•lier
chan•de•lier
chandileer : chan•de•lier
chaneled : chan•neled
chanelled : chan•neled
changable : change•able
change•able
changebal : change•able
changeble : change•able

change•ling
changible : **change•able**
changling : **change•ling**
chan•neled *or* **chan•nelled**
chan•nelled *or* **chan•neled**
chanseller : **chan•cel•lor**
chansellor : **chan•cel•lor**
chansillor : **chan•cel•lor**
cha•os
chaoss : **cha•os**
chaparone : **chap•er•on**
chap•el
chapelen : **chap•lain**
chapelin : **chap•lain**
chap•er•on *or* **chap•er•one**
chap•er•one *or* **chap•er•on**
chaperown : **chap•er•on**
chapil : **chap•el**
chap•lain
chaplan : **chap•lain**
chaplin : **chap•lain**
chappel : **chap•el**
char•ac•ter
charactor : **char•ac•ter**
cha•rade
charaid : **cha•rade**
charatable : **char•i•ta•ble**
charaty : **char•i•ty**
char•coal
charcole : **char•coal**
charecter : **char•ac•ter**
charector : **char•ac•ter**
chareot : **char•i•ot**
chareoteer : **char•i•o•teer**
charetable : **char•i•ta•ble**
charety : **char•i•ty**
chargable : **charge•able**
chargeabel : **charge•able**
charge•able
chargible : **charge•able**
charicter : **char•ac•ter**
chariet : **char•i•ot**

charieteer : **char•i•o•teer**
char•i•ot
char•i•o•teer
chariotere : **char•i•o•teer**
chariotier : **char•i•o•teer**
charish : **cher•ish**
char•is•ma
char•i•ta•ble
chariteble : **char•i•ta•ble**
charitible : **char•i•ta•ble**
char•i•ty
charkcole : **char•coal**
char•la•tan
charlaten : **char•la•tan**
charlatin : **char•la•tan**
charletan : **char•la•tan**
charleten : **char•la•tan**
charlitan : **char•la•tan**
charrade : **cha•rade**
charrcoal : **char•coal**
charriot : **char•i•ot**
charrioteer : **char•i•o•teer**
charrish : **cher•ish**
charry : **cher•ry**
char•treuse
chartroose : **char•treuse**
chartruese : **char•treuse**
chartruse : **char•treuse**
charub : **cher•ub**
chasiss : **chas•sis**
chasm
chasses : **chas•sis**
chassey : **chas•sis**
chas•sis
chassiss : **chas•sis**
chasstise : **chas•tise**
chassy : **chas•sis**
chast : **chaste**
chaste
chastety : **chas•ti•ty**
chas•tise
chastitty : **chas•ti•ty**

chas·ti·ty
chastize : chas·tise
Chatannooga : Chat·ta·noo·ga
Chatanooga : Chat·ta·noo·ga
cha·teau
chatel : chat·tel
chatieu : cha·teau
chatle : chat·tel
chatoe : cha·teau
Chat·ta·noo·ga
Chattanuga : Chat·ta·noo·ga
chatteau : cha·teau
chat·tel
Chattenooga : Chat·ta·noo·ga
Chattinooga : Chat·ta·noo·ga
chattle : chat·tel
chattow : cha·teau
chauder : chow·der
chauffer : chauf·feur
chauf·feur
chauffuer : chauf·feur
chauvanism : chau·vin·ism
chauvenism : chau·vin·ism
chau·vin·ism
chavinism : chau·vin·ism
cheaky : cheeky
cheap·en
cheapin : cheap·en
chearful : cheer·ful
cheary : cheery
cheatah : chee·tah
cheat·er
Checago : Chi·ca·go
Chechoslovakia :
   Czech·o·slo·va·kia
check·er
cheeftain : chief·tain
cheekey : cheeky
cheeky
cheepen : cheap·en
cheer·ful
cheerfull : cheer·ful

cheery
cheeta : chee·tah
chee·tah
cheeter : cheat·er
cheiftain : chief·tain
cheipen : cheap·en
chekey : cheeky
Chele : Chile
chello : cel·lo
chemacal : chem·i·cal
chemastry : chem·is·try
chemecal : chem·i·cal
chemeese : che·mise
chemeleon : cha·me·leon
chemelion : cha·me·leon
chemese : che·mise
chemestry : chem·is·try
chem·i·cal
chemicle : chem·i·cal
che·mise
chemistery : chem·is·try
chem·is·try
chentz : chintz
chequer (*Brit.*) : check·er
cherade : cha·rade
Cherakee : Cher·o·kee
cherib : cher·ub
cheriot : char·i·ot
cherioteer : char·i·o·teer
cher·ish
cherlish : churl·ish
Cher·o·kee
Cherokey : Cher·o·kee
cherrish : cher·ish
cherrub : cher·ub
cher·ry
cher·ub
chery : cher·ry
Ches·a·peake
Chesapeeke : Ches·a·peake
Chesipeake : Ches·a·peake
Chesipeeke : Ches·a·peake

chesnut : **chest•nut**
Chessapeake : **Ches•a•peake**
chessnut : **chest•nut**
chest•nut
chetah : **chee•tah**
Cheyanne : **Chey•enne**
Chey•enne
Chicaggo : **Chi•ca•go**
Chi•ca•go
chicainery : **chi•ca•nery**
chicanary : **chi•ca•nery**
chicanerry : **chi•ca•nery**
chi•ca•nery
chickery : **chic•o•ry**
chickory : **chic•o•ry**
chic•o•ry
chief•tain
chieftan : **chief•tain**
chieftin : **chief•tain**
chikanery : **chi•ca•nery**
chikery : **chic•o•ry**
childern : **chil•dren**
chil•dren
Chile
Chille : **Chile**
chimese : **che•mise**
chimnee : **chim•ney**
chim•ney
chimny : **chim•ney**
chimpansey : **chim•pan•zee**
chimpansie : **chim•pan•zee**
chimpansy : **chim•pan•zee**
chim•pan•zee
chimpanzy : **chim•pan•zee**
Chinease : **Chi•nese**
Chineese : **Chi•nese**
Chi•nese
Chineze : **Chi•nese**
chints : **chintz**
chintz
chior : **choir**
chipmonck : **chip•munk**

chipmonk : **chip•munk**
chip•munk
chirapractor : **chi•ro•prac•tor**
chire : **choir**
chiropracktor : **chi•ro•prac•tor**
chiropracter : **chi•ro•prac•tor**
chi•ro•prac•tor
chisal : **chis•el**
chis•el
chisle : **chis•el**
chissel : **chis•el**
chitah : **chee•tah**
chivalery : **chiv•al•ry**
chivalrey : **chiv•al•ry**
chiv•al•ry
chivelry : **chiv•al•ry**
chivilry : **chiv•al•ry**
Chiyenne : **Chey•enne**
chizel : **chis•el**
chizzel : **chis•el**
chloesterol : **cho•les•ter•ol**
chloraform : **chlo•ro•form**
chloreen : **chlo•rine**
chloresterol : **cho•les•ter•ol**
chlo•ride
chloriform : **chlo•ro•form**
chlo•rine
chlo•ro•form
chlouride : **chlo•ride**
chlourine : **chlo•rine**
chluoride : **chlo•ride**
chluorine : **chlo•rine**
chluoroform : **chlo•ro•form**
choake : **choke**
choas : **cha•os**
choir
choiral : **cho•ral**
choireographer :
    cho•re•og•ra•pher
choke
chol•era
cholerra : **chol•era**

cholesteral : **cho·les·ter·ol**
cholesteroil : **cho·les·ter·ol**
cho·les·ter·ol
cholestral : **cho·les·ter·ol**
choot : **chute**
chop sooie : **chop su·ey**
chop sooy : **chop su·ey**
chop su·ey
cho·ral (relating to a choir);
   cho·rale (hymn); **cor·al**
   (reef); **cor·ral** (horse pen)
cho·rale (hymn); **cho·ral**
   (relating to a choir); **cor·al**
   (reef); **cor·ral** (horse pen)
chord (music); **cord** (rope)
chorel : **cho·ral** (relating to a
   choir) *or* **cho·rale** (hymn) *or*
   cor·al (reef) *or* **cor·ral** (horse
   pen)
choreografer :
   cho·re·og·ra·pher
cho·re·og·ra·pher
choriographer :
   cho·re·og·ra·pher
choris : **cho·rus**
choriss : **cho·rus**
cho·rus
chouder : **chow·der**
chovinism : **chau·vin·ism**
chow·der
chrisanthamem :
   chry·san·the·mum
chrisanthamum :
   chry·san·the·mum
chrisanthemum :
   chry·san·the·mum
christhanimum :
   chry·san·the·mum
Chris·tian
Christianety : **Chris·tian·i·ty**
Christianitty : **Chris·tian·i·ty**
Chris·tian·i·ty

Christien : **Chris·tian**
Christienity : **Chris·tian·i·ty**
Christion : **Chris·tian**
Christionity : **Chris·tian·i·ty**
chromeum : **chro·mi·um**
chromiem : **chro·mi·um**
chro·mi·um
chronalogy : **chro·nol·o·gy**
chron·ic
chronical : **chron·i·cle**
chronick : **chron·ic**
chronickal : **chron·i·cle**
chron·i·cle
chronikal : **chron·i·cle**
chronnic : **chron·ic**
chronnicle : **chron·i·cle**
chronnology : **chro·nol·o·gy**
chronollogy : **chro·nol·o·gy**
chronologgy : **chro·nol·o·gy**
chro·nol·o·gy
chrysanthamum :
   chry·san·the·mum
chrysanthemem :
   chry·san·the·mum
chry·san·the·mum
chuckal : **chuck·le**
chuckel : **chuck·le**
chuck·le
chukle : **chuck·le**
churl·ish
churllish : **churl·ish**
chute
cianide : **cy·a·nide**
Ciaro : **Cai·ro**
cibernetics : **cy·ber·net·ics**
cicle : **cy·cle**
ciclone : **cy·clone**
cieling : **ceil·ing**
ciello : **cel·lo**
cifer : **ci·pher**
ci·gar
cigarete : **cig·a·rette**

cig•a•rette
ciger : ci•gar
cigerette : cig•a•rette
ciggar : ci•gar
ciggarette : cig•a•rette
cignet : cyg•net (swan) *or*
 sig•net (ring)
Ciltic : Cel•tic
cilynder : cyl•in•der
cimbal : cym•bal (brass plate)
 or sym•bol (meaningful
 image)
cimball : cym•bal (brass plate)
 or sym•bol (meaningful
 image)
cimbol : cym•bal (brass plate)
 or sym•bol (meaningful
 image)
cinama : cin•e•ma
cinamin : cin•na•mon
cinamon : cin•na•mon
Cincanati : Cin•cin•nati
Cincenati : Cin•cin•nati
Cincennati : Cin•cin•nati
Cincinati : Cin•cin•nati
Cin•cin•nati
Cincinnatti : Cin•cin•nati
Cincinnaty : Cin•cin•nati
cin•e•ma
cineman : cin•na•mon
cinemon : cin•na•mon
cinicism : cyn•i•cism
cinnama : cin•e•ma
cinnamen : cin•na•mon
cinnamin : cin•na•mon
cin•na•mon
Cinncinati : Cin•cin•nati
Cinncinnati : Cin•cin•nati
cinnema : cin•e•ma
cinneman : cin•na•mon
cinnemon : cin•na•mon
Cinsanati : Cin•cin•nati

Cinsinnati : Cin•cin•nati
ci•pher
cipress : cy•press
cir•ca
circamspect : cir•cum•spect
circemspect : cir•cum•spect
circemstance : cir•cum•stance
circis : cir•cus
circka : cir•ca
cir•cu•late
cir•cum•spect
circumstanse : cir•cum•stance
cir•cus
circuss : cir•cus
cirhosis : cir•rho•sis
cirka : cir•ca
cirkus : cir•cus
Ciro : Cai•ro
ciropractor : chi•ro•prac•tor
cirosis : cir•rho•sis
cirqulate : cir•cu•late
cirrcus : cir•cus
cir•rho•ses (*plur.*); cir•rho•sis
 (*sing.*)
cir•rho•sis (*sing.*); cir•rho•ses
 (*plur.*)
cirrhosiss : cir•rho•sis
cirrosis : cir•rho•sis
cisstern : cis•tern
cisstirn : cis•tern
cissturn : cis•tern
cis•tern
cistirn : cis•tern
cisturn : cis•tern
cit•a•del
citadell : cit•a•del
citazen : cit•i•zen
citecen : cit•i•zen
citedel : cit•a•del
citezen : cit•i•zen
citicen : cit•i•zen
citicin : cit•i•zen

citidel : **cit•a•del**
cit•ies
cit•i•zen
citrous : **cit•rus**
cit•rus
citties : **cit•ies**
cittizen : **cit•i•zen**
citys : **cit•ies**
cityzen : **cit•i•zen**
civalization : **civ•i•li•za•tion**
civec : **civ•ic**
civelization : **civ•i•li•za•tion**
civ•ic
civick : **civ•ic**
civilisation (*Brit.*) :
　civ•i•li•za•tion
civ•i•li•za•tion
civillization : **civ•i•li•za•tion**
clairet : **clar•et**
clairity : **clar•i•ty**
clair•voy•ance
clairvoyanse : **clair•voy•ance**
clairvoyence : **clair•voy•ance**
clairvoyince : **clair•voy•ance**
clamer : **clam•or**
clamity : **ca•lam•i•ty**
clammer : **clam•or**
clammor : **clam•or**
clam•or
clamour (*Brit.*) : **clam•or**
clarafication : **clar•i•fi•ca•tion**
claranet : **clar•i•net**
clarat : **clar•et**
clarefication : **clar•i•fi•ca•tion**
clarenet : **clar•i•net**
clareon : **clar•i•on**
clar•et
clarety : **clar•i•ty**
clarifacation : **clar•i•fi•ca•tion**
clarifecation : **clar•i•fi•ca•tion**
clarificasion : **clar•i•fi•ca•tion**
clar•i•fi•ca•tion

clar•i•fy
clar•i•net
clar•i•on
clarit : **clar•et**
claritty : **clar•i•ty**
clar•i•ty
clarrion : **clar•i•on**
clarrity : **clar•i•ty**
clarvoyance : **clair•voy•ance**
clasefy : **clas•si•fy**
clasic : **clas•sic**
clasify : **clas•si•fy**
classec : **clas•sic**
classefy : **clas•si•fy**
clas•sic
classick : **clas•sic**
classiffy : **clas•si•fy**
clas•si•fy
clastrophobia :
　claus•tro•pho•bia
Claus (Santa); **clause** (sentence
　part); **claws** (talons)
clause (sentence part); **Claus**
　(Santa); **claws** (talons)
claustraphobia :
　claus•tro•pho•bia
claustrephobia :
　claus•tro•pho•bia
claustrofobia :
　claus•tro•pho•bia
claustrophobea :
　claus•tro•pho•bia
claus•tro•pho•bia
claws (talons); **Claus** (Santa);
　clause (sentence part)
clawstrophobia :
　claus•tro•pho•bia
clean•li•ness
cleanliniss : **clean•li•ness**
cleanlyness : **clean•li•ness**
cleansed
clear•ance

clearanse : **clear·ance**
clearence : **clear·ance**
clearense : **clear·ance**
clearify : **clar·i·fy**
clearrance : **clear·ance**
clearvoyance : **clair·voy·ance**
cleav·age
cleave
cleav·er
cleavidge : **cleav·age**
cleavige : **cleav·age**
cleche : **cli·ché**
cleeche : **cli·ché**
cleerance : **clear·ance**
cleeranse : **clear·ance**
cleerence : **clear·ance**
cleerense : **clear·ance**
cleevage : **cleav·age**
cleeve : **cleave**
cleeveage : **cleav·age**
cleever : **cleav·er**
cleint : **cli·ent**
cleive : **cleave**
cleiver : **cleav·er**
clem·en·cy
clemensy : **clem·en·cy**
clemincy : **clem·en·cy**
cleminsy : **clem·en·cy**
clemmency : **clem·en·cy**
clenliness : **clean·li·ness**
clensed : **cleansed**
cleptomaniac : **klep·to·ma·ni·ac**
cliant : **cli·ent**
cliantele : **cli·en·tele**
cliantell : **cli·en·tele**
clichay : **cli·ché**
cli·ché
click (sound); **clique** (group)
cli·ent
cli·en·tele
clientell : **cli·en·tele**
clientelle : **cli·en·tele**

clieve : **cleave**
cli·mac·tic (of a climax);
   cli·ma·tic (of a climate)
climat : **cli·mate**
cli·mate
cli·ma·tic (of a climate);
   cli·mac·tic (of a climax)
climency : **clem·en·cy**
climet : **cli·mate**
climite : **cli·mate**
climmat : **cli·mate**
climmate : **cli·mate**
climmit : **cli·mate**
clinec : **clin·ic**
clin·ic
clinick : **clin·ic**
clinliness : **clean·li·ness**
clinnic : **clin·ic**
clinsed : **cleansed**
clique (group); **click** (sound)
clishay : **cli·ché**
clishee : **cli·ché**
cloak·room
cloasure : **clo·sure**
cloathing : **cloth·ing**
cloisster : **clois·ter**
clois·ter
clokeroom : **cloak·room**
clokroom : **cloak·room**
cloride : **chlo·ride**
clorine : **chlo·rine**
cloroform : **chlo·ro·form**
close (to shut); **clothes**
   (apparel)
closhure : **clo·sure**
clostrophobia :
   claus·tro·pho·bi·a
clo·sure
clothes (apparel); **close** (to
   shut); **cloths** (fabrics)
cloth·ing

cloths (fabrics); **clothes**
 (apparel)
clouride : **chlo·ride**
clourine : **chlo·rine**
cloyster : **clois·ter**
coaco : **co·coa**
coaficcient : **co·ef·fi·cient**
coalece : **co·alesce**
co·alesce
coalese : **co·alesce**
coaless : **co·alesce**
coalicion : **co·ali·tion**
coalishion : **co·ali·tion**
co·ali·tion
coalittion : **co·ali·tion**
coarse (rough); **course**
 (direction)
coaterie : **co·te·rie**
cocaign : **co·caine**
cocain : **co·caine**
co·caine
cocane : **co·caine**
cocanut : **co·co·nut**
cocaonut : **co·co·nut**
coccaine : **co·caine**
cochroach : **cock·roach**
cock·ney
cocknie : **cock·ney**
cockny : **cock·ney**
cock·roach
cockroch : **cock·roach**
cocney : **cock·ney**
cocny : **cock·ney**
co·co (palm); **co·coa**
 (beverage)
co·coa
cocoanut : **co·co·nut**
co·co·nut
co·coon
cocune : **co·coon**
codafy : **cod·i·fy**
coddafy : **cod·i·fy**

coddefy : **cod·i·fy**
coddify : **cod·i·fy**
codeen : **co·deine**
codefy : **cod·i·fy**
co·deine
codene : **co·deine**
cod·ger .
codiene : **co·deine**
cod·i·fy
codine : **co·deine**
coefficiant : **co·ef·fi·cient**
co·ef·fi·cient
coeffisient : **co·ef·fi·cient**
coeffitiant : **co·ef·fi·cient**
coeffitient : **co·ef·fi·cient**
coeficient : **co·ef·fi·cient**
coefisient : **co·ef·fi·cient**
coelesce : **co·alesce**
coelition : **co·ali·tion**
co·erce
coercian : **co·er·cion**
coercien : **co·er·cion**
co·er·cion
coerse : **co·erce**
coersion : **co·er·cion**
coertion : **co·er·cion**
cofee : **cof·fee**
coff : **cough**
cof·fee
coffen : **cof·fin**
cofficient : **co·ef·fi·cient**
cof·fin
cofin : **cof·fin**
co·gen·cy
cogensy : **co·gen·cy**
cogentcy : **co·gen·cy**
cogentsy : **co·gen·cy**
coger : **cod·ger**
co·gnac
cognezant : **cog·ni·zant**
cognisant : **cog·ni·zant**
cog·ni·zant

coharence : **co•her•ence**
coharent : **co•her•ent**
cohecion : **co•he•sion**
coheerence : **co•her•ence**
coheerent : **co•her•ent**
coheesion : **co•he•sion**
coheirence : **co•her•ence**
coheirent : **co•her•ent**
coherance : **co•her•ence**
coheranse : **co•her•ence**
coherant : **co•her•ent**
coherce : **co•erce**
co•her•ence
coherense : **co•her•ence**
co•her•ent
coherse : **co•erce**
co•he•sion
cohhession : **co•he•sion**
cohision : **co•he•sion**
coin•age
coincedence : **co•in•ci•dence**
co•in•cide
co•in•ci•dence
coincidense : **co•in•ci•dence**
coincidince : **co•in•ci•dence**
coincied : **co•in•cide**
coinege : **coin•age**
coinige : **coin•age**
coinsedence : **co•in•ci•dence**
coinside : **co•in•cide**
coinsidence : **co•in•ci•dence**
cokaine : **co•caine**
cokney : **cock•ney**
cokny : **cock•ney**
cokonut : **co•co•nut**
colaborate : **col•lab•o•rate**
colaborator : **col•lab•o•ra•tor**
colan : **col•on**
col•an•der (drainer); **cal•en•dar**
  (chart of dates); **cal•en•der**
  (pressing machine)
colapse : **col•lapse**

colapsible : **col•laps•ible**
colar : **col•lar**
Colarado : **Col•o•ra•do**
colassal : **co•los•sal**
colateral : **col•lat•er•al**
coldslaw : **cole•slaw**
coleague : **col•league**
colection : **col•lec•tion**
colector : **col•lec•tor**
colege : **col•lege**
colen : **col•on**
colender : **col•an•der**
colera : **chol•era**
cole•slaw
colesterol : **cho•les•ter•ol**
col•ic
coliceum : **col•i•se•um**
colicion : **co•ali•tion**
colick : **col•ic**
col•icky
colicy : **col•icky**
colide : **col•lide**
col•i•se•um (amphitheater);
  Col•os•se•um (amphitheater
  in Rome)
colision : **col•li•sion**
colisium : **col•i•se•um**
colisseum : **col•i•se•um**
colission : **co•a•lition**
colition : **co•a•lition**
collabborate : **col•lab•o•rate**
collabborator : **col•lab•o•ra•tor**
collaberate : **col•lab•o•rate**
collaberator : **col•lab•o•ra•tor**
collabirate : **col•lab•o•rate**
collabirator : **col•lab•o•ra•tor**
col•lab•o•rate
collaborater : **col•lab•o•ra•tor**
col•lab•o•ra•tor
col•lage (composite work);
  col•league (associate);
  col•lege (school)

collander : **col·an·der**
collapce : **col·lapse**
collapsable : **col·laps·ible**
col·lapse
col·laps·ible
col·lar
col·lat·er·al
collaterel : **col·lat·er·al**
colleage : **col·lage** (composite work) *or* **col·league** (associate) *or* **col·lege** (school)
col·league (associate); **col·lage** (composite work); **col·lege** (school)
collecion : **col·lec·tion**
collecktion : **col·lec·tion**
collecter : **col·lec·tor**
col·lec·tion
col·lec·tor
colledge : **col·lage** (composite work) *or* **col·lege** (school)
colleegue : **col·league**
col·lege (school); **col·lage** (composite work); **col·league** (associate)
collegue : **col·league**
colleigue : **col·league**
collender : **col·an·der**
coller : **col·lar**
collerteral : **col·lat·er·al**
collesterol : **cho·les·ter·ol**
collic : **col·ic**
collicky : **col·icky**
col·lide
col·lie
collied : **col·lide**
colliflauer : **cau·li·flow·er**
colliflour : **cau·li·flow·er**
colliflower : **cau·li·flow·er**
collige : **col·lege**
colliseum : **col·i·se·um**

col·li·sion
collisium : **col·i·se·um**
collisseum : **col·i·se·um**
collission : **col·li·sion**
collizion : **col·li·sion**
collocial : **col·lo·qui·al**
collon : **col·on**
collonade : **col·on·nade**
collonel : **col·o·nel**
collonial : **co·lo·nial**
colloqial : **col·lo·qui·al**
colloqueal : **col·lo·qui·al**
col·lo·qui·al
colloquiel : **col·lo·qui·al**
Collorado : **Col·o·ra·do**
collossal : **co·los·sal**
collslaw : **cole·slaw**
collucion : **col·lu·sion**
collumbine : **col·um·bine**
Collumbus : **Co·lum·bus**
collumn : **col·umn**
col·lu·sion
colly : **col·lie**
Co·lom·bia (South American nation); **Co·lum·bia** (federal district)
colombine : **col·um·bine**
Colombus : **Co·lum·bus**
co·lon
colonade : **col·on·nade**
coloneal : **co·lo·nial**
col·o·nel (military officer); **ker·nel** (seed)
co·lo·nial
col·on·nade
colonnaid : **col·on·nade**
colonnel : **col·o·nel**
colonnial : **co·lo·nial**
coloquial : **col·lo·qui·al**
Coloraddo : **Col·o·ra·do**
Col·o·ra·do
coloride : **chlo·ride**

colorine : **chlo·rine**
Colorrado : **Col·o·ra·do**
colosal : **co·los·sal**
co·los·sal
Col·os·se·um (amphitheater in
 Rome); **col·i·se·um**
 (amphitheater)
colum : **col·umn**
Co·lum·bia (federal district);
 Co·lom·bia (South American
 nation)
col·um·bine
Co·lum·bus
Columbuss : **Co·lum·bus**
col·umn
columnade : **col·on·nade**
colusion : **col·lu·sion**
co·ma (unconscious state);
 com·ma (,)
comady : **com·e·dy**
comandant : **com·man·dant**
combenation : **com·bi·na·tion**
com·bi·na·tion
combinnation : **com·bi·na·tion**
combonation : **com·bi·na·tion**
combustable : **com·bus·ti·ble**
com·bus·ti·ble
comecal : **com·i·cal**
comeddy : **com·e·dy**
comedean : **co·me·di·an**
co·me·di·an
com·e·dy
comeedian : **co·me·di·an**
come·ly
comememorate :
 com·mem·o·rate
comemmorate :
 com·mem·o·rate
comemorate : **com·mem·o·rate**
comence : **com·mence**
comendable : **com·mend·able**
coment : **com·ment**

comentary : **com·men·tary**
comerce : **com·merce**
comercial : **com·mer·cial**
comersial : **com·mer·cial**
com·et (celestial body);
 com·mit (to entrust)
comfert : **com·fort**
comfertable : **com·fort·able**
com·fort
com·fort·able
comforteble : **com·fort·able**
comfortible : **com·fort·able**
com·ic
com·i·cal
comick : **com·ic**
comince : **com·mence**
comint : **com·ment**
comintary : **com·men·tary**
comiserate : **com·mis·er·ate**
comissar : **com·mis·sar**
comissary : **com·mis·sary**
comit : **com·et** (celestial body)
 or **com·mit** (to entrust)
comite : **com·mit·tee**
comittee : **com·mit·tee**
com·it·y (civility); **com·mit·tee**
 (task force)
comly : **come·ly**
com·ma (,); **co·ma**
 (unconscious state)
commady : **com·e·dy**
com·man·dant
commandaunt : **com·man·dant**
com·man·deer (to take by
 force); **com·mand·er** (leader)
com·mand·er (leader);
 com·man·deer (to take by
 force)
commant : **com·ment**
commantary : **com·men·tary**
commedian : **co·me·di·an**
commedy : **com·e·dy**

commeidian : **co•me•di•an**
commemerate :
  com•mem•o•rate
com•mem•o•rate
com•mence
com•mend•able
commendeble : **com•mend•able**
commendible : **com•mend•able**
commense : **com•mence**
com•ment
com•men•tary
commenterry : **com•men•tary**
commentery : **com•men•tary**
com•merce
com•mer•cial
commerse : **com•merce**
commershal : **com•mer•cial**
commersial : **com•mer•cial**
commet : **com•et** (celestial
  body) *or* **com•mit** (to
  entrust)
commic : **com•ic**
commical : **com•i•cal**
commince : **com•mence**
commindable : **com•mend•able**
comminse : **com•mence**
commint : **com•ment**
commintary : **com•men•tary**
commisar : **com•mis•sar**
commisary : **com•mis•sary**
com•mis•er•ate
commisirate : **com•mis•er•ate**
com•mis•sar
commissare : **com•mis•sar**
com•mis•sary
commisserate : **com•mis•er•ate**
commisserry : **com•mis•sary**
commissery : **com•mis•sary**
commisurate : **com•mis•er•ate**
commiszar : **com•mis•sar**
com•mit (to entrust); **com•et**
  (celestial body)

commite : **com•mit•tee**
com•mit•tee
committy : **com•mit•tee**
commoddity : **com•mod•i•ty**
commoddore : **com•mo•dore**
com•mode
commodety : **com•mod•i•ty**
commoditty : **com•mod•i•ty**
com•mod•i•ty
commodoar : **com•mo•dore**
commodoor : **com•mo•dore**
commodor : **com•mo•dore**
com•mo•dore
com•mon•er
com•mon•place
commonplaise : **com•mon•place**
commonplase : **com•mon•place**
com•mon•weal
com•mon•wealth
commonweel : **com•mon•weal**
commonweil : **com•mon•weal**
commonwellth :
  com•mon•wealth
commonwelth :
  com•mon•wealth
commoon : **com•mune**
commoonicable :
  com•mu•ni•ca•ble
commoonion : **com•mu•nion**
commoot : **com•mute**
com•mo•tion
com•mune
communety : **com•mu•ni•ty**
communian : **com•mu•nion**
com•mu•ni•ca•ble
com•mu•ni•cate
communiceble :
  com•mu•ni•ca•ble
communickable :
  com•mu•ni•ca•ble
communikate : **com•mu•ni•cate**
com•mu•nion

com•mu•nism
communitty : com•mu•ni•ty
com•mu•ni•ty
communiun : com•mu•nion
communnity : com•mu•ni•ty
communplace : com•mon•place
communyon : com•mu•nion
commurce : com•merce
commurse : com•merce
com•mute
comoddity : com•mod•i•ty
comode : com•mode
comodore : com•mo•dore
comoner : com•mon•er
comonplace : com•mon•place
comotion : com•mo•tion
compair : com•pare
compairable : com•pa•ra•ble
compairative : com•par•a•tive
compairison : com•par•i•son
com•pan•ion
companiun : com•pan•ion
compannion : com•pan•ion
companyon : com•pan•ion
com•pa•ra•ble
comparason : com•par•i•son
com•par•a•tive
com•pare
compareable : com•pa•ra•ble
compareble : com•pa•ra•ble
compareson : com•par•i•son
comparetive : com•par•a•tive
comparible : com•pa•ra•ble
comparisen : com•par•i•son
com•par•i•son
comparisun : com•par•i•son
comparitive : com•par•a•tive
compas : com•pass
compashion : com•pas•sion
compasion : com•pas•sion
com•pass
com•pas•sion

compatable : com•pat•i•ble
compateble : com•pat•i•ble
com•pat•i•ble
compeet : com•pete
compeit : com•pete
com•pel
compell : com•pel
compelsory : com•pul•so•ry
compencate : com•pen•sate
compendeum : com•pen•di•um
compendiom : com•pen•di•um
com•pen•di•um
com•pen•sate
compesition : com•po•si•tion
compess : com•pass
competator : com•pet•i•tor
com•pete
com•pe•tence
competense : com•pe•tence
competicion : com•pe•ti•tion
competince : com•pe•tence
competirer : com•pet•i•tor
competision : com•pe•ti•tion
com•pe•ti•tion
com•pet•i•tor
compindium : com•pen•di•um
compinsate : com•pen•sate
compis : com•pass
compisition : com•po•si•tion
compitence : com•pe•tence
compitition : com•pe•ti•tion
com•pla•cen•cy
complacensy : com•pla•cen•cy
com•pla•cent (self-satisfied);
    com•plai•sant (eager to
    please)
complacincy : com•pla•cen•cy
complaicency : com•pla•cen•cy
complaicent : com•pla•cent
    (self-satisfied) or
    com•plai•sant (eager to
    please)

com·plain
com·plai·sant (eager to please);
  com·pla·cent (self-satisfied)
complaisency : **com·pla·cen·cy**
complane : **com·plain**
complasency : **com·pla·cen·cy**
complasent : **com·pla·cent**
  (self-satisfied) *or*
  com·plai·sant (eager to
  please)
compleat : **com·plete**
complection : **com·plex·ion**
compleet : **com·plete**
compleetion : **com·ple·tion**
com·ple·ment (that which
  completes); **com·pli·ment**
  (flattering remark)
complesion : **com·ple·tion**
com·plete
completian : **com·ple·tion**
com·ple·tion
complexian : **com·plex·ion**
com·plex·ion
com·pli·ance
complianse : **com·pli·ance**
com·pli·ant
complicitty : **com·plic·i·ty**
com·plic·i·ty
complience : **com·pli·ance**
compliense : **com·pli·ance**
complient : **com·pli·ant**
com·pli·ment (flattering
  remark); **com·ple·ment** (that
  which completes)
complisitty : **com·plic·i·ty**
complisity : **com·plic·i·ty**
complition : **com·ple·tion**
compoanent : **com·po·nent**
componant : **com·po·nent**
com·po·nent
composate : **com·pos·ite**
composet : **com·pos·ite**

composhure : **com·po·sure**
composicion : **com·po·si·tion**
composit : **com·pos·ite**
com·pos·ite
com·po·si·tion
compossite : **com·pos·ite**
com·po·sure
compozure : **com·po·sure**
comprahend : **com·pre·hend**
comprahensible :
  com·pre·hen·si·ble
compramise : **com·pro·mise**
compramize : **com·pro·mise**
comprehenceble :
  com·pre·hen·si·ble
comprehencible :
  com·pre·hen·si·ble
com·pre·hend
comprehensable :
  com·pre·hen·si·ble
comprehenseble :
  com·pre·hen·si·ble
com·pre·hen·si·ble
compremise : **com·pro·mise**
compremize : **com·pro·mise**
compreshion : **com·pres·sion**
compresible : **com·press·ible**
compresion : **com·pres·sion**
compresor : **com·pres·sor**
compressable : **com·press·ible**
compresser : **com·pres·sor**
com·press·ible
com·pres·sion
com·pres·sor
comprimise : **com·pro·mise**
comprimize : **com·pro·mise**
com·prise
comprize : **com·prise**
com·pro·mise
compromize : **com·pro·mise**
comp·trol·ler *or* **con·trol·ler**
compulcery : **com·pul·so·ry**

compulsery : **com·pul·so·ry**
com·pul·so·ry
compuss : **com·pass**
comraderie : **ca·ma·ra·de·rie**
comradry : **ca·ma·ra·de·rie**
comroderie : **ca·ma·ra·de·rie**
comune : **com·mune**
comunicable :
  com·mu·ni·ca·ble
comunicate : **com·mu·ni·cate**
comunion : **com·mu·nion**
comunism : **com·mu·nism**
comunity : **com·mu·ni·ty**
comute : **com·mute**
conafer : **co·ni·fer**
concard : **con·cord**
con·ceal
conceave : **con·ceive**
con·cede
conceed : **con·cede**
conceel : **con·ceal**
conceeve : **con·ceive**
conceil : **con·ceal**
con·ceit
con·ceiv·able
con·ceive
conceiveable : **con·ceiv·able**
concensus : **con·sen·sus**
concentrait : **con·cen·trate**
con·cen·trate
con·cen·tric
concentrick : **con·cen·tric**
con·cept
con·cep·tu·al
conceptuel : **con·cep·tu·al**
conceptule : **con·cep·tu·al**
con·cern
con·cert
con·ces·sion
conciderable : **con·sid·er·able**
conciel : **con·ceal**
conciet : **con·ceit**

concieve : **con·ceive**
con·cil·i·ate
conciliatorry : **con·cil·ia·to·ry**
con·cil·ia·to·ry
concillatory : **con·cil·ia·to·ry**
concilleate : **con·cil·i·ate**
concilliate : **con·cil·i·ate**
concilliatory : **con·cil·ia·to·ry**
concillitory : **con·cil·ia·to·ry**
concintrate : **con·cen·trate**
concirt : **con·cert**
con·cise
concomatant : **con·com·i·tant**
concometent : **con·com·i·tant**
con·com·i·tant
concomitent : **con·com·i·tant**
concommitant : **con·com·i·tant**
concommitent : **con·com·i·tant**
con·cord
concreet : **con·crete**
concreit : **con·crete**
con·crete
con·cur
concure : **con·cur**
concurent : **con·cur·rent**
concurn : **con·cern**
concurr : **con·cur**
concurrant : **con·cur·rent**
con·cur·rent
concushion : **con·cus·sion**
concusion : **con·cus·sion**
concussien : **con·cus·sion**
con·cus·sion
concution : **con·cus·sion**
condament : **con·di·ment**
condaminium :
  con·do·min·i·um
condamint : **con·di·ment**
condascend : **con·de·scend**
condascension :
  con·de·scen·sion
condement : **con·di·ment**

condeminium :
   con·do·min·i·um
condemm : con·demn
con·demn
condence : con·dense
con·dense
con·de·scend
con·de·scen·sion
condescinsion :
   con·de·scen·sion
condesend : con·de·scend
condesension : con·de·scen·sion
condessend : con·de·scend
condicion : con·di·tion
con·di·ment
condiscend : con·de·scend
condission : con·di·tion
con·di·tion
condolance : con·do·lence
condolanse : con·do·lence
con·do·lence
condolense : con·do·lence
condomenium :
   con·do·min·i·um
condominiem :
   con·do·min·i·um
con·do·min·i·um
condominnium :
   con·do·min·i·um
conduceve : con·du·cive
con·du·cive
conducter : con·duc·tor
con·duc·tor
conduet : con·duit
con·duit
condusive : con·du·cive
condute : con·duit
coneac : co·gnac
confadence : con·fi·dence
confadential : con·fi·den·tial
confedaracy : con·fed·er·a·cy
confedence : con·fi·dence

confedential : con·fi·den·tial
con·fed·er·a·cy
confederasy : con·fed·er·a·cy
con·fed·er·ate
confederet : con·fed·er·ate
confederissy : con·fed·er·a·cy
confederisy : con·fed·er·a·cy
confedirate : con·fed·er·ate
conferance : con·fer·ence
conferanse : con·fer·ence
confered : con·ferred
con·fer·ee
con·fer·ence
conferense : con·fer·ence
conferie : con·fer·ee
con·ferred
conferree : con·fer·ee
conferrence : con·fer·ence
confery : con·fer·ee
confesion : con·fes·sion
confessian : con·fes·sion
con·fes·sion
confeti : con·fet·ti
con·fet·ti
con·fi·dant *or* con·fi·dante (one
   confided in); con·fi·dent
   (assured)
con·fi·dante *or* con·fi·dant (one
   confided in); con·fi·dent
   (assured)
con·fi·dence
confidense : con·fi·dence
confidenshial : con·fi·den·tial
confidensial : con·fi·den·tial
confident (assured);
   con·fi·dant (one confided in)
con·fi·den·tial
confidintial : con·fi·den·tial
configeration :
   con·fig·u·ra·tion
configguration :
   con·fig·u·ra·tion

con•fig•u•ra•tion
con•fla•gra•tion
conflagretion : con•fla•gra•tion
conflegration : con•fla•gra•tion
confligration : con•fla•gra•tion
confuree : con•fer•ee
confurred : con•ferred
con•fused
confuzed : con•fused
con•geal
congeel : con•geal
congeenial : con•ge•nial
congeil : con•geal
con•ge•nial
conginial : con•ge•nial
congizant : cog•ni•zant
congnac : co•gnac
congradulate : con•grat•u•late
congragate : con•gre•gate
congragration : con•gre•ga•tion
congratalate : con•grat•u•late
con•grat•u•late
congregacion : con•gre•ga•tion
con•gre•gate
con•gre•ga•tion
congres : con•gress
con•gress
congrigate : con•gre•gate
congrigation : con•gre•ga•tion
congriss : con•gress
congruance : con•gru•ence
congruanse : con•gru•ence
con•gru•ence
congruense : con•gru•ence
congugal : con•ju•gal
coniac : co•gnac
con•ic
con•i•fer
conivance : con•niv•ance
conjagle : con•ju•gal
conjigal : con•ju•gal
con•ju•gal

conker : con•quer
conkeror : con•quer•or
connatation : con•no•ta•tion
Connectacutt : Con•nect•i•cut
Connectecut : Con•nect•i•cut
Con•nect•i•cut
Connetacut : Con•nect•i•cut
Conneticut : Con•nect•i•cut
connic : con•ic
connifer : co•ni•fer
con•niv•ance
connivanse : con•niv•ance
connivence : con•niv•ance
con•nois•seur
connoser : con•nois•seur
connossure : con•nois•seur
con•no•ta•tion
con•note
conosseur : con•nois•seur
conotation : con•no•ta•tion
conote : con•note
conpare : com•pare
con•quer
conquerer : con•quer•or
con•quer•or
conquor : con•quer
conqur : con•quer
conqurer : con•quer•or
consacrate : con•se•crate
consalate : con•sul•ate
consalation : con•so•la•tion
consarn : con•cern
con•science (moral sense);
   con•scious (awake)
con•scious (awake);
   con•science (moral sense)
conseal : con•ceal
con•se•crate
consede : con•cede
conseed : con•cede
conseel : con•ceal
conseeve : con•ceive

conseil : **con·ceal**
conseit : **con·ceit**
conseive : **con·ceive**
consensis : **con·sen·sus**
con·sen·sus
consentrate : **con·cen·trate**
consentric : **con·cen·tric**
consept : **con·cept**
conseptual : **con·cep·tu·al**
con·se·quence
consequense : **con·se·quence**
consequince : **con·se·quence**
consern : **con·cern**
consert : **con·cert**
conservatian : **con·ser·va·tion**
con·ser·va·tion
con·ser·va·tive
conservatorry : **con·ser·va·to·ry**
con·ser·va·to·ry
conservetive : **con·ser·va·tive**
conservetory : **con·ser·va·to·ry**
conservitive : **con·ser·va·tive**
conseshion : **con·ces·sion**
consesion : **con·ces·sion**
consession : **con·ces·sion**
consice : **con·cise**
consicrate : **con·se·crate**
con·sid·er·able
considerible : **con·sid·er·able**
consieve : **con·ceive**
consilate : **con·sul·ate**
consilation : **con·so·la·tion**
consilatory : **con·cil·ia·to·ry**
consiliate : **con·cil·i·ate**
consiliatory : **con·cil·ia·to·ry**
consilitory : **con·cil·ia·to·ry**
consillatory : **con·cil·ia·to·ry**
consilliate : **con·cil·i·ate**
consilliatory : **con·cil·ia·to·ry**
consillitory : **con·cil·ia·to·ry**
consintrate : **con·cen·trate**
consise : **con·cise**

consistancy : **con·sis·ten·cy**
consistansy : **con·sis·ten·cy**
consistant : **con·sis·tent**
con·sis·ten·cy
consistensy : **con·sis·ten·cy**
con·sis·tent
consoladate : **con·sol·i·date**
con·so·la·tion
consoledate : **con·sol·i·date**
con·sol·i·date
consoomer : **con·sum·er**
conspeeracy : **con·spir·a·cy**
consperacy : **con·spir·a·cy**
con·spir·a·cy
conspirasy : **con·spir·a·cy**
conspirater : **con·spir·a·tor**
con·spir·a·tor
conspirisy : **con·spir·a·cy**
constabble : **con·sta·ble**
con·sta·ble
constallation : **con·stel·la·tion**
con·stan·cy
constapate : **con·sti·pate**
constatute : **con·sti·tute**
consteble : **con·sta·ble**
constelation : **con·stel·la·tion**
con·stel·la·tion
constency : **con·stan·cy**
constensy : **con·stan·cy**
constepate : **con·sti·pate**
constetue : **con·sti·tute**
con·sti·pate
constituancy : **con·stit·u·en·cy**
con·stit·u·en·cy
constituensy : **con·stit·u·en·cy**
con·sti·tute
con·sul (diplomat); **coun·cil**
  (assembly); **coun·sel** (advice;
  lawyer)
con·sul·ate
consulltane: con·sul·tant
con·sul·tant

consultent : **con•sul•tant**
con•sum•er
consumor : **con•sum•er**
consurn : **con•cern**
consurvation : **con•ser•va•tion**
contageous : **con•ta•gious**
con•ta•gious
containence : **con•ti•nence**
   (self-restraint) *or*
   coun•te•nance (face)
contajious : **con•ta•gious**
contamenate : **con•tam•i•nate**
con•tam•i•nate
contemperary :
   con•tem•po•rary
contempirary : **con•tem•po•rary**
contemporarry :
   con•tem•po•rary
con•tem•po•rary
contemporery :
   con•tem•po•rary
contenence : **con•ti•nence**
   (self-restraint) *or*
   coun•te•nance (face)
contenent : **con•ti•nent**
contenentel : **con•ti•nen•tal**
contengent : **con•tin•gent**
con•tes•tant
contestent : **con•tes•tant**
contestint : **con•tes•tant**
contimporary :
   con•tem•po•rary
continance : **con•ti•nence**
   (self-restraint) *or*
   coun•te•nance (face)
con•ti•nence (self-restraint);
   coun•te•nance (face)
con•ti•nent
con•ti•nen•tal
continentle : **con•ti•nen•tal**
con•tin•gent
contingint : **con•tin•gent**

con•tin•u•al
continuel : **con•tin•u•al**
continule : **con•tin•u•al**
con•tour
con•tra•band
con•tra•cep•tive
contracter : **con•trac•tor**
con•trac•tor
con•tra•dict
contradictery : **con•tra•dic•to•ry**
contradictorry :
   con•tra•dic•to•ry
con•tra•dic•to•ry
contrarry : **con•trary**
con•trary
contraseptive : **con•tra•cep•tive**
contravercial : **con•tro•ver•sial**
contravercy : **con•tro•ver•sy**
contraverseal : **con•tro•ver•sial**
contraversial : **con•tro•ver•sial**
contraversy : **con•tro•ver•sy**
contreband : **con•tra•band**
contreceptive : **con•tra•cep•tive**
contredict : **con•tra•dict**
contredictory : **con•tra•dic•to•ry**
contrery : **con•trary**
contreversial : **con•tro•ver•sial**
contreversy : **con•tro•ver•sy**
contriband : **con•tra•band**
contridict : **con•tra•dict**
contridictory : **con•tra•dic•to•ry**
con•triv•ance
contrivence : **con•triv•ance**
contrivense : **con•triv•ance**
con•trol
controll : **con•trol**
con•trol•ler *or* **comp•trol•ler**
con•tro•ver•sial
con•tro•ver•sy
contry : **coun•try**
contur : **con•tour**
conture : **con•tour**

convacation : **con•vo•ca•tion**
con•va•les•cence
convalescense : **con•va•les•cence**
convalesence : **con•va•les•cence**
convalessence : **con•va•les•cence**
convay : **con•vey**
convayance : **con•vey•ance**
convean : **con•vene**
conveen : **con•vene**
conveenience : **con•ve•nience**
convelescence : **con•va•les•cence**
con•vene
conveneance : **con•ve•nience**
con•ve•nience
conveniense : **con•ve•nience**
con•ve•nient
con•ver•gence
convergince : **con•ver•gence**
convertable : **con•vert•ible**
con•vert•er (one that converts);
  con•vert•or (electrical device)
con•vert•ible
con•vert•or (electrical device);
  con•vert•er (one that
  converts)
convexety : **con•vex•i•ty**
convexitty : **con•vex•i•ty**
con•vex•i•ty
con•vey
con•vey•ance
conveyence : **con•vey•ance**
convication : **con•vo•ca•tion**
convience : **con•ve•nience**
convient : **con•ve•nient**
convilescence : **con•va•les•cence**
convine : **con•vene**
convinience : **con•ve•nience**
convinient : **con•ve•nient**
con•vo•ca•tion
convurgence : **con•ver•gence**
conyac : **co•gnac**
coocumber : **cu•cum•ber**

coogar : **cou•gar**
cooger : **cou•gar**
cookoo : **cuck•oo**
coo•lie (laborer); **cool•ly** (in a
  cool manner)
cool•ly (in a cool manner);
  coo•lie (laborer)
co•op•er•ate
coopon : **cou•pon**
co•or•di•nate
corage : **cour•age**
corageous : **cou•ra•geous**
cor•al (reef); **cho•ral** (relating
  to a choir); **cho•rale** (hymn);
  cor•ral (horse pen)
corale : **cho•ral** (relating to a
  choir) *or* **cho•rale** (hymn) *or*
  cor•al (reef) *or* **cor•ral** (horse
  pen)
coralle : **cho•ral** (relating to a
  choir) *or* **cho•rale** (hymn) *or*
  cor•al (reef) *or* **cor•ral** (horse
  pen)
coranation : **cor•o•na•tion**
cord (rope); **chord** (music)
cordaroy : **cor•du•roy**
cordeal : **cor•dial**
cordeality : **cor•dial•i•ty**
corderoy : **cor•du•roy**
cordialety : **cor•dial•i•ty**
cor•dial•i•ty
cordiallity : **cor•dial•i•ty**
cordiroy : **cor•du•roy**
cor•du•roy
corect : **cor•rect**
corel : **cho•ral** (relating to a
  choir) *or* **cho•rale** (hymn) *or*
  cor•al (reef) *or* **cor•ral** (horse
  pen)
corelate : **cor•re•late**
coreographer :
  cho•re•og•ra•pher

corespondence :
  cor·re·spon·dence
corgeality : **cor·dial·i·ty**
corgial : **cor·dial**
coridor : **cor·ri·dor**
coriographer :
  cho·re·og·ra·pher
cornace : **cor·nice**
cornation : **cor·o·na·tion**
cor·nea
cornia : **cor·nea**
cor·nice
cornise : **cor·nice**
corobarate : **cor·rob·o·rate**
corode : **cor·rode**
corolary : **cor·ol·lary**
cor·ol·lary
cor·o·na·tion
cor·o·ner
cororoborate : **cor·rob·o·rate**
corparate : **cor·po·rate**
corperal : **cor·po·ral**
corperate : **cor·po·rate**
cor·po·ral
cor·po·rate
corporel : **cor·po·ral**
corps (military unit); **corpse**
  (dead body)
corpse (dead body); **corps**
  (military unit)
corrador : **cor·ri·dor**
corragation : **cor·ru·ga·tion**
cor·ral (horse pen); **cho·ral**
  (relating to a choir);
  cho·rale (hymn); **cor·al** (reef)
corralate : **cor·re·late**
corrallary : **cor·ol·lary**
cor·rect
correl : **cho·ral** (relating to a
  choir) *or* **cho·rale** (hymn) *or*
  cor·al (reef) *or* **cor·ral** (horse
  pen)

cor·re·late
corresponanse :
  cor·re·spon·dence
correspondance :
  cor·re·spon·dence
cor·re·spon·dence
corridoor : **cor·ri·dor**
cor·ri·dor
corrobborate : **cor·rob·o·rate**
corroberate : **cor·rob·o·rate**
cor·rob·o·rate
cor·rode
corroll : **cho·ral** (relating to a
  choir) *or* **cho·rale** (hymn) *or*
  cor·al (reef) *or* **cor·ral** (horse
  pen)
corrollary : **cor·ol·lary**
corrollery : **cor·ol·lary**
corroner : **cor·o·ner**
cor·ru·ga·tion
cor·rupt
corrus : **cho·rus**
corteous : **cour·te·ous**
cortesy : **cour·te·sy**
corugation : **cor·ru·ga·tion**
corupt : **cor·rupt**
corus : **cho·rus**
corvet : **cor·vette**
cor·vette
cosmapolitan :
  cos·mo·pol·i·tan
cosmepolitan : **cos·mo·pol·i·tan**
cos·met·ic
cosmettic : **cos·met·ic**
cos·mo·pol·i·tan
cosmopoliten :
  cos·mo·pol·i·tan
cosmopollitan :
  cos·mo·pol·i·tan
cotarie : **co·te·rie**
coteree : **co·te·rie**
co·te·rie

cotery : **co•te•rie**
cot•tage
cottege : **cot•tage**
cotten : **cot•ton**
cottige : **cot•tage**
cot•ton
cou•gar
couger : **cou•gar**
cough
coun•cil (assembly); **con•sul**
(diplomat); **coun•sel** (advice;
lawyer)
coun•sel (advice; lawyer);
con•sul (diplomat); **coun•cil**
(assembly)
counseler : **coun•sel•or**
counsellor : **coun•sel•or**
coun•sel•or
counsillor : **coun•sel•or**
coun•te•nance (face);
con•ti•nence (self-restraint)
countenanse : **con•ti•nence**
(self-restraint) *or*
coun•te•nance (face)
countenence : **con•ti•nence**
(self-restraint) *or*
coun•te•nance (face)
coun•ter•feit
counterfet : **coun•ter•feit**
counterfiet : **coun•ter•feit**
counterfit : **coun•ter•feit**
count•ess
countinance : **con•ti•nence**
(self-restraint) *or*
coun•te•nance (face)
countiss : **count•ess**
coun•try
coupan : **cou•pon**
coupelet : **coup•let**
coupeling : **coup•ling**
coupleing : **coup•ling**
coup•let

coup•ling
cou•pon
couponn : **cou•pon**
cour•age
cou•ra•geous
couragious : **cou•ra•geous**
courege : **cour•age**
cou•ri•er
courige : **cour•age**
courrier : **cou•ri•er**
course (direction); **coarse**
(rough)
courtasy : **cour•te•sy**
(politeness) *or* **curt•sy** (bow)
cour•te•ous
courtessy : **cour•te•sy**
(politeness) *or* **curt•sy** (bow)
cour•te•sy (politeness); **curt•sy**
(bow)
courtious : **cour•te•ous**
courtisy : **cour•te•sy**
(politeness) *or* **curt•sy** (bow)
courtmarshall : **court-mar•tial**
court-mar•tial
cousen : **cous•in**
cous•in
cov•e•nant
covenent : **cov•e•nant**
covennant : **cov•e•nant**
cov•er•age
coverege : **cov•er•age**
coverige : **cov•er•age**
covrage : **cov•er•age**
cowardace : **cow•ard•ice**
cow•ard•ice
cowardise : **cow•ard•ice**
cowardiss : **cow•ard•ice**
cowerdice : **cow•ard•ice**
coy•ote
coyotee : **coy•ote**
coyotie : **coy•ote**
crainium : **cra•ni•um**

cranbary : **cran•ber•ry**
cran•ber•ry
cranbery : **cran•ber•ry**
craniem : **cra•ni•um**
cra•ni•um
cra•ter
crator : **cra•ter**
cra•vat
cravatt : **cra•vat**
creak (noise); **creek** (stream)
creamary : **cream•ery**
creamerry : **cream•ery**
cream•ery
creamory : **cream•ery**
crease
creater : **cre•ator**
cre•ator
crea•ture
crecent : **cres•cent**
credability : **cred•i•bil•i•ty**
credable : **cred•i•ble**
cre•dence
credense : **cre•dence**
credibilety : **cred•i•bil•i•ty**
cred•i•bil•i•ty
credibillity : **cred•i•bil•i•ty**
cred•i•ble
credince : **cre•dence**
cre•do
creedence : **cre•dence**
creedo : **cre•do**
creek (stream); **creak** (noise);
    crick (pain in neck)
creemery : **cream•ery**
creep
creese : **crease**
creeture : **crea•ture**
cre•scen•do
cres•cent
creshendo : **cre•scen•do**
cressant : **cres•cent**
cressendo : **cre•scen•do**

cressent : **cres•cent**
creture : **crea•ture**
crev•asse (crack in ice);
    crev•ice (narrow crack)
crevat : **cra•vat**
crevatte : **cra•vat**
crev•ice (narrow crack);
    crev•asse (crack in ice)
crevisse : **crev•asse** (crack in
    ice) *or* **crev•ice** (narrow
    crack)
criator : **cre•ator**
crick (pain in neck); **creek**
    (stream)
crimenal : **crim•i•nal**
crim•i•nal
crimminal : **crim•i•nal**
crimsen : **crim•son**
crim•son
criptic : **cryp•tic**
crisanthamum :
    chry•san•the•mum
crisanthemum :
    chry•san•the•mum
cri•ses (*plur.*); **cri•sis** (*sing.*)
cri•sis (*sing.*); **cri•ses** (*plur.*)
crissis : **cri•sis**
cristal : **crys•tal**
Cristian : **Chris•tian**
Cristianity : **Chris•tian•i•ty**
critacism : **crit•i•cism**
critearia : **cri•te•ria**
critearion : **cri•te•ri•on**
criteek : **cri•tique**
criteeque : **cri•tique**
criteeria : **cri•te•ria**
criteerion : **cri•te•ri•on**
cri•te•ria (*plur.*); **cri•te•ri•on**
    (*sing.*)
cri•te•ri•on (*sing.*); **cri•te•ria**
    (*plur.*)
crit•ic

criticise (*Brit.*) : **crit•i•cize**
crit•i•cism
crit•i•cize
cri•tique
critiria : **cri•te•ria**
critirion : **cri•te•ri•on**
critisism : **crit•i•cism**
critisize : **crit•i•cize**
crittacize : **crit•i•cize**
crittic : **crit•ic**
critticism : **crit•i•cism**
critticize : **crit•i•cize**
crocadial : **croc•o•dile**
crocadile : **croc•o•dile**
crockodile : **croc•o•dile**
croc•o•dile
cromeum : **chro•mi•um**
cromiem : **chro•mi•um**
cromium : **chro•mi•um**
cronic : **chron•ic**
cronicle : **chron•i•cle**
cronollogy : **chro•nol•o•gy**
cronologgy : **chro•nol•o•gy**
cronology : **chro•nol•o•gy**
croose : **cruise**
croud : **crowd**
crowd
crucefy : **cru•ci•fy**
cru•cial
crucibal : **cru•ci•ble**
cru•ci•ble
cruciffy : **cru•ci•fy**
cru•ci•fy
cruise
cruse : **cruise**
crushall : **cru•cial**
crusial : **cru•cial**
crusible : **cru•ci•ble**
crusify : **cru•ci•fy**
crus•ta•cean
crustacion : **crus•ta•cean**
crustashean : **crus•ta•cean**

cruze : **cruise**
cryp•tic
cryptick : **cryp•tic**
crysanthamum :
    chry•san•the•mum
crysanthemum :
    chry•san•the•mum
crys•tal
crystall : **crys•tal**
crystell : **crys•tal**
csar : **czar**
cuadrant : **quad•rant**
cuarto : **quar•to**
cubbard : **cup•board**
cub•i•cal (cube-shaped);
    cub•i•cle (compartment)
cub•i•cle (compartment);
    cub•i•cal (cube-shaped)
cuck•oo
cucomber : **cu•cum•ber**
cucoo : **cuck•oo**
cu•cum•ber
cud•gel
cudgle : **cud•gel**
cue (signal; poolstick); **queue**
    (pigtail; line)
Cuebec : **Que•bec**
cujel : **cud•gel**
culenery : **cu•li•nary**
cu•li•nary
cullenery : **cu•li•nary**
cullinary : **cu•li•nary**
cullmination : **cul•mi•na•tion**
cullprit : **cul•prit**
culltivate : **cul•ti•vate**
culmanation : **cul•mi•na•tion**
culmenation : **cul•mi•na•tion**
cul•mi•na•tion
culpabal : **cul•pa•ble**
cul•pa•ble
culpible : **cul•pa•ble**
culpret : **cul•prit**

cul·prit
cultavate : **cul·ti·vate**
cul·ti·vate
cummercial : **com·mer·cial**
cumpass : **com·pass**
cup·board
cupbord : **cup·board**
cup·ful
cupfull : **cup·ful**
cuplet : **coup·let**
cupling : **coup·ling**
cupon : **cou·pon**
curafe : **ca·rafe**
curage : **cour·age**
curdal : **cur·dle**
curdel : **cur·dle**
cur·dle
cureo : **cu·rio**
curiculum : **cur·ric·u·lum**
cu·rio
curios : **cu·ri·ous**
curiosety : **cu·ri·os·i·ty**
cu·ri·os·i·ty
curiossity : **cu·ri·os·i·ty**
cu·ri·ous
curnel : **col·o·nel** (military officer) *or* **ker·nel** (seed)
cur·rant (berry); **cur·rent** (*noun,* flow; *adj.,* contemporary)
cur·rent (*noun,* flow; *adj.,* contemporary); **cur·rant** (berry)
cur·ric·u·lum
currier : **cou·ri·er**
cursary : **cur·so·ry**
curserry : **cur·so·ry**
cursery : **cur·so·ry**
cur·so·ry
curteous : **cour·te·ous**
curt·sey *or* **curt·sy** (bow); **cour·te·sy** (politeness)

curt·sy *or* **curt·sey** (bow); **cour·te·sy** (politeness)
cusin : **cous·in**
cus·tard
custerd : **cus·tard**
custodean : **cus·to·di·an**
cus·to·di·an
cus·tom·er
custommer : **cus·tom·er**
cut·lass
cutless : **cut·lass**
cutliss : **cut·lass**
cuzzin : **cous·in**
cwire : **choir**
cy·a·nide
cyanied : **cy·a·nide**
cy·ber·net·ics
cybernettics : **cy·ber·net·ics**
cycal : **cy·cle**
cy·cle (rotation); **sick·le** (knife)
cycloan : **cy·clone**
cy·clone
cyg·net (swan); **sig·net** (ring)
cyl·in·der
cyllinder : **cyl·in·der**
cym·bal (brass plate); **sym·bol** (meaningful image)
cymbol : **cym·bal** (brass plate) *or* **sym·bol** (meaningful image)
cyn·i·cism
cynisism : **cyn·i·cism**
cyote : **coy·ote**
cy·press
cypriss : **cy·press**
czar *or* **tsar**
Czechoslavokia : **Czecho·slo·va·kia**
Czecho·slo·va·kia
Czeckoslovakia : **Czecho·slo·va·kia**

D

dachshound : **dachs•hund**
dachs•hund
dackshund : **dachs•hund**
dad•dy
dady : **dad•dy**
daery : **dairy** (milk farm) *or*
  di•a•ry (daybook)
daffadil : **daf•fo•dil**
daffault : **de•fault**
daf•fo•dil
daffodill : **daf•fo•dil**
dafodil : **daf•fo•dil**
daggerotype : **da•guerre•o•type**
da•guerre•o•type
daguerrotype :
  da•guerre•o•type
dahl•ia
dai•ly
dai•qui•ri
daiquiry : **dai•qui•ri**
dairdevil : **dare•dev•il**
dairy (milk farm); **di•a•ry**
  (daybook)
Dalas : **Dal•las**
daley : **dai•ly**
dalinquent : **de•lin•quent**
Dal•las
Dalles : **Dal•las**
dallia : **dahl•ia**
dal•li•ance
dallianse : **dal•li•ance**
dallience : **dal•li•ance**
Dallis : **Dal•las**
Dallmatian : **Dal•ma•tian**
dallyance : **dal•li•ance**
Dalmashin : **Dal•ma•tian**
Dal•ma•tian
Dalmation : **Dal•ma•tian**
daly : **dai•ly**
damadge : **dam•age**

dam•age
damidge : **dam•age**
damige : **dam•age**
dammed (blocked); **damned**
  (condemned)
damned (condemned);
  dammed (blocked)
damozel : **dam•sel**
dam•sel
damsill : **dam•sel**
damsul : **dam•sel**
damzel : **dam•sel**
danc•er
dandalion : **dan•de•li•on**
dan•de•li•on
dandilion : **dan•de•li•on**
dandreff : **dan•druff**
dandriff : **dan•druff**
dan•druff
dandylion : **dan•de•li•on**
Danemark : **Den•mark**
Danesh : **Dan•ish**
dangeriss : **dan•ger•ous**
dan•ger•ous
Dan•ish
Dannish : **Dan•ish**
Dannube : **Dan•ube**
danser : **danc•er**
Dan•ube
dapravity : **de•prav•i•ty**
daquerri : **dai•qui•ri**
daquiri : **dai•qui•ri**
daralict : **der•e•lict**
daredevel : **dare•dev•il**
dare•dev•il
dary : **dairy** (milk farm) *or*
  di•a•ry (daybook)
da•ta (*plur.*); **da•tum** (*sing.*)
da•tum (*sing.*); **da•ta** (*plur.*)
daugh•ter

82

dauter : **daugh•ter**
dautter : **daugh•ter**
dazle : **daz•zle**
dazzal : **daz•zle**
dazzel : **daz•zle**
daz•zle
deacan : **dea•con**
dea•con
deadicate : **ded•i•cate**
dead•li•er
deadlyer : **dead•li•er**
deaf•en
deaf•ness
deafniss : **deaf•ness**
deakon : **dea•con**
dealt
deapth : **depth**
dear (precious); **deer** (animal)
dearth
death
deaty : **de•i•ty**
debachery : **de•bauch•ery**
de•ba•cle
debait : **de•bate**
debakle : **de•ba•cle**
debanair : **deb•o•nair**
de•bate
debauchary : **de•bauch•ery**
de•bauch•ery
debawchery : **de•bauch•ery**
debbacle : **de•ba•cle**
debbate : **de•bate**
debbonair : **deb•o•nair**
debbonare : **deb•o•nair**
debbris : **de•bris**
debecal : **de•ba•cle**
debinair : **deb•o•nair**
deb•o•nair
debonare : **deb•o•nair**
debree : **de•bris**
debres : **de•bris**

de•bris
debter : **debt•or**
debt•or (one who owes); **de•ter**
  (to prevent)
debue : **de•but**
de•but
decadance : **de•ca•dence**
decadanse : **de•ca•dence**
de•cade
de•ca•dence
decadense : **de•ca•dence**
decaid : **de•cade**
decapatate : **de•cap•i•tate**
decapetate : **de•cap•i•tate**
decapitait : **de•cap•i•tate**
de•cap•i•tate
decappitate : **de•cap•i•tate**
decarate : **dec•o•rate**
decathalon : **de•cath•lon**
decathelon : **de•cath•lon**
de•cath•lon
deccade : **de•cade**
deccadence : **de•ca•dence**
deccorate : **dec•o•rate**
de•ceased
deceatful : **de•ceit•ful**
deceave : **de•ceive**
decebel : **dec•i•bel**
deceble : **dec•i•bel**
decedence : **de•ca•dence**
deceesed : **de•ceased**
deceised : **de•ceased**
de•ceit•ful
deceitfull : **de•ceit•ful**
de•ceive
decemal : **dec•i•mal**
De•cem•ber
de•cen•cy
decendant : **de•scen•dant**
decendent : **de•scen•dant**
decensy : **de•cen•cy**

de•cent (respectable); de•scent
(act of going down);
dis•sent (disagreement)
decesed : de•ceased
decetful : de•ceit•ful
deceve : de•ceive
decibal : dec•i•bel
dec•i•bel
decibell : dec•i•bel
de•cide
decidewous : de•cid•u•ous
deciduiss : de•cid•u•ous
de•cid•u•ous
decietful : de•ceit•ful
decietfull : de•ceit•ful
decieve : de•ceive
decifer : de•ci•pher
dec•i•mal
decimel : dec•i•mal
decimmal : dec•i•mal
decincy : de•cen•cy
de•ci•pher
deciphur : de•ci•pher
deciple : dis•ci•ple
decisian : de•ci•sion
de•ci•sion
decission : de•ci•sion
decizion : de•ci•sion
deckade : de•cade
decklaration : dec•la•ra•tion
deckorate : dec•o•rate
declair : de•clare
declaratian : dec•la•ra•tion
dec•la•ra•tion
de•clare
decleration : dec•la•ra•tion
decliration : dec•la•ra•tion
decontamanate :
   de•con•tam•i•nate
decontamenate :
   de•con•tam•i•nate
de•con•tam•i•nate

decontamminate :
   de•con•tam•i•nate
de•cor
decoram : de•co•rum
dec•o•rate
decore : de•cor
decorem : de•co•rum
decorr : de•cor
decorrum : de•co•rum
de•co•rum
decreace : de•crease
de•crease
decreece : de•crease
decreese : de•crease
decreise : de•crease
decrepatude : de•crep•i•tude
decrepet : de•crep•it
decrepid : de•crep•it
de•crep•it
de•crep•i•tude
decreppit : de•crep•it
decreppitude : de•crep•i•tude
decrese : de•crease
dedacate : ded•i•cate
deddicate : ded•i•cate
dedduce : de•duce
dedduction : de•duc•tion
dedecate : ded•i•cate
ded•i•cate
dedlier : dead•li•er
dedoose : de•duce
de•duce
deducktion : de•duc•tion
de•duc•tion
deduse : de•duce
deecon : dea•con
deer (animal); dear (precious)
deesall : die•sel
deesel : die•sel
deeth : death
de•face
defacit : def•i•cit

defallt : **de•fault**
defalt : **de•fault**
def•a•ma•tion
defammation : **def•a•ma•tion**
defanitely : **def•i•nite•ly**
defanition : **def•i•ni•tion**
defase : **de•face**
defaullt : **de•fault**
de•fault
de•feat
defeet : **de•feat**
defeit : **de•feat**
defemation : **def•a•ma•tion**
defence (*Brit.*) : **de•fense**
defencible : **de•fen•si•ble**
de•fen•dant
defendent : **de•fen•dant**
defendint : **de•fen•dant**
defensable : **de•fen•si•ble**
de•fense
defenseble : **de•fen•si•ble**
defensibal : **de•fen•si•ble**
de•fen•si•ble
defered : **de•ferred**
de•ferred
defete : **de•feat**
defface : **de•face**
deffamation : **def•a•ma•tion**
deffeat : **de•feat**
deffen : **deaf•en**
deffenatly : **def•i•nite•ly**
deffendent : **de•fen•dant**
deffense : **de•fense**
deffered : **de•ferred**
defferred : **de•ferred**
defficit : **def•i•cit**
deffinitely : **def•i•nite•ly**
deffinition : **def•i•ni•tion**
deffness : **deaf•ness**
de•fi•ance
defianse : **de•fi•ance**
de•fi•cient

def•i•cit
defience : **de•fi•ance**
defiense : **de•fi•ance**
defimation : **def•a•ma•tion**
de•fin•able
definately : **def•i•nite•ly**
definatly : **def•i•nite•ly**
defineable : **de•fin•able**
defineble : **de•fin•able**
definetion : **def•i•ni•tion**
definetly : **def•i•nite•ly**
definibal : **de•fin•able**
definible : **de•fin•able**
def•i•nite•ly
def•i•ni•tion
definitly : **def•i•nite•ly**
defiset : **def•i•cit**
defisient : **de•fi•cient**
defisit : **def•i•cit**
defrad : **de•fraud**
de•fraud
defrod : **de•fraud**
defth : **depth**
defyance : **de•fi•ance**
degenarate : **de•gen•er•ate**
de•gen•er•ate
degennerate : **de•gen•er•ate**
deginerate : **de•gen•er•ate**
deginnerate : **de•gen•er•ate**
deg•ra•da•tion
degradeation : **deg•ra•da•tion**
degredation : **deg•ra•da•tion**
dehidrate : **de•hy•drate**
dehli : **Del•hi** (city) *or* deli
  (delicatessen)
dehydrait : **de•hy•drate**
de•hy•drate
deiffy : **de•i•fy**
de•i•fy
deisel : **die•sel**
deitary : **di•etary**
de•i•ty

dekathalon : **de·cath·lon**
dekathlon : **de·cath·lon**
delacacy : **del·i·ca·cy**
delacate : **del·i·cate**
delagate : **del·e·gate**
delaget : **del·e·gate**
delapidated : **di·lap·i·dat·ed**
delaterious : **del·e·te·ri·ous**
Delawair : **Del·a·ware**
Del·a·ware
Delawear : **Del·a·ware**
delearious : **de·lir·i·ous**
deleat : **de·lete**
delecacy : **del·i·ca·cy**
delecktable : **de·lec·ta·ble**
de·lec·ta·ble
delectibal : **de·lec·ta·ble**
delectible : **de·lec·ta·ble**
deleerious : **de·lir·i·ous**
deleet : **de·lete**
del·e·gate
delerious : **de·lir·i·ous**
de·lete
del·e·te·ri·ous
Deleware : **Del·a·ware**
Del·hi (city); **deli** (delicatessen)
deli (delicatessen); **Del·hi** (city)
delibberate : **de·lib·er·ate**
de·lib·er·ate
deliberet : **de·lib·er·ate**
del·i·ca·cy
delicasy : **del·i·ca·cy**
del·i·cate
delicatessan : **del·i·ca·tes·sen**
del·i·ca·tes·sen
deliceous : **de·li·cious**
delicet : **del·i·cate**
delicetessen : **del·i·ca·tes·sen**
de·li·cious
delinguent : **de·lin·quent**
delinquant : **de·lin·quent**
de·lin·quent

de·lir·i·ous
delishous : **de·li·cious**
deliterious : **del·e·te·ri·ous**
de·liv·er·ance
deliveranse : **de·liv·er·ance**
deliverence : **de·liv·er·ance**
dellaterious : **del·e·te·ri·ous**
Dellaware : **Del·a·ware**
dellegate : **del·e·gate**
Delleware : **Del·a·ware**
dellhi : **Del·hi** (city) *or* **deli**
   (delicatessen)
delli : **Del·hi** (city) *or* **deli**
   (delicatessen)
dellicacy : **del·i·ca·cy**
dellicate : **del·i·cate**
dellicatessen : **del·i·ca·tes·sen**
delliverence : **de·liv·er·ance**
delt : **dealt**
demacracy : **de·moc·ra·cy**
demagod : **demi·god**
dem·a·gog *or* **dem·a·gogue**
dem·a·gogue *or* **dem·a·gog**
demalition : **dem·o·li·tion**
demanstrate : **dem·on·strate**
de·mean
demeen : **de·mean**
demenshia : **de·men·tia**
demension : **di·men·sion**
de·men·tia
demeret : **de·mer·it**
de·mer·it
demerrit : **de·mer·it**
demi·god
demigogue : **dem·a·gogue**
demilition : **de·mo·li·tion**
de·mise
demize : **de·mise**
demmagogue : **dem·a·gogue**
demmigod : **demi·god**
demmise : **de·mise**
demmocracy : **de·moc·ra·cy**

demmolition : **de•mo•li•tion**
demmonstrate : **dem•on•strate**
de•moc•ra•cy
democrasy : **de•moc•ra•cy**
democricy : **de•moc•ra•cy**
democrisy : **de•moc•ra•cy**
demogod : **demi•god**
demogogue : **dem•a•gogue**
demolission : **de•mo•li•tion**
demolitian : **de•mo•li•tion**
de•mo•li•tion
demolizion : **de•mo•li•tion**
demonstrait : **dem•on•strate**
dem•on•strate
demuir : **de•mur** (to disagree)
  or **de•mure** (modest)
de•mur (to disagree); **de•mure**
  (modest)
de•mure (modest); **de•mur** (to
  disagree)
denam : **den•im**
denazen : **den•i•zen**
dence : **dense**
dencity : **den•si•ty**
denezen : **den•i•zen**
den•im
denisen : **den•i•zen**
den•i•zen
Denmarck : **Den•mark**
Den•mark
dennim : **den•im**
dennizen : **den•i•zen**
dennotation : **de•no•ta•tion**
dennote : **de•note**
dennounce : **de•nounce**
denntal : **den•tal**
dennum : **den•im**
denomanation :
  de•nom•i•na•tion
denomenation :
  de•nom•i•na•tion
de•nom•i•na•tion

denommination :
  de•nom•i•na•tion
de•no•ta•tion
de•note
denottation : **de•no•ta•tion**
de•nounce
denounciation :
  de•nun•ci•a•tion
denounse : **de•nounce**
denownce : **de•nounce**
densaty : **den•si•ty**
dense
densety : **den•si•ty**
densitty : **den•si•ty**
den•si•ty
den•tal
dentel : **den•tal**
dentestry : **den•tist•ry**
dentistery : **den•tist•ry**
den•tist•ry
denum : **den•im**
de•nun•ci•a•tion
denunsiation : **de•nun•ci•a•tion**
deoderant : **de•odor•ant**
deodirant : **de•odor•ant**
de•odor•ant
deodorent : **de•odor•ant**
depaty : **dep•u•ty**
dependabal : **de•pend•able**
de•pend•able
dependant : **de•pen•dent**
dependible : **de•pend•able**
depety : **dep•u•ty**
depewty : **dep•u•ty**
dephth : **depth**
de•plor•able
deploreble : **de•plor•able**
deplorible : **de•plor•able**
depopalate : **de•pop•u•late**
depoppulate : **de•pop•u•late**
de•pop•u•late
deposet : **de•pos•it**

de·pos·it
depossit : **de·pos·it**
depozit : **de·pos·it**
depposit : **de·pos·it**
depprivation : **de·pri·va·tion**
depravety : **de·prav·i·ty**
depravitty : **de·prav·i·ty**
de·prav·i·ty
depresent : **de·pres·sant**
de·pres·sant
depressent : **de·pres·sant**
deprevation : **de·pri·va·tion**
deprivatian : **de·pri·va·tion**
de·pri·va·tion
depth
deputty : **dep·u·ty**
dep·u·ty
deralict : **der·e·lict**
derelect : **der·e·lict**
derelick : **der·e·lict**
der·e·lict
derick : **der·rick**
derilict : **der·e·lict**
derishion : **de·ri·sion**
de·ri·sion
derission : **de·ri·sion**
derizion : **de·ri·sion**
dermatoligist : **der·ma·tol·o·gist**
dermatollogist :
  der·ma·tol·o·gist
der·ma·tol·o·gist
dermetologist :
  der·ma·tol·o·gist
dermitologist :
  der·ma·tol·o·gist
derreck : **der·rick**
derrelict : **der·e·lict**
der·rick
derrik : **der·rick**
derth : **dearth**
desacrate : **des·e·crate**
de·scen·dant or **de·scen·dent**

de·scen·dent or **de·scen·dant**
de·scent (act of going down);
  de·cent (respectable);
  dis·sent (disagreement)
describtion : **de·scrip·tion**
descriptian : **de·scrip·tion**
de·scrip·tion
deseased : **de·ceased**
des·e·crate
deseive : **de·ceive**
Desember : **De·cem·ber**
de·sert (arid land); **des·sert**
  (sweet dish)
desibel : **dec·i·bel**
desible : **dec·i·bel**
deside : **de·cide**
desiduous : **de·cid·u·ous**
desifer : **de·ci·pher**
de·sign
de·sign·er
designor : **de·sign·er**
desimal : **dec·i·mal**
desimel : **dec·i·mal**
desine : **de·sign**
desiner : **de·sign·er**
desipher : **de·ci·pher**
desirabal : **de·sir·able**
de·sir·able
desireble : **de·sir·able**
de·spair
desparado : **des·per·a·do**
desparate : **des·per·ate**
despare : **de·spair**
des·per·a·do
des·per·ate
desperato : **des·per·a·do**
despirate : **des·per·ate**
de·spise
despize : **de·spise**
des·pot
dessecrate : **des·e·crate**
dessect : **dis·sect**

dessendant : **de•scen•dant**

des•sert (sweet dish); **de•sert** (arid land)

dessign : **de•sign**

dessirable : **de•sir•able**

destanation : **des•ti•na•tion**

destany : **des•ti•ny**

destatute : **des•ti•tute**

desteny : **des•ti•ny**

destetute : **des•ti•tute**

des•ti•na•tion

destinct : **dis•tinct**

destinnation : **des•ti•na•tion**

destinny : **des•ti•ny**

des•ti•ny

des•ti•tute

destructable : **de•struc•ti•ble**

de•struc•ti•ble

de•tach

de•tain

detaintion : **de•ten•tion**

detanate : **det•o•nate**

detane : **de•tain**

detatch : **de•tach**

deteariorate : **de•te•ri•o•rate**

de•ten•tion

de•ter (to prevent); **debt•or** (one who owes)

deterent : **de•ter•rent**

detereorate : **de•te•ri•o•rate**

de•te•ri•o•rate

determen : **de•ter•mine**

determin : **de•ter•mine**

de•ter•mine

deterr : **debt•or** (one who owes) or **de•ter** (to prevent)

deterrant : **de•ter•rent**

de•test•able

detestible : **de•test•able**

deth : **death**

detinate : **det•o•nate**

detiriorate : **de•te•ri•o•rate**

det•o•nate

detramental : **det•ri•men•tal**

detremental : **det•ri•men•tal**

det•ri•men•tal

dettain : **de•tain**

detter : **debt•or** (one who owes) or **de•ter** (to prevent)

dettermine : **de•ter•mine**

dettonate : **det•o•nate**

dettor : **debt•or** (one who owes) or **de•ter** (to prevent)

devan : **di•van**

dev•as•tate

deveate : **de•vi•ate**

devel : **dev•il**

devellop : **de•vel•op**

de•vel•op

de•vel•oped

developped : **de•vel•oped**

deveous : **de•vi•ous**

devest : **di•vest**

devestate : **dev•as•tate**

de•vi•ate

de•vice (*noun*); **de•vise** (*verb*)

devide : **di•vide**

dev•il

devine : **di•vine**

devinity : **di•vin•i•ty**

de•vi•ous

de•vise (*verb*); **de•vice** (*noun*)

devision : **di•vi•sion**

devistate : **dev•as•tate**

devorce : **di•vorce**

devorse : **di•vorce**

dev•o•tee

devotie : **dev•o•tee**

devoty : **dev•o•tee**

de•vour

devowr : **de•vour**

devulge : **di•vulge**

devvil : **dev•il**

dexteriss : **dex•ter•ous**

dex·ter·ous
dexterus : **dex·ter·ous**
dextrous : **dex·ter·ous**
dezine : **de·sign**
diabalical : **di·a·bol·i·cal**
diabeates : **di·a·be·tes**
diabeetes : **di·a·be·tes**
di·a·be·tes
diabetese : **di·a·be·tes**
di·a·bet·ic
diabetis : **di·a·be·tes**
di·a·bol·i·cal
diabollical : **di·a·bol·i·cal**
di·ag·no·sis
di·a·gram
dialate : **di·late**
di·a·log *or* **di·a·logue**
di·a·logue *or* **di·a·log**
diamater : **di·am·e·ter**
diameater : **di·am·e·ter**
diameeter : **di·am·e·ter**
diameiter : **di·am·e·ter**
diamend : **di·a·mond**
di·am·e·ter
diamiter : **di·am·e·ter**
di·a·mond
diamund : **di·a·mond**
di·a·per
diarea : **di·ar·rhea**
diarhea : **di·ar·rhea**
di·ar·rhea
diarrhia : **di·ar·rhea**
di·a·ry (daybook); **dairy** (milk farm)
diaty : **de·i·ty**
dibetes : **di·a·be·tes**
dibetic : **di·a·bet·ic**
dibolical : **di·a·bol·i·cal**
Dicksie : **Dix·ie**
dicktator : **dic·ta·tor**
dictater : **dic·ta·tor**
dic·ta·tor

dic·tio·nary
dictionery : **dic·tio·nary**
die (perish); **dye** (color)
diefy : **de·i·fy**
diery : **dairy** (milk farm) *or*
  di·a·ry (daybook)
die·sel
diesell : **die·sel**
dietarry : **di·etary**
di·etary
dieterry : **di·etary**
dietery : **di·etary**
diety : **de·i·ty**
diferent : **dif·fer·ent**
diffacult : **dif·fi·cult**
diffecult : **dif·fi·cult**
differant : **dif·fer·ent**
dif·fer·ent
dif·fi·cult
diffrent : **dif·fer·ent**
dificult : **dif·fi·cult**
digestable : **di·gest·ible**
digesteble : **di·gest·ible**
di·gest·ible
dig·i·tal
digitel : **dig·i·tal**
digittal : **dig·i·tal**
dignafied : **dig·ni·fied**
dignatary : **dig·ni·tary**
dignaty : **dig·ni·ty**
dignefied : **dig·ni·fied**
dignetary : **dig·ni·tary**
dignety : **dig·ni·ty**
dig·ni·fied
dignifyed : **dig·ni·fied**
dignitarry : **dig·ni·tary**
dig·ni·tary
dignitery : **dig·ni·tary**
dignitty : **dig·ni·ty**
dig·ni·ty
dignosis : **di·ag·no·sis**
digram : **di·a·gram**

dijestible : **di•gest•ible**
dike
dilapedated : **di•lap•i•dat•ed**
di•lap•i•dat•ed
dilappidated : **di•lap•i•dat•ed**
di•late
dilectable : **de•lec•ta•ble**
dilema : **di•lem•ma**
di•lem•ma
dilemna : **di•lem•ma**
dil•i•gence
diligense : **dil•i•gence**
dilimma : **di•lem•ma**
dilirious : **de•lir•i•ous**
dilligence : **dil•i•gence**
dilogue : **di•a•logue**
dimend : **di•a•mond**
dimensian : **di•men•sion**
di•men•sion
dimond : **di•a•mond**
dinamic : **dy•nam•ic**
dinamite : **dy•na•mite**
dinasaur : **di•no•saur**
dinasty : **dy•nas•ty**
dinesaur : **di•no•saur**
di•no•saur
dinosore : **di•no•saur**
diodorant : **de•odor•ant**
diper : **di•a•per**
diplamat : **dip•lo•mat**
diplimat : **dip•lo•mat**
dip•lo•mat
directer : **di•rec•tor**
di•rec•tor
dirrea : **di•ar•rhea**
dirrhea : **di•ar•rhea**
dirth : **dearth**
diry : **di•a•ry**
disapearance : **dis•ap•pear•ance**
disapearence : **dis•ap•pear•ance**
disapoint : **dis•ap•point**
dis•ap•pear•ance

disappearanse :
  dis•ap•pear•ance
dis•ap•point
disasster : **dis•as•ter**
dis•as•ter
disasterous : **di•sas•trous**
di•sas•trous
disatisfy : **dis•sat•is•fy**
disberse : **dis•burse**
disbirse : **dis•burse**
disburce : **dis•burse**
dis•burse
disc *or* disk
discerage : **dis•cour•age**
dis•cern
discipal : **dis•ci•ple**
dis•ci•ple
dis•ci•pline
discloshure : **dis•clo•sure**
dis•clo•sure
dis•cour•age
discourige : **dis•cour•age**
dis•creet (prudent); **dis•crete**
  (separate)
dis•crep•an•cy
discrepency : **dis•crep•an•cy**
dis•crete (separate); **dis•creet**
  (prudent)
discurage : **dis•cour•age**
dis•ease
disect : **dis•sect**
diseese : **dis•ease**
disent : **de•cent** (respectable) *or*
  de•scent (act of going down)
  or **dis•sent** (disagreement)
disese : **dis•ease**
disgise : **dis•guise**
dis•guise
disguize : **dis•guise**
dis•in•fec•tant
disinfectent : **dis•in•fec•tant**
disintagrate : **dis•in•te•grate**

dis•in•te•grate
disipline : **dis•ci•pline**
disk *or* **disc**
dis•mal
dismel : **dis•mal**
disobediance : **dis•obe•di•ence**
dis•obe•di•ence
disobediense : **dis•obe•di•ence**
disobeedience : **dis•obe•di•ence**
dispair : **de•spair**
dis•par•age
dispare : **de•spair**
disparige : **dis•par•age**
disparrage : **dis•par•age**
dis•pel
dispell : **dis•pel**
dispence : **dis•pense**
dispencible : **dis•pen•sable**
dispensabal : **dis•pen•sable**
dis•pen•sable
dis•pense
dispensible : **dis•pen•sable**
dispise : **de•spise**
dis•pos•al
disposel : **dis•pos•al**
dispot : **des•pot**
dis•put•able
disputible : **dis•put•able**
disqualefy : **dis•qual•i•fy**
dis•qual•i•fy
disrubt : **dis•rupt**
dis•rupt
dis•sat•is•fy
dis•sect
dis•sent (disagreement);
  de•cent (respectable);
    de•scent (act of going down)
dissern : **dis•cern**
dissiple : **dis•ci•ple**
dis•tance
distanse : **dis•tance**
distence : **dis•tance**

distilary : **dis•till•ery**
distilery : **dis•till•ery**
distillary : **dis•till•ery**
dis•till•ery
dis•tinct
distributer : **dis•trib•u•tor**
dis•trib•u•tor
distructible : **de•struc•ti•ble**
diury : **di•a•ry**
di•van
divann : **di•van**
divedend : **div•i•dend**
divergance : **di•ver•gence**
di•ver•gence
divergense : **di•ver•gence**
di•vest
divet : **div•ot**
di•vide
div•i•dend
dividind : **div•i•dend**
divied : **di•vide**
di•vine
divinety : **di•vin•i•ty**
divinitty : **di•vin•i•ty**
di•vin•i•ty
divinnity : **di•vin•i•ty**
divishion : **di•vi•sion**
di•vi•sion
division : **di•vi•sion**
divit : **div•ot**
divizion : **di•vi•sion**
di•vorce
divorse : **di•vorce**
div•ot
divour : **de•vour**
di•vulge
divurgence : **di•ver•gence**
divvest : **di•vest**
divvide : **di•vide**
divvot : **div•ot**
Dixee : **Dix•ie**
Dix•ie

Dixy : **Dix·ie**
diziness : **diz·zi·ness**
dizmal : **dis·mal**
diz·zi·ness
dizziniss : **diz·zi·ness**
dizzyness : **diz·zi·ness**
docell : **doc·ile**
dochshund : **dachs·hund**
doc·ile
docilitty : **do·cil·i·ty**
do·cil·i·ty
docill : **doc·ile**
docillety : **do·cil·i·ty**
docillity : **do·cil·i·ty**
docksology : **dox·ol·o·gy**
docter : **doc·tor**
docterate : **doc·tor·ate**
doc·tor
doc·tor·ate
doctoret : **doc·tor·ate**
doctorit : **doc·tor·ate**
doctren : **doc·trine**
doctrenaire : **doc·tri·naire**
doctrin : **doc·trine**
doc·tri·naire
doctrinare : **doc·tri·naire**
doc·trine
doctrinnaire : **doc·tri·naire**
documentarry :
    doc·u·men·ta·ry
doc·u·men·ta·ry
documentery : **doc·u·men·ta·ry**
documentry : **doc·u·men·ta·ry**
documintary : **doc·u·men·ta·ry**
dogerel : **dog·ger·el**
doggarel : **dog·ger·el**
doggeral : **dog·ger·el**
dog·ger·el
doggerle : **dog·ger·el**
doilie : **doi·ly**
doi·ly
dolar : **dol·lar**

doldrams : **dol·drums**
doldrems : **dol·drums**
dol·drums
doledrums : **dol·drums**
doler : **dol·lar**
dolfin : **dol·phin**
dol·lar
dolldrums : **dol·drums**
doller : **dol·lar**
dollphin : **dol·phin**
dolphen : **dol·phin**
dol·phin
do·main
domanant : **dom·i·nant**
domane : **do·main**
domaneering : **dom·i·neer·ing**
domenance : **dom·i·nance**
domeno : **dom·i·no**
domesstic : **do·mes·tic**
domessticity : **do·mes·tic·i·ty**
do·mes·tic
domesticety : **do·mes·tic·i·ty**
domesticitty : **do·mes·tic·i·ty**
do·mes·tic·i·ty
domestick : **do·mes·tic**
domestisity : **do·mes·tic·i·ty**
do·mi·cile
domicill : **do·mi·cile**
dom·i·nance
dominanse : **dom·i·nance**
dom·i·nant
dominearing : **dom·i·neer·ing**
dom·i·neer·ing
domineiring : **dom·i·neer·ing**
dominence : **dom·i·nance**
dominense : **dom·i·nance**
dominent : **dom·i·nant**
dom·i·no
dominoe : **dom·i·no**
domisile : **do·mi·cile**
domminance : **dom·i·nance**
domminant : **dom·i·nant**

dommino : **dom·i·no**
domocile : **do·mi·cile**
domosile : **do·mi·cile**
doner : **do·nor**
donkee : **don·key**
don·key
donkie : **don·key**
do·nor
doormouse : **dor·mouse**
dooty : **du·ty**
dor·mant
dormatory : **dor·mi·to·ry**
dorment : **dor·mant**
dormetory : **dor·mi·to·ry**
dormitorry : **dor·mi·to·ry**
dor·mi·to·ry
dor·mouse
dor·sal
dorsel : **dor·sal**
dorssal : **dor·sal**
dosadge : **dos·age**
dos·age
dosege : **dos·age**
dosier : **dos·sier**
dosige : **dos·age**
dosile : **doc·ile**
dosility : **do·cil·i·ty**
dosill : **doc·ile**
dossage : **dos·age**
dossiay : **dos·sier**
dos·sier
dossiey : **dos·sier**
dot·age
dotege : **dot·age**
dotige : **dot·age**
dottage : **dot·age**
doubal : **dou·ble**
doubel : **dou·ble**
doubious : **du·bi·ous**
dou·ble
doubley : **dou·bly**
dou·bloon

doublune : **dou·bloon**
dou·bly
doubt·ful
doubtfull : **doubt·ful**
doubt·less
doubtliss : **doubt·less**
doughter : **daugh·ter**
doul : **dow·el** (peg) or **du·al**
    (double) or **du·el** (fight)
douplex : **du·plex**
doutful : **doubt·ful**
doutless : **doubt·less**
dow·a·ger
dowajer : **dow·a·ger**
doweger : **dow·a·ger**
dow·el
dowell : **dow·el**
dowerry : **dow·ry**
dowery : **dow·ry**
dowger : **dow·a·ger**
dowiger : **dow·a·ger**
dowl : **dow·el**
downpore : **down·pour**
down·pour
down·ward
downwerd : **down·ward**
downword : **down·ward**
dow·ry
doxhund : **dachs·hund**
doxolagy : **dox·ol·o·gy**
doxoligy : **dox·ol·o·gy**
doxollogy : **dox·ol·o·gy**
dox·ol·o·gy
doyly : **doi·ly**
doz·en
dozin : **doz·en**
dozzen : **doz·en**
draft
dragen : **drag·on**
draggon : **drag·on**
dragin : **drag·on**
drag·on

dra·ma
dra·mat·i·cal·ly
dramaticaly : **dra·mat·i·cal·ly**
dramaticly : **dra·mat·i·cal·ly**
dramatise (*Brit.*) : **dra·ma·tize**
dra·ma·tize
dramattically : **dra·mat·i·cal·ly**
drametize : **dra·ma·tize**
dramitize : **dra·ma·tize**
dramma : **dra·ma**
drammatically : **dra·mat·i·cal·ly**
drammatize : **dra·ma·tize**
drapary : **drap·ery**
draperry : **drap·ery**
drap·ery
drapry : **drap·ery**
dras·ti·cal·ly
drasticaly : **dras·ti·cal·ly**
drastickally : **dras·ti·cal·ly**
drasticly : **dras·ti·cal·ly**
drastikally : **dras·ti·cal·ly**
draught (*Brit.*) : **draft**
dread·ful
dreadfull : **dread·ful**
dream
drearally : **drea·ri·ly**
drearely : **drea·ri·ly**
drea·ri·ly
drearly : **drea·ri·ly**
drea·ry
dredful : **dread·ful**
dreem : **dream**
dreerily : **drea·ri·ly**
dreery : **drea·ry**
dreiry : **drea·ry**
dreser : **dress·er**
dress·er
dressor : **dress·er**
dri·er (more dry); dry·er
  (device for drying)
drily : **dry·ly**
drinkabel : **drink·able**

drink·able
drinkeble : **drink·able**
drinkibal : **drink·able**
drinkible : **drink·able**
drival : **driv·el**
driv·el
drivle : **driv·el**
drivvel : **driv·el**
drizle : **driz·zle**
drizzal : **driz·zle**
driz·zle
drousiness : **drow·si·ness**
drow·si·ness
drowsiniss : **drow·si·ness**
drowsyness : **drow·si·ness**
drowziness : **drow·si·ness**
drudgerry : **drudg·ery**
drudg·ery
drudgiry : **drudg·ery**
drudgry : **drudg·ery**
drudjery : **drudg·ery**
drugery : **drudg·ery**
druggest : **drug·gist**
drug·gist
drugist : **drug·gist**
drunk·ard
drunkerd : **drunk·ard**
dry·er (device for drying);
  dri·er (more dry)
dry·ly
du·al (double); du·el (fight)
dubble : **dou·ble**
dubbloon : **dou·bloon**
dubblune : **dou·bloon**
dubbly : **dou·bly**
dubeous : **du·bi·ous**
du·bi·ous
dubloon : **dou·bloon**
dubly : **dou·bly**
Duch : **Dutch**
duch·ess
duchiss : **duch·ess**

duchuss : **duch•ess**
ducktile : **duc•tile**
ductel : **duc•tile**
duc•tile
ductill : **duc•tile**
ductle : **duc•tile**
du•el (fight); **du•al** (double)
dufel : **duf•fel**
duf•fel
duffle : **duf•fel**
dulard : **dull•ard**
dull•ard
dullerd : **dull•ard**
dullird : **dull•ard**
dul•ly (with dullness); **du•ly** (as
  is due)
du•ly (as is due); **dul•ly** (with
  dullness)
dumb•bell
dumbell : **dumb•bell**
dumb•found or **dum•found**
dumb•wait•er
dumbwaitor : **dumb•wait•er**
dumby : **dum•my**
dum•found or **dumb•found**
dummey : **dum•my**
dummie : **dum•my**
dum•my
dumwaiter : **dumb•wait•er**
dunce
dun•ga•ree
dungarey : **dun•ga•ree**
dungarie : **dun•ga•ree**
dungary : **dun•ga•ree**
dungean : **dun•geon**
dungen : **dun•geon**
dun•geon
dungeree : **dun•ga•ree**
dungin : **dun•geon**
dungiree : **dun•ga•ree**
dunjeon : **dun•geon**
dunse : **dunce**

duplacator : **du•pli•ca•tor**
duplecate : **du•pli•cate**
duplects : **du•plex**
du•plex
du•plic•ate
du•pli•ca•tor
duplicety : **du•plic•i•ty**
duplicitty : **du•plic•i•ty**
du•plic•i•ty
duplisity : **du•plic•i•ty**
durabal : **du•ra•ble**
durabilety : **du•ra•bil•i•ty**
du•ra•bil•i•ty
durabillity : **du•ra•bil•i•ty**
du•ra•ble
durebility : **du•ra•bil•i•ty**
dureble : **du•ra•ble**
du•ress
durible : **du•ra•ble**
durrable : **du•ra•ble**
durress : **du•ress**
durth : **dearth**
dutaful : **du•ti•ful**
Dutch
dutchess : **duch•ess**
du•te•ous
du•ti•ful
dutifull : **du•ti•ful**
dutious : **du•te•ous**
dutius : **du•te•ous**
dutty : **du•ty**
du•ty
dutyful : **du•ti•ful**
dutyous : **du•te•ous**
duzen : **doz•en**
duzzen : **doz•en**
dye (color); **die** (perish)
dye•ing (coloring); **dy•ing**
  (perishing)
dy•ing (perishing); **dye•ing**
  (coloring)
dyke : **dike**

dy•nam•ic
dynamick : **dy•nam•ic**
dynamight : **dy•na•mite**
dy•na•mite
dynammic : **dy•nam•ic**
dynassty : **dy•nas•ty**

dy•nas•ty
dynesty : **dy•nas•ty**
dynimite : **dy•na•mite**
dynisty : **dy•nas•ty**
dynomite : **dy•na•mite**
dyrea : **di•ar•rhea**

E

eagel : **ea·gle**
ea·ger
eagger : **ea·ger**
ea·gle
eaked : **eked**
eaking : **ek·ing**
ear·ache
earacke : **ear·ache**
earaik : **ear·ache**
earake : **ear·ache**
earie : **ae·rie** (nest) *or* **ee·rie** (weird) *or* **Erie** (lake and canal)
earing : **ear·ring** (jewelry) *or* **err·ing** (mistaking)
ear·li·er
ear·ly
earlyier : **ear·li·er**
earn (to work to gain); **urn** (vase)
ear·nest (sincere); **Er·nest** (name)
ear·ring (jewelry); **err·ing** (mistaking)
earth·en·ware
earthenwear : **earth·en·ware**
earth·ly
easal : **ea·sel**
ea·sel
easell : **ea·sel**
easill : **ea·sel**
eas·i·ly
easyly : **eas·i·ly**
eat·able
eather : **ei·ther** (one or the other) *or* **ether** (gas)
eatible : **eat·able**
eaves·drop·ping
ebbony : **eb·o·ny**
eboney : **eb·o·ny**

ebonie : **eb·o·ny**
ebonny : **eb·o·ny**
eb·o·ny
ebulient : **ebul·lient**
ebulliant : **ebul·lient**
ebul·lient
eccede : **ac·cede** (to give in) *or* **ex·ceed** (to surpass)
ecceed : **ac·cede** (to give in) *or* **ex·ceed** (to surpass)
ec·cen·tric
eccentrick : **ec·cen·tric**
eccept : **ac·cept** (to take) *or* **ex·cept** (to leave out)
eccerpt : **ex·cerpt**
eccert : **ex·cerpt** (to extract) *or* **ex·ert** (to put forth)
eccise : **ex·cise**
ecco : **echo**
eccology : **ecol·o·gy**
ecconomy : **econ·o·my**
Eccuador : **Ec·ua·dor**
Eccuadorian : **Ec·ua·do·re·an**
ecentric : **ec·cen·tric**
echalon : **ech·e·lon**
ech·e·lon
echilon : **ech·e·lon**
echo
echoe : **echo**
ecko : **echo**
eclec·tic
eclectick : **eclec·tic**
eclexic : **eclec·tic**
eclips : **eclipse**
eclipse
ecolagy : **ecol·o·gy**
ecollogy : **ecol·o·gy**
ecol·o·gy
econamy : **econ·o·my**
econimy : **econ·o·my**

econnomy : **econ•o•my**
econ•o•my
Ecquador : **Ec•ua•dor**
Ecquadorian : **Ec•ua•dor•ean**
ecsentric : **ec•cen•tric**
ecsort : **es•cort** (to accompany)
  or **ex•hort** (to urge)
ecstacy : **ec•sta•sy**
ecstassy : **ec•sta•sy**
ec•sta•sy
ec•stat•ic
ecstattic : **ec•stat•ic**
ecstesy : **ec•sta•sy**
ecstisy : **ec•sta•sy**
Ec•ua•dor
Ec•ua•dor•ean
Ecudor : **Ec•ua•dor**
Ecudore : **Ec•ua•dor**
Ecudorian : **Ec•ua•dor•ean**
ec•ze•ma
eczemma : **ec•ze•ma**
edable : **ed•i•ble**
edafy : **ed•i•fy**
Edanburgh : **Ed•in•burgh**
edator : **ed•i•tor**
eddible : **ed•i•ble**
eddify : **ed•i•fy**
Eddinburgh : **Ed•in•burgh**
eddit : **ed•it**
edditor : **ed•i•tor**
edditorial : **ed•it•or•i•al**
edducation : **ed•u•ca•tion**
edefy : **ed•i•fy**
ed•i•ble
ed•i•fy
Edinborough : **Ed•in•burgh**
Edinburg : **Ed•in•burgh**
Ed•in•burgh
Edinburo : **Ed•in•burgh**
edit
editer : **ed•i•tor**

edi•tion (book); **ad•di•tion**
  (adding)
ed•i•tor
editoreal : **ed•i•to•ri•al**
ed•i•to•ri•al
educatian : **ed•u•ca•tion**
ed•u•ca•tion
eegle : **ea•gle**
eeked : **eked**
eeking : **ek•ing**
ee•rie *or* **ee•ry** (weird);
  ae•rie(nest); **Erie** (lake and
  canal)
ee•ry *or* **ee•rie**
eesel : **ea•sel**
eevesdropping : **eaves•drop•ping**
Efel : **Eif•fel**
efemininate : **ef•fem•i•nate**
efervescent : **ef•fer•ves•cent**
efete : **ef•fete**
effeat : **ef•fete**
ef•fect (result); **af•fect** (to
  influence)
effegy : **ef•fi•gy**
effemanate : **ef•fem•i•nate**
ef•fem•i•nate
effeminent : **ef•fem•i•nate**
effemminate : **ef•fem•i•nate**
effervecent : **ef•fer•ves•cent**
effervesant : **ef•fer•ves•cent**
ef•fer•ves•cent
effervessent : **ef•fer•ves•cent**
ef•fete
efficency : **ef•fi•cien•cy**
efficiancy : **ef•fi•cien•cy**
ef•fi•cien•cy
efficiensy : **ef•fi•cien•cy**
ef•fi•gy
effiminant : **ef•fem•i•nate**
effinity : **af•fin•i•ty**
effishiency : **ef•fi•cien•cy**
effite : **ef•fete**

effrontary : **ef•fron•tery**
ef•fron•tery
effrontry : **ef•fron•tery**
eficiency : **ef•fi•cien•cy**
efigy : **ef•fi•gy**
efrontery : **ef•fron•tery**
eger : **ea•ger**
eggress : **egress** (exit) *or*
　ag•gress (to attack)
Egipt : **Egypt**
Egiptian : **Egyp•tian**
Egiypt : **Egypt**
Egiyptian : **Egyp•tian**
egle : **ea•gle**
egreegrious : **egre•grious**
egre•gious
egregous : **egre•grious**
egreigious : **egre•grious**
egrejious : **egre•grious**
egress (exit); **ag•gress** (to
　attack)
Eguador : **Ec•ua•dor**
Eguadorean : **Ec•ua•dor•ean**
eguana : **igua•na**
Egypt
Egyp•tian
Egyption : **Egyp•tian**
egzalt : **ex•alt** (to honor) *or*
　ex•ult (to rejoice)
egzema : **ec•ze•ma**
Eifel : **Eif•fel**
Eif•fel
Eiffle : **Eif•fel**
eightean : **eigh•teen**
eigh•teen
eightteen : **eigh•teen**
eiked : **eked**
eir : **err** (to mistake) *or* **heir**
　(inheritor)
eiress : **heir•ess**
eiriss : **heir•ess**
eirloom : **heir•loom**

eirlume : **heir•loom**
eisel : **ea•sel**
ei•ther (one or the other);
　ether (gas)
ejecktion : **ejec•tion**
ejec•tion
ekcentric : **ec•cen•tric**
eked
ekeing : **ek•ing**
ek•ing
eklectic : **eclec•tic**
ekstasy : **ec•sta•sy**
elabarate : **elab•o•rate**
elaberate : **elab•o•rate**
elab•o•rate
elaboret : **elab•o•rate**
elaborite : **elab•o•rate**
elagance : **el•e•gance**
elagy : **el•e•gy**
elament : **el•e•ment**
elamental : **el•e•men•tal**
elaphant : **el•e•phant**
elaquence : **el•o•quence**
elasstic : **elas•tic**
elastec : **elas•tic**
elas•tic
elastick : **elas•tic**
elavate : **el•e•vate**
elavator : **el•e•va•tor**
El•ba (island); **El•be** (river)
El•be (river); **El•ba** (island)
elbo : **el•bow**
elboe : **el•bow**
el•bow
el•dest
eldist : **el•dest**
elead : **elide**
eleaven : **elev•en**
electefy : **elec•tri•fy**
electokute : **elec•tro•cute**
electracute : **elec•tro•cute**
electrafy : **elec•tri•fy**

electrecute : **elec·tro·cute**
elec·tric
electricety : **elec·tric·i·ty**
elec·tri·cian
electricion : **elec·tri·cian**
electricitty : **elec·tric·i·ty**
elec·tric·i·ty
electricute : **elec·tro·cute**
elec·tri·fy
electrision : **elec·tri·cian**
electrisity : **elec·tric·i·ty**
electrition : **elec·tri·cian**
elec·tro·cute
elede : **elide**
elefant : **el·e·phant**
el·e·gance
eleganse : **el·e·gance**
elegants : **el·e·gance**
elegence : **el·e·gance**
elegible : **el·i·gi·ble** (qualified)
   or **il·leg·i·ble** (unreadable)
el·e·gy
elejy : **el·e·gy**
elektric : **elec·tric**
el·e·ment
el·e·men·tal
elementel : **el·e·men·tal**
elementle : **el·e·men·tal**
elemintal : **el·e·men·tal**
el·e·phant
elephent : **el·e·phant**
elephunt : **el·e·phant**
elete : **elite**
elevait : **el·e·vate**
elevan : **elev·en**
el·e·vate
elevater : **el·e·va·tor**
el·e·va·tor
elev·en
elicet : **elic·it** (to draw out) *or*
   il·lic·it (unlawful)

elic·it (to draw out); **il·lic·it**
   (unlawful)
elickser : **elix·ir**
elide
eligance : **el·e·gance**
eligeble : **el·i·gi·ble** (qualified)
   or **il·leg·i·ble** (unreadable)
eli·gi·ble (qualified); **il·leg·i·ble**
   (unreadable)
eligy : **el·e·gy**
elijible : **el·i·gi·ble** (qualified)
   or **il·leg·i·ble** (unreadable)
elimental : **el·e·men·tal**
elim·i·nate
eliphant : **el·e·phant**
eliquence : **el·o·quence**
elisit : **elic·it** (to draw out) *or*
   il·lic·it (unlawful)
elite
elivate : **el·e·vate**
elivator : **el·e·va·tor**
elixer : **elix·ir**
elix·ir
elixor : **elix·ir**
ellagy : **el·e·gy**
ellbow : **el·bow**
ellectrify : **elec·tri·fy**
ellectrocute : **elec·tro·cute**
ellegance : **el·e·gance**
ellegy : **el·e·gy**
ellement : **el·e·ment**
ellemental : **el·e·men·tal**
ellephant : **el·e·phant**
ellevate : **el·e·vate**
ellevator : **el·e·va·tor**
elleven : **elev·en**
ellicit : **elic·it** (to draw out) *or*
   il·lic·it (unlawful)
ellide : **elide**
elligible : **el·i·gi·ble** (qualified)
   or **il·leg·i·ble** (unreadable)
ellite : **elite**

ellixir : **elix·ir**
elloquence : **el·o·quence**
ellucidate : **elu·ci·date**
ellusive : **elu·sive**
eloapment : **elope·ment**
elope·ment
elopment : **elope·ment**
el·o·quence
eloquense : **el·o·quence**
eloquince : **el·o·quence**
elucedate : **elu·ci·date**
elu·ci·date
elucive : **al·lu·sive** (making
    references) *or* **elu·sive**
    (avoiding) *or* **il·lu·sive**
    (deceptive)
elude (to escape); **al·lude** (to
    refer)
elusidate : **elu·ci·date**
elu·sion (evasion); **al·lu·sion**
    (reference); **il·lu·sion** (false
    idea or image)
elu·sive (avoiding); **al·lu·sive**
    (making references);
    il·lu·sive (deceptive)
emaceated : **ema·ci·at·ed**
ema·ci·at·ed
emagrant : **em·i·grant**
emancepate : **eman·ci·pate**
eman·ci·pate
emanent : **em·i·nent** (famous)
    or **im·ma·nent** (dwelling
    within) *or* **im·mi·nent**
    (impending)
emansipate : **eman·ci·pate**
emarald : **em·er·ald**
emasarry : **em·is·sary**
emas·cu·late
emasiate : **ema·ci·ate**
embacy : **em·bas·sy**
em·balm
embam : **em·balm**

em·bank·ment
embarass : **em·bar·rass**
embaress : **em·bar·rass**
em·bar·go
embariss : **em·bar·rass**
em·bark
em·bar·rass
embarriss : **em·bar·rass**
embasey : **em·bas·sy**
em·bas·sy
embasy : **em·bas·sy**
embelish : **em·bel·lish**
embellash : **em·bel·lish**
embellesh : **em·bel·lish**
em·bel·lish
embezel : **em·bez·zle**
embezle : **em·bez·zle**
embezzal : **em·bez·zle**
embezzel : **em·bez·zle**
em·bez·zle
embibe : **im·bibe**
emblam : **em·blem**
emblazen : **em·bla·zon**
em·bla·zon
em·blem
emblim : **em·blem**
emblum : **em·blem**
em·bodi·ment
embodimint : **em·bodi·ment**
embodyment : **em·bodi·ment**
embom : **em·balm**
embracable : **em·brace·able**
em·brace
em·brace·able
embracible : **em·brace·able**
embraice : **em·brace**
embrase : **em·brace**
embrasible : **em·brace·able**
embreo : **em·bryo**
embrio : **em·bryo**
embroidary : **em·broi·dery**
embroiderry : **em·broi·dery**

em·broi·dery
embroydery : em·broi·dery
em·bryo
embue : im·bue
emcumbrance : en·cum·brance
emegrant : em·i·grant (one
    leaving) *or* im·mi·grant (one
    coming in)
emend (to correct); amend (to
    change or add to)
em·er·ald
emeratus : emer·i·tus
emeretus : emer·i·tus
emer·gen·cy
emergensy : emer·gen·cy
emergincy : emer·gen·cy
emeritas : emer·i·tus
emeritis : emer·i·tus
emer·i·tus
emerold : em·er·ald
emerritus : emer·i·tus
emesarry : em·is·sary
emfeeble : en·fee·ble
emgagement : en·gage·ment
em·i·grant (one leaving);
    im·mi·grant (one coming in)
emind : emend
em·i·nent (famous);
    im·ma·nent (dwelling
    within); im·mi·nent
    (impending)
emisary : em·is·sary
emision : emis·sion
em·is·sary
emisserry : em·is·sary
emissery : em·is·sary
emissian : emis·sion
emis·sion
emition : emis·sion
emity : en·mi·ty
emmaculate : im·mac·u·late
emmancipate : eman·ci·pate

emmasculate : emas·cu·late
emmend : emend
emmerald : em·er·ald
emmergency : emer·gen·cy
emmeritus : emer·i·tus
emmigrant : em·i·grant (one
    leaving) *or* im·mi·grant (one
    coming in)
emminent : em·i·nent (famous)
    or im·ma·nent (dwelling
    within) *or* im·mi·nent
    (impending)
emmissary : em·is·sary
emmity : en·mi·ty
emmusion : emul·sion
emorald : em·er·ald
empact : im·pact
empair : im·pair
empale : im·pale
empanel : im·pan·el
empart : im·part
empassioned : im·pas·sioned
empeach : im·peach
empearian : em·py·re·an
empeccable : im·pec·ca·ble
empede : im·pede
empediment : im·ped·i·ment
emperial : im·pe·ri·al
emperil : im·pe·ri·al (relating
    to empire) *or* im·per·il (to
    endanger)
emphisema : em·phy·se·ma
emphisima : em·phy·se·ma
emphyseama : em·phy·se·ma
em·phy·se·ma
emphysima : em·phy·se·ma
emphyzema : em·phy·se·ma
empier : em·pire
empierian : em·py·re·an
em·pire
empirial : im·pe·ri·al
empirian : em·py·re·an

emplant : **im·plant**
emporeum : **em·po·ri·um**
emporiam : **em·po·ri·um**
em·po·ri·um
emposter : **im·pos·tor**
empouarium : **em·po·ri·um**
empound : **im·pound**
empoureum : **em·po·ri·um**
empoverish : **im·pov·er·ish**
empyre : **em·pire**
em·py·re·an
empyrian : **em·py·re·an**
emullsion : **emul·sion**
emulsian : **emul·sion**
emul·sion
emultion : **emul·sion**
emvironment : **en·vi·ron·ment**
emzyme : **en·zyme**
enamal : **enam·el**
enam·el
enamell : **enam·el**
enamerd : **enam·ored**
enamered : **enam·ored**
enamil : **enam·el**
enammel : **enam·el**
enammored : **enam·ored**
enam·ored
enamoured (*Brit.*) : **enam·ored**
enamy : **en·e·my**
enargy : **en·er·gy**
enbalm : **em·balm**
enbam : **em·balm**
enbankment : **em·bank·ment**
enbargo : **em·bar·go**
enbark : **em·bark**
enbarrass : **em·bar·rass**
enbassy : **em·bas·sy**
enbelish : **em·bel·lish**
enbellish : **em·bel·lish**
enbezzle : **em·bez·zle**
enblazon : **em·bla·zon**
enblem : **em·blem**

enbodiment : **em·bodi·ment**
enbrace : **em·brace**
enbraceable : **em·brace·able**
enbroidery : **em·broi·dery**
enbryo : **em·bryo**
encantation : **in·can·ta·tion**
encendiary : **in·cen·di·ary**
encercle : **en·cir·cle**
encessant : **in·ces·sant**
enciclopedia : **en·cyc·lo·pe·dia**
encinerate : **in·cin·er·ate**
encircel : **en·cir·cle**
en·cir·cle
encirkal : **en·cir·cle**
encirkle : **en·cir·cle**
encite : **in·cite** (to urge on) *or*
    in·sight (discernment)
encouradge : **en·cour·age**
en·cour·age
encourege : **en·cour·age**
encourige : **en·cour·age**
en·cum·brance
encumbranse : **en·cum·brance**
encumbrence : **en·cum·brance**
encumbrince : **en·cum·brance**
encurage : **en·cour·age**
encyclapedia : **en·cy·clo·pe·dia**
encyclepedia : **en·cy·clo·pe·dia**
encyclipedia : **en·cy·clo·pe·dia**
encyclopeadia :
    en·cy·clo·pe·dia
encyclopedea : **en·cy·clo·pe·dia**
en·cy·clo·pe·dia
encyclopeedia : **en·cy·clo·pe·dia**
endeaver : **en·deav·or**
en·deav·or
endevor : **en·deav·or**
endevvor : **en·deav·or**
endite : **in·dict** (to charge with
    a crime) *or* **in·dite** (to write)
endolent : **in·do·lent**
endomitable : **in·dom·i·ta·ble**

endoument : **en•dow•ment**
endowmate : **en•dow•ment**
endowmeant : **en•dow•ment**
en•dow•ment
endowmint : **en•dow•ment**
endulge : **in•dulge**
en•dur•ance
enduranse : **en•dur•ance**
endurence : **en•dur•ance**
endurrance : **en•dur•ance**
endurrence : **en•dur•ance**
endustrial : **in•dus•tri•al**
enebriate : **ine•bri•ate**
enemmy : **en•e•my**
en•e•my
en•er•gy
enerjy : **en•er•gy**
enerrgy : **en•er•gy**
enert : **in•ert**
enertia : **in•er•tia**
enfallible : **in•fal•li•ble**
enfatuate : **in•fat•u•ate**
enfeable : **en•fee•ble**
enfeebal : **en•fee•ble**
en•fee•ble
enfeible : **en•fee•ble**
enferior : **in•fe•ri•or**
enferno : **in•fer•no**
enfidel : **in•fi•del**
enfinite : **in•fi•nite**
enfirmary : **in•fir•ma•ry**
enfirmity : **in•fir•mi•ty**
enflammable : **in•flam•ma•ble**
enflexible : **in•flex•i•ble**
enfluence : **in•flu•ence**
enfuriate : **in•fu•ri•ate**
en•gage•ment
engagment : **en•gage•ment**
engeneer : **en•gi•neer**
engenious : **in•ge•nious**
engenue : **in•ge•nue**
engenuous : **in•gen•u•ous**

engest : **in•gest**
en•gi•neer
enginier : **en•gi•neer**
En•gland
englorious : **in•glo•ri•ous**
Englund : **En•gland**
engredient : **in•gre•di•ent**
enhabit : **in•hab•it**
enhale : **in•hale**
enhancemeant : **en•hance•ment**
en•hance•ment
enhancemint : **en•hance•ment**
enhansement : **en•hance•ment**
enherent : **in•her•ent**
enherit : **in•her•it**
enhibit : **in•hib•it**
eniggma : **enig•ma**
enig•ma
enimical : **in•im•i•cal**
enimy : **en•e•my**
enitial : **ini•tial**
enitiate : **ini•ti•ate**
enjineer : **en•gi•neer**
enmaty : **en•mi•ty**
enmety : **en•mi•ty**
enmitty : **en•mi•ty**
en•mi•ty
ennamel : **enam•el**
ennamored : **enam•ored**
ennate : **in•nate**
ennemy : **en•e•my**
ennigma : **enig•ma**
ennocence : **in•no•cence**
ennovate : **in•no•vate**
ennue : **en•nui**
ennuee : **en•nui**
en•nui
ennumerable : **in•nu•mer•a•ble**
ennumerate : **enu•mer•ate**
enoomerate : **enu•mer•ate**
enoui : **en•nui**
enounciate : **enun•ci•ate**

enperil : **im•pe•ri•al** (relating to empire) *or* **im•per•il** (to endanger)

enphysema : **em•phy•se•ma**

enpire : **em•pire**

enpireal : **im•pe•ri•al**

enporium : **em•po•ri•um**

enpyrean : **em•py•re•an**

enscrutable : **in•scru•ta•ble**

ensiclopedia : **en•cy•clo•pe•dia**

en•sign

ensine : **en•sign**

ensipid : **in•sip•id**

ensircle : **en•cir•cle**

ensolence : **in•so•lence**

ensoluble : **in•sol•u•ble**

ensolvent : **in•sol•vent**

ensomnia : **in•som•nia**

ensouciant : **in•sou•ci•ant**

enstill : **in•still**

ensular : **in•su•lar**

ensulin : **in•su•lin**

ensurance : **in•sur•ance**

ensurgent : **in•sur•gent**

ensyclopedia : **en•cy•clo•pe•dia**

ensyme : **en•zyme**

entegrate : **in•te•grate**

entellect : **in•tel•lect**

entelligent : **in•tel•li•gent**

enteprise : **en•ter•prise**

enterance : **en•trance**

enterence : **en•trance**

enterpreneur : **en•tre•pre•neur**

enterpretation : **in•ter•pre•ta•tion**

en•ter•prise

enterprize : **en•ter•prise**

enterrogate : **in•ter•ro•gate**

en•ter•tain

entertane : **en•ter•tain**

enterval : **in•ter•val**

entervene : **in•ter•vene**

enterview : **in•ter•view**

entestine : **in•tes•tine**

entimacy : **in•ti•ma•cy**

entimate : **in•ti•mate**

entolerable : **in•tol•er•a•ble**

entolerance : **in•tol•er•ance**

entolerant : **in•tol•er•ant**

entouradge : **en•tou•rage**

en•tou•rage

entouraje : **en•tou•rage**

entouroge : **en•tou•rage**

entoxicate : **in•tox•i•cate**

en•trance

entranse : **en•trance**

entransigent : **in•tran•si•gent**

entrapreneur : **en•tre•pre•neur**

entraypreneur : **en•tre•pre•neur**

entrence : **en•trance**

entrense : **en•trance**

entrepeneur : **en•tre•pre•neur**

entrepid : **in•trep•id**

en•tre•pre•neur

entreprenoir : **en•tre•pre•neur**

entreprenoor : **en•tre•pre•neur**

entreprineur : **en•tre•pre•neur**

entricacy : **in•tri•ca•cy**

entricate : **in•tri•cate**

entrigue : **in•trigue**

entrince : **en•trance**

entrinse : **en•trance**

entroduce : **in•tro•duce**

entuition : **in•tu•ition**

enturage : **en•tou•rage**

enui : **en•nui**

enumarate : **enu•mer•ate**

enu•mer•ate

enunceate : **enun•ci•ate**

enun•ci•ate

enundate : **in•un•date**

enunsiate : **enun•ci•ate**

envade : **in•vade**

envalid : **in•va•lid** (sick or disabled) *or* **in•val•id** (not valid)

envalope : **en•ve•lope** (*noun*)

envellope : **en•ve•lope** (*noun*)

enveloap : **en•ve•lope** (*noun*)

en•vel•op (*verb*); **en•ve•lope** (*noun*)

en•ve•lope (*noun*); **en•vel•op** (*verb*)

enventory : **in•ven•to•ry**

enveous : **en•vi•ous**

envestigate : **in•ves•ti•gate**

enveterate : **in•vet•er•ate**

enviernment : **en•vi•ron•ment**

envigorate : **in•vig•o•rate**

envilope : **en•ve•lope** (*noun*)

envincible : **in•vin•ci•ble**

enviolable : **in•vi•o•la•ble**

enviolate : **in•vi•o•late**

enviornment : **en•vi•ron•ment**

enviorns : **en•vi•rons**

en•vi•ous

enviran : **en•vi•rons**

enviranment : **en•vi•ron•ment**

envirenment : **en•vi•ron•ment**

envirens : **en•vi•rons**

envirnment : **en•vi•ron•ment**

envirns : **en•vi•rons**

en•vi•ron•ment

en•vi•rons

enviruns : **en•vi•rons**

en•vis•age

envisege : **en•vis•age**

envisible : **in•vis•i•ble**

envisige : **en•vis•age**

envissage : **en•vis•age**

envius : **en•vi•ous**

envizage : **en•vis•age**

en•voy

envyous : **en•vi•ous**

enwee : **en•nui**

enzime : **en•zyme**

en•zyme

epacurean : **ep•i•cu•re•an**

epasode : **ep•i•sode**

epataph : **ep•i•taph**

epathet : **ep•i•thet**

epecurean : **ep•i•cu•re•an**

epesode : **ep•i•sode**

ep•ic (narrative); **ep•och** (era)

epick : **ep•ic** (narrative) *or* **ep•och** (era)

ep•i•cu•re•an

epicurian : **ep•i•cu•re•an**

ep•i•gram

Episcapalian : **Epis•co•pa•lian**

Episcipalian : **Epis•co•pa•lian**

Epis•co•pa•lian

episoad : **ep•i•sode**

ep•i•sode

epissel : **epis•tle**

epissle : **epis•tle**

epis•tle

epistol : **epis•tle**

epitaff : **ep•i•taph**

ep•i•taph

ep•i•thet

ep•och (era); **ep•ic** (narrative)

eppic : **ep•ic** (narrative) *or* **ep•och** (era)

eppicurean : **ep•i•cu•re•an**

eppigram : **ep•i•gram**

Eppiscopalian : **Epis•co•pa•lian**

eppisode : **ep•i•sode**

eppistle : **epis•tle**

eppitaph : **ep•i•taph**

eppithet : **ep•i•thet**

eqal : **equal**

eqity : **eq•ui•ty**

Equador : **Ec•ua•dor**

Equadorian : **Ec•ua•dor•ean**

equal

equall : **equal**

equassion : **equa·tion**
equater : **equa·tor**
equatian : **equa·tion**
equa·tion
equa·tor
equaty : **eq·ui·ty**
equel : **equal**
equetty : **eq·ui·ty**
equety : **eq·ui·ty**
equil : **equal**
equitty : **eq·ui·ty**
eq·ui·ty
erand : **er·rand**
erase
eratic : **er·rat·ic**
eratick : **er·rat·ic**
erb : **herb**
erbage : **herb·age**
erbal : **herb·al**
erbege : **herb·age**
erbel : **herb·al**
erbige : **herb·age**
Erie (lake and canal); **ee·rie** (weird)
erlier : **ear·li·er**
erly : **ear·ly**
ermen : **er·mine**
ermin : **er·mine**
er·mine
ern : **earn** (to work to gain) *or* **urn** (vase)
Er·nest (name); **ear·nest** (sincere)
eroodite : **er·u·dite**
eror : **er·ror**
erosean : **ero·sion**
erosian : **ero·sion**
erosien : **ero·sion**
ero·sion
erossion : **ero·sion**
er·otic
erotick : **erot·ic**

erotion : **ero·sion**
erottic : **erot·ic**
err (to mistake); **heir** (inheritor)
er·rand
errase : **erase**
er·rat·ic
errattic : **er·rat·ic**
errend : **er·rand**
errer : **er·ror**
errind : **er·rand**
errir : **er·ror**
errlier : **ear·li·er**
er·ror
errosion : **ero·sion**
errotic : **erot·ic**
errudite : **er·u·dite**
erthenware : **earth·en·ware**
erthly : **earth·ly**
er·u·dite
esay : **es·say**
es·cape
eschoir : **es·quire**
es·cort
escuire : **es·quire**
esel : **ea·sel**
esence : **es·sence**
esential : **es·sen·tial**
eshelon : **ech·e·lon**
eshilon : **ech·e·lon**
Eskamo : **Es·ki·mo**
Eskemo : **Es·ki·mo**
Eskimmo : **Es·ki·mo**
Es·ki·mo
Eskimoe : **Es·ki·mo**
eskwire : **es·quire**
esofagus : **esoph·a·gus**
esophagas : **esoph·a·gus**
esophages : **esoph·a·gus**
esophagis : **esoph·a·gus**
esoph·a·gus
esophegus : **esoph·a·gus**
esophigus : **esoph·a·gus**

esophogus : **esoph•a•gus**
especialy : **es•pe•cial•ly**
es•pe•cial•ly
esquier : **es•quire**
es•quire
essance : **es•sence**
es•say
es•sence
essencial : **es•sen•tial**
essense : **es•sence**
essenshial : **es•sen•tial**
es•sen•tial
essintial : **es•sen•tial**
essophagus : **esoph•a•gus**
essquire : **es•quire**
estamate : **es•ti•mate**
estatic : **ec•stat•ic**
es•teem
estemate : **es•ti•mate**
esteme : **es•teem**
es•thet•ic *or* **aes•thet•ic**
estimant : **es•ti•mate**
es•ti•mate
estiment : **es•ti•mate**
etaquette : **et•i•quette**
etequette : **et•i•quette**
eter•nal
eternall : **eter•nal**
eternel : **eter•nal**
eternetty : **eter•ni•ty**
eternety : **eter•ni•ty**
eternitty : **eter•ni•ty**
eter•ni•ty
ethacal : **eth•i•cal**
etheareal : **ethe•re•al**
ethecal : **eth•i•cal**
etheerial : **ethe•re•al**
etheirial : **ethe•re•al**
Etheopia : **Ethi•o•pia**
ether (gas); **ei•ther** (one or the other)
ethe•re•al

etherial : **ethe•re•al**
eth•i•cal
ethicle : **eth•i•cal**
ethikal : **eth•i•cal**
Ethiopea : **Ethi•o•pia**
Ethi•o•pia
ethnec : **eth•nic**
eth•nic
ethnick : **eth•nic**
etikit : **et•i•quette**
etiquet : **et•i•quette**
et•i•quette
etiquit : **et•i•quette**
etiquitte : **et•i•quette**
etternal : **eter•nal**
ettiquette : **et•i•quette**
eturnal : **eter•nal**
Eucarist : **Eu•cha•rist**
Eu•cha•rist
Euchrist : **Eu•cha•rist**
eufemism : **eu•phe•mism**
eufonious : **eu•pho•ni•ous**
euforia : **eu•pho•ria**
eulagy : **eu•lo•gy**
eulegy : **eu•lo•gy**
euligy : **eu•lo•gy**
euloggy : **eu•lo•gy**
eu•lo•gy
eunach : **eu•nuch**
eunech : **eu•nuch**
euneck : **eu•nuch**
eunich : **eu•nuch**
eunick : **eu•nuch**
eu•nuch
euphamism : **eu•phe•mism**
euphemesm : **eu•phe•mism**
eu•phe•mism
euphimism : **eu•phe•mism**
euphoneous : **eu•pho•ni•ous**
eu•pho•ni•ous
euphonius : **eu•pho•ni•ous**
euphorea : **eu•pho•ria**

eu·pho·ria
euphorria : eu·pho·ria
eureaka : eu·re·ka
eureeka : eu·re·ka
eu·re·ka
eurika : eu·re·ka
Euroap : Eu·rope
Europ : Eu·rope
Eu·rope
euthanacia : eu·tha·na·sia
eu·tha·na·sia
euthanazia : eu·tha·na·sia
euthenasia : eu·tha·na·sia
euthinasia : eu·tha·na·sia
evacion : eva·sion
evacive : eva·sive
evacooate : evac·u·ate
evacuait : evac·u·ate
evac·u·ate
evadence : ev·i·dence
evakauate : evac·u·ate
evalution : ev·o·lu·tion
evalutionary : ev·o·lu·tion·ary
ev·a·nes·cence
evanescense : ev·a·nes·cence
evanesense : ev·a·nes·cence
evanessance : ev·a·nes·cence
evanessence : ev·a·nes·cence
evangelesm : evan·ge·lism
evan·ge·lism
evangellism : evan·ge·lism
evanjelism : evan·ge·lism
evaparate : evap·o·rate
evaperate : evap·o·rate
evapirate : evap·o·rate
evaporait : evap·o·rate
evap·o·rate
evapperate : evap·o·rate
evapporate : evap·o·rate
Evarest : Ev·er·est
Evarist : Ev·er·est
evaseve : eva·sive

eva·sion
eva·sive
evassion : eva·sion
evassive : eva·sive
evation : eva·sion
evazion : eva·sion
evedence : ev·i·dence
eveneng : eve·ning
evenescence : ev·a·nes·cence
eve·ning
event·ful
eventfull : event·ful
eventially : even·tu·al·ly
even·tu·al·ly
eventualy : even·tu·al·ly
eventuelly : even·tu·al·ly
eventuilly : even·tu·al·ly
eventuily : even·tu·al·ly
Ev·er·est
Everist : Ev·er·est
evesdropping : eaves·drop·ping
evidanse : ev·i·dence
ev·i·dence
evidense : ev·i·dence
evilution : ev·o·lu·tion
evilutionary : ev·o·lu·tion·ary
evinescence : ev·a·nes·cence
evintful : event·ful
Evirest : Ev·er·est
evning : eve·ning
evolusion : ev·o·lu·tion
evolusionary : ev·o·lu·tion·ary
evolutian : ev·o·lu·tion
evolutianary : ev·o·lu·tion·ary
ev·o·lu·tion
evolutionarry : ev·o·lu·tion·ary
ev·o·lu·tion·ary
evolutionerry : ev·o·lu·tion·ary
evolutionery : ev·o·lu·tion·ary
Evrist : Ev·er·est
ewe (female sheep); yew (tree);
  you (pron.)

exacution : **ex•e•cu•tion**

exacutive : **ex•ec•u•tive**

exadus : **ex•o•dus**

exagerate : **ex•ag•ger•ate**

exaggarate : **ex•ag•ger•ate**

ex•ag•ger•ate

exaggirate : **ex•ag•ger•ate**

exajerate : **ex•ag•ger•ate**

exale : **ex•hale**

ex•alt (to honor); **ex•ult** (to rejoice)

examplary : **ex•em•pla•ry**

exaqution : **ex•e•cu•tion**

exasparate : **ex•as•per•ate**

exasperait : **ex•as•per•ate**

ex•as•per•ate

exasperrate : **ex•as•per•ate**

exaspirate : **ex•as•per•ate**

exassperate : **ex•as•per•ate**

exaust : **ex•haust**

excape : **es•cape**

excasperate : **ex•as•per•ate**

excavatian : **ex•ca•va•tion**

ex•ca•va•tion

excede : **ac•cede** (to give in) *or* **ex•ceed** (to surpass)

ex•ceed (to surpass); **ac•cede** (to give in)

ex•cel

excelence : **ex•cel•lence**

excell : **ex•cel**

excellance : **ex•cel•lence**

excellanse : **ex•cel•lence**

ex•cel•lence

excellense : **ex•cel•lence**

excemplify : **ex•em•pli•fy**

excempt : **ex•empt**

ex•cept (to leave out); **ac•cept** (to take)

excercise : **ex•er•cise**

ex•cerpt

excersise : **ex•er•cise**

excert : **ex•cerpt** (extract) *or* **ex•ert** (to put forth)

excertion : **ex•er•tion**

excevation : **ex•ca•va•tion**

excibition : **ex•hi•bi•tion**

excilarate : **ex•hil•a•rate**

excilaration : **ex•hil•a•ra•tion**

excile : **ex•ile**

excirpt : **ex•cerpt**

ex•cise

excist : **ex•ist**

excistence : **ex•is•tence**

excistentialism : **ex•is•ten•tial•ism**

excitemeant : **ex•cite•ment**

ex•cite•ment

excitment : **ex•cite•ment**

excize : **ex•cise**

ex•claim

exclaimation : **ex•cla•ma•tion**

exclamasion : **ex•cla•ma•tion**

exclamatian : **ex•cla•ma•tion**

ex•cla•ma•tion

exclame : **ex•claim**

exclemation : **ex•cla•ma•tion**

exclimation : **ex•cla•ma•tion**

excloosive : **ex•clu•sive**

exclucive : **ex•clu•sive**

excluseve : **ex•clu•sive**

ex•clu•sive

excort : **es•cort** (to accompany) *or* **ex•hort** (to urge)

excrament : **ex•cre•ment**

excremant : **ex•cre•ment**

ex•cre•ment

excriment : **ex•cre•ment**

excroosiating : **ex•cru•ci•at•ing**

excruceating : **ex•cru•ci•at•ing**

ex•cru•ci•at•ing

excrusiating : **ex•cru•ci•at•ing**

excume : **ex•hume**

exebition : **ex•hi•bi•tion**

execkutive : **ex·ec·u·tive**
execusion : **ex·e·cu·tion**
executeve : **ex·ec·u·tive**
executian : **ex·e·cu·tion**
ex·e·cu·tion
ex·ec·u·tive
exedus : **ex·o·dus**
exeed : **ac·cede** (to give in) *or*
   ex·ceed (to surpass)
exel : **ax·le** (wheel shaft) *or*
   ex·cel (to be superior)
exelence : **ex·cel·lence**
exellence : **ex·cel·lence**
exema : **ec·ze·ma**
exemplafy : **ex·em·pli·fy**
exemplarry : **ex·em·pla·ry**
ex·em·pla·ry
exemplerry : **ex·em·pla·ry**
exemplery : **ex·em·pla·ry**
exempley : **ex·em·pli·fy**
ex·em·pli·fy
exemplury : **ex·em·pla·ry**
ex·empt
exept : **ac·cept** (to take) *or*
   ex·cept (to leave out)
exeqution : **ex·e·cu·tion**
exercion : **ex·er·tion**
ex·er·cise
exercize : **ex·er·cise**
exerpt : **ex·cerpt**
exersion : **ex·er·tion**
exersise : **ex·er·cise**
ex·ert (to put forth); **ex·cerpt**
   (extract)
exertian : **ex·er·tion**
ex·er·tion
exhail : **ex·hale**
exhailation : **ex·ha·la·tion**
ex·ha·la·tion
ex·hale
ex·haust
exhawst : **ex·haust**

exhibbit : **ex·hib·it**
exhibet : **ex·hib·it**
ex·hib·it
ex·hi·bi·tion
ex·hil·a·rate
ex·hil·a·ra·tion
exhile : **ex·ile**
exhilerate : **ex·hil·a·rate**
exhileration : **ex·hil·a·ra·tion**
exhilirate : **ex·hil·a·rate**
exhorbitant : **ex·or·bi·tant**
ex·hort
exhuberance : **ex·u·ber·ance**
ex·hume
exibbet : **ex·hib·it**
exibit : **ex·hib·it**
exibition : **ex·hi·bi·tion**
exicution : **ex·e·cu·tion**
exidus : **ex·o·dus**
exigancy : **ex·i·gen·cy**
ex·i·gen·cy
exigensy : **ex·i·gen·cy**
exilarait : **ex·hil·a·rate**
exilarate : **ex·hil·a·rate**
exilaration : **ex·hil·a·ra·tion**
ex·ile
exileration : **ex·hil·a·ra·tion**
exise : **ex·cise**
exishency : **ex·i·gen·cy**
ex·ist
existance : **ex·is·tence**
existanse : **ex·is·tence**
existantialism :
   ex·is·ten·tial·ism
ex·is·tence
existencialism :
   ex·is·ten·tial·ism
existense : **ex·is·tence**
existensialism :
   ex·is·ten·tial·ism
ex·is·ten·tial·ism

existentiallism :
  ex•is•ten•tial•ism
exitement : **ex•cite•ment**
exize : **ex•cise**
exodas : **ex•o•dus**
exodis : **ex•o•dus**
exodos : **ex•o•dus**
ex•o•dus
ex•or•bi•tant
exort : **ex•hort**
expance : **ex•panse**
ex•panse
expeadient : **ex•pe•di•ent**
expearience : **ex•pe•ri•ence**
expeariment : **ex•per•i•ment**
ex•pec•tant
expectent : **ex•pec•tant**
expeddition : **ex•pe•di•tion**
expediant : **ex•pe•di•ent**
ex•pe•di•ent
expedision : **ex•pe•di•tion**
ex•pe•di•tion
expedittion : **ex•pe•di•tion**
expeedient : **ex•pe•di•ent**
expeerience : **ex•pe•ri•ence**
expeeriment : **ex•per•i•ment**
expeirience : **ex•pe•ri•ence**
expeiriment : **ex•per•i•ment**
expence : **ex•pense**
expencive : **ex•pen•sive**
expendachure : **ex•pen•di•ture**
expendature : **ex•pen•di•ture**
expendeture : **ex•pen•di•ture**
ex•pen•di•ture
ex•pense
expenseve : **ex•pen•sive**
ex•pen•sive
experament : **ex•per•i•ment**
experement : **ex•per•i•ment**
experiance : **ex•pe•ri•ence**
experianse : **ex•pe•ri•ence**
ex•pe•ri•ence

experiense : **ex•pe•ri•ence**
ex•per•i•ment
ex•pert
expier : **ex•pire**
ex•plain
explaination : **ex•pla•na•tion**
ex•pla•na•tion
explane : **ex•plain**
explannation : **ex•pla•na•tion**
explenation : **ex•pla•na•tion**
explination : **ex•pla•na•tion**
expload : **ex•plode**
exploasion : **ex•plo•sion**
ex•plode
explosian : **ex•plo•sion**
ex•plo•sion
explotion : **ex•plo•sion**
explozion : **ex•plo•sion**
expurt : **ex•pert**
exquesite : **ex•qui•site**
exquisate : **ex•qui•site**
exquiset : **ex•qui•site**
ex•qui•site
exquizite : **ex•qui•site**
exsasperate : **ex•as•per•ate**
exsel : **ex•cel**
exsellanse : **ex•cel•lence**
exsellence : **ex•cel•lence**
exsercise : **ex•er•cise**
exsertion : **ex•er•tion**
exsibition : **ex•hi•bi•tion**
exsilaration : **ex•hil•a•ra•tion**
exsile : **ex•ile**
exsileration : **ex•hil•a•ra•tion**
exsise : **ex•cise**
exsist : **ex•ist**
exsistence : **ex•is•tence**
exsistentialism :
  ex•is•ten•tial•ism
exsitement : **ex•cite•ment**
exsize : **ex•cise**
exsort : **ex•hort**

exspire : **ex·pire**
exstol : **ex·tol**
exsume : **ex·hume**
extenguish : **ex·tin·guish**
extermanate : **ex·ter·mi·nate**
extermenate : **ex·ter·mi·nate**
exterminait : **ex·ter·mi·nate**
ex·ter·mi·nate
extinguesh : **ex·tin·guish**
ex·tin·guish
extinquish : **ex·tin·guish**
ex·tol
extoll : **ex·tol**
extraordenary :
  ex·traor·di·nary
extraordinarry :
  ex·traor·di·nary
ex·traor·di·nary
extraordinery : **ex·traor·di·nary**
ex·trav·a·gance
extravaganse : **ex·trav·a·gance**

extravagence : **ex·trav·a·gance**
extravegance : **ex·trav·a·gance**
extravert : **ex·tro·vert**
extravigance : **ex·trav·a·gance**
extravirt : **ex·tro·vert**
extream : **ex·treme**
extreem : **ex·treme**
ex·treme
extrivert : **ex·tro·vert**
extroardinary : **ex·traor·di·nary**
extrordinary : **ex·traor·di·nary**
ex·tro·vert
exubarance : **ex·u·ber·ance**
ex·u·ber·ance
exuberanse : **ex·u·ber·ance**
exuberence : **ex·u·ber·ance**
exuberense : **ex·u·ber·ance**
ex·ult (to rejoice); **ex·alt** (to
  honor)
exume : **ex·hume**
exurpt : **ex·cerpt**

F

fabble : **fa•ble**
fabbric : **fab•ric**
fabel : **fa•ble**
fa•ble
fabrec : **fab•ric**
fab•ric
fabrick : **fab•ric**
fa•cade
facaid : **fa•cade**
facalty : **fa•cil•i•ty** (aptitude;
   building) *or* **fac•ul•ty** (ability;
   teachers)
faceal : **fa•cial** (relating to the
   face) *or* **fac•ile** (superficial)
faceatious : **fa•ce•tious**
faceetious : **fa•ce•tious**
faceitious : **fa•ce•tious**
facelty : **fa•cil•i•ty** (aptitude;
   building) *or* **fac•ul•ty** (ability;
   teachers)
faceshious : **fa•ce•tious**
fac•et
fa•ce•tious
facetius : **fa•ce•tious**
fa•cial (relating to the face);
   fac•ile (superficial)
fac•ile (superficial); **fa•cial**
   (relating to the face)
facilety : **fa•cil•i•ty**
fa•cil•i•ty
facillity : **fa•cil•i•ty**
facimile : **fac•sim•i•le**
facination : **fas•ci•na•tion**
facism : **fas•cism**
facit : **fac•et**
facksimile : **fac•sim•i•le**
fackulty : **fac•ul•ty**
facsimely : **fac•sim•i•le**
fac•sim•i•le
facsimily : **fac•sim•i•le**

facsimmile : **fac•sim•i•le**
factary : **fac•to•ry**
factery : **fac•to•ry**
fac•to•ry
fac•ul•ty
faery : **fairy** (sprite) *or* **fer•ry**
   (boat)
Fahr•en•heit
Fahrenhiet : **Fahr•en•heit**
Fahrenhite : **Fahr•en•heit**
faign : **feign**
faimous : **fa•mous**
fair (equitable; bazaar); **fare**
   (fee)
Fairenheit : **Fahr•en•heit**
fairwell : **fare•well**
fairy (sprite); **fer•ry** (boat)
falacious : **fal•la•cious**
falacy : **fal•la•cy**
falcan : **fal•con**
falcify : **fal•si•fy**
fal•con
falible : **fal•li•ble**
falken : **fal•con**
falkon : **fal•con**
fallable : **fal•li•ble**
fal•la•cious
fallacius : **fal•la•cious**
fal•la•cy
fallashious : **fal•la•cious**
fallasy : **fal•la•cy**
fallatious : **fal•la•cious**
fallcon : **fal•con**
falleble : **fal•li•ble**
fallecy : **fal•la•cy**
fallesy : **fal•la•cy**
fallibal : **fal•li•ble**
fallibel : **fal•li•ble**
fal•li•ble
fallic : **phal•lic**

fallicy : **fal•la•cy**
fallisy : **fal•la•cy**
fallsify : **fal•si•fy**
fallty : **faulty**
falsafy : **fal•si•fy**
falsefy : **fal•si•fy**
falsety : **fal•si•ty**
fal•si•fy
falsitty : **fal•si•ty**
fal•si•ty
famaly : **fam•i•ly**
famely : **fam•i•ly**
famen : **fam•ine**
fameous : **fa•mous**
famesh : **fam•ish**
familar : **fa•mil•iar**
fa•mil•iar
familier : **fa•mil•iar**
familliar : **fa•mil•iar**
familly : **fam•i•ly**
fam•i•ly
famin : **fam•ine**
fam•ine
fam•ish
fammiliar : **fa•mil•iar**
fammily : **fam•i•ly**
fammine : **fam•ine**
fammish : **fam•ish**
fa•mous
fanatec : **fa•nat•ic**
fa•nat•ic
fanatick : **fa•nat•ic**
fanattic : **fa•nat•ic**
fan•ci•ful
fancifull : **fan•ci•ful**
fan•cy
fancyful : **fan•ci•ful**
fane : **feign**
fanfair : **.fan•fare**
fan•fare
fannatic : **fa•nat•ic**
fansiful : **fan•ci•ful**

fansy : **fan•cy**
fantasstic : **fan•tas•tic**
fantassy : **fan•ta•sy**
fantastec : **fan•tas•tic**
fan•tas•tic
fantastick : **fan•tas•tic**
fan•ta•sy *or* **phan•ta•sy**
fantesy : **fan•ta•sy**
fantissy : **fan•ta•sy**
fantisy : **fan•ta•sy**
fantom : **phan•tom**
farce
farcecal : **far•ci•cal**
far•ci•cal
farcicle : **far•ci•cal**
fare (fee); **fair** (equitable;
    bazaar)
fare•well
farmacy : **phar•ma•cy**
Farrenheit : **Fahr•en•heit**
farry : **fairy** (sprite) *or* **fer•ry**
    (boat)
farse : **farce**
farsecal : **far•ci•cal**
farsical : **far•ci•cal**
fasade : **fa•cade**
fascenation : **fas•ci•na•tion**
fascesm : **fas•cism**
fascinacion : **fas•ci•na•tion**
fascinatian : **fas•ci•na•tion**
fas•ci•na•tion
fas•cism
faset : **fac•et**
fasetious : **fa•ce•tious**
fashial : **fa•cial**
fashianable : **fash•ion•able**
fashienable : **fash•ion•able**
fash•ion•able
fashionibal : **fash•ion•able**
fashionible : **fash•ion•able**
fasility : **fa•cil•i•ty**
fasination : **fas•ci•na•tion**

fasit : **fac•et**
fasodd : **fa•cade**
fassetious : **fa•ce•tious**
fassination : **fas•ci•na•tion**
fassionable : **fash•ion•able**
fassism : **fas•cism**
fasteadious : **fas•tid•i•ous**
fasteedious : **fas•tid•i•ous**
fastideous : **fas•tid•i•ous**
fas•tid•i•ous
fastidius : **fas•tid•i•ous**
fat•al
fateague : **fa•tigue**
fategue : **fa•tigue**
fatel : **fa•tal**
fatham : **fa•thom**
fathem : **fa•thom**
fa•thom
fatige : **fa•tigue**
fa•tigue
fatique : **fa•tigue**
fatteague : **fa•tigue**
fattigue : **fa•tigue**
fau•cet
faucit : **fau•cet**
faul•ty
faun (mythical being); **fawn** (young deer)
fauset : **fau•cet**
favarable : **fa•vor•able**
faverable : **fa•vor•able**
faverite : **fa•vor•ite**
fa•vor•able
favorate : **fa•vor•ite**
favoret : **fa•vor•ite**
favorible : **fa•vor•able**
fa•vor•ite
fawn (young deer); **faun** (mythical being)
faze (to disturb); **phase** (step in a process)
feable : **fee•ble**

feacundity : **fe•cun•di•ty**
Feaji : **Fi•ji**
feance : **fi•an•cé** (*masc.*) *or* **fi•an•cée** (*fem.*)
fear•ful
fearfull : **fear•ful**
feasable : **fea•si•ble**
feasco : **fi•as•co**
feaseble : **fea•si•ble**
feasibal : **fea•si•ble**
fea•si•ble
feath•er
feazible : **fea•si•ble**
Feb•ru•ary
Februery : **Feb•ru•ary**
Febuarry : **Feb•ru•ary**
Febuery : **Feb•ru•ary**
fecundety : **fe•cun•di•ty**
fecunditty : **fe•cun•di•ty**
fe•cun•di•ty
fedaral : **fed•er•al**
fedderal : **fed•er•al**
fedelity : **fi•del•i•ty**
fed•er•al
federel : **fed•er•al**
federil : **fed•er•al**
fediral : **fed•er•al**
fedrel : **fed•er•al**
feebal : **fee•ble**
fee•ble
Feegee : **Fi•ji**
Feejee : **Fi•ji**
feerful : **fear•ful**
feesible : **fea•si•ble**
feetus : **fe•tus**
feign
feild : **field**
fein : **feign**
feirful : **fear•ful**
felan : **fel•on**
felany : **fel•o•ny**
felen : **fel•on**

feleny : **fel•o•ny**
felicety : **fe•lic•i•ty**
felicitty : **fe•lic•i•ty**
fe•lic•i•ty
felisity : **fe•lic•i•ty**
fellicity : **fe•lic•i•ty**
fellisity : **fe•lic•i•ty**
fellon : **fel•on**
fellony : **fel•o•ny**
fel•on
fel•o•ny
femail : **fe•male**
fe•male
femaminity : **fem•i•nin•i•ty**
femanine : **fem•i•nine**
femenine : **fem•i•nine**
feminen : **fem•i•nine**
feminenity : **fem•i•nin•i•ty**
feminin : **fem•i•nine**
fem•i•nine
femininety : **fem•i•nin•i•ty**
femininitty : **fem•i•nin•i•ty**
fem•i•nin•i•ty
feminity : **fem•i•nin•i•ty**
feminnine : **fem•i•nine**
femminine : **fem•i•nine**
femmininity : **fem•i•nin•i•ty**
fenagle : **fi•na•gle**
fence
Fenix : **Phoe•nix**
fennagle : **fi•na•gle**
fenomenal : **phe•nom•e•nal**
fenomenon : **phe•nom•e•non**
fense : **fence**
ferlough : **fur•lough**
ferlow : **fur•lough**
fernace : **fur•nace**
fe•ro•cious
feroshious : **fe•ro•cious**
ferotious : **fe•ro•cious**
ferrocious : **fe•ro•cious**
fer•ry (boat); **fairy** (sprite)

fertalizer : **fer•til•iz•er**
fer•tile
fertilety : **fer•til•i•ty**
fertiliser : **fer•til•iz•er**
fertilitty : **fer•til•i•ty**
fer•til•i•ty
fer•til•iz•er
fertill : **fer•tile**
fertillity : **fer•til•i•ty**
fertillizer : **fer•til•iz•er**
fervant : **fer•vent**
fer•vent
ferver : **fer•vor**
fer•vor
fesible : **fea•si•ble**
festaval : **fes•ti•val**
festeval : **fes•ti•val**
fes•ti•val
festivall : **fes•ti•val**
festivel : **fes•ti•val**
festivle : **fes•ti•val**
fether : **feath•er**
fetis : **fe•tus**
fetther : **feath•er**
fe•tus
feud
feu•dal (medieval social order);
  fu•tile (without success)
feudel : **feu•dal** (medieval social
  order) *or* **fu•tile** (without
  success)
feushia : **fuch•sia**
Fevruary : **Feb•ru•ary**
fewd : **feud**
fi•an•cé (*masc.*); **fi•an•cée**
  (*fem.*)
fi•an•cée (*fem.*); **fi•an•cé**
  (*masc.*)
fiancey : **fiancé** (*masc.*) *or*
  fi•an•cée (*fem.*)
fianse : **fi•an•cé** (*masc.*) *or*
  fi•an•cée (*fem.*)

fiansey : **fi·an·cé** (*masc.*) *or*
  fi·an·cée (*fem.*)
fiary : **fi·ery**
fi·as·co
fiasko : **fi·as·co**
fickal : **fick·le**
fickel : **fick·le**
fick·le
ficsion : **fis·sion**
fidelety : **fi·del·i·ty**
fidelitty : **fi·del·i·ty**
fi·del·i·ty
fidellity : **fi·del·i·ty**
field
fi·ery
fiftean : **fif·teen**
fif·teen
fiftene : **fif·teen**
fif·ti·eth
fif·ty
fiftyeth : **fif·ti·eth**
Figi : **Fi·ji**
Fi·ji
fikle : **fick·le**
filabuster : **fi·li·bus·ter**
fil·a·ment
filamete : **fil·a·ment**
Filapino : **Fil·i·pi·no**
filay : **fi·let** (filet mignon) *or*
  fil·let (boneless meat or fish)
fileal : **fil·ial**
filement : **fil·a·ment**
Filepino : **Fil·i·pi·no**
fi·let (filet mignon); **fil·let**
  (boneless meat or fish)
filey : **fi·let** (filet mignon) *or*
  fil·let (boneless meat or fish)
fil·ial
fi·li·bus·ter
filiel : **fil·ial**
filiment : **fil·a·ment**
Filipeno : **Fil·i·pi·no**

Fil·i·pi·no
fillabuster : **fi·li·bus·ter**
fillay : **fi·let** (filet mignon) *or*
  fil·let (boneless meat or fish)
fil·let (boneless meat or fish);
  fi·let (filet mignon)
filley : **fi·let** (filet mignon) *or*
  fil·let (boneless meat or fish)
fillial : **fil·ial**
fillibuster : **fi·li·bus·ter**
filliment : **fil·a·ment**
Fillipino : **Fil·i·pi·no**
fimale : **fe·male**
finagal : **fi·na·gle**
fi·na·gle
finaly : **fi·nal·ly**
fi·nal·ly
fi·nance
financeer : **fi·nan·cier**
financeir : **fi·nan·cier**
fi·nan·cial
fi·nan·cier
finanse : **fi·nance**
finanseir : **fi·nan·cier**
finanshial : **fi·nan·cial**
finansier : **fi·nan·cier**
finantial : **fi·nan·cial**
finesce : **fi·nesse**
finess : **fi·nesse**
fi·nesse
fin·icky
finicy : **fin·icky**
fin·ish (to complete); **Finn·ish**
  (from Finland)
Fin·land
finnagle : **fi·na·gle**
finnally : **fi·nal·ly**
finness : **fi·nesse**
finnicky : **fin·icky**
Finn·ish (from Finland);
  fin·ish (to complete)
Finnland : **Fin·land**

fiord *or* fjord
firey : **fi•ery**
firlough : **fur•lough**
firtile : **fer•tile**
firtility : **fer•til•i•ty**
firy : **fi•ery**
fishary : **fish•ery**
fisherry : **fish•ery**
fish•ery
fishion : **fis•sion**
fision : **fis•sion**
fis•sion
fistacuffs : **fist•i•cuffs**
fistecuffs : **fist•i•cuffs**
fist•i•cuffs
fitus : **fe•tus**
fivteen : **fif•teen**
fivtieth : **fif•ti•eth**
fivty : **fif•ty**
fixety : **fix•i•ty**
fixitty : **fix•i•ty**
fix•i•ty
fizion : **fis•sion**
fjord *or* **fiord**
flac•cid
flacid : **flac•cid**
flagan : **flag•on**
flagen : **flag•on**
flaggon : **flag•on**
flag•on
fla•grant
flagrent : **fla•grant**
flair (talent); **flare** (torch)
flamboiant : **flam•boy•ant**
flam•boy•ant
flamboyent : **flam•boy•ant**
flambuoyant : **flam•boy•ant**
flameboyant : **flam•boy•ant**
flanel : **flan•nel**
flannal : **flan•nel**
flan•nel
flare (torch); **flair** (talent)

flasid : **flac•cid**
flassid : **flac•cid**
flautest : **flut•ist**
flaut•ist *or* **flut•ist**
flaver : **fla•vor**
fla•vor
fleacy : **fleecy**
flecksible : **flex•i•ble**
fledgleng : **fledg•ling**
fledg•ling
fleecy
fleesy : **fleecy**
flertatious : **flir•ta•tious**
flexable : **flex•i•ble**
flexeble : **flex•i•ble**
flex•i•ble
flimsey : **flim•sy**
flim•si•ness
flimssness : **flim•si•ness**
flimziness : **flim•si•ness**
flimzy : **flim•sy**
flipant : **flip•pant**
flip•pant
flippent : **flip•pant**
flippint : **flip•pant**
flirtacious : **flir•ta•tious**
flirtashious : **flir•ta•tious**
flir•ta•tious
flirtatius : **flir•ta•tious**
floatsam : **flot•sam**
floora : **flo•ra**
Floorida : **Flor•i•da**
flo•ra
flored : **flor•id** (ornate; ruddy) *or* **flu•o•ride** (dental treatment)
Floreda : **Flor•i•da**
flo•res•cent (flowering); **flu•o•res•cent** (emitting light)
floresh : **flour•ish**
florest : **flo•rist**

flor·id (ornate; ruddy);
  flu·o·ride (dental treatment)
Flor·i·da
floridation : **flu·o·ri·da·tion**
floride : **flor·id** (ornate; ruddy)
  or **flu·o·ride** (dental
  treatment)
florish : **flour·ish**
flo·rist
florra : **flo·ra**
florrescent : **flo·res·cent**
  (flowering) *or* **flu·o·res·cent**
  (emitting light)
florressent : **flo·res·cent**
  (flowering) *or* **flu·o·res·cent**
  (emitting light)
florrid : **flor·id** (ornate; ruddy)
  or **flu·o·ride** (dental
  treatment)
Florrida : **Flor·i·da**
florridation : **flu·o·ri·da·tion**
florride : **flor·id** (ornate;
  ruddy) *or* **flu·o·ride** (dental
  treatment)
florrish : **flour·ish**
florrist : **flo·rist**
flot·sam
flotsem : **flot·sam**
flotsum : **flot·sam**
flottsam : **flot·sam**
floun·der
flour (grain meal); **flow·er**
  (plant)
flourescent : **flu·o·res·cent**
flouresh : **flour·ish**
flouridation : **flu·o·ri·da·tion**
flouride : **flor·id** (ornate;
  ruddy) *or* **flu·o·ride** (dental
  treatment)
flour·ish
flourrish : **flour·ish**
floutest : **flut·ist**

floutist : **flut·ist**
flow·er (plant); **flour** (grain
  meal)
flowera : **flo·ra**
flowerist : **flo·rist**
flownder : **floun·der**
fluancy : **flu·en·cy**
fluansy : **flu·en·cy**
fluant : **flu·ent**
flu·en·cy
fluensy : **flu·en·cy**
flu·ent
fluoradation : **flu·o·ri·da·tion**
fluoredation : **flu·o·ri·da·tion**
flu·o·res·cent (emitting light);
  flo·res·cent (flowering)
fluoresent : **flo·res·cent**
  (flowering) *or* **flu·o·res·cent**
  (emitting light)
fluoressent : **flo·res·cent**
  (flowering) *or* **flu·o·res·cent**
  (emitting light)
fluorid : **flor·id** (ornate; ruddy)
  or **flu·o·ride** (dental
  treatment)
flu·o·ri·da·tion
flu·o·ride (dental treatment);
  flor·id (ornate; ruddy)
fluoried : **flor·id** (ornate;
  ruddy) *or* **flu·o·ride** (dental
  treatment)
flutest : **flut·ist**
flut·ist *or* **flaut·ist**
fluttist : **flut·ist**
foacal : **fo·cal**
foacused : **fo·cused**
foam
fobia : **pho·bia**
fo·cal
focel : **fo·cal**
fo·cused

fo·cus·ing
focussed : **fo·cused**
focussing : **fo·cus·ing**
Foenix : **Phoe·nix**
foe·tus (*Brit.*) : **fe·tus**
fog·ey (old-fashioned person);
  fog·gy (misty) *or* **fo·gy**
  (old-fashioned person)
fog·gy (misty); **fo·gy**
  (old-fashioned person)
fo·gy *or* **fog·ey** (old-fashioned
  person); **fog·gy** (misty)
foibal : **foi·ble**
foibel : **foi·ble**
foi·ble
foilage : **fo·liage**
foilege : **fo·liage**
foilige : **fo·liage**
fokal : **fo·cal**
fokissed : **fo·cused**
fokle : **fo·cal**
fokused : **fo·cused**
folage : **fo·liage**
foleo : **fo·lio**
fo·liage
folicle : **fol·li·cle**
folige : **fo·liage**
fo·lio
follacle : **fol·li·cle**
follakle : **fol·li·cle**
follecle : **fol·li·cle**
follekle : **fol·li·cle**
folleo : **fo·lio**
follical : **fol·li·cle**
fol·li·cle
follikle : **fol·li·cle**
follio : **fo·lio**
folyage : **fo·liage**
fome : **foam**
fonetic : **pho·net·ic**
foram : **fo·rum**

forarm : **fore·arm**
forbare : **for·bear** (to restrain
  oneself) *or* **fore·bear**
  (ancestor)
forbarence : **for·bear·ance**
for·bear (to restrain oneself);
  fore·bear (ancestor)
for·bear·ance
forbearanse : **for·bear·ance**
forbearence : **for·bear·ance**
forbearense : **for·bear·ance**
forberance : **for·bear·ance**
for·bid
forbode : **fore·bode**
forcast : **fore·cast**
forcaster : **fore·cast·er**
forceble : **forc·ible**
force·ful
forcefull : **force·ful**
forcibal : **forc·ible**
forcibel : **forc·ible**
forc·ible
fore·arm
forebare : **for·bear** (to restrain
  oneself) *or* **fore·bear**
  (ancestor)
fore·bear (ancestor); **for·bear**
  (to restrain oneself)
forebearance : **for·bear·ance**
forebid : **for·bid**
foreboad : **fore·bode**
fore·bode
fore·cast
fore·cast·er
forecastor : **fore·cast·er**
fore·fa·ther
forefeit : **for·feit**
forefet : **for·feit**
forefit : **for·feit**
foregetful : **for·get·ful**
foregive : **for·give**
foregn : **for·eign**

foregner : **for•eign•er**
fore•go *or* **for•go**
fore•gone
foregotten : **for•got•ten**
fore•head
for•eign
for•eign•er
foreignor : **for•eign•er**
forelorn : **for•lorn**
forem : **fo•rum**
fore•man
foremat : **for•mat**
foremidable : **for•mi•da•ble**
foremula : **for•mu•la**
foren : **for•eign**
forencic : **fo•ren•sic**
forener : **for•eign•er**
forenicate : **for•ni•cate**
forensec : **fo•ren•sic**
fo•ren•sic
forensick : **fo•ren•sic**
fore•see
foreshadoe : **fore•shad•ow**
fore•shad•ow
for•est
fore•stall
forestary : **for•est•ry**
foresterry : **for•est•ry**
forestery : **for•est•ry**
for•est•ry
foreswear : **for•swear**
foresythia : **for•syth•ia**
foreteen : **four•teen**
fore•tell
foretification : **for•ti•fi•ca•tion**
foretress : **for•tress**
foretuitious : **for•tu•itous**
foretunate : **for•tu•nate**
foretune : **for•tune**
foreward : **fore•word** (preface)
or **for•ward** (ahead)
fore•warn

fore•word (preface); **for•ward**
(ahead)
forfather : **fore•fa•ther**
for•feit
forfet : **for•feit**
forfiet : **for•feit**
forfit : **for•feit**
forgary : **forg•ery**
forgerry : **forg•ery**
forg•ery
for•get•ful
forgetfull : **for•get•ful**
forgeting : **for•get•ting**
for•get•ting
forgitful : **for•get•ful**
forgiting : **for•get•ting**
forgitting : **for•get•ting**
for•give
for•go *or* **fore•go**
forgone : **fore•gone**
for•got•ten
forgry : **forg•ery**
forhead : **fore•head**
forign : **for•eign**
forigner : **for•eign•er**
forim : **fo•rum**
forin : **for•eign**
foriner : **for•eign•er**
forinsic : **fo•ren•sic**
forist : **for•est**
foristry : **for•est•ry**
forjery : **forg•ery**
for•lorn
formadyhide : **form•al•de•hyde**
formaldehide : **form•al•de•hyde**
formaldehied : **form•al•de•hyde**
form•al•de•hyde
formaldihyde : **form•al•de•hyde**
formalldehyde :
form•al•de•hyde
forman : **fore•man**
for•mat

formeldehyde : **form·al·de·hyde**
for·mi·da·ble
formiddable : **for·mi·da·ble**
formideble : **for·mi·da·ble**
formidibal : **for·mi·da·ble**
formidibel : **for·mi·da·ble**
formidible : **for·mi·da·ble**
formoola : **for·mu·la**
for·mu·la
formulah : **for·mu·la**
formulla : **for·mu·la**
fornacate : **for·ni·cate**
fornecate : **for·ni·cate**
fornicait : **for·ni·cate**
for·ni·cate
forram : **fo·rum**
forrem : **fo·rum**
forrensic : **fo·ren·sic**
forrest : **for·est**
forrestry : **for·est·ry**
forrim : **fo·rum**
forrist : **for·est**
forristry : **for·est·ry**
forrum : **fo·rum**
forsee : **fore·see**
forseful : **force·ful**
forshadow : **fore·shad·ow**
forsible : **forc·ible**
forsithea : **for·syth·ia**
forsithia : **for·syth·ia**
forstall : **fore·stall**
forsware : **for·swear**
for·swear
forsythea : **for·syth·ia**
for·syth·ia
fort (bulwark); **forte** (strong point)
fortafication : **for·ti·fi·ca·tion**
fortafy : **for·ti·fy**
fortatude : **for·ti·tude**
forte (strong point); **fort** (bulwark)

forteen : **four·teen**
fortefication : **for·ti·fi·ca·tion**
fortefy : **for·ti·fy**
fortell : **fore·tell**
fortetude : **for·ti·tude**
forth (forward); **fourth** (4th)
fortien : **for·tune**
for·ti·eth
fortifacation : **for·ti·fi·ca·tion**
for·ti·fi·ca·tion
fortifikation : **for·ti·fi·ca·tion**
for·ti·fy
fortifycation : **for·ti·fi·ca·tion**
fortine : **for·tune**
fortitood : **for·ti·tude**
for·ti·tude
fortooitous : **for·tu·itous**
fortoon : **for·tune**
fortoonate : **for·tu·nate**
fortres : **for·tress**
fortrese : **for·tress**
for·tress
fortriss : **for·tress**
fortruss : **for·tress**
fortuatous : **for·tu·itous**
fortuetous : **for·tu·itous**
fortuitious : **for·tu·itous**
for·tu·itous
fortuitus : **for·tu·itous**
for·tu·nate
for·tune
fortunet : **for·tu·nate**
fortunete : **for·tu·nate**
fortunit : **for·tu·nate**
for·ty
fortyeth : **for·ti·eth**
fortyith : **for·ti·eth**
fo·rum
forust : **for·est**
forustry : **for·est·ry**
for·ward (ahead); **fore·word** (preface)

forwarn : **fore·warn**
fosell : **fos·sil**
fosil : **fos·sil**
fosile : **fos·sil**
fossel : **fos·sil**
fossell : **fos·sil**
fos·sil
fossile : **fos·sil**
fossill : **fos·sil**
fotagrafy : **pho·tog·ra·phy**
foul (offensive); **fowl** (bird)
foundary : **found·ry**
founderry : **found·ry**
foundery : **found·ry**
foundiry : **found·ry**
found·ry
foun·tain
founten : **foun·tain**
fountian : **foun·tain**
fountin : **foun·tain**
fourarm : **fore·arm**
fourbid : **for·bid**
fourbode : **fore·bode**
fourcast : **fore·cast**
fourcaster : **fore·cast·er**
fourensic : **fo·ren·sic**
fourfather : **fore·fa·ther**
fourtean : **four·teen**
four·teen
fourtene : **four·teen**
fourth (4th); **forth** (forward)
fourtieth : **for·ti·eth**
fourtification : **for·ti·fi·ca·tion**
fourtify : **for·ti·fy**
fourtine : **four·teen**
fourtress : **for·tress**
fourtuitous : **for·tu·itous**
fourtunate : **for·tu·nate**
fourtune : **for·tune**
fourty : **for·ty**
fowl (bird); **foul** (offensive)
foyble : **foi·ble**

fra·cas
frachion : **frac·tion**
frachure : **frac·ture**
fracis : **fra·cas**
frackas : **fra·cas**
fracktion : **frac·tion**
frackture : **frac·ture**
frackus : **fra·cas**
fractian : **frac·tion**
frac·tion
frac·ture
fracus : **fra·cas**
fragell : **frag·ile**
fraggile : **frag·ile**
fragil : **frag·ile**
frag·ile
fragill : **frag·ile**
fra·grance
fragranse : **fra·grance**
fra·grant
fragrence : **fra·grance**
fragrense : **fra·grance**
fragrent : **fra·grant**
fragrince : **fra·grance**
fragrinse : **fra·grance**
fragrint : **fra·grant**
fragrunce : **fra·grance**
fragrunse : **fra·grance**
fragrunt : **fra·grant**
fraighter : **freight·er**
frail
fraiter : **freight·er**
frajile : **frag·ile**
frakas : **fra·cas**
frale : **frail**
franc (money); **frank** (honest)
fran·chise
franchize : **fran·chise**
franetic : **fre·net·ic**
frank (honest); **franc** (money)
franshise : **fran·chise**
frater : **freight·er**

fraternety : **fra•ter•ni•ty**
fraternitty : **fra•ter•ni•ty**
fra•ter•ni•ty
fraturnity : **fra•ter•ni•ty**
fraudulant : **fraud•u•lent**
fraud•u•lent
frawdulent : **fraud•u•lent**
fraxion : **frac•tion**
fraxure : **frac•ture**
freak
freckal : **freck•le**
freckel : **freck•le**
freck•le
freek : **freak**
freight•er
freightor : **freight•er**
freik : **freak**
freind : **friend**
freiter : **freight•er**
freke : **freak**
frekkle : **freck•le**
frend : **friend**
fre•net•ic
frenetick : **fre•net•ic**
frenettic : **fre•net•ic**
frennetic : **fre•net•ic**
frensy : **fren•zy**
fren•zy
frequancy : **fre•quen•cy**
frequansy : **fre•quen•cy**
fre•quen•cy
frequensy : **fre•quen•cy**
fri•ar (monk); **fry•er** (fried
   fowl)
frieghter : **freight•er**
friend
fri•er or **fry•er** (fried fowl);
   fri•ar (monk)
frigat : **frig•ate**
frig•ate
friged : **frig•id**
frigedity : **fri•gid•i•ty**

friget : **frig•ate**
friggate : **frig•ate**
frigget : **frig•ate**
friggid : **frig•id**
friggidity : **fri•gid•i•ty**
friggit : **frig•ate**
frig•id
frigidety : **fri•gid•i•ty**
frigiditty : **fri•gid•i•ty**
fri•gid•i•ty
frigit : **frig•ate** (ship) or **frig•id**
   (cold)
frinetic : **fre•net•ic**
friquency : **fre•quen•cy**
frivalous : **friv•o•lous**
frivalus : **friv•o•lous**
frivelous : **friv•o•lous**
frivilous : **friv•o•lous**
frivilus : **friv•o•lous**
frivolety : **fri•vol•i•ty**
frivolis : **friv•o•lous**
fri•vol•i•ty
frivollity : **fri•vol•i•ty**
friv•o•lous
frol•ic
frolick : **frol•ic**
frollic : **frol•ic**
frontadge : **front•age**
front•age
fron•tal
frontear : **fron•tier**
fronteer : **fron•tier**
frontege : **front•age**
fronteir : **fron•tier**
frontel : **fron•tal**
frontespiece : **fron•tis•piece**
frontidge : **front•age**
fron•tier
frontige : **front•age**
frontispeace : **fron•tis•piece**
frontispeice : **fron•tis•piece**
frontispice : **fron•tis•piece**

fron·tis·piece
frontspiece : **fron·tis·piece**
frovolitty : **fri·vol·i·ty**
fru·gal
frugel : **fru·gal**
fruit·ful
fruitfull : **fruit·ful**
frutful : **fruit·ful**
fry·er *or* **fri·er** (fried fowl);
   fri·ar (monk)
fuchea : **fuch·sia**
fuchia : **fuch·sia**
fuch·sia
fucilage : **fu·se·lage**
fuciloge : **fu·se·lage**
fudal : **feu·dal** (medieval social
   order) *or* **fu·tile** (without
   success)
fued : **feud**
fuedal : **feu·dal** (medieval
   social order) *or* **fu·tile**
   (without success)
fugative : **fu·gi·tive**
fugetive : **fu·gi·tive**
fugiteve : **fu·gi·tive**
fu·gi·tive
fujitive : **fu·gi·tive**
fulcram : **ful·crum**
fulcrem : **ful·crum**
fulcrim : **ful·crum**
ful·crum
ful·fil *or* **ful·fill**
ful·fill *or* **ful·fil**
fullcrem : **ful·crum**
fullcrum : **ful·crum**
fullfil : **ful·fill**
fullfill : **ful·fill**
fullsome : **ful·some**
ful·some
fumagate : **fum·i·gate**
fumegate : **fum·i·gate**
fumigait : **fum·i·gate**

fum·i·gate
fun·da·men·tal
fundamintal : **fun·da·men·tal**
fundemental : **fun·da·men·tal**
fundimental : **fun·da·men·tal**
funel : **fun·nel**
funell : **fun·nel**
funil : **fun·nel**
funill : **fun·nel**
funnal : **fun·nel**
fun·nel
funnell : **fun·nel**
funnil : **fun·nel**
furer : **fu·ror**
fur·lough
furlowe : **fur·lough**
fur·nace
furnature : **fur·ni·ture**
furnece : **fur·nace**
furness : **fur·nace**
furneture : **fur·ni·ture**
furnice : **fur·nace**
furniss : **fur·nace**
fur·ni·ture
furoar : **fu·ror**
fu·ror
furrer : **fu·ror**
furror : **fu·ror**
fusalage : **fu·se·lage**
fu·se·lage
fuselodge : **fu·se·lage**
fuseloge : **fu·se·lage**
fushea : **fuch·sia**
fushia : **fuch·sia**
fusilage : **fu·se·lage**
fusiloge : **fu·se·lage**
fu·sion
fussion : **fu·sion**
futele : **feu·dal** (medieval social
   order) *or* **fu·tile** (without
   success)

futell : **feu·dal** (medieval social
order) *or* **fu·tile** (without
success)
fu·tile (without success);
feu·dal (medieval social
order)
futilety : **fu·til·i·ty**

futilitty : **fu·til·i·ty**
fu·til·i·ty
futill : **fu·tile**
futillity : **fu·til·i·ty**
fuzion : **fu·sion**
fyord : **fjord**

G

gabardeen : **gab•ar•dine**
gabardene : **gab•ar•dine**
gab•ar•dine *or* **gab•er•dine**
gabbardine : **gab•ar•dine**
gabberdine : **gab•ar•dine**
gab•ble (to babble); **ga•ble**
  (roof feature)
gabel : **gab•ble** (to babble) *or*
  ga•ble (roof feature)
gab•er•dine *or* **gab•ar•dine**
ga•ble (roof feature); **gab•ble**
  (to babble)
gache : **gauche**
gad•get
gadgit : **gad•get**
gadjet : **gad•get**
Gaelec : **Gael•ic**
Gael•ic
gaget : **gad•get**
gai•ety *or* **gay•ety**
Gailic : **Gael•ic**
gai•ly *or* **gay•ly**
gait (way of walking); **gate**
  (door)
ga•la
galactec : **ga•lac•tic**
ga•lac•tic
galary : **gal•lery**
gal•axy
galen : **gal•lon**
galery : **gal•lery**
Galic : **Gael•ic**
galion : **gal•le•on** (ship) *or*
  gal•lon (measure)
galip : **gal•lop**
galla : **ga•la**
gallacksy : **gal•axy**
gallactic : **ga•lac•tic**
gallantery : **gal•lant•ry**
gal•lant•ry

gallap : **gal•lop**
gallary : **gal•lery**
gallaxy : **gal•axy**
gallen : **gal•le•on** (ship) *or*
  gal•lon (measure)
gallentry : **gal•lant•ry**
gal•le•on (ship); **gal•lon**
  (measure)
gallep : **gal•lop**
gal•lery
gallexy : **gal•axy**
gal•ley
gallin : **gal•le•on** (ship) *or*
  gal•lon (measure)
gallintry : **gal•lant•ry**
gallion : **gal•le•on** (ship) *or*
  gal•lon (measure)
gallip : **gal•lop**
gallixy : **gal•axy**
gal•lon (measure); **gal•le•on**
  (ship)
gal•lop (canter); **Gal•lup** (poll)
gallosh : **ga•losh** (footwear) *or*
  gou•lash (stew)
galluntry : **gal•lant•ry**
Gal•lup (poll); **gal•lop** (canter)
gally : **gal•ley**
galon : **gal•le•on** (ship) *or*
  gal•lon (measure)
galop : **gal•lop**
ga•losh (footwear); **gou•lash**
  (stew)
galvanise : **gal•va•nize**
gal•va•nize
galvenize : **gal•va•nize**
galvinize : **gal•va•nize**
gambet : **gam•bit**
gam•bit
gam•ble (to risk or bet);
  gam•bol (to frolic)

gam·bol (to frolic); **gam·ble** (to risk or bet)
gamet : **gam·ut**
gamit : **gam·ut**
gammet : **gam·ut**
gammit : **gam·ut**
gammut : **gam·ut**
gam·ut
gandola : **gon·do·la**
gangrean : **gan·grene**
gangreen : **gan·grene**
gan·grene
gangrine : **gan·grene**
gaol (*Brit.*) : **jail**
ga·rage
garantee : **guar·an·tee**
garason : **gar·ri·son**
gardeenia : **gar·de·nia**
gar·den
gar·de·nia
gardian : **guard·ian**
gardin : **gar·den**
gardinia : **gar·de·nia**
garentee : **guar·an·tee**
garesh : **gar·ish**
garet : **gar·ret**
gargoil : **gar·goyle**
gargoyl : **gar·goyle**
gar·goyle
garintee : **guar·an·tee**
gar·ish
garison : **gar·ri·son**
garit : **gar·ret**
gar·land
garlec : **gar·lic**
garlend : **gar·land**
gar·lic
garlick : **gar·lic**
garlind : **gar·land**
garlund : **gar·land**
garmant : **gar·ment**
gar·ment

garmet : **gar·ment**
garmint : **gar·ment**
gar·net
garnit : **gar·net**
garodge : **ga·rage**
garoge : **ga·rage**
garrage : **ga·rage**
garrentee : **guar·an·tee**
garreson : **gar·ri·son**
gar·ret
garrisen : **gar·ri·son**
garrish : **gar·ish**
gar·ri·son
garrit : **gar·ret**
gar·ru·lous
garulous : **gar·ru·lous**
gasaleen : **gas·o·line**
gasalene : **gas·o·line**
gasaline : **gas·o·line**
gas·e·ous
gasiline : **gas·o·line**
gasious : **gas·e·ous**
gas·ket
gaskit : **gas·ket**
gasolean : **gas·o·line**
gasoleen : **gas·o·line**
gasolene : **gas·o·line**
gas·o·line
gasseous : **gas·e·ous**
gassoline : **gas·o·line**
gastly : **ghast·ly**
gate (door); **gait** (way of walking)
gauche
gaudy
gauge
gauky : **gawky**
gaurantee : **guar·an·tee**
gaurd : **guard**
gaurdian : **guard·ian**
gause : **gauze**
gauze

gaval : **gav·el**
gav·el
gavell : **gav·el**
gavil : **gav·el**
gavvel : **gav·el**
gavvil : **gav·el**
gawdy : **gaudy**
gawky
gawze : **gauze**
gay·ety *or* **gai·ety**
gay·ly *or* **gai·ly**
gazet : **ga·zette**
gazett : **ga·zette**
ga·zette
gazzette : **ga·zette**
geagraphy : **ge·og·ra·phy**
Gealic : **Gael·ic**
gealogy : **ge·ol·o·gy**
geametry : **ge·om·e·try**
geanology : **ge·ne·al·o·gy**
gear
gearth : **girth**
geer : **gear**
gehad : **ji·had**
geir : **gear**
geiser : **gey·ser**
gel *or* jell
gelaten : **gel·a·tin**
gel·a·tin
gelitin : **gel·a·tin**
gellatin : **gel·a·tin**
Gem·i·ni
Geminie : **Gem·i·ni**
Geminni : **Gem·i·ni**
gemnasium : **gym·na·si·um**
gemnasstics : **gym·nas·tics**
gemnast : **gym·nast**
gemnastecs : **gym·nas·tics**
gemnasticks : **gym·nas·tics**
gemnest : **gym·nast**
gemnist : **gym·nast**
genarator : **gen·er·a·tor**

ge·ne·al·o·gy
Geneava : **Ge·ne·va**
Geneeva : **Ge·ne·va**
geneology : **ge·ne·al·o·gy**
gen·era (*plur.*, class or kind);
   genre (class of literature)
gen·er·al
generater : **gen·er·a·tor**
gen·er·a·tor
generel : **gen·er·al**
ge·ner·ic
generick : **ge·ner·ic**
generil : **gen·er·al**
gen·er·ous
generric : **gen·er·ic**
generus : **gen·er·ous**
gen·e·sis
geneticks : **ge·net·ics**
ge·net·ics
genettics : **ge·net·ics**
Ge·ne·va
Genieva : **Ge·ne·va**
genious : **gen·ius**
geniral : **gen·er·al**
genirator : **gen·er·a·tor**
genirous : **gen·er·ous**
genisis : **gen·e·sis**
gen·ius (intellectual power);
   ge·nus (*sing.*, class or kind)
Geniva : **Ge·ne·va**
gennerate : **gen·er·ate**
gennerator : **gen·er·a·tor**
genneric : **ge·ner·ic**
gennerous : **gen·er·ous**
gennesis : **gen·e·sis**
gennetics : **ge·net·ics**
gennirate : **gen·er·ate**
genooine : **gen·u·ine**
genre (class of literature);
   gen·era (*plur.*, class or kind)
genteal : **gen·teel**

gen·teel (polite); gen·tile (not Jewish)

gentele : gen·teel (polite) or gen·tile (not Jewish)

gen·tile (not Jewish); gen·teel (polite)

genuin : gen·u·ine

gen·u·ine

ge·nus (*sing.*, class or kind); gen·ius (intellectual power)

genuwine : gen·u·ine

geoggrapy : ge·og·ra·phy

geografy : ge·og·ra·phy

ge·og·ra·phy

geogrefy : ge·og·ra·phy

geogrephy : ge·og·ra·phy

geogriphy : ge·og·ra·phy

geolegy : ge·ol·o·gy

geollogy : ge·ol·o·gy

geologgy : ge·ol·o·gy

ge·ol·o·gy

ge·om·e·try

geomettry : ge·om·e·try

geommetry : ge·om·e·try

geonoligy : ge·ne·al·o·gy

geonollogy : ge·ne·al·o·gy

geonre : genre

Georga : Geor·gia

Geor·gia

gerage : ga·rage

gerand : ger·und

geraneum : ge·ra·ni·um

geraniam : ge·ra·ni·um

geraniem : ge·ra·ni·um

ge·ra·ni·um

gerantology : ger·on·tol·o·gy

gerder : gird·er

gerdle : gir·dle

gerend : ger·und

gerkin : gher·kin

Germanny : Ger·ma·ny

Ger·ma·ny

Germeny : Ger·ma·ny

gerontolegy : ger·on·tol·o·gy

gerontoligy : ger·on·tol·o·gy

gerontollogy : ger·on·tol·o·gy

ger·on·tol·o·gy

gerranium : ge·ra·ni·um

gerrund : ger·und

gerth : girth

ger·und

gess : guess

gessture : ges·ture

gest : gist (essence) or jest (joke)

gester : ges·ture (movement) or jest·er (joker)

ges·ture (movement); jest·er (joker)

gesyr : gey·ser

gettho : ghet·to

Gettisburg : Get·tys·burg

getto : ghet·to

Gettysberg : Get·tys·burg

Get·tys·burg

Gettysburgh : Get·tys·burg

geuss : guess

gey·ser

ghast·ly

gherken : gher·kin

gher·kin

ghet·to

ghoul·ish

ghulish : ghoul·ish

ghurkin : gher·kin

gi·ant

gibe (to taunt); jibe (to change course in boat; to agree)

Gibralltar : Gi·bral·tar

Gi·bral·tar

Gibralter : Gi·bral·tar

gidance : guid·ance

gient : gi·ant

gier : gear

gieser : **gey·ser**

gihad : **ji·had**

gild (to cover with gold); **gilled** (having gills); **guild** (union)

gillatine : **guil·lo·tine**

gilled (having gills); **gild** (to cover with gold); **guild** (union)

gilliteen : **guil·lo·tine**

gillotine : **guil·lo·tine**

gilt (covered with gold); **guilt** (shame)

gimick : **gim·mick**

Gimini : **Gem·i·ni**

gimmeck : **gim·mick**

gimmic : **gim·mick**

gim·mick

gimnasium : **gym·na·si·um**

gimnasstics : **gym·nas·tics**

gimnast : **gym·nast**

gimnastecs : **gym·nas·tics**

gimnasticks : **gym·nas·tics**

gimnest : **gym·nast**

gimnist : **gym·nast**

ginacology : **gy·ne·col·o·gy**

ginasis : **gen·e·sis**

gincolijy : **gy·ne·col·o·gy**

ginecolligy : **gy·ne·col·o·gy**

ginecollogy : **gy·ne·col·o·gy**

gingam : **ging·ham**

ging·ham

ginghem : **ging·ham**

gingum : **ging·ham**

ginicology : **gy·ne·col·o·gy**

ginocology : **gy·ne·col·o·gy**

gipcem : **gyp·sum**

gipcim : **gyp·sum**

gipsam : **gyp·sum**

gipsem : **gyp·sum**

gipsey : **gyp·sy**

gipsim : **gyp·sum**

gipsy : **gyp·sy**

girafe : **gi·raffe**

gi·raffe

girage : **ga·rage**

giraph : **gi·raffe**

girascope : **gy·ro·scope**

girate : **gy·rate**

gird·er

gir·dle

girgle : **gur·gle**

girocompass : **gy·ro·com·pass**

girocompess : **gy·ro·com·pass**

girrate : **gy·rate**

girth

giser : **gey·ser**

gist (essence); **jest** (joke)

gister : **ges·ture** (movement) *or* **jest·er** (joker)

gitar : **gui·tar**

gittar : **gui·tar**

giullotine : **guil·lo·tine**

giutar : **gui·tar**

glaceir : **gla·cier**

glacher : **gla·cier**

gla·cier

gladdiator : **glad·i·a·tor**

gladeator : **glad·i·a·tor**

gladiater : **glad·i·a·tor**

glad·i·a·tor

glamarous : **glam·or·ous**

glamerous : **glam·or·ous**

glammorous : **glam·or·ous**

glam·or *or* **glam·our**

glam·or·ous

glamorus : **glam·or·ous**

glam·our *or* **glam·or**

glamourous : **glam·or·ous**

glance

glanse : **glance**

Glasco : **Glas·gow**

Glascoe : **Glas·gow**

Glascow : **Glas·gow**

Glas·gow

glasher : **gla•cier**
Glasscow : **Glas•gow**
glass•ware
glasswear : **glass•ware**
glasware : **glass•ware**
gleam
gleem : **gleam**
gleim : **gleam**
glemmer : **glim•mer**
glimer : **glim•mer**
glim•mer
glimpce : **glimpse**
glimpse
glimse : **glimpse**
glissen : **glis•ten**
glissten : **glis•ten**
glis•ten
gloabal : **glob•al**
gloat
glob•al
globall : **glob•al**
globel : **glob•al**
glorafication : **glo•ri•fi•ca•tion**
glorafy : **glo•ri•fy**
glorefication : **glo•ri•fi•ca•tion**
glorefy : **glo•ri•fy**
gloreous : **glo•ri•ous**
glorifacation : **glo•ri•fi•ca•tion**
glorifecation : **glo•ri•fi•ca•tion**
glo•ri•fi•ca•tion
glo•ri•fy
glo•ri•ous
glorius : **glo•ri•ous**
glorrification : **glo•ri•fi•ca•tion**
glorrify : **glo•ri•fy**
glorrious : **glo•ri•ous**
glorry : **glo•ry**
glo•ry
glosary : **glos•sa•ry**
glosery : **glos•sa•ry**
glos•sa•ry
glossery : **glos•sa•ry**

glote : **gloat**
gluton : **glut•ton**
glutonny : **glut•tony**
gluttan : **glut•ton**
glutten : **glut•ton**
gluttenny : **glut•tony**
glutteny : **glut•tony**
gluttin : **glut•ton**
gluttiny : **glut•tony**
glut•ton
glut•tony
gnarled
gnarreled : **gnarled**
gnarrled : **gnarled**
gnash
gnat
gnaw
gnoam : **gnome**
gnome (dwarf); **Nome** (city)
gnu (antelope); **knew** (was
    aware); **new** (not old)
goache : **gauche**
goal
goard : **gourd**
goashe : **gauche**
goa•tee
goatey : **goa•tee**
goatie : **goa•tee**
gobblen : **gob•lin**
gobblet : **gob•let**
gobblin : **gob•lin**
gobblit : **gob•let**
goblen : **gob•lin**
gob•let
gob•lin
goblit : **gob•let**
goche : **gauche**
goddes : **god•dess**
god•dess
goddiss : **god•dess**
godess : **god•dess**
god•li•ness

godlyness : **god•li•ness**
gofer : **go•pher**
gole : **goal**
gon•do•la
gondolla : **gon•do•la**
gooce : **goose**
good-by *or* **good-bye**
good-bye *or* **good-by**
goose
go•pher
gophur : **go•pher**
gord : **gourd**
gorey : **gory**
gor•geous
Gorgia : **Geor•gia**
gorgious : **gor•geous**
gorgius : **gor•geous**
gorila : **go•ril•la** (ape) *or*
   guer•ril•la (warrior)
go•ril•la (ape); **guer•ril•la**
   (warrior)
gorjeous : **gor•geous**
gormay : **gour•met**
gormet : **gour•met**
gorry : **gory**
gory
gosamer : **gos•sa•mer**
gosemer : **gos•sa•mer**
gosimer : **gos•sa•mer**
gosip : **gos•sip**
gos•pel
gospell : **gos•pel**
gospil : **gos•pel**
gospul : **gos•pel**
gos•sa•mer
gossamere : **gos•sa•mer**
gossamir : **gos•sa•mer**
gossemer : **gos•sa•mer**
gossep : **gos•sip**
gossimer : **gos•sa•mer**
gos•sip
gosspel : **gos•pel**

gossup : **gos•sip**
gosup : **gos•sip**
gotee : **goa•tee**
gothec : **goth•ic**
goth•ic
gothick : **goth•ic**
gou•lash (stew); **ga•losh**
   (footwear)
goulosh : **ga•losh** (footwear) *or*
   gou•lash (stew)
goun : **gown**
gourd
gourmay : **gour•met**
gour•met
gourmey : **gour•met**
govanor : **gov•er•nor**
govenor : **gov•er•nor**
goverment : **gov•ern•ment**
gov•ern
gov•er•nance
governanse : **gov•er•nance**
governence : **gov•er•nance**
governense : **gov•er•nance**
governer : **gov•er•nor**
governince : **gov•er•nance**
governmant : **gov•ern•ment**
gov•ern•ment
gov•er•nor
govirn : **gov•ern**
govirnance : **gov•er•nance**
govner : **gov•er•nor**
govurn : **gov•ern**
govurnor : **gov•er•nor**
govvern : **gov•ern**
govvernance : **gov•er•nance**
govvernment : **gov•ern•ment**
govvernnor : **gov•er•nor**
gown
grace•ful
gracefull : **grace•ful**
graceous : **gra•cious**
gra•cious

gracius : **gra·cious**
graddual : **grad·u·al**
gradduate : **grad·u·ate**
gradeant : **gra·di·ent**
gradiant : **gra·di·ent**
gra·di·ent
graduait : **grad·u·ate**
grad·u·al
grad·u·ate
graduel : **grad·u·al**
graduill : **grad·u·al**
graduwel : **grad·u·al**
graffec : **graph·ic**
graffete : **graf·fi·ti** (writing) *or*
  graph·ite (carbon)
graffic : **graph·ic**
graffically : **graph·i·cal·ly**
graf·fi·ti (writing); **graph·ite**
  (carbon)
graffitti : **graf·fi·ti**
grafitti : **graf·fi·ti**
gragarious : **gre·gar·i·ous**
graiceful : **grace·ful**
grainarry : **gra·na·ry**
grainary : **gra·na·ry**
grainerry : **gra·na·ry**
grainery : **gra·na·ry**
grainular : **gran·u·lar**
grainule : **gran·ule**
graitful : **grate·ful**
graiven : **grav·en**
graize : **graze**
gramar : **gram·mar**
gramer : **gram·mar**
gram·mar
grammer : **gram·mar**
grammir : **gram·mar**
granade : **gre·nade**
granaid : **gre·nade**
gra·na·ry
grandelaquence :
  gran·dil·o·quence

grandelloquence :
  gran·dil·o·quence
grandeloquance :
  gran·dil·o·quence
grandeloquence :
  gran·dil·o·quence
grandeoce : **gran·di·ose**
grandeose : **gran·di·ose**
gran·deur
grandilaquence :
  gran·dil·o·quence
gran·dil·o·quence
grandiloquense :
  gran·dil·o·quence
grandiloquince :
  gran·dil·o·quence
grandioce : **gran·di·ose**
gran·di·ose
grandoor : **gran·deur**
grandur : **gran·deur**
grandure : **gran·deur**
granerry : **gra·na·ry**
granery : **gra·na·ry**
grannule : **gran·ule**
granool : **gran·ule**
granoolar : **gran·u·lar**
gran·u·lar
gran·ule
granuler : **gran·u·lar**
granulir : **gran·u·lar**
graphec : **graph·ic**
graphecally : **graph·i·cal·ly**
grapheit : **graph·ite**
graph·ic
graph·i·cal·ly
graphick : **graph·ic**
graphickelly : **graph·i·cal·ly**
graphicly : **graph·i·cal·ly**
graph·ite (carbon); **graf·fi·ti**
  (writing)
graple : **grap·ple**
grappal : **grap·ple**

grappel : **grap·ple**
grap·ple
graseful : **grace·ful**
grasious : **grac·ious**
gratafication : **grat·i·fi·ca·tion**
gratafy : **grat·i·fy**
gratatude : **grat·i·tude**
grate (framework); **great** (large)
grate·ful
gratefull : **grate·ful**
gratefy : **grat·i·fy**
gratetude : **grat·i·tude**
gratful : **grate·ful**
gratiffication : **grat·i·fi·ca·tion**
grat·i·fi·ca·tion
grat·i·fy
grat·is
gratitood : **grat·i·tude**
grat·i·tude
gratitued : **grat·i·tude**
gratiutous : **gra·tu·itous**
grattafication : **grat·i·fi·ca·tion**
grattatude : **grat·i·tude**
grattifacation : **grat·i·fi·ca·tion**
grattification : **grat·i·fi·ca·tion**
grattify : **grat·i·fy**
grattis : **grat·is**
grattitude : **grat·i·tude**
grattuitous : **gra·tu·itous**
grattus : **grat·is**
gratuetous : **gra·tu·itous**
gratuitious : **gra·tu·itous**
gra·tu·itous
gratus : **grat·is**
gravatate : **grav·i·tate**
grav·el
gravell : **grav·el**
grav·en
gravetate : **grav·i·tate**
gravety : **grav·i·ty**
gravil : **grav·el**
grav·i·tate

gravitty : **grav·i·ty**
grav·i·ty
gravvel : **grav·el**
gravvitate : **grav·i·tate**
gravvity : **grav·i·ty**
gray or **grey**
grayhound : **grey·hound**
graze
gready : **greedy**
greanery : **green·ery**
Greasian : **Gre·cian**
greasy
great (large); **grate** (framework)
greatful : **grate·ful**
greating : **greet·ing**
greavance : **griev·ance**
greave (armored legging);
    grieve (to mourn)
Gre·cian
Greecian : **Gre·cian**
greedy
greenary : **green·ery**
greenerry : **green·ery**
green·ery
Greenich : **Green·wich**
Green·wich
Greenwitch : **Green·wich**
Greesian : **Gre·cian**
greesy : **greasy**
greet·ing
greevance : **griev·ance**
grefitti : **graf·fi·ti**
gregairious : **gre·gar·i·ous**
gregareous : **gre·gar·i·ous**
gre·gar·i·ous
gregarius : **gre·gar·i·ous**
greggarious : **gre·gar·i·ous**
greif : **grief**
greisy : **greasy**
greivance : **griev·ance**
greive : **greave** (armored
    legging) or **grieve** (to mourn)

greivence : **griev•ance**
gremlan : **grem•lin**
gremlen : **grem•lin**
grem•lin
gremlun : **grem•lin**
gre•nade
grenaid : **gre•nade**
Grennich : **Green•wich**
Grenwich : **Green•wich**
Grenwitch : **Green•wich**
greve : **greave** (armored
   legging) *or* **grieve** (to mourn)
grey *or* **gray**
grey•hound
gridiern : **grid•iron**
gridiren : **grid•iron**
gridirn : **grid•iron**
grid•iron
grief
griefance : **griev•ance**
griefitti : **graf•fi•ti**
griev•ance
grievanse : **griev•ance**
grieve (to mourn); **greave**
   (armored legging)
grievense : **griev•ance**
grif•fin *or* **grif•fon** *or* **gryph•on**
griffiti : **graf•fi•ti**
grif•fon *or* **grif•fin** *or* **gryph•on**
grigarious : **gre•gar•i•ous**
grill (to broil); **grille** (screen)
grille (screen); **grill** (to broil)
gri•mace
grimece : **gri•mace**
grimice : **gri•mace**
grimise : **gri•mace**
grimlin : **grem•lin**
grimmace : **gri•mace**
grisled : **griz•zled**
gris•ly (gruesome); **griz•zly**
   (grayish, as the bear)
grissel : **gris•tle**

grissle : **gris•tle**
gris•tle
grivance : **griev•ance**
griz•zled
griz•zly (grayish, as the bear);
   gris•ly (gruesome)
groacer : **gro•cer**
groacery : **gro•cery**
groaned
groap : **grope**
groape : **grope**
groatesque : **gro•tesque**
gro•cer
grocerry : **gro•cery**
gro•cery
grociary : **gro•cery**
grociery : **gro•cery**
groned : **groaned**
grooling : **gru•el•ing**
grope
groser : **gro•cer**
grotesk : **gro•tesque**
groteske : **gro•tesque**
gro•tesque
grouchy
grov•eled *or* **grov•elled**
grov•el•ing *or* **grov•el•ling**
grov•elled *or* **grov•eled**
grov•el•ling *or* **grov•el•ing**
groviled : **grov•eled**
grovilling : **grov•el•ing**
grovveled : **grov•eled**
growchy : **grouchy**
gru•el•ing
gruesom : **grue•some**
grue•some
gruling : **gru•el•ing**
grulling : **gru•el•ing**
grusome : **grue•some**
grusum : **grue•some**
gryph•on *or* **grif•fin** *or* **grif•fon**
guage : **gauge**

guar·an·tee
guard
guard·ian
guardien : **guard·ian**
guarintie : **guar·an·tee**
Guatamala : **Gua·te·ma·la**
Gua·te·ma·la
Guatemalla : **Gua·te·ma·la**
Guattemala : **Gua·te·ma·la**
guerila : **go·ril·la** (ape) or
  guer·ril·la (warrior)
guer·ril·la (warrior); **go·ril·la**
  (ape)
guess
guetar : **gui·tar**
guid·ance
guidanse : **guid·ance**
guiddance : **guid·ance**
guidence : **guid·ance**
guidense : **guid·ance**
guild (union); **gild** (to cover
  with gold); **gilled** (having
  gills)
guillatine : **guil·lo·tine**
guilletine : **guil·lo·tine**
guillotene : **guil·lo·tine**
guil·lo·tine
guilt (shame); **gilt** (covered with
  gold)
gui·tar
gulash : **ga·losh** (footwear) or
  gou·lash (stew)
gulet : **gul·let**
gulible : **gul·li·ble**
gullable : **gul·li·ble**
gullat : **gul·let**
gulleble : **gul·li·ble**
gul·let
gullibal : **gul·li·ble**
gul·li·ble
gullit : **gul·let**

gulosh : **ga·losh** (footwear) or
  gou·lash (stew)
gunery : **gun·nery**
gunnary : **gun·nery**
gun·nel or **gun·wale**
gunnerry : **gun·nery**
gun·nery
gun·wale or **gun·nel**
guord : **gourd**
guormet : **gour·met**
gurgal : **gur·gle**
gurgel : **gur·gle**
gur·gle
gurilla : **go·ril·la** (ape) or
  guer·ril·la (warrior)
gurkin : **gher·kin**
gurth : **girth**
guse : **goose**
Gwatemala : **Gua·te·ma·la**
gymnaisium : **gym·na·si·um**
gymnaseum : **gym·na·si·um**
gymnasiem : **gym·na·si·um**
gym·na·si·um
gymnasstics : **gym·nas·tics**
gym·nast
gymnastecs : **gym·nas·tics**
gymnasticks : **gym·nas·tics**
gym·nas·tics
gymnest : **gym·nast**
gymnist : **gym·nast**
gynacology : **gy·ne·col·o·gy**
gyncolijy : **gy·ne·col·o·gy**
gynecolligy : **gy·ne·col·o·gy**
gynecollogy : **gy·ne·col·o·gy**
gy·ne·col·o·gy
gynicology : **gy·ne·col·o·gy**
gynocology : **gy·ne·col·o·gy**
gyp
gypcem : **gyp·sum**
gypcim : **gyp·sum**
gyped : **gypped**
gypped

gypsam : **gyp•sum**
gypsem : **gyp•sum**
gypsey : **gyp•sy**
gypsie : **gyp•sy**
gypsim : **gyp•sum**
gyp•sum
gyp•sy
gyracompass : **gy•ro•com•pass**
gyrait : **gy•rate**
gyrascope : **gy•ro•scope**

gy•rate
gyricompass : **gy•ro•com•pass**
gyriscope : **gy•ro•scope**
gy•ro•com•pass
gyrocompess : **gy•ro•com•pass**
gyrocompiss : **gy•ro•com•pass**
gyroscoap : **gy•ro•scope**
gy•ro•scope
gyrrate : **gy•rate**
gyser : **gey•ser**

H

habbet : **hab·it**
habbit : **hab·it**
habbitable : **hab·it·able**
habetable : **hab·it·able**
hab·it
habitabel : **hab·it·able**
hab·it·able
habitibal : **hab·it·able**
habitible : **hab·it·able**
haceinda : **ha·ci·en·da**
hachery : **hatch·ery**
hachet : **hatch·et**
hachit : **hatch·et**
ha·ci·en·da
haciendah : **ha·ci·en·da**
hack·neyed
hacknied : **hack·neyed**
hackny : **hack·neyed**
haddeck : **had·dock**
haddoc : **had·dock**
had·dock
hadj *or* hajj (pilgrimage); **hag**
   (witch); **Hague** (city)
hadock : **had·dock**
Haeti : **Hai·ti**
haf : **half**
hafhazard : **hap·haz·ard**
hag (witch); **Hague** (city); **hajj**
   (pilgrimage)
hagard : **hag·gard**
haggal : **hag·gle**
hag·gard
haggel : **hag·gle**
haggerd : **hag·gard**
haggird : **hag·gard**
hag·gle
Hague (city); **hag** (witch); **hajj**
   (pilgrimage)
hailo : **ha·lo**
hailstoan : **hail·stone**

hail·stone
hair (on head); **heir** (inheritor)
hairbrained : **hare·brained**
hairbraned : **hare·brained**
hairlip : **hare·lip**
haissen : **has·ten**
haisten : **has·ten**
Haitee : **Hai·ti**
Hai·ti
Haity : **Hai·ti**
hajj *or* **hadj** (pilgrimage); **hag**
   (witch); **Hague** (city)
halabut : **hal·i·but**
halatosis : **hal·i·to·sis**
halceon : **hal·cy·on**
halcion : **hal·cy·on**
hal·cy·on
halebut : **hal·i·but**
halestone : **hail·stone**
haletosis : **hal·i·to·sis**
half (*sing.*); **halve** (*verb*);
   halves (*plur.*)
halfhazard : **hap·haz·ard**
halfs : **halves**
haliard : **hal·yard**
halibet : **hal·i·but**
hal·i·but
halitoses : **hal·i·to·sis**
hal·i·to·sis
hallabet : **hal·i·but**
hallalujah : **hal·le·lu·jah**
Hallaween : **Hal·low·een**
hallcyon : **hal·cy·on**
halleloojah : **hal·le·lu·jah**
hal·le·lu·jah
halleluyah : **hal·le·lu·jah**
hal·liard *or* **hal·yard**
hallibut : **hal·i·but**
hallierd : **hal·yard**
hallilujah : **hal·le·lu·jah**

hallitosis : **hal·i·to·sis**
Halloeen : **Hal·low·een**
halloocination :
   hal·lu·ci·na·tion
Hallowean : **Hal·low·een**
Hal·low·een
Hallowene : **Hal·low·een**
hallucenation : **hal·lu·ci·na·tion**
hal·lu·ci·na·tion
hallusination : **hal·lu·ci·na·tion**
hallyard : **hal·yard**
ha·lo
Haloween : **Hal·low·een**
halseon : **hal·cy·on**
halsion : **hal·cy·on**
halucination : **hal·lu·ci·na·tion**
halve (*verb*); **half** (*sing.*);
   halves (*plur.*)
halves (*plur.*); **half** (*sing.*);
   halve (*verb*)
hal·yard *or* **hal·liard**
hamberger : **ham·burg·er**
hambirger : **ham·burg·er**
ham·burg·er
hamburgur : **ham·burg·er**
hamer : **ham·mer**
hammack : **ham·mock**
hammar : **ham·mer**
hammeck : **ham·mock**
ham·mer
ham·mock
hamock : **ham·mock**
handal : **han·dle**
handecap : **hand·i·cap**
handecraft : **hand·i·craft**
Han·del (composer); **han·dle**
  (part for grasping)
handework : **hand·i·work**
hand·ful
handfull : **hand·ful**
hand·i·cap
hand·i·craft

handikraft : **hand·i·craft**
handil : **han·dle**
handiwerk : **hand·i·work**
hand·i·work
handiwurk : **hand·i·work**
handkercheif : **hand·ker·chief**
hand·ker·chief
handkerchiff : **hand·ker·chief**
handkirchief : **hand·ker·chief**
handkurchief : **hand·ker·chief**
han·dle (part for grasping);
  Han·del (composer)
hand·made (made by hand);
  hand·maid (female servant)
hand·maid (female servant);
  hand·made (made by hand)
hand·some (good-looking);
  han·som (cab)
handycap : **hand·i·cap**
handycraft : **hand·i·craft**
handywork : **hand·i·work**
han·gar (airplane shed);
  hang·er (device for hanging)
hang·er (device for hanging);
  han·gar (airplane shed)
hankercheif : **hand·ker·chief**
hankerchief : **hand·ker·chief**
hankerchiff : **hand·ker·chief**
hanndle : **han·dle**
han·som (cab); **hand·some**
  (good-looking)
hant : **haunt**
hanted : **haun·ted**
hap·haz·ard
haphazerd : **hap·haz·ard**
haphazzard : **hap·haz·ard**
haphazzerd : **hap·haz·ard**
hapiness : **hap·pi·ness**
hap·less
hapliss : **hap·less**
hap·pi·ness
happiniss : **hap·pi·ness**

happless : **hap·less**
happyness : **hap·pi·ness**
haram : **har·em**
harasment : **ha·rass·ment**
ha·rass
ha·rass·ment
harbar : **har·bor**
harbenger : **har·bin·ger**
harber : **har·bor**
har·bin·ger
harbinjer : **har·bin·ger**
harboar : **har·bor**
har·bor
har·di·ness
hardiniss : **har·di·ness**
hard·ware
hardwear : **hard·ware**
hardwere : **hard·ware**
hardwhere : **hard·ware**
hardyness : **har·di·ness**
hare·brained
harebraned : **hare·brained**
hare·lip
har·em
haress : **ha·rass** (to annoy) *or*
  heir·ess (inheritor)
haretic : **her·e·tic**
harim : **har·em**
Harlam : **Har·lem**
harlaquin : **har·le·quin**
Har·lem
harlequen : **har·le·quin**
har·le·quin
harlequine : **har·le·quin**
harlet : **har·lot**
harliquin : **har·le·quin**
harlit : **har·lot**
har·lot
Harlum : **Har·lem**
harmoanious : **har·mo·ni·ous**
harmoneous : **har·mo·ni·ous**
har·mon·i·ca

harmonicka : **har·mon·i·ca**
harmonika : **har·mon·i·ca**
har·mo·ni·ous
harmonius : **har·mo·ni·ous**
harmonnica : **har·mon·i·ca**
harnass : **har·ness**
harnes : **har·ness**
har·ness
harniss : **har·ness**
harnuss : **har·ness**
Har·old (name); **her·ald**
  (messenger)
har·poon
harpsachord : **harp·si·chord**
harpsechord : **harp·si·chord**
harp·si·chord
harpsicord : **harp·si·chord**
harpune : **har·poon**
harram : **har·em**
harrasment : **ha·rass·ment**
harrass : **ha·rass** (to annoy) *or*
  heir·ess (inheritor)
harrassment : **ha·rass·ment**
harrbinger : **har·bin·ger**
harrbor : **har·bor**
harrem : **har·em**
harress : **ha·rass** (to annoy) *or*
  heir·ess (inheritor)
harrim : **har·em**
harring : **her·ring**
Harrlem : **Har·lem**
harrlequin : **har·le·quin**
harrlot : **har·lot**
harrum : **har·em**
hart (male deer); **heart** (body
  organ)
hartbeat : **heart·beat**
hartbroken : **heart·bro·ken**
hartburn : **heart·burn**
harten : **heart·en**
harth : **hearth**
harty : **hearty**

harum : **har•em**
har•vest
harvist : **har•vest**
harvust : **har•vest**
hasard : **haz•ard**
hasienda : **ha•ci•en•da**
hasle : **has•sle**
hassal : **has•sle**
hassel : **has•sle**
hassen : **has•ten**
hassienda : **ha•ci•en•da**
has•sle
has•ten
hatchary : **hatch•ery**
hatcherry : **hatch•ery**
hatch•ery
hatch•et
hatchit : **hatch•et**
Hati : **Hai•ti**
haugh•ty
haunt•ed
havec : **hav•oc**
haveck : **hav•oc**
havic : **hav•oc**
havick : **hav•oc**
hav•oc
havock : **hav•oc**
havvoc : **hav•oc**
Hawahi : **Ha•waii**
Hawai : **Ha•waii**
Ha•waii
Hawiei : **Ha•waii**
Hawii : **Ha•waii**
hawnt : **haunt**
haw•thorn (shrub);
  Haw•thorne (author)
Haw•thorne (author);
  haw•thorn (shrub)
hawtty : **haugh•ty**
Hawyii : **Ha•waii**
hayday : **hey•day**
haz•ard

hazellnut : **ha•zel•nut**
ha•zel•nut
hazerd : **haz•ard**
hazilnut : **ha•zel•nut**
hazird : **haz•ard**
hazzard : **haz•ard**
hazzerd : **haz•ard**
heackle : **heck•le**
head•ache
headacke : **head•ache**
headake : **head•ache**
head•dress
head•line
headonism : **he•do•nism**
headress : **head•dress**
heafer : **heif•er**
heal (to cure); **heel** (back of the
  foot)
healix : **he•lix**
healpful : **help•ful**
health
heanous : **hei•nous**
heap
hearce : **hearse**
heard (*past of* to hear); **herd**
  (group of animals)
hear•ing
hear•say (rumor); **her•e•sy**
  (dissent)
hearse (funeral car); **hers**
  (belonging to her)
heart (body organ); **hart** (male
  deer)
heart•beat
heart•bro•ken
heart•burn
hearth
hearty
heath
hea•then
heath•er
heave

heav•en
heavi•ly
heaviweight : **heavy•weight**
heaviwieght : **heavy•weight**
heavy
heavyly : **heavi•ly**
heavywaight : **heavy•weight**
heavy•weight
heccle : **heck•le**
heckal : **heck•le**
heckel : **heck•le**
heck•le
hecktic : **hec•tic**
hectec : **hec•tic**
hec•tic
hectick : **hec•tic**
hedache : **head•ache**
heddonism : **he•do•nism**
hedline : **head•line**
hedonesm : **he•do•nism**
he•do•nism
heed•ful
heedfull : **heed•ful**
heel (back of the foot); **heal** (to cure)
heep : **heap**
heering : **hear•ing**
heeth : **heath**
heethen : **hea•then**
heffer : **heif•er**
hegeminny : **he•ge•mo•ny**
hegemone : **he•ge•mo•ny**
he•ge•mo•ny
hegimony : **he•ge•mo•ny**
heif•er
height
hei•nous
heir (inheritor); **hair** (on head)
heir•ess (inheritor); **ha•rass** (to annoy)
heiriss : **heir•ess**
heir•loom

heirlume : **heir•loom**
heirse : **hearse**
heithen : **hea•then**
heive : **heave**
hejemony : **he•ge•mo•ny**
hejiminy : **he•ge•mo•ny**
helacopter : **hel•i•cop•ter**
helecopter : **hel•i•cop•ter**
heleum : **he•li•um**
helicks : **he•lix**
hel•i•cop•ter
heliem : **he•li•um**
helikopter : **hel•i•cop•ter**
he•li•um
he•lix
hellacopter : **hel•i•cop•ter**
hellecopter : **hel•i•cop•ter**
hellicopter : **hel•i•cop•ter**
hellium : **he•li•um**
hellix : **he•lix**
hellmet : **hel•met**
hellth : **health**
hel•met
helmit : **hel•met**
helmut : **hel•met**
help•ful
helpfull : **help•ful**
helth : **health**
hemasphere : **hemi•sphere**
hemesphere : **hemi•sphere**
hemisfere : **hemi•sphere**
hemispear : **hemi•sphere**
hemispfere : **hemi•sphere**
hemisphear : **hemi•sphere**
hemispheir : **hemi•sphere**
hemi•sphere
hemmisphere : **hemi•sphere**
hemmophilia : **he•mo•phil•ia**
hemmorrhage : **hem•or•rhage**
hemmorroid : **hem•or•rhoid**
hemofilia : **he•mo•phil•ia**
hemophealia : **he•mo•phil•ia**

hemophelea : **he·mo·phil·ia**
hemophelia : **he·mo·phil·ia**
he·mo·phil·ia
hemophillia : **he·mo·phil·ia**
hemorhoid : **hem·or·rhoid**
hemoridge : **hem·or·rhage**
hemorige : **hem·or·rhage**
hemoroid : **hem·or·rhoid**
hemorredge : **hem·or·rhage**
hemorrege : **hem·or·rhage**
hem·or·rhage
hemorrhige : **hem·or·rhage**
hem·or·rhoid
hemorrige : **hem·or·rhage**
hemorroid : **hem·or·rhoid**
hencefoarth : **hence·forth**
hence·forth
hencefourth : **hence·forth**
henseforth : **hence·forth**
her·ald (messenger); **Har·old** (name)
heraldery : **her·ald·ry**
her·ald·ry
herass : **ha·rass** (to annoy) *or* **heir·ess** (inheritor)
herassment : **ha·rass·ment**
herasy : **her·e·sy**
heratage : **her·i·tage**
heratic : **her·e·tic**
herb·age
herb·al
herbedge : **herb·age**
herbege : **herb·age**
herbel : **herb·al**
herbiage : **herb·age**
herbige : **herb·age**
herd (group of animals); **heard** (past *of* to hear)
herdle : **hur·dle** (to leap a barrier) *or* **hur·tle** (to dash)
heredditary : **he·red·i·tary**
heredetery : **he·red·i·tary**

heredety : **he·red·i·ty**
he·red·i·tary
herediterry : **he·red·i·tary**
herediterry : **he·red·i·tary**
hereditery : **he·red·i·tary**
hereditty : **he·red·i·ty**
he·red·i·ty
heresay : **hear·say** (rumor) *or* **her·e·sy** (dissent)
heresey : **hear·say** (rumor) *or* **her·e·sy** (dissent)
her·e·sy (dissent); **hear·say** (rumor)
heretage : **her·i·tage**
her·e·tic
heretick : **her·e·tic**
hering : **her·ring**
herissy : **her·e·sy**
her·i·tage
heritedge : **her·i·tage**
heritege : **her·i·tage**
heritige : **her·i·tage**
hermat : **her·mit**
hermatige : **her·mit·age**
hermet : **her·mit**
hermetage : **her·mit·age**
hermett : **her·mit**
her·mit
her·mit·age
hermut : **her·mit**
hernea : **her·nia**
her·nia
hernya : **her·nia**
her·o·in (drug); **her·o·ine** (great woman)
her·o·ine (great woman); **her·o·in** (drug)
heroldery : **her·ald·ry**
heroldry : **her·ald·ry**
her·on
Heroshima : **Hi·ro·shi·ma**
herrald : **her·ald**
herraldry : **her·ald·ry**

herreditary : **he•red•i•tary**

herredity : **he•red•i•ty**

herress : **ha•rass** (to annoy) *or* **heir•ess** (inheritor)

herressy : **her•e•sy**

herresy : **her•e•sy**

herretic : **her•e•tic**

herrin : **her•on**

her•ring

herritage : **her•i•tage**

herron : **her•on**

herrse : **hearse**

hers (belonging to her); **hearse** (funeral car)

her's : **hers**

herse : **hearse**

herth : **hearth**

hertle : **hur•dle** (to leap a barrier) *or* **hur•tle** (to dash)

he's (he is); **his** (belonging to him)

hesatant : **hes•i•tant**

hesatate : **hes•i•tate**

hes•i•tant

hes•i•tate

hesitent : **hes•i•tant**

hessitant : **hes•i•tant**

hessitate : **hes•i•tate**

het•er•o•ge•neous *or* **het•er•og•e•nous**

heterogenius : **het•er•o•ge•neous**

het•er•og•e•nous *or* **het•er•o•ge•neous**

hether : **heath•er**

heve : **heave**

heven : **heav•en**

hevven : **heav•en**

hevvy : **heavy**

hevvyweight : **heavy•weight**

hevy : **heavy**

hevywait : **heavy•weight**

hey•day

hezitant : **hes•i•tant**

hiacenth : **hy•a•cinth**

hiacinth : **hy•a•cinth**

hiararchy : **hi•er•ar•chy**

hiasenth : **hy•a•cinth**

hiasinth : **hy•a•cinth**

hiatis : **hi•a•tus**

hi•a•tus

hibernait : **hi•ber•nate**

hi•ber•nate

hibred : **hy•brid**

hibryd : **hy•brid**

hiburnate : **hi•ber•nate**

hiccough (*Brit.*) : **hic•cup**

hic•cup

hickarry : **hick•o•ry**

hickary : **hick•o•ry**

hickerry : **hick•o•ry**

hickery : **hick•o•ry**

hick•o•ry

hiddeous : **hid•eous**

hiddious : **hid•eous**

hid•eous

hidious : **hid•eous**

hidius : **hid•eous**

hidrant : **hy•drant**

hidraulic : **hy•draul•ic**

hidrent : **hy•drant**

hidrint : **hy•drant**

hidrogen : **hy•dro•gen**

hieana : **hy•e•na**

hiefer : **heif•er**

hieght : **height**

hiena : **hy•e•na**

hienous : **hei•nous**

hi•er•ar•chy

hierarky : **hi•er•ar•chy**

hieress : **heir•ess**

hierloom : **heir•loom**

hifen : **hy•phen**

higene : **hy•giene**

highjack : **hi•jack**
high•ness
highniss : **high•ness**
hight : **height**
higiene : **hy•giene**
hi•jack
hilairious : **hi•lar•i•ous**
hilareous : **hi•lar•i•ous**
hi•lar•i•ous
hillarious : **hi•lar•i•ous**
him (that man); **hymn** (song)
himmorroid : **hem•or•rhoid**
himn : **hymn**
himnal : **hym•nal**
himnel : **hym•nal**
himorhoid : **hem•or•rhoid**
himoroid : **hem•or•rhoid**
himorrhage : **hem•or•rhage**
himorroid : **hem•or•rhoid**
hinderance : **hin•drance**
hinderense : **hin•drance**
hin•drance
hindranse : **hin•drance**
hindrence : **hin•drance**
hindrense : **hin•drance**
hiness : **high•ness**
hinotism : **hyp•no•tism**
hipadermic : **hy•po•der•mic**
hiphen : **hy•phen**
hipnatism : **hyp•no•tism**
hipnetism : **hyp•no•tism**
hipnosis : **hyp•no•sis**
hipnotism : **hyp•no•tism**
hipocrisy : **hy•poc•ri•sy**
hipocrite : **hyp•o•crite**
hipodermic : **hy•po•der•mic**
hipothesis : **hy•poth•e•sis**
hirarchy : **hi•er•ar•chy**
Hiroshema : **Hi•ro•shi•ma**
Hi•ro•shi•ma
his (belonging to him); **he's** (he is)

hisstory : **his•to•ry**
histarical : **hys•ter•i•cal**
histeria : **hys•te•ria**
histerical : **hys•ter•i•cal**
histericle : **hys•ter•i•cal**
histerikal : **hys•ter•i•cal**
histery : **his•to•ry**
historey : **his•to•ry**
historry : **his•to•ry**
his•to•ry
histry : **his•to•ry**
hite : **height**
hoard (cache); **horde** (multitude)
hoarmone : **hor•mone**
hoarse (rough-voiced); **horse** (animal)
hoary
hoastess : **hos•tess**
holacaust : **hol•o•caust**
ho•li•ness
hollacaust : **hol•o•caust**
hollocaust : **hol•o•caust**
hollocost : **hol•o•caust**
Holloween : **Hal•low•een**
hol•ly (tree); **ho•ly** (sacred); **whol•ly** (completely)
hol•o•caust
holocost : **hol•o•caust**
ho•ly (sacred); **hol•ly** (tree); **whol•ly** (completely)
holyness : **ho•li•ness**
homacidal : **ho•mi•cid•al**
homacide : **ho•mi•cide**
homadge : **hom•age**
hom•age
homage : **hom•age**
homagenious : **ho•mo•ge•neous**
homaly : **hom•i•ly**
homasidal : **ho•mi•cid•al**
homaside : **ho•mi•cide**
homasidel : **ho•mi•cid•al**

homege : **hom•age**
home•ly (plain); **hom•i•ly**
  (sermon)
homesidal : **ho•mi•cid•al**
homeside : **ho•mi•cide**
home•stead
homested : **home•stead**
ho•mi•cid•al
ho•mi•cide
homidge : **hom•age**
homige : **hom•age**
hom•i•ly (sermon); **home•ly**
  (plain)
hommage : **hom•age**
hommige : **hom•age**
hommily : **hom•i•ly**
hommonim : **hom•onym**
hommonym : **hom•onym**
homocidal : **ho•mi•cid•al**
homocide : **hom•i•cide**
ho•mo•ge•neous *or*
  ho•mog•e•nous
homogenious : **ho•mo•ge•neous**
homogenius : **ho•mo•ge•neous**
ho•mog•e•nize
ho•mog•e•nous *or*
  ho•mo•ge•neous
homogonize : **ho•mog•e•nize**
homonim : **hom•onym**
hom•onym
homosidal : **ho•mi•cid•al**
homoside : **ho•mi•cide**
homosidel : **ho•mi•cid•al**
Honalulu : **Ho•no•lu•lu**
honarary : **hon•or•ary**
honasty : **hon•es•ty**
Honelulu : **Ho•no•lu•lu**
honer : **hon•or**
honerary : **hon•or•ary**
hon•est
hon•esty
hon•ey

honie : **hon•ey**
honist : **hon•est**
Honnelulu : **Ho•no•lu•lu**
honnest : **hon•est**
honnesty : **hon•es•ty**
honney : **hon•ey**
honnist : **hon•est**
Honnolulu : **Ho•no•lu•lu**
honnor : **hon•or**
honnorable : **hon•or•able**
honnorary : **hon•or•ary**
Ho•no•lu•lu
hon•or
hon•or•able
hon•or•ary
honorery : **hon•or•ary**
honorible : **hon•or•able**
hoodlam : **hood•lum**
hoodlem : **hood•lum**
hoodlim : **hood•lum**
hood•lum
hoolagan : **hoo•li•gan**
hoolegan : **hoo•li•gan**
hoo•li•gan
horascope : **horo•scope**
horde (multitude); **hoard**
  (cache)
horey : **hoary**
horible : **hor•ri•ble**
horify : **hor•ri•fy**
horizen : **ho•ri•zon**
ho•ri•zon
horizun : **ho•ri•zon**
hormoan : **hor•mone**
hor•mone
hor•net
hornit : **hor•net**
hornut : **hor•net**
horo•scope
horrable : **hor•ri•ble**
horrafy : **hor•ri•fy**
horreble : **hor•ri•ble**

horred : **hor·rid**
horrefy : **hor·ri·fy**
horribal : **hor·ri·ble**
hor·ri·ble
hor·rid
hor·ri·fy
horrizon : **ho·ri·zon**
horroscope : **horo·scope**
horry : **hoary**
horse (animal); **hoarse**
   (rough-voiced)
hortaculture : **hor·ti·cul·ture**
horteculture : **hor·ti·cul·ture**
hor·ti·cul·ture
hosary : **ho·siery**
hoserry : **ho·siery**
hosery : **ho·siery**
ho·siery
hospece : **hos·pice**
hospetal : **hos·pi·tal**
hos·pice
hospise : **hos·pice**
hos·pi·ta·ble
hos·pi·tal
hospiteble : **hos·pi·ta·ble**
hospitibal : **hos·pi·ta·ble**
hospitible : **hos·pi·ta·ble**
hospitle : **hos·pi·tal**
hospittable : **hos·pi·ta·ble**
hospittal : **hos·pi·tal**
hospittle : **hos·pi·tal**
hos·tage
hostege : **hos·tage**
hos·tel (lodging house);
   hos·tile (antagonistic)
hostes : **host·ess**
host·ess
hostige : **hos·tage**
hostil : **hos·tel** (lodging house)
   or **hos·tile** (antagonistic)
hos·tile (antagonistic); **hos·tel**
   (lodging house)

hostilety : **hos·til·i·ty**
hostilitty : **hos·til·i·ty**
hos·til·i·ty
hostill : **hos·tel** (lodging house)
   or **hos·tile** (antagonistic)
hostillity : **hos·til·i·ty**
hostiss : **host·ess**
houghty : **haugh·ty**
hour (60 minutes); **our**
   (belonging to us)
Housten : **Hous·ton**
Hous·ton
hoval : **hov·el**
hov·el
hovil : **hov·el**
hovvel : **hov·el**
huligan : **hoo·li·gan**
humain : **hu·mane**
hu·man (human being);
   hu·mane (compassionate)
hu·mane (compassionate);
   hu·man (human being)
humanety : **hu·man·i·ty**
humanitty : **hu·man·i·ty**
hu·man·i·ty
humannity : **hu·man·i·ty**
humed : **hu·mid**
humer : **hu·mor**
humerous : **hu·mer·us** (arm
   bone) *or* **hu·mor·ous** (funny)
hu·mer·us (arm bone);
   hu·mor·ous (funny)
humess : **hu·mus**
hu·mid
humiddity : **hu·mid·i·ty**
humidefy : **hu·mid·i·fy**
humidetty : **hu·mid·i·ty**
humidety : **hu·mid·i·ty**
humidiffy : **hu·mid·i·fy**
hu·mid·i·fy
humiditty : **hu·mid·i·ty**
hu·mid·i·ty

humileate : **hu•mil•i•ate**
humilety : **hu•mil•i•ty**
hu•mil•i•ate
humilitty : **hu•mil•i•ty**
hu•mil•i•ty
humilliate : **hu•mil•i•ate**
humillity : **hu•mil•i•ty**
humis : **hu•mus**
hummid : **hu•mid**
hummidify : **hu•mid•i•fy**
hummor : **hu•mor**
hu•mor
hu•mor•ous (funny);
  hu•mer•us (arm bone)
humorus : **hu•mer•us** (arm
  bone) *or* **hu•mor•ous** (funny)
humous : **hu•mus**
hu•mus
Hun•ga•ry (nation); **hun•gry**
  (having hunger)
hungery : **Hun•ga•ry** (nation)
  or **hun•gry** (having hunger)
hun•gry (having hunger);
  Hun•ga•ry (nation)
hunta : **jun•ta**
hurdel : **hur•dle** (to leap a
  barrier) *or* **hur•tle** (to dash)
hurdil : **hur•dle** (to leap a
  barrier) *or* **hur•tle** (to dash)
hurdill : **hur•dle** (to leap a
  barrier) *or* **hur•tle** (to dash)
hur•dle (to leap a barrier);
  hur•tle (to dash)
hurecane : **hur•ri•cane**
huricane : **hur•ri•cane**
hurracane : **hur•ri•cane**
hurrecane : **hur•ri•cane**
hurricain : **hur•ri•cane**
hur•ri•cane
hur•tle (to dash); **hur•dle** (to
  leap a barrier)
hus•band

husbandery : **hus•band•ry**
hus•band•ry
husbend : **hus•band**
husbendry : **hus•band•ry**
husbind : **hus•band**
husbindry : **hus•band•ry**
hussband : **hus•band**
hussel : **hus•tle**
hussle : **hus•tle**
husstle : **hus•tle**
Husston : **Hous•ton**
hustal : **hus•tle**
hustel : **hus•tle**
hus•tle
Huston : **Hous•ton**
hy•a•cinth
hyatus : **hi•a•tus**
hybred : **hy•brid**
hy•brid
hydragen : **hy•dro•gen**
hydrallic : **hy•drau•lic**
hy•drant
hydraulec : **hy•drau•lic**
hy•drau•lic
hydraulick : **hy•drau•lic**
hydrawlic : **hy•drau•lic**
hydregen : **hy•dro•gen**
hydrent : **hy•drant**
hydrigen : **hy•dro•gen**
hydrint : **hy•drant**
hy•dro•gen
hydrojen : **hy•dro•gen**
hydrojin : **hy•dro•gen**
hydrollic : **hy•drau•lic**
hyeana : **hy•e•na**
hyeena : **hy•e•na**
hy•e•na
hyfen : **hy•phen**
hyfin : **hy•phen**
hygeine : **hy•giene**
hygene : **hy•giene**
hy•giene

hyicinth : **hy•a•cinth**
hyina : **hy•e•na**
hymn (song); **him** (that man)
hym•nal
hymnel : **hym•nal**
hymnul : **hym•nal**
hypacrite : **hyp•o•crite**
hypedermic : **hy•po•der•mic**
hy•per•bo•la (curved line);
  hy•per•bo•le (exaggeration)
hy•per•bo•le (exaggeration);
  hy•per•bo•la (curved line)
hy•phen
hyphin : **hy•phen**
hypnetism : **hyp•no•tism**
hypnitism : **hyp•no•tism**
hypnoasis : **hyp•no•sis**
hyp•no•sis
hyp•no•tism
hypockrisy : **hy•poc•ri•sy**
hypocracy : **hy•poc•ri•sy**
hypocrassy : **hy•poc•ri•sy**
hypocrasy : **hy•poc•ri•sy**

hypocresy : **hy•poc•ri•sy**
hypocrete : **hyp•o•crite**
hypocricy : **hy•poc•ri•sy**
hy•poc•ri•sy
hypocrit : **hyp•o•crite**
hyp•o•crite
hy•po•der•mic
hypodermick : **hy•po•der•mic**
hypodirmic : **hy•po•der•mic**
hypothasis : **hy•poth•e•sis**
hy•poth•e•ses (*plur.*);
  hy•poth•e•sis (*sing.*)
hy•poth•e•sis (*sing.*);
  hy•poth•e•ses (*plur.*)
hystaria : **hys•te•ria**
hystarical : **hys•ter•i•cal**
hysterea : **hys•te•ria**
hys•te•ria
hys•ter•i•cal
hystericle : **hys•ter•i•cal**
hysterikal : **hys•ter•i•cal**
hysterria : **hys•te•ria**

I

iadine : **io·dine**
Iawa : **Io·wa**
icecle : **ici·cle**
icecycle : **ici·cle**
icical : **ici·cle**
ici·cle
ic·ing
icon *or* **ikon**
iconaclast : **icon·o·clast**
iconiclast : **icon·o·clast**
iconnoclast : **icon·o·clast**
icon·o·clast
iconoklast : **icon·o·clast**
icycle : **ici·cle**
Ida·ho
iddiocy : **id·i·o·cy**
iddiom : **id·i·om**
iddiosyncrasy : **id·io·syn·cra·sy**
iddiot : **id·i·ot**
ide·al
idealise (*Brit.*) : **ide·al·ize**
idealogy : **ide·ol·o·gy**
ideel : **ide·al**
ideelize : **ide·al·ize**
Ideho : **Ida·ho**
idele : **ide·al**
idelize : **ide·al·ize**
ideloigy : **ide·ol·o·gy**
identacal : **iden·ti·cal**
identecal : **iden·ti·cal**
identety : **iden·ti·ty**
iden·ti·cal
identicle : **iden·ti·cal**
identidy : **iden·ti·ty**
identikal : **iden·ti·cal**
identikle : **iden·ti·cal**
identitty : **iden·ti·ty**
iden·ti·ty
ideocy : **id·i·o·cy**
ideolijy : **ide·ol·o·gy**

ideollogy : **ide·ol·o·gy**
ide·ol·o·gy
ideom : **id·i·om**
ideosyncrasy : **id·io·syn·cra·sy**
idiacy : **id·i·o·cy**
idiam : **id·i·om**
idiasy : **id·i·o·cy**
idiasyncrasy : **id·io·syn·cra·sy**
idiel : **ide·al**
idielize : **ide·al·ize**
Idiho : **Ida·ho**
idine : **io·dine**
id·i·o·cy
idiology : **ide·ol·o·gy**
id·i·om
idiosincrasy : **id·io·syn·cra·sy**
idiosincresy : **id·io·syn·cra·sy**
idiosy : **id·i·o·cy**
idiosyncrassy : **id·io·syn·cra·sy**
id·io·syn·cra·sy
idiosyncrissy : **id·io·syn·cra·sy**
id·i·ot
idium : **id·i·om**
idle (inactive); **idol** (image);
   idyll (pastoral)
idol (image); **idle** (inactive);
   idyll (pastoral)
idol·a·ter
idolator : **idol·a·ter**
idoliter : **idol·a·ter**
idyl *or* **idyll** (pastoral); **idle**
   (inactive); **idol** (image)
idyll *or* **idyl** (pastoral); **idle**
   (inactive); **idol** (image)
Ifel : **Eif·fel**
iffete : **ef·fete**
Iffle : **Eif·fel**
ig·loo
iglu : **ig·loo**
ig·ne·ous

153

ignetion : **ig•ni•tion**
ignight : **ig•nite**
ignious : **ig•ne•ous**
ignishion : **ig•ni•tion**
ignission : **ig•ni•tion**
ig•nite
ignitian : **ig•ni•tion**
ig•ni•tion
ignittion : **ig•ni•tion**
ignius : **ig•ne•ous**
ignobal : **ig•no•ble**
ignobel : **ig•no•ble**
ig•no•ble
ignomenious : **ig•no•min•i•ous**
ignomineous : **ig•no•min•i•ous**
ig•no•min•i•ous
ignominius : **ig•no•min•i•ous**
ignominnious : **ig•no•min•i•ous**
ignoraimus : **ig•no•ra•mus**
ignorammis : **ig•no•ra•mus**
ignorammus : **ig•no•ra•mus**
ig•no•ra•mus
ig•no•rance
ignoranse : **ig•no•rance**
ignoremus : **ig•no•ra•mus**
ignorence : **ig•no•rance**
ignorense : **ig•no•rance**
igua•na
iguanna: igua•na
igwana : igua•na
ikon or **icon**
ikonoclast : **icon•o•clast**
iland : **is•land**
ilastic : **elas•tic**
ilectefy : **elec•tri•fy**
ilectracute : **elec•tro•cute**
ilectrafy : **elec•tri•fy**
ilectrecute : **elec•tro•cute**
ilectric : **elec•tric**
ilectricety : **elec•tric•i•ty**
ilectricion : **elec•tri•cian**
ilectricitty : **elec•tric•i•ty**

ilectricity : **elec•tric•i•ty**
ilectricute : **elec•tro•cute**
ilectrify : **elec•tri•fy**
ilectrision : **elec•tri•cian**
ilectrisity : **elec•tric•i•ty**
ilectrition : **elec•tri•cian**
ilectrocute : **elec•tro•cute**
ilectrokute : **elec•tro•cute**
ilegible : **el•i•gi•ble** (qualified)
 or **il•leg•i•ble** (unreadable)
ilektric : **elec•tric**
ilicit : **elic•it** (to draw out) or
 il•lic•it (unlawful)
ilickser : **elix•ir**
iliminate : **elim•i•nate**
Ilinois : **Il•li•nois**
iliterate : **il•lit•er•ate**
ilixer : **elix•ir**
ilixir : **elix•ir**
ilixor : **elix•ir**
Illanois : **Il•li•nois**
illastic : **elas•tic**
illastrate : **il•lus•trate**
illeagal : **il•le•gal**
illectrify : **elec•tri•fy**
illectrocute : **elec•tro•cute**
illeegal : **il•le•gal**
il•le•gal
illegeble : **el•i•gi•ble** (qualified)
 or **il•leg•i•ble** (unreadable)
illegel : **il•le•gal**
illegibal : **el•i•gi•ble** (qualified)
 or **il•leg•i•ble** (unreadable)
il•leg•i•ble (unreadable);
 el•i•gi•ble (qualified)
illegitemant : **il•le•git•i•mate**
illegitemate : **il•le•git•i•mate**
il•le•git•i•mate
illegitimet : **il•le•git•i•mate**
illegle : **il•le•gal**
illejitimate : **il•le•git•i•mate**
illestrate : **il•lus•trate**

il·lic·it (unlawful); elic·it (to draw out)

Il·li·nois

Illinoy : Il·li·nois

illistrate : il·lus·trate

il·lit·er·ate

illixir : elix·ir

illude : elude (to escape) or al·lude (to refer)

illumanate : il·lu·mi·nate

illumenate : il·lu·mi·nate

il·lu·mi·nate

Illunois : Il·li·nois

illusary : il·lu·so·ry

illusery : il·lu·so·ry

il·lu·sion (false idea or image); al·lu·sion (reference); elu·sion (evasion)

il·lu·sive (deceptive); al·lu·sive (making references); elu·sive (avoiding)

il·lu·so·ry

illusry : il·lu·so·ry

illustrait : il·lus·trate

il·lus·trate

iloapment : elope·ment

ilopement : elope·ment

ilopment : elope·ment

ilude : elude (to escape) or al·lude (to refer)

iluminate : il·lu·mi·nate

ilusion : al·lu·sion (reference) or elu·sion (evasion) or il·lu·sion (false idea or image)

ilusive : al·lu·sive (making references) or elu·sive (avoiding) or il·lu·sive (deceptive)

ilusory : il·lu·so·ry

imaculate : im·mac·u·late

imaculet : im·mac·u·late

imagary : im·ag·ery

im·age

imagenation : imag·i·na·tion

imagene : imag·ine

im·ag·ery

imagin : imag·ine

imag·i·na·tion

imagry : im·ag·ery

imancepate : eman·ci·pate

imancipate : eman·ci·pate

imanent : em·i·nent (famous) or im·ma·nent (dwelling within) or im·mi·nent (impending)

imansipate : eman·ci·pate

imarald : em·er·ald

imasarry : em·is·sary

imatate : im·i·tate

imbacile : im·be·cile

imbacy : em·bas·sy

imbalm : em·balm

imbam : em·balm

imbankment : em·bank·ment

imbargo : em·bar·go

imbark : em·bark

imbasey : em·bas·sy

imbassy : em·bas·sy

imbasy : em·bas·sy

im·be·cile

imbecill : im·be·cile

imbelish : em·bel·lish

imbellash : em·bel·lish

imbellesh : em·bel·lish

imbellish : em·bel·lish

imbesill : im·be·cile

imbezel : em·bez·zle

imbezle : em·bez·zle

imbezzal : em·bez·zle

imbezzel : em·bez·zle

imbezzle : em·bez·zle

im·bibe

imbicile : im·be·cile

imblam : **em·blem**
imblazen : **em·bla·zon**
imblazon : **em·bla·zon**
imblem : **em·blem**
imblim : **em·blem**
imblum : **em·blem**
imbodiment : **em·bod·i·ment**
imbodimint : **em·bod·i·ment**
imbodyment : **em·bod·i·ment**
imbom : **em·balm**
imbrace : **em·brace**
imbrase : **em·brace**
imbreo : **em·bryo**
imbrio : **em·bryo**
imbroidary : **em·broi·dery**
imbroiderry : **em·broi·dery**
imbroidery : **em·broi·dery**
imbryo : **em·bryo**
im·bue
imediate : **im·me·di·ate**
imege : **im·age**
imerald : **em·er·ald**
imeratus : **emer·i·tus**
imeritus : **emer·i·tus**
imerold : **em·er·ald**
imerritus : **emer·i·tus**
imesarry : **em·is·sary**
imige : **im·age**
imigery : **im·ag·ery**
iminent : **em·i·nent** (famous) *or*
　im·ma·nent (dwelling within)
　or **im·mi·nent** (impending)
imisary : **em·is·sary**
imissary : **em·is·sary**
im·i·tate
imity : **en·mi·ty**
im·mac·u·late
immaculet : **im·mac·u·late**
immage : **im·age**
immagery : **im·ag·ery**
immagination : **imag·i·na·tion**
immakulate : **im·mac·u·late**

immancipate : **eman·ci·pate**
im·ma·nent (dwelling within);
　em·i·nent (famous);
　im·mi·nent (impending)
immeadiate : **im·me·di·ate**
immedeate : **im·me·di·ate**
im·me·di·ate
immediet : **im·me·di·ate**
immeediate : **im·me·di·ate**
immerald : **em·er·ald**
im·mi·grant (one coming in);
　em·i·grant (one leaving)
im·mi·nent (impending);
　em·i·nent (famous);
　im·ma·nent (dwelling within)
immissary : **em·is·sary**
immitate : **im·i·tate**
immity : **en·mi·ty**
im·mor·al
immorel : **im·mor·al**
im·mor·tal
immortel : **im·mor·tal**
im·mov·able
immovibal : **im·mov·able**
immovible : **im·mov·able**
im·mune
imoral : **im·mor·al**
imorald : **em·er·ald**
imortal : **im·mor·tal**
imovable : **im·mov·able**
impacient : **im·pa·tient**
impail : **im·pale**
im·pair
impairious : **im·pe·ri·ous**
impairitive : **im·per·a·tive**
impaitient : **im·pa·tient**
im·pale
im·pal·pa·ble
impalpeble : **im·pal·pa·ble**
impalpibal : **im·pal·pa·ble**
impalpible : **im·pal·pa·ble**
imparative : **im·per·a·tive**

imparcial : **im·par·tial**
impare : **im·pair**
imparil : **im·per·il**
imparious : **im·pe·ri·ous**
imparshial : **im·par·tial**
im·part
im·par·tial
impashient : **im·pa·tient**
impashioned : **im·pas·sioned**
impass : **im·passe**
im·passe
im·pas·sioned
impatiant : **im·pa·tient**
im·pa·tient
impatus : **im·pe·tus**
im·peach
impead : **im·pede**
impearian : **em·py·re·an**
impecable : **im·pec·ca·ble**
im·pec·ca·ble
impeccibal : **im·pec·ca·ble**
impeccible : **im·pec·ca·ble**
impeckable : **im·pec·ca·ble**
impeckible : **im·pec·ca·ble**
impeddament : **im·ped·i·ment**
impeddement : **im·ped·i·ment**
impeddiment : **im·ped·i·ment**
im·pede
impedimant : **im·ped·i·ment**
im·ped·i·ment
impeech : **im·peach**
impeerial : **im·pe·ri·al**
impeid : **im·pede**
impeirial : **im·pe·ri·al**
impenatent : **im·pen·i·tent**
impenitant : **im·pen·i·tent**
im·pen·i·tent
im·per·a·tive
impereal : **im·pe·ri·al**
imperel : **im·per·il**
im·pe·ri·al
im·per·il

imperill : **im·per·il**
im·pe·ri·ous
imperitive : **im·per·a·tive**
imperril : **im·per·il**
impertenent : **im·per·ti·nent**
impertinant : **im·per·ti·nent**
im·per·ti·nent
imperveous : **im·per·vi·ous**
im·per·vi·ous
impervius : **im·per·vi·ous**
impetis : **im·pe·tus**
impettis : **im·pe·tus**
im·pe·tus
imphisema : **em·phy·se·ma**
imphisima : **em·phy·se·ma**
imphyseama : **em·phy·se·ma**
imphysema : **em·phy·se·ma**
imphysima : **em·phy·se·ma**
impiatty : **im·pi·e·ty**
impier : **em·pire**
impierian : **em·py·re·an**
impietty : **im·pi·e·ty**
im·pi·e·ty
impinitent : **im·pen·i·tent**
impire : **em·pire**
impirian : **em·py·re·an**
impitus : **im·pe·tus**
implament : **im·ple·ment**
im·plant
im·ple·ment
impliment : **im·ple·ment**
imporeum : **em·po·ri·um**
imporiam : **em·po·ri·um**
imporium : **em·po·ri·um**
im·por·tant
importent : **im·por·tant**
im·pos·ter or **im·pos·tor**
im·pos·tor or **im·pos·ter**
impotance : **im·po·tence**
im·po·tence
impotense : **im·po·tence**
impouarium : **em·po·ri·um**

impoureum : **em•po•ri•um**
impoveresh : **im•pov•er•ish**
im•pov•er•ish
impovrish : **im•pov•er•ish**
impracate : **im•pre•cate**
impractacle : **im•prac•ti•cal**
impractecle : **im•prac•ti•cal**
im•prac•ti•cal
impracticle : **im•prac•ti•cal**
impravise : **im•pro•vise**
im•pre•cate
impreshion : **im•pres•sion**
impresion : **im•pres•sion**
impressian : **im•pres•sion**
im•pres•sion
impricate : **im•pre•cate**
imprisen : **im•pris•on**
im•pris•on
imprisson : **im•pris•on**
imprivise : **im•pro•vise**
imprizen : **im•pris•on**
imprizon : **im•pris•on**
impromptoo : **im•promp•tu**
im•promp•tu
impromptue : **im•promp•tu**
impromtu : **im•promp•tu**
im•pro•vise
improvize : **im•pro•vise**
im•pugn
impune : **im•pugn**
impunety : **im•pu•ni•ty**
impunitty : **im•pu•ni•ty**
im•pu•ni•ty
impurvious : **im•per•vi•ous**
impyre : **em•pire**
impyrean : **em•py•re•an**
inagurate : **in•au•gu•rate**
inain : **inane**
inamerd : **en•am•ored**
inamered : **en•am•ored**
inammored : **en•am•ored**
inamored : **en•am•ored**

inamoured : **en•am•ored**
inamy : **en•e•my**
inane
in•apt (not apt); **in•ept**
   (unskilled)
inargy : **en•er•gy**
inate : **in•nate**
inaugarate : **in•au•gu•rate**
inaugerate : **in•au•gu•rate**
inaugurait : **in•au•gu•rate**
in•au•gu•rate
inawgurate : **in•au•gu•rate**
inbalm : **en•balm**
inbankment : **em•bank•ment**
inbargo : **em•bar•go**
inbark : **em•bark**
inbassy : **em•bas•sy**
inbelish : **em•bel•lish**
inbellish : **em•bel•lish**
inbezzle : **em•bez•zle**
inbibe : **im•bibe**
inblazon : **em•bla•zon**
inblem : **em•blem**
inbodiment : **em•bodi•ment**
inbrace : **em•brace**
inbroidery : **em•broi•dery**
inbryo : **em•bryo**
incandecent : **in•can•des•cent**
incandescant : **in•can•des•cent**
in•can•des•cent
incandessent : **in•can•des•cent**
incapabal : **in•ca•pa•ble**
in•ca•pa•ble
incapeble : **in•ca•pa•ble**
incapibal : **in•ca•pa•ble**
incapible : **in•ca•pa•ble**
in•car•cer•ate
incarcirate : **in•car•cer•ate**
incarserate : **in•car•cer•ate**
in•cen•di•ary
incendierry : **in•cen•di•ary**
incendiery : **in•cen•di•ary**

incenerate : **in•cin•er•ate**
incercle : **en•cir•cle**
incert : **in•sert**
incesant : **in•ces•sant**
in•ces•sant
incessent : **in•ces•sant**
incessint : **in•ces•sant**
in•cest
inciclopedia : **en•cy•clo•pe•dia**
in•ci•dent
incinarate : **in•cin•er•ate**
in•cin•er•ate
incinnerate : **in•cin•er•ate**
incinuate : **in•sin•u•ate**
incipiant : **in•cip•i•ent**
in•cip•i•ent
incippient : **in•cip•i•ent**
incircel : **en•cir•cle**
incircle : **en•cir•cle**
incirkal : **en•cir•cle**
incirkle : **en•cir•cle**
inciser : **in•ci•sor**
in•ci•sion
in•ci•sor
incission : **in•ci•sion**
in•cite (to urge on); **in•sight**
  (discernment)
incizion : **in•ci•sion**
incizor : **in•ci•sor**
inclament : **in•cle•ment**
inclemant : **in•cle•ment**
in•cle•ment
incliment : **in•cle•ment**
incohairent : **in•co•her•ent**
incoharent : **in•co•her•ent**
incoherant : **in•co•her•ent**
in•co•her•ent
incredable : **in•cred•i•ble**
in•cred•i•ble
incumbrance : **en•cum•brance**
incumbranse : **en•cum•brance**
incumbrence : **en•cum•brance**

incumbrince : **en•cum•brance**
incyclapedia : **en•cy•clo•pe•dia**
incyclepedia : **en•cy•clo•pe•dia**
incyclipedia : **en•cy•clo•pe•dia**
incyclopeadia : **en•cy•clo•pe•dia**
incyclopedea : **en•cy•clo•pe•dia**
incyclopedia : **en•cy•clo•pe•dia**
incyclopeedia : **en•cy•clo•pe•dia**
indago : **in•di•go**
indalent : **in•do•lent**
indavidual : **in•di•vid•u•al**
Indeana : **In•di•ana**
indeaver : **en•deav•or**
indeavor : **en•deav•or**
indegent : **in•di•gent**
indego : **in•di•go**
indelable : **in•del•i•ble**
indeleble : **in•del•i•ble**
indelent : **in•do•lent**
in•del•i•ble
indellible : **in•del•i•ble**
independance : **in•de•pen•dence**
independanse : **in•de•pen•dence**
in•de•pen•dence
independense : **in•de•pen•dence**
indepindence : **in•de•pen•dence**
indevidual : **in•di•vid•u•al**
indevor : **en•deav•or**
indevvor : **en•deav•or**
in•dex
in•dex•es or **in•di•ces**
In•di•ana
Indianaplis : **In•di•a•nap•o•lis**
In•di•a•nap•o•lis
Indianappolis :
  In•di•a•nap•o•lis
Indianna : **In•di•ana**
Indiannapolis :
  In•di•a•nap•o•lis
in•di•ces or **in•dex•es**
in•dict (to charge with a
  crime); **in•dite** (to write)

in·dict·ment
in·di·gent
indiggo : **in·di·go**
indigint : **in·di·gent**
in·dig·nant
indignate : **in·dig·nant**
indignent : **in·dig·nant**
indignety : **in·dig·ni·ty**
indignint : **in·dig·nant**
indignitty : **in·dig·ni·ty**
in·dig·ni·ty
in·di·go
in·dis·pens·able
indispensible : **in·dis·pens·able**
in·dite (to write); **in·dict** (to charge with a crime)
inditement : **in·dict·ment**
inditment : **in·dict·ment**
in·di·vid·u·al
individuel : **in·di·vid·u·al**
individule : **in·di·vid·u·al**
indivvidual : **in·di·vid·u·al**
indolant : **in·do·lent**
in·do·lent
indolint : **in·do·lent**
indomatable : **in·dom·i·ta·ble**
indometable : **in·dom·i·ta·ble**
in·dom·i·ta·ble
indomitibal : **in·dom·i·ta·ble**
indomitible : **in·dom·i·ta·ble**
indommitable : **in·dom·i·ta·ble**
indoument : **en·dow·ment**
indowmate : **en·dow·ment**
indowmeant : **en·dow·ment**
indowment : **en·dow·ment**
indowmint : **en·dow·ment**
in·dulge
indurance : **en·dur·ance**
induranse : **en·dur·ance**
indurence : **en·dur·ance**
indurrance : **en·dur·ance**
indurrence : **en·dur·ance**

industreal : **in·dus·tri·al**
in·dus·tri·al
industriel : **in·dus·tri·al**
ineabriate : **ine·bri·ate**
inebreate : **ine·bri·ate**
ine·bri·ate
inecksorable : **in·ex·o·ra·ble**
inedable : **in·ed·i·ble**
ineddible : **in·ed·i·ble**
inedeble : **in·ed·i·ble**
inedibal : **in·ed·i·ble**
in·ed·i·ble
inefable : **in·ef·fa·ble**
in·ef·fa·ble
ineffeble : **in·ef·fa·ble**
ineffibal : **in·ef·fa·ble**
ineffible : **in·ef·fa·ble**
inemmy : **en·e·my**
inemy : **en·e·my**
in·ept (unskilled); **in·apt** (not apt)
inercia : **in·er·tia**
inergy : **en·er·gy**
inerjy : **en·er·gy**
inerrgy : **en·er·gy**
inershia : **in·er·tia**
in·ert
inertea : **in·er·tia**
in·er·tia
inetible : **in·ed·i·ble**
inettible : **in·ed·i·ble**
inevatable : **in·ev·i·ta·ble**
in·ev·i·ta·ble
ineviteble : **in·ev·i·ta·ble**
inevitibal : **in·ev·i·ta·ble**
inevitible : **in·ev·i·ta·ble**
inexerable : **in·ex·o·ra·ble**
in·ex·o·ra·ble
inexorible : **in·ex·o·ra·ble**
infadel : **in·fi·del**
infalible : **in·fal·li·ble**
infallable : **in·fal·li·ble**

infalleble : **in·fal·li·ble**
infallibal : **in·fal·li·ble**
in·fal·li·ble
infammous : **in·fa·mous**
infammus : **in·fa·mous**
in·fa·mous
infamus : **in·fa·mous**
in·fan·cy
infansy : **in·fan·cy**
infantary : **in·fan·try**
infantcy : **in·fan·cy**
infantery : **in·fan·try**
in·fan·try
infantsy : **in·fan·cy**
infattuate : **in·fat·u·ate**
in·fat·u·ate
infeable : **en·fee·ble**
infearior : **in·fe·ri·or**
infechion : **in·fec·tion**
infectian : **in·fec·tion**
in·fec·tion
infedel : **in·fi·del**
infeebal : **en·fee·ble**
infeeble : **en·fee·ble**
infeerior : **in·fe·ri·or**
infeible : **en·fee·ble**
infemous : **in·fa·mous**
infency : **in·fan·cy**
infensy : **in·fan·cy**
infentry : **in·fan·try**
infereor : **in·fe·ri·or**
inferier : **in·fe·ri·or**
in·fe·ri·or
infermary : **in·fir·ma·ry**
infermity : **in·fir·mi·ty**
in·fer·nal
infernel : **in·fer·nal**
in·fer·no
infexion : **in·fec·tion**
in·fi·del
infidelety : **in·fi·del·i·ty**
infidelitty : **in·fi·del·i·ty**

in·fi·del·i·ty
infidell : **in·fi·del**
infidellity : **in·fi·del·i·ty**
infinate : **in·fi·nite**
infincy : **in·fan·cy**
infinet : **in·fi·nite**
infinete : **in·fi·nite**
infinety : **in·fin·i·ty**
in·fi·nite
in·fin·i·ty
infinnite : **in·fi·nite**
infinnity : **in·fin·i·ty**
infinsy : **in·fan·cy**
infintry : **in·fan·try**
in·fir·ma·ry
infirmery : **in·fir·ma·ry**
infirmety : **in·fir·mi·ty**
infirmitty : **in·fir·mi·ty**
in·fir·mi·ty
infirmry : **in·fir·ma·ry**
infirory : **in·fir·ma·ry**
inflaimable : **in·flam·ma·ble**
inflamable : **in·flam·ma·ble**
inflamatory : **in·flam·ma·to·ry**
inflameble : **in·flam·ma·ble**
inflametory : **in·flam·ma·to·ry**
in·flam·ma·ble
inflammatorry :
   in·flam·ma·to·ry
in·flam·ma·to·ry
inflammetory :
   in·flam·ma·to·ry
inflammibal : **in·flam·ma·ble**
inflammible : **in·flam·ma·ble**
inflammitory :
   in·flam·ma·to·ry
inflecksible : **in·flex·i·ble**
inflexable : **in·flex·i·ble**
inflexeble : **in·flex·i·ble**
inflexibal : **in·flex·i·ble**
in·flex·i·ble
inflooence : **in·flu·ence**

influance : **in•flu•ence**
influanse : **in•flu•ence**
in•flu•ence
influense : **in•flu•ence**
infureate : **in•fu•ri•ate**
in•fu•ri•ate
infurnal : **in•fer•nal**
infurno : **in•fer•no**
infurriate : **in•fu•ri•ate**
ingagement : **en•gage•ment**
ingagment : **en•gage•ment**
ingat : **in•got**
ingeanious : **in•ge•nious**
ingeenious : **in•ge•nious**
ingeneer : **en•gi•neer**
ingeneous : **in•ge•nious**
ingenew : **in•ge•nue**
in•ge•nious (intelligent);
   in•gen•u•ous (simple-minded)
ingenius : **in•ge•nious**
ingenoo : **in•ge•nue**
in•ge•nue
in•gen•u•ous (simple-minded);
   in•ge•nious (intelligent)
in•gest
inget : **in•got**
ingineer : **en•gi•neer**
inginier : **en•gi•neer**
inginue : **in•ge•nue**
ingloreous : **in•glo•ri•ous**
in•glo•ri•ous
inglorius : **in•glo•ri•ous**
Inglund : **En•gland**
in•got
ingott : **in•got**
ingreadient : **in•gre•di•ent**
ingredeant : **in•gre•di•ent**
ingrediant : **in•gre•di•ent**
in•gre•di•ent
ingreedient : **in•gre•di•ent**
ingridient : **in•gre•di•ent**
ingure : **in•jure**

inhabbet : **in•hab•it**
inhabbit : **in•hab•it**
inhabet : **in•hab•it**
in•hab•it
inhail : **in•hale**
in•hale
inhancement : **en•hance•ment**
inhancemint : **en•hance•ment**
inhansement : **en•hance•ment**
inharent : **in•her•ent**
inharit : **in•her•it**
inharitance : **in•her•i•tance**
inharrit : **in•her•it**
inharritance : **in•her•i•tance**
inhear : **in•here**
inhearent : **in•her•ent**
inherant : **in•her•ent**
in•here
in•her•ent
inheret : **in•her•it**
inheretance : **in•her•i•tance**
inherint : **in•her•ent**
in•her•it
in•her•i•tance
inheritanse : **in•her•i•tance**
inheritence : **in•her•i•tance**
inheritense : **in•her•i•tance**
inherrit : **in•her•it**
inherritance : **in•her•i•tance**
inhibbet : **in•hib•it**
inhibbit : **in•hib•it**
inhibet : **in•hib•it**
in•hib•it
inhirent : **in•her•ent**
inibit : **in•hib•it**
inicial : **ini•tial**
iniciate : **ini•tiate**
iniggma : **enig•ma**
inigma : **enig•ma**
inimacal : **in•im•i•cal**
inimecal : **in•im•i•cal**
in•im•i•cal

inimicle : **in•im•i•cal**
inimikal : **in•im•i•cal**
inimmical : **in•im•i•cal**
inimy : **en•e•my**
inindate : **in•un•date**
iniqiety : **in•iq•ui•ty**
iniquitty : **in•iq•ui•ty**
in•iq•ui•ty
inishall : **ini•tial**
inishiate : **ini•tiate**
initeate : **ini•tiate**
ini•tial
ini•tiate
injere : **in•jure**
injery : **in•ju•ry**
injest : **in•gest**
injineer : **en•gi•neer**
injur : **in•jure**
in•jure
injurry : **in•ju•ry**
in•ju•ry
inmaty : **en•mi•ty**
inmety : **en•mi•ty**
inmitty : **en•mi•ty**
inmity : **en•mi•ty**
innacence : **in•no•cence**
innait : **in•nate**
innamored : **enam•ored**
in•nate
innavate : **in•no•vate**
innemy : **en•e•my**
innert : **in•ert**
innervene : **in•ter•vene**
innerview : **in•ter•view**
innigma : **enig•ma**
innitial : **ini•tial**
innitiate : **ini•tiate**
innivate : **in•no•vate**
in•no•cence
innocense : **in•no•cence**
innocince : **in•no•cence**
innocinse : **in•no•cence**

innovait : **in•no•vate**
in•no•vate
in•nu•en•do
innuindo: **in•nu•en•do**
in•nu•mer•a•ble
innumerible : **in•nu•mer•a•ble**
innumirable : **in•nu•mer•a•ble**
inocence : **in•no•cence**
inovate : **in•no•vate**
inphysema : **em•phy•se•ma**
inpire : **em•pire**
inporium : **em•po•ri•um**
inquisator : **in•quis•i•tor**
inquisiter : **in•quis•i•tor**
in•quis•i•tor
inquissitor : **in•quis•i•tor**
inquizitor : **in•quis•i•tor**
in•road
inrode : **in•road**
insain : **in•sane**
in•sane
in•scru•ta•ble
inscruteble : **in•scru•ta•ble**
inscrutibal : **in•scru•ta•ble**
inscrutible : **in•scru•ta•ble**
inseart : **in•sert**
insectacide : **in•sec•ti•cide**
in•sec•ti•cide
insectiside : **in•sec•ti•cide**
insendiary : **in•cen•di•ary**
insenerate : **in•cin•er•ate**
insenuate : **in•sin•u•ate**
insergent : **in•sur•gent**
in•sert
insessant : **in•ces•sant**
insessent : **in•ces•sant**
insest : **in•cest**
inshurance : **in•sur•ance**
insiclopedia : **en•cy•clo•pe•dia**
insiddious : **in•sid•i•ous**
insident : **in•ci•dent**
insideous : **in•sid•i•ous**

in·sid·i·ous
insidius : **in·sid·i·ous**
in·sight (discernment); **in·cite**
  (to urge on)
insign : **en·sign**
insinarate : **in·cin·er·ate**
insine : **en·sign**
insinerate : **in·cin·er·ate**
insinnuate : **in·sin·u·ate**
in·sin·u·ate
insiped : **in·sip·id**
insipiant : **in·cip·i·ent**
in·sip·id
insipient : **in·cip·i·ent**
insippid : **in·sip·id**
insippient : **in·cip·i·ent**
insircle : **en·cir·cle**
insision : **in·ci·sion**
insisor : **in·ci·sor**
insistance : **in·sis·tence**
in·sis·tence
insistense : **in·sis·tence**
insizor : **in·ci·sor**
insoalence : **in·so·lence**
in·so·lence
insolense : **in·so·lence**
insollance : **in·so·lence**
insollence : **in·so·lence**
insolluble : **in·sol·u·ble**
insoluable : **in·sol·u·ble**
insolubal : **in·sol·u·ble**
in·sol·u·ble
insolvant : **in·sol·vent**
in·sol·vent
insomnea : **in·som·nia**
in·som·nia
insouceant : **in·sou·ci·ant**
in·sou·ci·ant
insoucient : **in·sou·ci·ant**
inspecter : **in·spec·tor**
in·spec·tor
instagate : **in·sti·gate**

in·stance
instanse : **in·stance**
instantaineous :
  in·stan·ta·neous
in·stan·ta·neous
instantanious : **in·stan·ta·neous**
instantanius : **in·stan·ta·neous**
instatute : **in·sti·tute**
in·stead
insted : **in·stead**
instegate : **in·sti·gate**
instence : **in·stance**
instetute : **in·sti·tute**
instigait : **in·sti·gate**
in·sti·gate
instil : **in·still**
in·still
in·sti·tute
instructer : **in·struc·tor**
in·struc·tor
insuciant : **in·sou·ci·ant**
in·su·lar
insulen : **in·su·lin**
insuler : **in·su·lar**
in·su·lin
insullin : **in·su·lin**
in·sur·ance
insuranse : **in·sur·ance**
insurence : **in·sur·ance**
insurense : **in·sur·ance**
in·sur·gent
insurgient : **in·sur·gent**
insyclopedia : **en·cy·clo·pe·dia**
intagrate : **in·te·grate**
intallect : **in·tel·lect**
intarogate : **in·ter·ro·gate**
intarrogate : **in·ter·ro·gate**
intarrupt : **in·ter·rupt**
intearior : **in·te·ri·or**
inteerior : **in·te·ri·or**
integrait : **in·te·grate**
in·te·grate

intelect : **in•tel•lect**
inteligent : **in•tel•li•gent**
intellagent : **in•tel•li•gent**
in•tel•lect
intellegent : **in•tel•li•gent**
in•tel•li•gent
intence : **in•tense**
in•tense
inteprise : **en•ter•prise**
interagate : **in•ter•ro•gate**
interance : **en•trance**
in•ter•cede
interceed : **in•ter•cede**
in•ter•cept
interduce : **in•tro•duce**
interem : **in•ter•im**
interence : **en•trance**
in•ter•est
interfear : **in•ter•fere**
interfearence : **in•ter•fer•ence**
interfeer : **in•ter•fere**
interfeerence : **in•ter•fer•ence**
interferance : **in•ter•fer•ence**
interferanse : **in•ter•fer•ence**
in•ter•fere
in•ter•fer•ence
interferense : **in•ter•fer•ence**
interier : **in•te•ri•or**
in•ter•im
in•te•ri•or
interist : **in•ter•est**
interogate : **in•ter•ro•gate**
interpratation :
   in•ter•pre•ta•tion
in•ter•pre•ta•tion
interprise : **en•ter•prise**
interpritation :
   in•ter•pre•ta•tion
interprize : **en•ter•prise**
interragate : **in•ter•ro•gate**
interrigate : **in•ter•ro•gate**
interrim : **in•ter•im**

interrogait : **in•ter•ro•gate**
in•ter•ro•gate
interrum : **in•ter•im**
in•ter•rupt
intersede : **in•ter•cede**
interseed : **in•ter•cede**
intersept : **in•ter•cept**
in•ter•state (between states);
   in•tra•state (within a state)
intertain : **en•ter•tain**
intertane : **en•ter•tain**
interum : **in•ter•im**
interupt : **in•ter•rupt**
in•ter•val
intervean : **in•ter•vene**
interveen : **in•ter•vene**
interveiw : **in•ter•view**
intervel : **in•ter•val**
in•ter•vene
intervenous : **in•tra•ve•nous**
in•ter•view
intervil : **in•ter•val**
intesten : **in•tes•tine**
intestin : **in•tes•tine**
in•tes•tine
intigrate : **in•te•grate**
intillect : **in•tel•lect**
in•ti•ma•cy
intimant : **in•ti•mate**
intimassy : **in•ti•ma•cy**
intimasy : **in•ti•ma•cy**
in•ti•mate
intiment : **in•ti•mate**
intimet : **in•ti•mate**
intimissy : **in•ti•ma•cy**
intimisy : **in•ti•ma•cy**
intimit : **in•ti•mate**
intimmacy : **in•ti•ma•cy**
intirval : **in•ter•val**
intiution : **in•tu•ition**
intocksicate : **in•tox•i•cate**
in•tol•er•a•ble

in·tol·er·ance
intoleranse : **in·tol·er·ance**
in·tol·er·ant
intolerence : **in·tol·er·ance**
intolerent : **in·tol·er·ant**
intolerible : **in·tol·er·a·ble**
intolirable : **in·tol·er·a·ble**
intollarent : **in·tol·er·ant**
intollerable : **in·tol·er·a·ble**
intollerance : **in·tol·er·ance**
intollerant : **in·tol·er·ant**
intoxacate : **in·tox·i·cate**
intoxecate : **in·tox·i·cate**
in·tox·i·cate
intracacy : **in·tri·ca·cy**
intracate : **in·tri·cate**
intraduce : **in·tro·duce**
intrance : **en·trance**
intrancigent : **in·tran·si·gent**
intransagent : **in·tran·si·gent**
intranse : **en·trance**
intransegent : **in·tran·si·gent**
in·tran·si·gent
in·tra·state (within a state);
   in·ter·state (between states)
intravainous : **in·tra·ve·nous**
intravanous : **in·tra·ve·nous**
intraveinous : **in·tra·ve·nous**
intravenious : **in·tra·ve·nous**
in·tra·ve·nous
intravienous : **in·tra·ve·nous**
intreague : **in·trigue**
intrecacy : **in·tri·ca·cy**
intreeg : **in·trigue**
intrence : **en·trance**
intrense : **en·trance**
intrensic : **in·trin·sic**
intreped : **in·trep·id**
in·trep·id
intreppid : **in·trep·id**
intrest : **in·ter·est**
intrevenous : **in·tra·ve·nous**

in·tri·ca·cy
intricait : **in·tri·cate**
intricassy : **in·tri·ca·cy**
intricasy : **in·tri·ca·cy**
intricat : **in·tri·cate**
in·tri·cate
intricet : **in·tri·cate**
intricisy : **in·tri·ca·cy**
in·trigue
intrince : **en·trance**
intrinse : **en·trance**
in·trin·sic
intrinsick : **in·trin·sic**
in·tro·duce
introduse : **in·tro·duce**
intrupt : **in·ter·rupt**
intuishion : **in·tu·ition**
intuission : **in·tu·ition**
in·tu·ition
inuendo : **in·nu·en·do**
inumerable : **in·nu·mer·a·ble**
inunciate : **enun·ci·ate**
in·un·date
in·vade
invaid : **in·vade**
invaigh : **in·veigh**
invaled : **in·va·lid** (sick or
   disabled) *or* **in·val·id** (not
   valid)
in·va·lid (sick or disabled);
   in·val·id (not valid)
invallid : **in·va·lid** (sick or
   disabled) *or* **in·val·id** (not
   valid)
invalope : **en·vel·op** (*verb*) *or*
   en·ve·lope (*noun*)
in·va·sion
invassion : **in·va·sion**
invation : **in·va·sion**
invay : **in·veigh**
invazion : **in·va·sion**
in·veigh

invelid : **in•va•lid** (sick or
disabled) *or* **in•val•id** (not
valid)
invellope : **en•vel•op** (*verb*) *or*
en•ve•lope (*noun*)
inveloap : **en•vel•op** (*verb*) *or*
en•ve•lope (*noun*)
invelop : **en•vel•op** (*verb*) *or*
en•ve•lope (*noun*)
invelope : **en•vel•op** (*verb*) *or*
en•ve•lope (*noun*)
invencible : **in•vin•ci•ble**
inventorry : **in•ven•to•ry**
in•ven•to•ry
inveous : **en•vi•ous**
investagate : **in•ves•ti•gate**
investegate : **in•ves•ti•gate**
investigait : **in•ves•ti•gate**
in•ves•ti•gate
invetarate : **in•vet•er•ate**
inveterat : **in•vet•er•ate**
in•vet•er•ate
inveteret : **in•vet•er•ate**
invetterate : **in•vet•er•ate**
invey : **in•veigh**
invialable : **in•vi•o•la•ble**
invialate : **in•vi•o•late**
inviernment : **en•vi•ron•ment**
invigarate : **in•vig•o•rate**
invigerate : **in•vig•o•rate**
inviggorate : **in•vig•o•rate**
in•vig•o•rate
invilable : **in•vi•o•la•ble**
invilate : **in•vi•o•late**
invilope : **en•vel•op** (*verb*) *or*
en•ve•lope (*noun*)
invinceble : **in•vin•ci•ble**
in•vin•ci•ble
invinsible : **in•vin•ci•ble**
invintory : **in•ven•to•ry**
in•vi•o•la•ble
in•vi•o•late

inviolible : **in•vi•o•la•ble**
inviornment : **en•vi•ron•ment**
invious : **en•vi•ous**
inviranment : **en•vi•ron•ment**
invirenment : **en•vi•ron•ment**
invirirnment : **en•vi•ron•ment**
invirnment : **en•vi•ron•ment**
invironment : **en•vi•ron•ment**
invisable : **in•vis•i•ble**
in•vis•i•ble
invissible : **in•vis•i•ble**
invius : **en•vi•ous**
invizible : **in•vis•i•ble**
invyous : **en•vi•ous**
io•dine
Io•wa
Ioway : **Io•wa**
iracible : **iras•ci•ble**
iragate : **ir•ri•gate**
irasceble : **iras•ci•ble**
iras•ci•ble
irassible : **iras•ci•ble**
iratate : **ir•ri•tate**
irelevant : **ir•rel•e•vant**
irevocable : **ir•re•vo•ca•ble**
irie : **ae•rie** (nest) *or* **ee•rie**
(weird) *or* **Erie** (lake and
canal)
irigate : **ir•ri•gate**
iritate : **ir•ri•tate**
irn : **earn** (to work to gain) *or*
urn (vase)
irragate : **ir•ri•gate**
ir•rel•e•vant
irrelevent : **ir•rel•e•vant**
irretate : **ir•ri•tate**
ir•re•vo•ca•ble
irrevokable : **ir•re•vo•ca•ble**
ir•ri•gate
ir•ri•tate
isalation : **iso•la•tion**
isicle : **ici•cle**

ising : **ic•ing**
is•land
ismis : **isth•mus**
ismiss : **isth•mus**
ismus : **isth•mus**
iso•la•tion
iso•mer
isomere : **iso•mer**
isoscelees : **isos•ce•les**
isos•ce•les
isoseles : **isos•ce•les**
isoselles : **isos•ce•les**
isosseles : **isos•ce•les**
iso•tope
Is•ra•el
Israle : **Is•ra•el**
Isreal : **Is•ra•el**
issotope : **iso•tope**
isthmas : **isth•mus**
isthmis : **isth•mus**
isthmiss : **isth•mus**
isth•mus
italacize : **ital•i•cize**
italasize : **ital•i•cize**
italecize : **ital•i•cize**
ital•ic

italicise : **ital•i•cize**
ital•i•cize
italick : **ital•ic**
italisize : **ital•i•cize**
itallic : **ital•ic**
itallicize : **ital•i•cize**
itemise : **item•ize**
item•ize
itenerant : **itin•er•ant**
itenerent : **itin•er•ant**
ither : **ei•ther** (one or the
    other) *or* **ether** (gas)
ithsmis : **isth•mus**
itimize : **item•ize**
itinarant : **itin•er•ant**
itin•er•ant
itinerent : **itin•er•ant**
itomize : **item•ize**
its (belonging to it); **it's** (it is)
it's (it is); **its** (belonging to it)
itumize : **item•ize**
ivary : **ivo•ry**
ivery : **ivo•ry**
ivesdropping : **eaves•drop•ping**
ivo•ry
ivvory : **ivo•ry**

J

jack•al
jackel : jack•al
jackle : jack•al
jagaur : jag•uar
jaged : jag•ged
jag•ged
jaggid : jag•ged
jag•uar
jaguarr : jag•uar
jaguire : jag•uar
jagwar : jag•uar
jagwer : jag•uar
jail
jail•er *or* jail•or
jail•or *or* jail•er
jale : jail
jaler : jail•er
jallopy : ja•lopy
jaloppe : ja•lopy
ja•lopy
Jamaca : Ja•mai•ca
Jamaeca : Ja•mai•ca
Ja•mai•ca
Jamaika : Ja•mai•ca
Jamayka : Ja•mai•ca
jambaree : jam•bo•ree
jambiree : jam•bo•ree
jam•bo•ree
jamborie : jam•bo•ree
jambory : jam•bo•ree
janator : jan•i•tor
janatorial : jan•i•to•ri•al
jandice : jaun•dice
janetor : jan•i•tor
janetorial : jan•i•to•ri•al
jangal : jan•gle (harsh ringing
    sound) *or* jin•gle (pleasant
    ringing sound)

jangel : jan•gle (harsh ringing
    sound) *or* jin•gle (pleasant
    ringing sound)
jan•gle (harsh ringing sound);
    jin•gle (pleasant ringing
    sound)
janiter : jan•i•tor
janiterial : jan•i•to•ri•al
jan•i•tor
janitoreal : jan•i•to•ri•al
jan•i•to•ri•al
jannitor : jan•i•tor
jannitorial : jan•i•to•ri•al
Jannuary : Jan•u•ary
janquil : jon•quil
Januarry : Jan•u•ary
Jan•u•ary
Januerry : Jan•u•ary
Januery : Jan•u•ary
Januwary : Jan•u•ary
Januwery : Jan•u•ary
Ja•pan
Japaneese : Jap•a•nese
Jap•a•nese
Japaneze : Jap•a•nese
Japannese : Jap•a•nese
Jappan : Ja•pan
Jappanese : Jap•a•nese
jargan : jar•gon
jargen : jar•gon
jargin : jar•gon
jar•gon
jasmen : jas•mine
jasmin : jas•mine
jas•mine *or* jes•sa•mine
jassmine : jas•mine
jaudiss : jaun•dice
jaundace : jaun•dice
jaundase : jaun•dice
jaun•dice

jaundish : **jaun•dice**
javalen : **jav•e•lin**
javalin : **jav•e•lin**
javaline : **jav•e•lin**
javelen : **jav•e•lin**
jav•e•lin
javlen : **jav•e•lin**
javlin : **jav•e•lin**
jazmine : **jas•mine**
jazzmine : **jas•mine**
jealis : **jeal•ous**
jeallous : **jeal•ous**
jeal•ous
jealus : **jeal•ous**
jehad : **ji•had**
jejoon : **je•june**
je•june
jell *or* gel
jellitan : **gel•a•tin**
jellous : **jeal•ous**
jelopy : **ja•lopy**
jelous : **jeal•ous**
Jemaica : **Ja•mai•ca**
jemnasium : **gym•na•si•um**
jemnasstics : **gym•nas•tics**
jemnast : **gym•nast**
jemnastecs : **gym•nas•tics**
jemnasticks : **gym•nas•tics**
jemnest : **gym•nast**
jemnist : **gym•nast**
jengle : **jan•gle** (harsh ringing
    sound) *or* **jin•gle** (pleasant
    ringing sound)
jenre : **genre**
jeop•ar•dy
jeoprady : **jeop•ar•dy**
jeoprody : **jeop•ar•dy**
jepardy : **jeop•ar•dy**
jepordy : **jeop•ar•dy**
jepperdy : **jeop•ar•dy**
jepprady : **jeop•ar•dy**
jepprody : **jeop•ar•dy**

jeramiad : **jer•e•mi•ad**
jeremaid : **jer•e•mi•ad**
jer•e•mi•ad
jerimiad : **jer•e•mi•ad**
jernalism : **jour•nal•ism**
jerrand : **ger•und**
jerremiad : **jer•e•mi•ad**
jerrund : **ger•und**
Jerrusalem : **Je•ru•sa•lem**
jerrybilt : **jer•ry-built**
jer•ry-built
jersee : **jer•sey**
jer•sey
jersie : **jer•sey**
jerssey : **jer•sey**
jersy : **jer•sey**
jerund : **ger•und**
Je•ru•sa•lem
Jeruselem : **Je•ru•sa•lem**
Jerushalom : **Je•ru•sa•lem**
jerybuilt : **jer•ry-built**
jesamine : **jas•mine**
jessamen : **jas•mine**
jessamin : **jas•mine**
jes•sa•mine *or* **jas•mine**
jesster : **ges•ture** (movement) *or*
    jest•er (joker)
jessymine : **jas•mine**
jest (joke); **gist** (essence)
jest•er (joker); **ges•ture**
    (movement)
jestor : **jest•er** (joker) *or*
    ges•ture (movement)
jesture : **jest•er** (joker) *or*
    ges•ture (movement)
jetison : **jet•ti•son**
jet•sam
jetsem : **jet•sam**
jetsim : **jet•sam**
jetsum : **jet•sam**
jettason : **jet•ti•son**
jettisen : **jet•ti•son**

jet·ti·son
jettsam : jet·sam
jeuel : jew·el
jeueled : jew·eled
jeueler : jew·el·er
jeuelry : jew·el·ry
jewal : jew·el
jewaled : jew·eled
jewaler : jew·el·er
jewalry : jew·el·ry
jewbilee : ju·bi·lee
Jewdism : Ju·da·ism
Jewdyism : Ju·da·ism
jew·el
jew·eled or jew·elled
jew·el·er or jew·el·ler
jewelery : jew·el·ry
jew·elled or jew·eled
jew·el·ler or jew·el·er
jewellery (*Brit.*) : jew·el·ry
jewl : jew·el
jewled : jew·eled
jewler : jew·el·er
jewlry : jew·el·ry
jibe (to change course in boat;
    to agree); gibe (to taunt)
ji·had
jijune : je·june
jilopy : ja·lopy
Jimaica : Ja·mai·ca
Jimaka : Ja·mai·ca
jimnasium : gym·na·si·um
jimnasstics : gym·nas·tics
jimnast : gym·nast
jimnastecs : gym·nas·tics
jimnasticks : gym·nas·tics
jimnest : gym·nast
jimnist : gym·nast
jingal : jan·gle (harsh ringing
    sound) *or* jin·gle (pleasant
    ringing sound)

jingel : jan·gle (harsh ringing
    sound) *or* jin·gle (pleasant
    ringing sound)
jin·gle (pleasant ringing
    sound); jan·gle (harsh
    ringing sound)
jip : gyp
jipcem : gyp·sum
jipcim : gyp·sum
jipped : gypped
jipsam : gyp·sum
jipsem : gyp·sum
jipsey : gyp·sy
jipsim : gyp·sum
jipsy : gyp·sy
jirascope : gy·ro·scope
jirate : gy·rate
jirocompass : gy·ro·com·pass
jirocompess : gy·ro·com·pass
jirrate : gy·rate
jirsey : jer·sey
jist : gist (essence) *or* jest (joke)
jockee : jock·ey
jock·ey
jocky : jock·ey
jo·cose
joc·u·lar
joculer : joc·u·lar
joddper : jodh·pur
jodhper : jodh·pur
jodh·pur
jodper : jodh·pur
jodpur : jodh·pur
johdpur : jodh·pur
johnquil : jon·quil
joiful : joy·ful
joious : joy·ous
joist
jokose : jo·cose
jokular : joc·u·lar
jolity : jol·li·ty
jollety : jol·li·ty

jollitty : **jol•li•ty**
jol•li•ty
joncuil : **jon•quil**
jon•quil
jonquill : **jon•quil**
jonra : **genre**
joocy : **juicy**
joonta : **jun•ta**
jornalism : **jour•nal•ism**
jorneyman : **jour•ney•man**
jossel : **jos•tle**
jostel : **jos•tle**
jos•tle
jour•nal•ism
journelism : **jour•nal•ism**
jour•ney•man
jouryman : **jour•ney•man**
joveal : **jo•vial**
jo•vial
joy•ful
joyfull : **joy•ful**
joy•ous
joyst : **joist**
joyus : **joy•ous**
jubalant : **ju•bi•lant**
jubalee : **ju•bi•lee**
jubalint : **ju•bi•lant**
jubelant : **ju•bi•lant**
ju•bi•lant
ju•bi•lee
jubilent : **ju•bi•lant**
jubillee : **ju•bi•lee**
jubilly : **ju•bi•lee**
jucstapose : **jux•ta•pose**
jucy : **juicy**
Judahism : **Ju•da•ism**
Ju•da•ism
judeciary : **ju•di•cia•ry**
judge
judgement (*Brit.*) : **judg•ment**
judgerry : **ju•di•cia•ry**
judg•ment

judiceal : **ju•di•cial**
ju•di•cial
judiciarry : **ju•di•cia•ry**
ju•di•cia•ry
ju•di•cious
judishall : **ju•di•cial**
judishious : **ju•di•cious**
judisial : **ju•di•cial**
Judism : **Ju•da•ism**
judissiary : **ju•di•ci•ary**
judissious : **ju•di•cious**
judtial : **ju•di•cial**
juditiary : **ju•di•ci•ary**
juditious : **ju•di•cious**
juge : **judge**
jugement : **judg•ment**
jugernaut : **jug•ger•naut**
juggal : **jug•gle**
juggerknot : **jug•ger•naut**
jug•ger•naut
juggernot : **jug•ger•naut**
jugglar : **jug•gler** (one who
    juggles) *or* **jug•u•lar** (vein)
jug•gle
jug•gler (one who juggles);
    jug•u•lar (vein)
juggular : **jug•gler** (one who
    juggles) *or* **jug•u•lar** (vein)
jugguler : **jug•gler** (one who
    juggles) *or* **jug•u•lar** (vein)
jugler : **jug•gler** (one who
    juggles) *or* **jug•u•lar** (vein)
Ju•go•sla•via *or* **Yu•go•sla•via**
jugoular : **jug•gler** (one who
    juggles) *or* **jug•u•lar** (vein)
jug•u•lar (vein); **jug•gler** (one
    who juggles)
juguler : **jug•gler** (one who
    juggles) *or* **jug•u•lar** (vein)
jugulir : **jug•gler** (one who
    juggles) *or* **jug•u•lar** (vein)
juicy

ju•lep
julip : **ju•lep**
jullip : **ju•lep**
junaper : **ju•ni•per**
junchure : **junc•ture**
juncion : **junc•tion**
juncshion : **junc•tion**
juncshure : **junc•ture**
junc•tion
junc•ture
juncure : **junc•ture**
Ju•neau (city); **Ju•no** (goddess)
Juneoh : **Ju•neau**
juneper : **ju•ni•per**
jungal : **jun•gle**
jungel : **jun•gle**
jun•gle
junier : **jun•ior**
Junieu : **Ju•neau**
jun•ior
ju•ni•per
junipper : **ju•ni•per**
jun•ket
junkit : **jun•ket**
junktion : **junc•tion**
junkture : **junc•ture**
junnior : **ju•nior**
Ju•no (goddess); **Ju•neau** (city)
Junoe : **Ju•neau**
junquet : **jun•ket**
jun•ta
juntah : **jun•ta**
juntion : **junc•tion**
jurer : **ju•ror**
juresdiction : **ju•ris•dic•tion**
juressdiction : **ju•ris•dic•tion**
jurisdicion : **ju•ris•dic•tion**
jurisdicktion : **ju•ris•dic•tion**
ju•ris•dic•tion
jurissdiction : **ju•ris•dic•tion**
jurnalism : **jour•nal•ism**
jurneyman : **jour•ney•man**

ju•ror
jurrer : **ju•ror**
jurybuilt : **jer•ry-built**
justace : **jus•tice**
justafiable : **jus•ti•fi•able**
justefiable : **jus•ti•fi•able**
justefy : **jus•ti•fy**
jus•tice
justiffy : **jus•ti•fy**
justifiabel : **jus•ti•fi•able**
jus•ti•fi•able
jus•ti•fy
justifyable : **jus•ti•fi•able**
justis : **jus•tice**
justise : **jus•tice**
justiss : **jus•tice**
juvanile : **ju•ve•nile**
juvenial : **ju•ve•nile**
ju•ve•nile
juvinile : **ju•ve•nile**
jux•ta•pose
jymnaisium : **gym•na•si•um**
jymnaseum : **gym•na•si•um**
jymnasiem : **gym•na•si•um**
jymnasstics : **gym•nas•tics**
jymnastecs : **gym•nas•tics**
jymnasticks : **gym•nas•tics**
jymnest : **gym•nast**
jymnist : **gym•nast**
jyp : **gyp**
jypcem : **gyp•sum**
jypcim : **gyp•sum**
jyped : **gypped**
jypped : **gypped**
jypsam : **gyp•sum**
jypsem : **gyp•sum**
jypsey : **gyp•sy**
jypsie : **gyp•sy**
jypsim : **gyp•sum**
jyracompass : **gy•ro•com•pass**
jyrait : **gy•rate**
jyrascope : **gy•ro•scope**

jyricompass : **gy•ro•com•pass**
jyriscope : **gy•ro•scope**
jyrocompess : **gy•ro•com•pass**

jyrocompiss : **gy•ro•com•pass**
jyroscoap : **gy•ro•scope**
jyrrate : **gy•rate**

K

kacki : **kha•ki**
kactis : **cac•tus**
kactus : **cac•tus**
kadet : **ca•det**
kaffee : **cof•fee**
kahki : **kha•ki**
Kairo : **Cai•ro**
kakhi : **kha•ki**
kaki : **kha•ki**
kakki : **kha•ki**
kakky : **kha•ki**
kaky : **kha•ki**
kaleidascope : **ka•lei•do•scope**
kaleidescope : **ka•lei•do•scope**
ka•lei•do•scope
kalico : **cal•i•co**
kalidoscope : **ka•lei•do•scope**
kaliedoscope : **ka•lei•do•scope**
kalipso : **ca•lyp•so**
kalisthenics : **cal•is•then•ics**
kalisthinics : **cal•is•then•ics**
kalleidoscope : **ka•lei•do•scope**
kallisthenics : **cal•is•then•ics**
kalypso : **ca•lyp•so**
kan•ga•roo
kangarue : **kan•ga•roo**
kangeroo : **kan•ga•roo**
kangiroo : **kan•ga•roo**
kangroo : **kan•ga•roo**
kanguru : **kan•ga•roo**
kanine : **ca•nine**
kaos : **cha•os**
Kan•sas
Kansus : **Kan•sas**
kar•at *or* car•at (weight of
   gems); **car•et** (^); **car•rot**
   (vegetable)
karet : **kar•at** (weight of gems)
   or car•et (^) *or* **car•rot**
   (vegetable)

karisma : **char•is•ma**
karosene : **ker•o•sene**
karrat : **kar•at** (weight of gems)
   or **car•et** (^) *or* **car•rot**
   (vegetable)
karret : **kar•at** (weight of gems)
   or **car•et** (^) *or* **car•rot**
   (vegetable)
kataclism : **cat•a•clysm**
kataclysm : **cat•a•clysm**
katsup : **cat•sup**
kayac : **kay•ak**
kayack : **kay•ak**
kay•ak
keanness : **keen•ness**
keeness : **keen•ness**
keen•ness
keesh : **quiche**
kelogram : **ki•lo•gram**
Keltic : **Celt•ic**
kemono : **ki•mo•no**
ken (to know); **kin** (relatives)
kendal : **kin•dle**
kendengarten : **kin•der•gar•ten**
kendle : **kin•dle**
kendling : **kin•dling**
kendred : **kin•dred**
kenel : **ken•nel**
kenetic : **ki•net•ic**
kennal : **ken•nel**
ken•nel
kennle : **ken•nel**
Kentuckey : **Ken•tucky**
Ken•tucky
Kentuky : **Ken•tucky**
keosk : **ki•osk**
kerasene : **ker•o•sene**
kernal : **col•o•nel** (military
   officer) *or* **ker•nel** (seed)

ker·nel (seed); col·o·nel
(military officer)
kernele : col·o·nel (military
officer) or ker·nel (seed)
keroseen : ker·o·sene
ker·o·sene
kerosine : ker·o·sene
kerrosene : ker·o·sene
ketchap : cat·sup
ketchep : cat·sup
ketch·up or cat·sup
ketle : ket·tle
ketsup : cat·sup
kettal : ket·tle
kettel : ket·tle
ket·tle
keyosk : ki·osk
kha·ki
khaky : kha·ki
kiask : ki·osk
kibbits : kib·butz (collective
farm) or ki·bitz (to offer
advice)
kibbitz : kib·butz (collective
farm) or ki·bitz (to offer
advice)
kib·butz (collective farm);
ki·bitz (to offer advice)
kibetz : kib·butz (collective
farm) or ki·bitz (to offer
advice)
kibits : kib·butz (collective
farm) or ki·bitz (to offer
advice)
ki·bitz (to offer advice);
kib·butz (collective farm)
kiche : quiche
kichen : kitch·en
kichin : kitch·en
kiddergarden : kin·der·gar·ten
kiddney : kid·ney
kid·nap·er or kid·nap·per

kid·nap·ing or kid·nap·ping
kid·nap·per or kid·nap·er
kid·nap·ping or kid·nap·ing
kid·ney
kidnie : kid·ney
kidny : kid·ney
kilagram : ki·lo·gram
Kilamanjaro : Kil·i·man·ja·ro
kilameter : ki·lo·me·ter
kilegram : ki·lo·gram
Kilemanjaro : Kil·i·man·ja·ro
kiligram : ki·lo·gram
Kil·i·man·ja·ro
killogram : ki·lo·gram
killometer : ki·lo·me·ter
ki·lo·gram
kilomeater : ki·lo·me·ter
kilomeeter : ki·lo·me·ter
ki·lo·me·ter
kilometre (Brit.) : ki·lo·me·ter
kimmono : ki·mo·no
ki·mo·no
kin (relatives); ken (to know)
kindal : kin·dle
kindel : kin·dle
kindergarden : kin·der·gar·ten
kindergardin : kin·der·gar·ten
kin·der·gar·ten
kinderguarden : kin·der·gar·ten
kin·dle
kindleing : kin·dling
kin·dling
kindread : kin·dred
kin·dred
kindrid : kin·dred
kindrud : kin·dred
ki·net·ic
kinetick : ki·net·ic
kinettic : ki·net·ic
kingdam : king·dom
kingdem : king·dom
king·dom

kingdum : **king·dom**
kinnetic : **ki·net·ic**
kintergarden : **kin·der·gar·ten**
kintergarten : **kin·der·gar·ten**
Kintucky : **Ken·tucky**
ki·osk
kishe : **quiche**
kis·met
kismit : **kis·met**
kiss·able
kissible : **kiss·able**
kissmet : **kis·met**
kitch·en
kitchin : **kitch·en**
kitchun : **kitch·en**
kiten : **kit·ten**
kitshen : **kitch·en**
kit·ten
kittin : **kit·ten**
kiyak : **kay·ak**
kizmet : **kis·met**
klepptomaniac :
  klep·to·ma·ni·ac
kleptamaniac : **klep·to·ma·ni·ac**
kleptemaniac : **klep·to·ma·ni·ac**
kleptomainiac :
  klep·to·ma·ni·ac
kleptomaneac :
  klep·to·ma·ni·ac
klep·to·ma·ni·ac
kliptomaniac : **klep·to·ma·ni·ac**
knap·sack
knew (was aware); **gnu**
  (antelope); **new** (not old)
knicht : **knight**
knick·knack
knicknack : **knick·knack**
knife
knifes (verb); **knives** (*plur.*)
knight (medieval soldier);
  night (not day)
knigt : **knight**

knikknak : **knick·knack**
knite : **knight**
knives (*plur.*); **knifes** (*verb*)
knoal : **knoll**
knole : **knoll**
knoll
knolledge : **knowl·edge**
knollege : **knowl·edge**
knollegible : **knowl·edge·able**
knot (in rope; one nautical
  mile); **not** (negative)
knot·hole
know (to be aware of); **no**
  (negative); **now** (at this time)
knowledgable :
  knowl·edge·able
knowl·edge
knowl·edge·able
knowledgible : **knowl·edge·able**
knowlege : **knowl·edge**
knowlegeable : **knowl·edge·able**
knowlegible : **knowl·edge·able**
knowlidge : **knowl·edge**
knowlige : **knowl·edge**
knuckal : **knuck·le**
knuckel : **knuck·le**
knuck·le
knukkle : **knuck·le**
ko·ala
koalla : **ko·ala**
koff : **cough**
koffee : **cof·fee**
kohlrabbi : **kohl·ra·bi**
kohl·ra·bi
kohlrobbi : **kohl·ra·bi**
kohlrobi : **kohl·ra·bi**
kohlroby : **kohl·ra·bi**
koleidoscope : **ka·lei·do·scope**
kollidoscope : **ka·lei·do·scope**
kollrabi : **kohl·ra·bi**
kolrabi : **kohl·ra·bi**
komquat : **kum·quat**

Ko·rea
Koria : **Ko·rea**
Korrea : **Ko·rea**
kough : **cough**
kowala : **ko·ala**
kowalla : **ko·ala**
kremlen : **krem·lin**
krem·lin
krimlin : **krem·lin**
krimmlin : **krem·lin**
kripton : **kryp·ton**
kryppton : **kryp·ton**

kryp·ton
kumkwat : **kum·quat**
kum·quat
kumquot : **kum·quat**
kurnel : **col·o·nel** (military
    officer) *or* **ker·nel** (seed)
kwagmire : **quag·mire**
kwick : **quick**
kyack : **kay·ak**
kymono : **ki·mo·no**
kyosk : **ki·osk**

L

labal : **la•bel**
laballed : **la•beled**
labarinth : **lab•y•rinth**
labbel : **la•bel**
labbor : **la•bor**
labbored : **la•bored**
labborious : **la•bo•ri•ous**
la•bel
la•beled *or* **la•belled**
la•belled *or* **la•beled**
laber : **la•bor**
labered : **la•bored**
laberinth : **lab•y•rinth**
laberynth : **lab•y•rinth**
labil : **la•bel**
labirinth : **lab•y•rinth**
labirynth : **lab•y•rinth**
lable : **la•bel**
labled : **la•beled**
la•bor
laboratorry : **lab•o•ra•to•ry**
lab•o•ra•to•ry
la•bored
laboreous : **la•bo•ri•ous**
la•bo•ri•ous
laborratory : **lab•o•ra•to•ry**
laborred : **la•bored**
laborrious : **la•bo•ri•ous**
labortory : **lab•o•ra•to•ry**
Labradoor : **Lab•ra•dor**
Lab•ra•dor
Labradore : **Lab•ra•dor**
labratory : **lab•o•ra•to•ry**
Labredor : **Lab•ra•dor**
labretory : **lab•o•ra•to•ry**
Labridor : **Lab•ra•dor**
labrinth : **lab•y•rinth**
labritory : **lab•o•ra•to•ry**
labrotory : **lab•o•ra•to•ry**
labrynth : **lab•y•rinth**

labul : **la•bel**
lab•y•rinth
lacadaisical : **lack•a•dai•si•cal**
lacerait : **lac•er•ate**
lac•er•ate
lacey : **lacy**
lacivious : **las•civ•i•ous**
lack•a•dai•si•cal
lackadasical : **lack•a•dai•si•cal**
lacker : **lac•quer**
lacksitive : **lax•a•tive**
lacksity : **lax•i•ty**
lackydaisical : **lack•a•dai•si•cal**
lac•quer
lacuer : **lac•quer**
lacy
ladal : **la•dle**
ladel : **la•dle**
ladill : **la•dle**
laditude : **lat•i•tude**
la•dle
laff : **laugh**
laffable : **laugh•able**
laffible : **laugh•able**
laffter : **laugh•ter**
lagard : **lag•gard**
la•ger (beer); **log•ger** (tree
    cutter)
lag•gard
lagger : **la•ger** (beer) *or* **log•ger**
    (tree cutter)
laggerd : **lag•gard**
laggoon : **la•goon**
la•goon
lagune : **la•goon**
lair (nest, burrow); **lay•er** (one
    that lays; one thickness)
laith : **lath** (board) *or* **lathe**
    (machine)

179

laithe : **lath** (board) *or* **lathe**
(machine)
lamanate : **lam•i•nate**
lamenate : **lam•i•nate**
lam•i•nate
laminnate : **lam•i•nate**
lamminate : **lam•i•nate**
lam•poon
lampune : **lam•poon**
lanalen : **lan•o•lin**
lanalin : **lan•o•lin**
lance
lan•cet
lanch : **launch**
lancit : **lan•cet**
landlover : **land•lub•ber**
land•lub•ber
landluvver : **land•lub•ber**
landscaip : **land•scape**
land•scape
landskape : **land•scape**
lannolin : **lan•o•lin**
lanolen : **lan•o•lin**
lan•o•lin
lanse : **lance**
lanset : **lan•cet**
lansit : **lan•cet**
lapal : **la•pel**
la•pel
lapell : **la•pel**
lappel : **la•pel**
laquer : **lac•quer**
lar•ce•ny
larciny : **lar•ce•ny**
larengitis : **lar•yn•gi•tis**
larenx : **lar•ynx**
lar•gess *or* **lar•gesse**
lar•gesse *or* **lar•gess**
lar•i•at
lariet : **lar•i•at**
laringitis : **lar•yn•gi•tis**
larinks : **lar•ynx**

larinx : **lar•ynx**
larrangitis : **lar•yn•gi•tis**
larrengitus : **lar•yn•gi•tis**
larriat : **lar•i•at**
larriet : **lar•i•at**
larrinks : **lar•ynx**
larrinx : **lar•ynx**
larseny : **lar•ce•ny**
larsinny : **lar•ce•ny**
larsiny : **lar•ce•ny**
lar•va (*sing.*); **lar•vae** (*plur.*)
lar•vae (*plur.*); **lar•va** (*sing.*)
lar•yn•gi•tis
laryngitus : **lar•yn•gi•tis**
larynjitis : **lar•yn•gi•tis**
lar•ynx
lasarate : **lac•er•ate**
lasciveous : **las•civ•i•ous**
las•civ•i•ous
laserate : **lac•er•ate**
lasserate : **lac•er•ate**
lassivious : **las•civ•i•ous**
Latan : **Lat•in**
latancy : **la•ten•cy**
latansy : **la•ten•cy**
latant : **la•tent**
latarel : **lat•er•al**
latatude : **lat•i•tude**
Laten : **Lat•in**
la•ten•cy
latensy : **la•ten•cy**
la•tent
lat•er•al
laterel : **lat•er•al**
latetude : **lat•i•tude**
lath (board); **lathe** (machine)
lathe (machine); **lath** (board)
latice : **lat•tice**
Lat•in
latise : **lat•tice**
latiss : **lat•tice**
lat•i•tude

lattece : **lat·tice**
latteral : **lat·er·al**
lat·tice
Lattin : **Lat·in**
lattise : **lat·tice**
lattiss : **lat·tice**
lattiude : **lat·i·tude**
laud·able
laudible : **laud·able**
laugh
laugh·able
laughible : **laugh·able**
laugh·ter
launch
laundary : **laun·dry**
launderry : **laun·dry**
laundery : **laun·dry**
laun·dry
lavalear : **lav·a·liere**
lavaleer : **lav·a·liere**
lav·a·liere
lavander : **lav·en·der**
laveleer : **lav·a·liere**
lavelier : **lav·a·liere**
laveliere : **lav·a·liere**
lavendar : **lav·en·der**
lav·en·der
lavesh : **lav·ish**
lavinder : **lav·en·der**
lav·ish
lavvish : **lav·ish**
lawdable : **laud·able**
lawdible : **laud·able**
law·ful
lawfull : **law·ful**
lawnch : **launch**
lawndry : **laun·dry**
lax·a·tive
laxety : **lax·i·ty**
laxitive : **lax·a·tive**
laxitty : **lax·i·ty**
lax·i·ty

lay (to put down; *past of* to lie); **lie** (to recline)
lay·er (one that lays; one thickness); **lair** (nest, burrow)
lay·ing (act of putting down); **ly·ing** (act of reclining)
leace : **lease**
leach (to dissolve); **leech** (bloodsucker)
lead (to guide; a metal); **led** (*past of* to lead)
lead·en
leaf
leafs : **leaves**
leag : **league**
leagal : **le·gal**
leagality : **le·gal·i·ty**
leagion : **le·gion**
leagle : **le·gal**
league
leak (to let out); **leek** (vegetable)
lean (to incline); **lien** (legal claim)
leanient : **le·nient**
lean-to
leap
leapard : **leop·ard**
leaperd : **leop·ard**
leaque : **league**
learn
lear·y *or* **leer·y**
lease
leasure : **lei·sure**
leater : **li·ter**
leathal : **le·thal**
leath·er
leavel : **lev·el**
leaveled : **lev·eled**
leav·en
leaverage : **lev·er·age**
leaves

leavity : **lev•i•ty**

leaward : **lee•ward**

Lebannon : **Leb•a•non**

Leb•a•non

Lebbanon : **Leb•a•non**

Lebenon : **Leb•a•non**

Lebinon : **Leb•a•non**

lechary : **lech•ery**

lech•ery

led (*past of* to lead); **lead** (to guide; a metal)

ledden : **lead•en**

led•ger

leece : **lease**

leech (bloodsucker); **leach** (to dissolve)

leef : **leaf**

leefs : **leaves**

leegue : **league**

leek (vegetable); **leak** (to let out)

leen : **lean** (to incline) *or* **lien** (legal claim)

leento : **lean-to**

leep : **leap**

leer•y *or* **lear•y**

leese : **lease**

leesure : **lei•sure**

leeter : **li•ter**

leethal : **le•thal**

leeves : **leaves**

lee•ward

leewerd : **lee•ward**

leeword : **lee•ward**

leftenant : **lieu•ten•ant**

legability : **leg•i•bil•i•ty**

leg•a•cy

le•gal

legalety : **le•gal•i•ty**

legalitty : **le•gal•i•ty**

le•gal•i•ty

legallity : **le•gal•i•ty**

legassy : **leg•a•cy**

legasy : **leg•a•cy**

legebility : **leg•i•bil•i•ty**

legeble : **leg•i•ble**

legel : **le•gal**

leg•end

legendarry : **leg•end•ary**

leg•end•ary

legenderry : **leg•end•ary**

legendery : **leg•end•ary**

legeon : **le•gion**

leger : **led•ger**

legeslator : **leg•is•la•tor**

leggend : **leg•end**

leggendery : **leg•end•ary**

legger : **led•ger**

leggion : **le•gion**

leggislator : **leg•is•la•tor**

leggitimate : **le•git•i•mate**

legian : **le•gion**

legibal : **leg•i•ble**

legibel : **leg•i•ble**

legibilety : **leg•i•bil•i•ty**

legibilitty : **leg•i•bil•i•ty**

leg•i•bil•i•ty

legibillity : **leg•i•bil•i•ty**

leg•i•ble

legicy : **leg•a•cy**

legind : **leg•end**

le•gion

legislater : **leg•is•la•tor**

leg•is•la•tor

legissy : **leg•a•cy**

legitamacy : **le•git•i•ma•cy**

legitamet : **le•git•i•mate**

legitemacy : **le•git•i•ma•cy**

legitemate : **le•git•i•mate**

le•git•i•ma•cy

legitimassy : **le•git•i•ma•cy**

legitimasy : **le•git•i•ma•cy**

le•git•i•mate

legitimet : **le•git•i•mate**

legitimisy : **le•git•i•ma•cy**
legittimacy : **le•git•i•ma•cy**
legle : **le•gal**
leip : **leap**
leishure : **lei•sure**
lei•sure
lejend : **leg•end**
lejendary : **leg•end•ary**
lemen : **lem•on**
lemenade : **lem•on•ade**
lemin : **lem•on**
leminade : **lem•on•ade**
lemmon : **lem•on**
lemmonade : **lem•on•ade**
lemmur : **le•mur**
lem•on
lem•on•ade
lemonaid : **lem•on•ade**
le•mur
lemure : **le•mur**
lenghth : **length**
length
leniant : **le•nient**
le•nient
lental : **len•til** (legume) *or*
   lin•tel (door beam)
lenth : **length**
len•til (legume); **lin•tel** (door
   beam)
lentle : **lentil** (legume) *or*
   lin•tel (door beam)
leop•ard
leoperd : **leop•ard**
lepard : **leop•ard**
lep•er
leperd : **leop•ard**
leppard : **leop•ard**
lepper : **lep•er**
lepperd : **leop•ard**
lerch : **lurch**
lerk : **lurk**
lern : **learn**

les•sen (to decrease); **les•son**
   (thing studied)
les•son (thing studied); **les•sen**
   (to decrease)
letchery : **lech•ery**
leter : **li•ter**
le•thal
lethel : **le•thal**
lether : **leath•er**
lettise : **let•tuce**
lettiss : **let•tuce**
let•tuce
lettus : **let•tuce**
lettuse : **let•tuce**
leucimia : **leu•ke•mia**
leukeamia : **leu•ke•mia**
leukemea : **leu•ke•mia**
leu•ke•mia
leukimia : **leu•ke•mia**
leval : **lev•el**
levaled : **lev•eled**
levarage : **lev•er•age**
lev•el
lev•eled
levelled : **lev•eled**
leven : **leav•en**
lev•er•age
leverege : **lev•er•age**
leverige : **lev•er•age**
levety : **lev•i•ty**
le•vi•a•than
leviathen : **le•vi•a•than**
leviethan : **le•vi•a•than**
levirige : **lev•er•age**
levitty : **lev•i•ty**
lev•i•ty
levven : **leav•en**
levvity : **lev•i•ty**
lewdicrous : **lu•di•crous**
liabilety : **li•a•bil•i•ty**
li•a•bil•i•ty
liabillity : **li•a•bil•i•ty**

li·a·ble (responsible or susceptible); li·bel (damaging printed statements)
li·ai·son
li·ar (teller of lies); lyre (stringed instrument)
liason : li·ai·son
libaral : lib·er·al
libartine : lib·er·tine
libary : li·brary
libberal : lib·er·al
libbertine : lib·er·tine
libberty : lib·er·ty
libedo : li·bi·do
li·bel (damaging printed statements); li·a·ble (responsible or susceptible)
libelity : li·a·bil·i·ty
lib·er·al
liberall : lib·er·al
liberel : lib·er·al
libertean : lib·er·tine
liberteen : lib·er·tine
libertene : lib·er·tine
lib·er·tine
lib·er·ty
li·bi·do
librarry : li·brary
li·brary
librery : li·brary
licarish : lic·o·rice
licence : li·cense
li·cense
licenze : li·cense
licerice : lic·o·rice
li·chen (fungus); lik·en (to compare)
licken : li·chen (fungus) or lik·en (to compare)
lickerish : lic·o·rice
lic·o·rice
licorish : lic·o·rice

lie (to recline); lay (to put down)
lieing : lay·ing (act of putting down) or ly·ing (act of reclining)
lien (legal claim); lean (to incline)
lietenent : lieu·ten·ant
lieu·ten·ant
lieutennant : lieu·ten·ant
lifegard : life·guard
lifegaurd : life·guard
life·guard
lik·en (to compare); li·chen (fungus)
li·lac
lilack : li·lac
lilly : lily
lily
limarick : lim·er·ick
lim·er·ick
limet : lim·it
lim·it
limmerick : lim·er·ick
limmit : lim·it
limosine : lim·ou·sine
limouseen : lim·ou·sine
limousene : lim·ou·sine
lim·ou·sine
limozene : lim·ou·sine
limozine : lim·ou·sine
limph : lymph
limrick : lim·er·ick
limur : le·mur
linament : lin·ea·ment (outline) or lin·i·ment (painkiller)
Lin·coln
Lincon : Lin·coln
Linconn : Lin·coln
lin·ea·ment (outline); lin·i·ment (painkiller)
lin·ear

linement : **lin·ea·ment** (outline)
  or **lin·i·ment** (painkiller)
lin·en
lingeray : **lin·ge·rie**
lingerey : **lin·ge·rie**
lin·ge·rie
linght : **length**
liniar : **lin·ear**
linient : **le·nient**
lin·i·ment (painkiller);
  lin·ea·ment (outline)
linnament : **lin·e·a·ment**
  (outline) *or* **lin·i·ment**
  (painkiller)
linnear : **lin·ear**
linnen : **lin·en**
linniar : **lin·ear**
linnoleum : **li·no·leum**
li·no·leum
linoliem : **li·no·leum**
linolium : **li·no·leum**
linon : **lin·en**
linsherie : **lin·ge·rie**
lintal : **len·til** (legume) *or*
  lin·tel (door beam)
lin·tel (door beam); **len·til**
  (legume)
lintle : **len·til** (*legume*)**or** lin·tel
  (door beam)
linx : lynx
li·on·ess
lionness : **li·on·ess**
liquaffy : **liq·ue·fy**
liquafy : **liq·ue·fy**
liqued : **li·quid**
liq·ue·fy
liq·uid
liquiffy : **liq·ue·fy**
liquify : **liq·ue·fy**
liquorice (*Brit.*) : **lic·o·rice**
liquorish : **lic·o·rice**
lirk : **lurk**

lisense : **li·cense**
lissener : **lis·ten·er**
lis·ten·er
lit·a·ny
litaracy : **lit·er·a·cy**
litegate : **lit·i·gate**
liteny : **lit·a·ny**
li·ter
literachure : **lit·er·a·ture**
lit·er·a·cy
literassy : **lit·er·a·cy**
lit·er·a·ture
litergy : **lit·ur·gy**
litericy : **lit·er·a·cy**
literissy : **lit·er·a·cy**
literisy : **lit·er·a·cy**
literture : **lit·er·a·ture**
lit·i·gate
litiny : **lit·a·ny**
litrature : **lit·er·a·ture**
litre (*Brit.*) : **li·ter**
littany : **lit·a·ny**
littature : **lit·er·a·ture**
litteracy : **lit·er·a·cy**
litterature : **lit·er·a·ture**
littigate : **lit·i·gate**
litturgy : **lit·ur·gy**
lit·ur·gy
liturjy : **lit·ur·gy**
live·li·hood
livelyhood : **live·li·hood**
livlihood : **live·li·hood**
liz·ard
lizerd : **liz·ard**
lizzard : **liz·ard**
lizzerd : **liz·ard**
loathesome : **loath·some**
loath·some
lo·cal (regional); **lo·cale**
  (region, setting)
lo·cale (region, setting); **lo·cal**
  (regional)

locamotion : **lo•co•mo•tion**
lo•co•mo•tion
logarhythm : **log•a•rithm**
logarithem : **log•a•rithm**
log•a•rithm
logarythm : **log•a•rithm**
loggarithm : **log•a•rithm**
log•ger (tree cutter); **la•ger**
  (beer)
logorithm : **log•a•rithm**
loial : **loy•al**
Londen : **Lon•don**
Londin : **Lon•don**
Lon•don
lone•li•ness
lone•ly
longatude : **lon•gi•tude**
longerie : **lin•ge•rie**
longetude : **lon•gi•tude**
longevety : **lon•gev•i•ty**
longevitty : **lon•gev•i•ty**
lon•gev•i•ty
longitood : **lon•gi•tude**
lon•gi•tude
longitued : **lon•gi•tude**
longivity : **lon•gev•i•ty**
longue : **lounge**
lonliness : **lone•li•ness**
lonly : **lone•ly**
loobricant : **lu•bri•cant**
loodricrous : **lu•di•crous**
lookemia : **leu•ke•mia**
loominary : **lu•mi•nary**
loonacy : **lu•na•cy**
loonasy : **lu•na•cy**
loonatic : **lu•na•tic**
loose (not attached); **lose** (to
  misplace)
Loosiana : **Lou•i•si•ana**
lootenent : **lieu•ten•ant**
loquaceous : **lo•qua•cious**

lo•qua•cious
loquaicious : **lo•qua•cious**
loquasious : **lo•qua•cious**
loquatious : **lo•qua•cious**
loquecious : **lo•qua•cious**
lose (to misplace); **loose** (not
  attached)
losinge : **loz•enge**
lossinge : **loz•enge**
lotery : **lot•tery**
lothesome : **loath•some**
lothsome : **loath•some**
lotis : **lo•tus**
lottary : **lot•tery**
lotterry : **lot•tery**
lot•tery
lo•tus
Loueesiana : **Lou•i•si•ana**
Louiseana : **Lou•i•si•ana**
Lou•i•si•ana
Louiziana : **Lou•i•si•ana**
Lousiana : **Lou•i•si•ana**
lounge
loungue : **lounge**
lov•able
loveable : **lov•able**
love•li•er
loveloarn : **love•lorn**
love•lorn
lovelyer : **love•li•er**
lovible : **lov•able**
lovlier : **love•li•er**
lovlorn : **love•lorn**
lowngue : **lounge**
loy•al
loyel : **loy•al**
loyil : **loy•al**
loyl : **loy•al**
loz•enge
lozinge : **loz•enge**
lozzinge : **loz•enge**

lubracant : **lu·bri·cant**
lubrecant : **lu·bri·cant**
lu·bri·cant
lubricent : **lu·bri·cant**
luced : **lu·cid**
lucer : **lu·cre**
luchre : **lu·cre**
lu·cid
lucksuriant : **lux·u·ri·ant**
lucksury : **lux·u·ry**
lu·cra·tive
lu·cre
lucretive : **lu·cra·tive**
ludacrous : **lu·di·crous**
ludecrous : **lu·di·crous**
ludicrace : **lu·di·crous**
ludicrass : **lu·di·crous**
ludicris : **lu·di·crous**
lu·di·crous
ludicrus : **lu·di·crous**
luekemia : **leu·ke·mia**
luetenant : **lieu·ten·ant**
lugage : **lug·gage**
lugege : **lug·gage**
lug·gage
luggege : **lug·gage**
luggidge : **lug·gage**
luggige : **lug·gage**
lugguage : **lug·gage**
lugige : **lug·gage**
Luisiana : **Lou·i·si·ana**
lukemia : **leu·ke·mia**
luker : **lu·cre**
lukre : **lu·cre**
lulaby : **lul·la·by**
luliby : **lul·la·by**
lul·la·by
lulleby : **lul·la·by**
lulliby : **lul·la·by**
lum·bar (of the loins); **lum·ber** (timber)

lum·ber (timber); **lum·bar** (of the loins)
lumenary : **lu·mi·nary**
lumenescent : **lu·mi·nes·cent**
luminarry : **lu·mi·nary**
lu·mi·nary
luminecent : **lu·mi·nes·cent**
luminery : **lu·mi·nary**
lu·mi·nes·cent
luminescint : **lu·mi·nes·cent**
luminessent : **lu·mi·nes·cent**
lu·na·cy
lunasy : **lu·na·cy**
lu·na·tic
lunatick : **lu·na·tic**
lun·cheon
lunchin : **lun·cheon**
lunchion : **lun·cheon**
lunesy : **lu·na·cy**
lunetic : **lu·na·tic**
lunissy : **lu·na·cy**
lunisy : **lu·na·cy**
lunitic : **lu·na·tic**
lurch
lu·rid
lurk
lurn : **learn**
lurrid : **lu·rid**
lurtch : **lurch**
lused : **lu·cid**
lusid : **lu·cid**
lus·ter
lustre (*Brit.*) : **lus·ter**
lutenant : **lieu·ten·ant**
luxeriant : **lux·u·ri·ant**
luxerry : **lux·u·ry**
luxery : **lux·u·ry**
luxiry : **lux·u·ry**
luxureant : **lux·u·ri·ant**
lux·u·ri·ant
luxurient : **lux·u·ri·ant**

lux·u·ry
lying (act of reclining); **lay·ing**
  (act of putting down)
lymph

lynx
lyre (stringed instrument); **li·ar**
  (teller of lies)

M

macab : **ma·ca·bre**
macaber : **ma·ca·bre**
ma·ca·bre
macah : **ma·caw**
macanic : **me·chan·ic**
macanical : **me·chan·i·cal**
macannic : **me·chan·ic**
macannical : **me·chan·i·cal**
macaroney : **mac·a·ro·ni**
mac·a·ro·ni
macarony : **mac·a·ro·ni**
ma·caw
maccaroni : **mac·a·ro·ni**
machanic : **me·chan·ic**
machanical : **me·chan·i·cal**
macharel : **mack·er·el**
macharell : **mack·er·el**
macharil : **mack·er·el**
ma·chete
machetey : **ma·chete**
machetie : **ma·chete**
machette : **ma·chete**
machettie : **ma·chete**
machinary : **ma·chin·ery**
ma·chine
machinerry : **ma·chin·ery**
ma·chin·ery
macironi : **mac·a·ro·ni**
mackarel : **mack·er·el**
mackaroni : **mac·a·ro·ni**
mackeral : **mack·er·el**
mack·er·el
mackiral : **mack·er·el**
macob : **ma·ca·bre**
Mad·a·gas·car
Madagascer : **Mad·a·gas·car**
Madagaskar : **Mad·a·gas·car**
madamoiselle : **mad·e·moi·selle**
madamozel : **mad·e·moi·selle**
Maddagascar : **Mad·a·gas·car**

mademaselle : **ma·de·moi·selle**
mademoisell : **ma·de·moi·selle**
ma·de·moi·selle
mademoizelle : **ma·de·moi·selle**
mademoselle : **ma·de·moi·selle**
madragal : **mad·ri·gal**
madregal : **mad·ri·gal**
mad·ri·gal
madrigall : **mad·ri·gal**
madrigle : **mad·ri·gal**
maelstorm : **mael·strom**
mael·strom
maelstrum : **mael·strom**
mae·stro
magasine : **mag·a·zine**
magazean : **mag·a·zine**
magazene : **mag·a·zine**
mag·a·zine
magec : **mag·ic**
ma·gen·ta
magesstic : **ma·jes·tic**
magestic : **ma·jes·tic**
magestrate : **mag·is·trate**
magesty : **maj·es·ty**
magezine : **mag·a·zine**
maggazine : **mag·a·zine**
magget : **mag·got**
maggistrate : **mag·is·trate**
maggit : **mag·got**
mag·got
maggut : **mag·got**
mag·ic
magichian : **ma·gi·cian**
ma·gi·cian
magicion : **ma·gi·cian**
magick : **mag·ic**
maginta : **ma·gen·ta**
mag·is·trate
magizine : **mag·a·zine**
magnafy : **mag·ni·fy**

magnanamous :
 mag•nan•i•mous
magnanemous :
 mag•nan•i•mous
mag•nan•i•mous
magnanimus : **mag•nan•i•mous**
magnannimous :
 mag•nan•i•mous
mag•nate (important person);
 mag•net (something with
 attractive force)
magnatude : **mag•ni•tude**
magnefy : **mag•ni•fy**
mag•net (something with
 attractive force); **mag•nate**
 (important person)
mag•net•ic
magnettic : **mag•net•ic**
magnetude : **mag•ni•tude**
magniffy : **mag•ni•fy**
mag•ni•fy
magnitood : **mag•ni•tude**
mag•ni•tude
magnoalia : **mag•no•lia**
mag•no•lia
magnollia : **mag•no•lia**
magnolya : **mag•no•lia**
magot : **mag•got**
ma•ha•ra•ja *or* **ma•ha•ra•jah**
ma•ha•ra•jah *or* **ma•ha•ra•ja**
maharasha : **ma•ha•ra•ja**
maharoja : **ma•ha•ra•ja**
mahoganie : **ma•hog•a•ny**
ma•hog•a•ny
mahogeny : **ma•hog•a•ny**
mahoggany : **ma•hog•a•ny**
mahogginy : **ma•hog•a•ny**
mahoginy : **ma•hog•a•ny**
mailstrom : **mael•strom**
main (primary); **Maine** (state);
 mane (hair)

Maine (state); **main** (primary);
 mane (hair)
mainia : **ma•nia**
maintainence : **main•te•nance**
main•te•nance
maintenanse : **main•te•nance**
maintenence : **main•te•nance**
maintenense : **main•te•nance**
maintennance : **main•te•nance**
maintinance : **main•te•nance**
maintinence : **main•te•nance**
maistro : **mae•stro**
maitenance : **main•te•nance**
maize (corn); **maze** (labyrinth)
majaraja : **ma•ha•ra•ja**
majenta : **ma•gen•ta**
majessty : **maj•es•ty**
ma•jes•tic
majestick : **ma•jes•tic**
maj•es•ty
majorety : **ma•jor•i•ty**
majoritty : **ma•jor•i•ty**
ma•jor•i•ty
majorrity : **ma•jor•i•ty**
mal•a•dy
mal•aise
malaize : **mal•aise**
malard : **mal•lard**
malarea : **ma•lar•ia**
ma•lar•ia
malase : **mal•aise**
malaze : **mal•aise**
maleable : **mal•lea•ble**
maledy : **mal•a•dy**
malerd : **mal•lard**
maleria : **ma•lar•ia**
malestrom : **mael•strom**
malet : **mal•let**
malevalent : **ma•lev•o•lent**
malevelent : **ma•lev•o•lent**
ma•lev•o•lent
malevolint : **ma•lev•o•lent**

mal·fea·sance
malfeasanse : **mal·fea·sance**
malfeasence : **mal·fea·sance**
malfeasense : **mal·fea·sance**
malfeasince : **mal·fea·sance**
malfeazance : **mal·fea·sance**
malfeesance : **mal·fea·sance**
malfisance : **mal·fea·sance**
mal·ice
malidy : **mal·a·dy**
ma·lign
ma·lig·nant
malignent : **ma·lig·nant**
malignint : **ma·lig·nant**
malird : **mal·lard**
malise : **mal·ice**
maliss : **mal·ice**
mallady : **mal·a·dy**
mallaise : **mal·aise**
mal·lard
mallaria : **ma·lar·ia**
mallarria : **ma·lar·ia**
mallat : **mal·let**
malleabal : **mal·lea·ble**
mal·lea·ble
mallerd : **mal·lard**
malleria : **ma·lar·ia**
mal·let
malliable : **mal·lea·ble**
mallible : **mal·lea·ble**
mallice : **mal·ice**
mallign : **ma·lign**
mallignant : **ma·lig·nant**
mallird : **mal·lard**
mallit : **mal·let**
mallovolent : **ma·lev·o·lent**
mallyable : **mal·lea·ble**
malody : **mal·a·dy**
malstrom : **mael·strom**
mamal : **mam·mal**
mamel : **mam·mal**

mameth : **mam·moth**
mamil : **mam·mal**
mamith : **mam·moth**
mam·mal
mammel : **mam·mal**
mammeth : **mam·moth**
mammil : **mam·mal**
mammith : **mam·moth**
mam·moth
mamoth : **mam·moth**
man·a·cle
manacure : **man·i·cure**
manafest : **man·i·fest**
manafesto : **man·i·fes·to**
manafold : **man·i·fold**
man·age
manageabal : **man·age·able**
man·age·able
managible : **man·age·able**
manakin : **man·i·kin** (little
  man) *or* **man·ne·quin**
  (model)
mandalen : **man·do·lin**
mandalin : **man·do·lin**
mandatorry : **man·da·to·ry**
man·da·to·ry
mandelin : **man·do·lin**
mandetory : **man·da·to·ry**
mandilin : **man·do·lin**
manditory : **man·da·to·ry**
man·do·lin
mane (hair); **main** (primary);
  Maine (state)
manea : **ma·nia**
maneac : **ma·ni·ac**
manecle : **man·a·cle**
manecure : **man·i·cure**
manefest : **man·i·fest**
manefesto : **man·i·fes·to**
manefold : **man·i·fold**
manege : **man·age**

manekin : **man·i·kin** (little man) *or* **man·ne·quin** (model)

manequin : **man·i·kin** (little man) *or* **man·ne·quin** (model)

ma·neu·ver

Manhatan : **Man·hat·tan**

Manhaten : **Man·hat·tan**

Man·hat·tan

Manhatten : **Man·hat·tan**

Manhattin : **Man·hat·tan**

ma·nia

ma·ni·ac

maniack : **ma·ni·ac**

manicle : **man·a·cle**

man·i·cure

man·i·fest

man·i·fes·to

man·i·fold

manige : **man·age**

man·i·kin *or* **man·ni·kin** (little man); **man·ne·quin** (model)

Ma·nila

Manilla : **Ma·nila**

man·li·ness

manlynes : **man·li·ness**

mannacle : **man·a·cle**

mannafest : **man·i·fest**

mannafesto : **man·i·fes·to**

mannage : **man·age**

mannageable : **man·age·able**

mannaquin : **man·i·kin** (little man) *or* **man·ne·quin** (model)

mannefest : **man·i·fest**

mannefesto : **man·i·fes·to**

mannekin : **man·i·kin** (little man) *or* **man·ne·quin** (model)

man·ne·quin (model); **man·i·kin** (little man)

man·ner (a way of doing); **man·or** (estate)

manneuver : **ma·neu·ver**

mannia : **ma·nia**

manniac : **ma·ni·ac**

mannical : **man·a·cle**

mannicure : **man·i·cure**

mannifest : **man·i·fest**

mannifesto : **man·i·fes·to**

man·ni·kin *or* **man·i·kin** (little man); **man·ne·quin** (model)

Mannila : **Ma·nila**

mannual : **man·u·al**

mannure : **ma·nure**

manny : **many**

manoor : **ma·nure**

manoor : **ma·nure**

manoover : **ma·neu·ver**

man·or (estate); **man·ner** (a way of doing)

mantal : **man·tel** (shelf) *or* **man·tle** (cape)

man·tel (shelf); **man·tle** (cape)

mantil : **man·tel** (shelf) *or* **man·tle** (cape)

mantill : **man·tel** (shelf) *or* **man·tle** (cape)

man·tis

man·tle (cape); **man·tel** (shelf)

mantus : **man·tis**

man·u·al

manuer : **ma·nure**

manuever : **ma·neu·ver**

manule : **man·u·al**

ma·nure

manuver : **ma·neu·ver**

many

manyfold : **man·i·fold**

maraner : **mar·i·ner**

maratal : **mar·i·tal**

mar·a·thon

ma·raud·er

marawder : **ma·raud·er**
marbal : **mar·ble**
marbel : **mar·ble**
marbil : **mar·ble**
marbile : **mar·ble**
mar·ble
mareen : **ma·rine**
marene : **ma·rine**
marener : **mar·i·ner**
maretal : **mar·i·tal**
marethon : **mar·a·thon**
margaren : **mar·ga·rine**
margarene : **mar·ga·rine**
margarin : **mar·ga·rine**
mar·ga·rine
margenal : **mar·gin·al**
margeren : **mar·ga·rine**
margerene : **mar·ga·rine**
margerin : **mar·ga·rine**
margerine : **mar·ga·rine**
mar·gin·al
marginel : **mar·gin·al**
marginnal : **mar·gin·al**
mariage : **mar·riage**
marige : **mar·riage**
mari·gold
Mariland : **Mary·land**
ma·rine
mar·i·ner
marinner : **mar·i·ner**
mar·i·tal
maritel : **mar·i·tal**
marithon : **mar·a·thon**
mar·ket·able
marketibal : **mar·ket·able**
marketible : **mar·ket·able**
markitable : **mar·ket·able**
mar·lin (fish); **mar·line** (cord)
mar·line (cord); **mar·lin** (fish)
mar·ma·lade
marmalaid : **mar·ma·lade**
marmelade : **mar·ma·lade**

marmelaid : **mar·ma·lade**
marmilade : **mar·ma·lade**
marmolade : **mar·ma·lade**
marmolaid : **mar·ma·lade**
marodder : **ma·raud·er**
ma·roon
marrage : **mar·riage**
marratal : **mar·i·tal**
marrathon : **mar·a·thon**
marrauder : **ma·raud·er**
marrege : **mar·riage**
mar·riage
marrige : **mar·riage**
marrine : **ma·rine**
marriner : **mar·i·ner**
marrital : **mar·i·tal**
marroon : **ma·roon**
marrune : **ma·roon**
marryage : **mar·riage**
Marryland : **Mary·land**
marrytal : **mar·i·tal**
Marsailles : **Mar·seilles**
Marsay : **Mar·seilles**
Mar·seilles
Marselles : **Mar·seilles**
Marsey : **Mar·seilles**
mar·shal (leader of military or police force); **mar·tial** (pertaining to war or combat)
marshall : **mar·shal** (leader of military or police force) *or* **mar·tial** (pertaining to war or combat)
marsh·mal·low
marshmellow : **marsh·mal·low**
marsoopial : **mar·su·pi·al**
marsupeal : **mar·su·pi·al**
mar·su·pi·al
martar : **mar·tyr**
marteeni : **mar·ti·ni**
marter : **mar·tyr**

mar•tial (pertaining to war or combat); mar•shal (leader of military or police force)

mar•ti•ni

martiny : mar•ti•ni

martir : mar•tyr

martor : mar•tyr

mar•tyr

marune : ma•roon

marvalous : mar•vel•ous

mar•vel

marvell : mar•vel

mar•vel•lous or mar•vel•ous

mar•vel•ous or mar•vel•lous

marvelus : mar•vel•ous

marvle : mar•vel

marygold : mari•gold

Mary•land

marytal : mar•i•tal

Masachusetts : Mas•sa•chu•setts

masacre : mas•sa•cre

mascaline : mas•cu•line

mas•cara

mascarra : mas•cara

masceline : mas•cu•line

mas•cot

mascott : mas•cot

masculen : mas•cu•line

masculin : mas•cu•line

mas•cu•line

mashean : ma•chine

masheenery : ma•chin•ery

mashete : ma•chete

mashette : ma•chete

mashine : ma•chine

mashinery : ma•chin•ery

maskara : mas•cara

maskarade : mas•quer•ade

maskarra : mas•cara

maskerade : mas•quer•ade

maskott : mas•cot

maskulen : mas•cu•line

maskuline : mas•cu•line

mas•och•ism

masokism : mas•och•ism

ma•son

mas•quer•ade

masquirade : mas•quer•ade

massacer : mas•sa•cre

Massachoosetts : Mas•sa•chu•setts

Mas•sa•chu•setts

Massachusitts : Mas•sa•chu•setts

mas•sa•cre

massecre : mas•sa•cre

Massichusetts : Mas•sa•chu•setts

massochism : mas•och•ism

masson : ma•son

masstoddon : mast•odon

mastadon : mast•odon

mastedon : mast•odon

masterpeace : mas•ter•piece

masterpeece : mas•ter•piece

masterpeice : mas•ter•piece

mas•ter•piece

mas•tery

mastidon : mast•odon

mast•odon

mastodont : mast•odon

mastry : mas•tery

matadoor : mat•a•dor

mat•a•dor

matanee : mat•i•nee

matearial : ma•te•ri•al (matter) or ma•té•ri•el (military equipment)

matedor : mat•a•dor

mateirial : ma•te•ri•al (matter) or ma•té•ri•el (military equipment)

matenance : main•te•nance

matenee : **mat•i•nee**
ma•te•ri•al (matter);
　ma•té•ri•el (military
　equipment)
ma•té•ri•el *or* **ma•te•ri•el**
　(military equipment);
　ma•te•ri•al (matter)
ma•ter•nal
maternel : **ma•ter•nal**
maternety : **ma•ter•ni•ty**
maternitty : **ma•ter•ni•ty**
ma•ter•ni•ty
mathamatics : **math•e•mat•ics**
mathematicks : **math•e•mat•ics**
math•e•mat•ics
mathemattics : **math•e•mat•ics**
mathimathics : **math•e•mat•ics**
mathmatics : **math•e•mat•ics**
matidor : **mat•a•dor**
matinay : **mat•i•nee**
mat•i•nee *or* **mat•i•née**
matiney : **mat•i•nee**
matramony : **mat•ri•mo•ny**
matremony : **mat•ri•mo•ny**
matress : **mat•tress**
matriarc : **ma•tri•arch**
ma•tri•arch
matrimoney : **mat•ri•mo•ny**
mat•ri•mo•ny
matriss : **mat•tress**
mattador : **mat•a•dor**
matterial : **ma•te•ri•al** (matter)
　or **ma•té•ri•el** (military
　equipment)
matternal : **ma•ter•nal**
mattinee : **mat•i•nee**
mat•tress
mattriss : **mat•tress**
maturety : **ma•tu•ri•ty**
maturitty : **ma•tu•ri•ty**
ma•tu•ri•ty
maturnal : **ma•ter•nal**

maturnity : **ma•ter•ni•ty**
maudlen : **maud•lin**
maud•lin
mausaleum : **mau•so•le•um**
mau•so•le•um
mausoliem : **mau•so•le•um**
mausolium : **mau•so•le•um**
mauzoleum : **mau•so•le•um**
mavarick : **mav•er•ick**
mav•er•ick
mawdlin : **maud•lin**
maxamum : **max•i•mum**
maxem : **max•im**
maxemum : **max•i•mum**
max•im
maximem : **max•i•mum**
max•i•mum
maxum : **max•im**
mayennaise : **may•on•naise**
mayer : **may•or**
may•hem
mayhim : **may•hem**
mayinnaise : **may•on•naise**
maynaise : **may•on•naise**
mayonaise : **may•on•naise**
mayonaize : **may•on•naise**
may•on•naise
mayonnase : **may•on•naise**
may•or
maze (labyrinth); **maize** (corn)
mazerka : **ma•zur•ka**
mazochism : **mas•och•ism**
ma•zur•ka
meadian : **me•di•an**
meadiate : **me•di•ate**
meadiocre : **me•di•o•cre**
mead•ow
mea•ger
meagre : **mea•ger**
meanial : **me•nial**
meant
measels : **mea•sles**

mea•sles
measley : **mea•sly**
mea•sly
meastro : **mae•stro**
mea•sure
meazels : **mea•sles**
meazles : **mea•sles**
mecabre : **ma•ca•bre**
me•chan•ic
mechanick : **me•chan•ic**
mechannic : **me•chan•ic**
mechannical : **me•chan•i•cal**
medacal : **med•i•cal**
medacate : **med•i•cate**
medaeval : **me•di•eval**
medal (decoration); **med•dle** (to interfere); **met•tle** (spirit)
medalion : **me•dal•lion**
medallian : **me•dal•lion**
me•dal•lion
medatate : **med•i•tate**
medatation : **med•i•ta•tion**
meddeval : **me•di•eval**
meddevil : **me•di•eval**
meddic : **med•ic**
meddical : **med•i•cal**
meddicate : **med•i•cate**
meddicinal : **me•dic•i•nal**
medditate : **med•i•tate**
medditation : **med•i•ta•tion**
Medditerranean : **Med•i•ter•ra•nean**
med•dle (to interfere); **med•al** (decoration); **met•tle** (spirit)
med•dler (one who meddles); **med•lar** (tree)
meddley : **med•ley**
meddow : **mead•ow**
medeate : **me•di•ate**
medecate : **med•i•cate**
medeival : **me•di•eval**
medetate : **med•i•tate**

medetation : **med•i•ta•tion**
Medeterranean : **Med•i•ter•ra•nean**
medeval : **me•di•eval**
mediacrity : **me•di•oc•ri•ty**
me•di•ae•val or **me•di•eval**
mediam : **me•di•um**
me•di•an
me•di•ate
med•ic
med•i•cal
med•i•cate
medicen : **med•i•cine**
medicenal : **me•dic•i•nal**
medicin : **med•i•cine**
me•dic•i•nal
med•i•cine
medicinel : **me•dic•i•nal**
medick : **med•ic**
medicle : **med•i•cal**
mediem : **me•di•um**
medien : **me•di•an**
me•di•eval or **me•di•ae•val**
medievel : **me•di•eval**
mediocer : **me•di•o•cre**
mediocraty : **me•di•oc•ri•ty**
me•di•o•cre
mediocrety : **me•di•oc•ri•ty**
mediocritty : **me•di•oc•ri•ty**
me•di•oc•ri•ty
medioker : **me•di•o•cre**
medisinal : **me•dic•i•nal**
medissinal : **me•dic•i•nal**
meditacion : **med•i•ta•tion**
meditait : **med•i•tate**
meditashion : **med•i•ta•tion**
med•i•tate
meditatian : **med•i•ta•tion**
Mediteranean : **Med•i•ter•ra•nean**
Mediterrainian : **Med•i•ter•ra•nean**

Med·i·ter·ra·nean
Mediterranian :
  Med·i·ter·ra·nean
me·di·um
medival : **me·di·eval**
med·lar (tree); **med·dler** (one
  who meddles)
med·ley
medlie : **med·ley**
medly : **med·ley**
medow : **mead·ow**
meedian : **me·di·an**
meediate : **me·di·ate**
meediocre : **me·di·o·cre**
meedium : **me·di·um**
meeger : **mea·ger**
meer : **mere** (nothing more
  than) *or* **mir·ror** (glass)
meesles : **mea·sles**
meesly : **mea·sly**
meger : **mea·ger**
meidian : **me·di·an**
meiger : **mea·ger**
meinial : **me·nial**
meladrama : **melo·dra·ma**
melady : **mel·o·dy**
melaise : **mal·aise**
melan : **mel·on**
melanchaly : **mel·an·choly**
mel·an·choly
melancolly : **mel·an·choly**
melancoly : **mel·an·choly**
mé·lange
melay : **me·lee**
me·lee
melencholy : **mel·an·choly**
melidy : **mel·o·dy**
melincholy : **mel·an·choly**
mellady : **mel·o·dy**
mellan : **mel·on**
mellancholy : **mel·an·choly**
mellange : **mé·lange**

mellencholy : **mel·an·choly**
mellidy : **mel·o·dy**
mellincholy : **mel·an·choly**
mellodrama : **melo·dra·ma**
mellody : **mel·o·dy**
mellon : **mel·on**
mel·low
mellowdrama : **melo·dra·ma**
melo·dra·ma
melodramma : **melo·dra·ma**
mel·o·dy
mel·on
melonge : **mé·lange**
melow : **mel·low**
memarabilia : **mem·o·ra·bil·ia**
memarable : **mem·o·ra·ble**
memarize : **mem·o·rize**
memary : **mem·o·ry**
membrain : **mem·brane**
mem·brane
me·men·to
Memfis : **Mem·phis**
meminto : **me·men·to**
memior : **mem·oir**
memiry : **mem·o·ry**
memmento : **me·men·to**
memmoir : **mem·oir**
memmorabilia :
  mem·o·ra·bil·ia
memmorable : **mem·o·ra·ble**
memmorial : **me·mo·ri·al**
memmorize : **mem·o·rize**
memmory : **mem·o·ry**
mem·oir
memorabeelia : **mem·o·ra·bil·ia**
mem·o·ra·bil·ia
memorabillia : **mem·o·ra·bil·ia**
mem·o·ra·ble
memoreal : **me·mo·ri·al**
memoreble : **mem·o·ra·ble**
me·mo·ri·al
memoribal : **mem·o·ra·ble**

memoribilia : **mem•o•ra•bil•ia**
memorible : **mem•o•ra•ble**
memorise (*Brit.*) : **mem•o•rize**
mem•o•rize
memorrial : **me•mo•ri•al**
mem•o•ry
memorybilia : **mem•o•ra•bil•ia**
Mem•phis
Memphiss : **Mem•phis**
Memphus : **Mem•phis**
men•ace
me•nag•er•ie
menagerrie : **me•nag•er•ie**
menagery : **me•nag•er•ie**
menagirie : **me•nag•er•ie**
menajerie : **me•nag•er•ie**
menapause : **men•o•pause**
mendacety : **men•dac•i•ty**
mendacitty : **men•dac•i•ty**
men•dac•i•ty
mendasity : **men•dac•i•ty**
mendassity : **men•dac•i•ty**
meneal : **me•nial**
meneral : **min•er•al**
meneret : **min•a•ret**
me•nial
menice : **men•ace**
meniss : **men•ace**
menistrone : **min•e•stro•ne**
mennace : **men•ace**
mennagerie : **me•nag•er•ie**
menneret : **min•a•ret**
mennice : **men•ace**
mennopause : **men•o•pause**
mennow : **min•now**
men•o•pause
Menphis : **Mem•phis**
ment : **meant**
men•tal
mentalety : **men•tal•i•ty**
mentalitty : **men•tal•i•ty**
men•tal•i•ty

mentallity : **men•tal•i•ty**
mentel : **men•tal**
menter : **men•tor**
menthal : **men•thol**
menthall : **men•thol**
men•thol
mentholl : **men•thol**
men•tor
merage : **mi•rage**
merangue : **me•ringue**
mercary : **mer•cu•ry**
mer•ce•nary
mercenery : **mer•ce•nary**
mercerial : **mer•cu•ri•al**
merchandice : **mer•chan•dise**
mer•chan•dise
mer•chant
merchantdise : **mer•chan•dise**
merchendise : **mer•chan•dise**
merchent : **mer•chant**
merchindise : **mer•chan•dise**
merchint : **mer•chant**
mer•ci•ful
mercifull : **mer•ci•ful**
mercinary : **mer•ce•nary**
mercureal : **mer•cu•ri•al**
mer•cu•ri•al
mer•cu•ry
mer•cy
mercyful : **mer•ci•ful**
mere (nothing more than);
    mir•ror (glass)
merecle : **mir•a•cle**
meremaid : **mer•maid**
meret : **mer•it**
merg•er
meriad : **myr•i•ad**
meriddian : **me•rid•i•an**
me•rid•i•an
meridien : **me•rid•i•an**
meringe : **me•ringue**
me•ringue

mer•it
merky : **murky**
mermade : **mer•maid**
mer•maid
mermer : **mur•mur**
mermur : **mur•mur**
merrangue : **me•ringue**
merridian : **me•rid•i•an**
mer•ri•ly
mer•ri•ment
merringue : **me•ringue**
merrit : **mer•it**
merryment : **mer•ri•ment**
mersenary : **mer•ce•nary**
mersiful : **mer•ci•ful**
mersinary : **mer•ce•nary**
mersy : **mer•cy**
merth : **mirth**
me•sa
mesage : **mes•sage**
mesiah : **mes•si•ah**
meskeet : **mes•quite**
mes•mer•ism
mesmirism : **mes•mer•ism**
mesmurism : **mes•mer•ism**
mesquete : **mes•quite**
mes•quite
messa : **me•sa**
mes•sage
messege : **mes•sage**
messia : **mes•si•ah**
mes•si•ah
messige : **mes•sage**
messmerism : **mes•mer•ism**
messquite : **mes•quite**
messure : **mea•sure**
mesure : **mea•sure**
metabalism : **me•tab•o•lism**
metabelism : **me•tab•o•lism**
metablism : **me•tab•o•lism**
me•tab•o•lism
metafor : **met•a•phor**

metallergy : **me•tal•lur•gy**
me•tal•lur•gy
metalurgy : **me•tal•lur•gy**
metamorfosis :
   meta•mor•pho•sis
metamorphasis :
   meta•mor•pho•sis
metamorphisis :
   meta•mor•pho•sis
meta•mor•pho•sis
met•a•phor
metaphore : **met•a•phor**
me•te•or
meteorallogy : **me•te•o•rol•o•gy**
meteoralogy : **me•te•o•rol•o•gy**
meteorollogy : **me•te•o•rol•o•gy**
me•te•o•rol•o•gy
me•ter
methain : **meth•ane**
methal : **meth•yl**
meth•ane
methel : **meth•yl**
methil : **meth•yl**
meth•yl
metickulous : **me•tic•u•lous**
me•tic•u•lous
meticulus : **me•tic•u•lous**
metifor : **met•a•phor**
metior : **me•te•or**
metiorology : **me•te•o•rol•o•gy**
metiphor : **met•a•phor**
metir : **me•ter**
metre (*Brit.*) : **me•ter**
met•ric
metrick : **met•ric**
metropalis : **me•trop•o•lis**
metropolice : **me•trop•o•lis**
me•trop•o•lis
metropoliss : **me•trop•o•lis**
mettabolism : **me•tab•o•lism**
mettaphor : **met•a•phor**
metticulous : **me•tic•u•lous**

met·tle (spirit); med·al
(decoration); med·dle (to
interfere)

mettric : met·ric

mettropolis : me·trop·o·lis

Mexaco : Mex·i·co

Mex·i·co

mezmerism : mes·mer·ism

Mi·ami

Miammi : Mi·ami

Miamy : Mi·ami

Michagan : Mich·i·gan

Michegan : Mich·i·gan

Mich·i·gan

micraphone : mi·cro·phone

microcosem : mi·cro·cosm

microcosim : mi·cro·cosm

mi·cro·cosm

microcossm : mi·cro·cosm

microcozm : mi·cro·cosm

mi·cro·phone

midaeval : me·di·eval

middal : mid·dle

middel : mid·dle

mid·dle

midg·et

midgit : midg·et

midieval : me·di·eval

Miditerranean :
   Med·i·ter·ra·nean

midle : mid·dle

miestro : mae·stro

mighty

migrain : mi·graine

mi·graine

migrane : mi·graine

mi·grant

migratery : mi·gra·to·ry

migratorry : mi·gra·to·ry

mi·gra·to·ry

migrent : mi·grant

migretory : mi·gra·to·ry

migritory : mi·gra·to·ry

milage : mile·age

milameter : mil·li·met·er

milatant : mil·i·tant

milatary : mil·i·tary

mile·age

mileau : mi·lieu

milege : mile·age

milenium : mil·len·ni·um

milennium : mil·len·ni·um

miletant : mil·i·tant

miletary : mil·i·tary

miliage : mile·age

milicia : mi·li·tia

mi·lieu

milimeter : mil·li·me·ter

milionaire : mil·lion·aire

miliou : mi·lieu

milisha : mi·li·tia

mil·i·tant

militarry : mil·i·tary

mil·i·tary

militent : mil·i·tant

militery : mil·i·tary

mi·li·tia

milleniem : mil·len·ni·um

mil·len·ni·um

millieu : mi·lieu

mil·li·me·ter

millimetre (Brit.) : mil·li·me·ter

millinnium : mil·len·ni·um

millionair : mil·lion·aire

mil·lion·aire

millionare : mil·lion·aire

millionnaire : mil·lion·aire

millitant : mil·i·tant

millitary : mil·i·tary

millitia : mi·li·tia

Millwaukee : Mil·wau·kee

Millwauky : Mil·wau·kee

Milwakee : Mil·wau·kee

Mil·wau·kee

Milwuakee : **Mil·wau·kee**
mim·ic
mimick : **mim·ic**
mimickery : **mim·ic·ry**
mim·ic·ry
mimmic : **mim·ic**
mimmicry : **mim·ic·ry**
mimmosa : **mi·mo·sa**
mi·mo·sa
minace : **men·ace**
minagerie : **me·nag·er·ie**
minamum : **min·i·mum**
minarel : **min·er·al**
min·a·ret
minarette : **min·a·ret**
Minasota : **Min·ne·so·ta**
minastrone : **min·e·stro·ne**
minature : **min·ia·ture**
Mineapolis : **Min·ne·ap·o·lis**
minemum : **min·i·mum**
min·er (mine worker); **min·or**
  (not major)
min·er·al
min·er·al·o·gy
minerel : **min·er·al**
mineret : **min·a·ret**
minerollogy : **min·er·al·o·gy**
minerology : **min·er·al·o·gy**
Minesota : **Min·ne·so·ta**
minester : **min·is·ter**
min·e·stro·ne
minestroni : **min·e·stro·ne**
minestrony : **min·e·stro·ne**
min·ia·ture
minimem : **min·i·mum**
min·i·mum
miniret : **min·a·ret**
min·is·ter
ministrone : **min·e·stro·ne**
miniture : **min·ia·ture**
minnace : **men·ace**
minnaret : **min·a·ret**

Minnasota : **Min·ne·so·ta**
Min·ne·ap·o·lis
Minneapolus : **Min·ne·ap·o·lis**
minneral : **min·er·al**
minneret : **min·a·ret**
Minnesoda : **Min·ne·so·ta**
Min·ne·so·ta
Minniapolis : **Min·ne·ap·o·lis**
minniature : **min·ia·ture**
minnimum : **min·i·mum**
Minnisota : **Min·ne·so·ta**
minnister : **min·is·ter**
min·now
min·or (not major); **min·er**
  (mine worker)
minstral : **min·strel**
min·strel
minstrell : **min·strel**
minstril : **min·strel**
minthol : **men·thol**
miopic : **my·o·pic**
mioppic : **my·o·pic**
mir·a·cle
mir·age
mircenary : **mer·ce·nary**
mirchandise : **mer·chan·dise**
mirchant : **mer·chant**
mirciful : **mer·ci·ful**
mircurial : **mer·cu·ri·al**
mircury : **mer·cu·ry**
mirecle : **mir·a·cle**
mirger : **merg·er**
miriad : **myr·i·ad**
mirical : **mir·a·cle**
miricle : **mir·a·cle**
mirky : **murky**
mirmaid : **mer·maid**
mirmur : **mur·mur**
miror : **mir·ror**
mirracle : **mir·a·cle**
mirrage : **mi·rage**
mirrer : **mir·ror**

mirrh : **mir•ror** (glass) *or*
  myrrh (perfume)
mir•ror
mirth
misanthroape : **mis•an•thrope**
mis•an•thrope
misarable : **mis•er•a•ble**
misary : **mis•ery**
miscelaneous : **mis•cel•la•neous**
mis•cel•la•neous
miscellanious : **mis•cel•la•neous**
mischeff : **mis•chief**
mischeif : **mis•chief**
mischeivous : **mis•chie•vous**
mis•chief
mischiefous : **mis•chie•vous**
mischievious : **mis•chie•vous**
mis•chie•vous
mischiff : **mis•chief**
mischiffous : **mis•chie•vous**
misdameanor : **mis•de•mean•or**
misdemeaner : **mis•de•mean•or**
mis•de•mean•or
misdemeenor : **mis•de•mean•or**
misdemenor : **mis•de•mean•or**
misdimeanor : **mis•de•mean•or**
miselanious : **mis•cel•la•neous**
misellaneous : **mis•cel•la•neous**
misenthrope : **mis•an•thrope**
mis•er•a•ble
miserble : **mis•er•a•ble**
miserible : **mis•er•a•ble**
mis•ery
Mishigan : **Mich•i•gan**
misinanthrope : **mis•an•thrope**
misionary : **mis•sion•ary**
Misissippi : **Mis•sis•sip•pi**
misle : **mis•sal** (prayerbook) *or*
  mis•sile (projectile)
misogenist : **mi•sog•y•nist**
misoginist : **mi•sog•y•nist**
mi•sog•y•nist

misogynnist : **mi•sog•y•nist**
misojinist : **mi•sog•y•nist**
Misouri : **Mis•sou•ri**
mispell : **mis•spell**
mis•sal (prayerbook); **mis•sile**
  (projectile)
missel : **mis•sal** (prayerbook) *or*
  mis•sile (projectile)
misseltoe : **mis•tle•toe**
misserable : **mis•er•a•ble**
missery : **mis•ery**
missiah : **mes•si•ah**
mis•sile (projectile); **mis•sal**
  (prayerbook)
mis•sion•ary
missionery : **mis•sion•ary**
Missisipi : **Mis•sis•sip•pi**
Mississipi : **Mis•sis•sip•pi**
Mis•sis•sip•pi
missle : **mis•sal** (prayerbook) *or*
  mis•sile (projectile)
missletoe : **mis•tle•toe**
mis•spell
Mis•sou•ri
misstress : **mis•tress**
Missuri : **Mis•sou•ri**
mistery : **mys•tery**
mistic : **mys•tic**
misticism : **mys•ti•cism**
mis•tle•toe
mistletow : **mis•tle•toe**
mis•tress
mithical : **myth•i•cal**
mithology : **my•thol•o•gy**
mity : **mighty**
mizery : **mis•ery**
mne•mon•ic
mnemonnic : **mne•mon•ic**
mneumonic : **mne•mon•ic**
mnimonic : **mne•mon•ic**
moaring : **moor•ing**
mobil : **mo•bile**

mo·bile
mobilety : mo·bil·i·ty
mo·bil·i·ty
mobillity : mo·bil·i·ty
moble : mo·bile
moccasen : moc·ca·sin
moc·ca·sin
moccason : moc·ca·sin
mockasin : moc·ca·sin
modafy : mod·i·fy
modarate : mod·er·ate
moddel : mod·el
modderate : mod·er·ate
moddern : mod·ern
moddest : mod·est
moddify : mod·i·fy
moddist : mod·est
moddle : mod·el
modefy : mod·i·fy
mod·el
mod·er·ate
moderet : mod·er·ate
mod·ern
mod·est
modiffy : mod·i·fy
mod·i·fy
modirn : mod·ern
modist : mod·est
modle : mod·el
mogal : mo·gul
mogel : mo·gul
mogle : mo·gul
mo·gul
mogule : mo·gul
molacule : mol·e·cule
molaculer : mo·lec·u·lar
mo·lar
mo·lec·u·lar
mol·e·cule
molequle : mol·e·cule
moler : mo·lar
molify : mol·li·fy

mollafy : mol·li·fy
mollecular : mo·lec·u·lar
mollecule : mol·e·cule
mollefy : mol·li·fy
mollesk : mol·lusk
mol·li·fy
mol·lusk
molusk : mol·lusk
momento : me·men·to
monalog : mon·o·logue
monapoly : mo·nop·o·ly
mon·ar·chy
monarky : mon·ar·chy
monastary : mon·as·tery
monasterry : mon·as·tery
mon·as·tery
monater : mon·i·tor
monatery : mon·e·tary
Mon·day
monestery : mon·as·tery
mon·e·tary
monetery : mon·e·tary
mon·ey
mon·eys or mon·ies
mon·ies or mon·eys
monitary : mon·e·tary
moniter : mon·i·tor
mon·i·tor
monnastery : mon·as·tery
monnitor : mon·i·tor
monnogamy : mo·nog·a·my
monnolith : mon·o·lith
monnolog : mon·o·logue
monnopoly : mo·nop·o·ly
Monntana : Mon·tana
monnument : mon·u·ment
monogammy : mo·nog·a·my
mo·nog·a·my
monogemy : mo·nog·a·my
monoleth : mon·o·lith
mon·o·lith
monolog : mon·o·logue

mon•o•logue
monopaly : **mo•nop•o•ly**
monoply : **mo•nop•o•ly**
mo•nop•o•ly
monsterous : **mon•strous**
monstrocity : **mon•stros•i•ty**
mon•stros•i•ty
monstrossity : **mon•stros•i•ty**
mon•strous
monstrousity : **mon•stros•i•ty**
mon•tage
Mon•tana
Montanna : **Mon•tana**
montoge : **mon•tage**
Mon•tre•al
Montreall : **Mon•tre•al**
Montrial : **Mon•tre•al**
montrosety : **mon•stros•i•ty**
mon•u•ment
mony : **mon•ey**
moor•ing
moose (elk); **mousse** (dessert)
morabund : **mor•i•bund**
mor•al (ethical; lesson);
  mo•rale (emotional state)
mo•rale (emotional state);
  mor•al (ethical; lesson)
moralety : **mo•ral•i•ty**
mo•ral•i•ty
morallity : **mo•ral•i•ty**
mo•rass
morcel : **mor•sel**
mor•dant (biting); **mor•dent**
  (Musical)
mor•dent *(Musical)*; **mor•dant**
  (biting)
morfeen : **mor•phine**
morfine : **mor•phine**
morgage : **mort•gage**
morgege : **mort•gage**
mor•i•bund
morings : **moor•ing**

Morman : **Mor•mon**
Mormen : **Mor•mon**
Mor•mon
mornful : **mourn•ful**
Mo•roc•co
Morocko : **Mo•roc•co**
Moroco : **Mo•roc•co**
morpheen : **mor•phine**
morphene : **mor•phine**
mor•phine
morrality : **mo•ral•i•ty**
morrass : **mo•rass**
morribund : **mor•i•bund**
mor•sel
morsil : **mor•sel**
morsle : **mor•sel**
mortafy : **mor•ti•fy**
mor•tal
mor•tar
mortefy : **mor•ti•fy**
mortel : **mor•tal**
morter : **mor•tar**
mort•gage
mortiffy : **mor•ti•fy**
mor•ti•fy
mortor : **mor•tar**
mor•tu•ary
mortuery : **mor•tu•ary**
mosk : **mosque**
moskeeto : **mos•qui•to**
moskito : **mos•qui•to**
Mos•lem *or* **Mus•lim**
Moslim : **Mus•lim**
mosque
mos•qui•to
mossoleum : **mau•so•le•um**
motavate : **mo•ti•vate**
moter : **mo•tor**
mo•ti•vate
mot•ley
mo•tor
mottley : **mot•ley**

moun·tain
mountan : **moun·tain**
Mountana : **Mon·ta·na**
mountian : **moun·tain**
mountin : **moun·tain**
mourn·ful
mournfull : **mourn·ful**
mouse (rodent); **mousse**
  (dessert)
mousse (dessert); **moose** (elk);
  mouse (rodent)
mov·able *or* **move·able**
move·able *or* **mov·able**
movible : **mov·able**
Mozlem : **Mus·lim**
mu·cous (*adj.*); **mu·cus** (*noun*)
mu·cus (*noun*); **mu·cous** (*adj.*)
muffen : **muf·fin**
muf·fin
multaple : **mul·ti·ple**
multaply : **mul·ti·ply**
multeple : **mul·ti·ple**
multeply : **mul·ti·ply**
multipal : **mul·ti·ple**
mul·ti·ple
mul·ti·ply
multipple : **mul·ti·ple**
mundain : **mun·dane**
mun·dane
Munday : **Mon·day**
municions : **mu·ni·tions**
mu·nic·i·pal
municiple : **mu·nic·i·pal**
munisipal : **mu·nic·i·pal**
mu·ni·tions
mu·ral
murcenary : **mer·ce·nary**
murchandise : **mer·chan·dise**
murchant : **mer·chant**
murcury : **mer·cu·ry**
murger : **merg·er**
murky

murmaid : **mer·maid**
murmer : **mur·mur**
mur·mur
murral : **mu·ral**
murrel : **mu·ral**
mursenary : **mer·ce·nary**
murth : **mirth**
mus·cle (body tissue); **mus·sel**
  (bivalve mollusk)
musecal : **mu·si·cal**
mu·se·um
mu·si·cal
mu·si·cian
musicion : **mu·si·cian**
musicle : **mu·si·cal**
musiem : **mu·se·um**
musium : **mu·se·um**
mus·ket
mus·ke·teer
musketere : **mus·ke·teer**
musketier : **mus·ke·teer**
muskit : **mus·ket**
muskiteer : **mus·ke·teer**
muslen : **mus·lin**
Mus·lim *or* **Mos·lem**
mus·lin
mus·sel (bivalve mollusk);
  mus·cle (body tissue)
mussle : **mus·cle** (body tissue)
  or **mus·sel** (bivalve mollusk)
musstard : **mus·tard**
mus·tard
musterd : **mus·tard**
mustird : **mus·tard**
mu·ta·bil·i·ty
mutabillity : **mu·ta·bil·i·ty**
mutalate : **mu·ti·late**
mutaneer : **mu·ti·neer**
mu·tant
mutany : **mu·ti·ny**
muteneer : **mu·ti·neer**
mutent : **mu·tant**

muteny : **mu•ti•ny**
mutibility : **mu•ta•bil•i•ty**
mu•ti•late
mutillate : **mu•ti•late**
mu•ti•neer
mutinere : **mu•ti•neer**
mutinier : **mu•ti•neer**
mu•ti•ny
mutten : **mut•ton**
muttin : **mut•ton**
mut•ton
muzel : **muz•zle**
muzeum : **mu•se•um**
Muzlim : **Mus•lim**
muzlin : **mus•lin**
muzzel : **muz•zle**
muz•zle
Myami: Mi•ami
mygraine : mi•graine

myistisism : **mys•ti•cism**
my•o•pic
myopick : **my•o•pic**
myoppic : **my•o•pic**
myr•i•ad
myrrh
mysterry : **mys•tery**
mys•tery
mys•tic
mys•ti•cism
mystick : **mys•tic**
mythacal : **myth•i•cal**
mythalogy : **my•thol•o•gy**
mythecal : **myth•i•cal**
myth•i•cal
mythicle : **myth•i•cal**
mythollogy : **my•thol•o•gy**
my•thol•o•gy

N

na·bob
nacent : na·scent
nadar : na·dir
nadeer : na·dir
nader : na·dir
na·dir
naevete : na·ive·te
naevety : na·ive·te
naibob : na·bob
naife : na·ive
naighbor : neigh·bor
naipalm : na·palm
naipam : na·palm
naipom : na·palm
Nai·ro·bi
nai·ve or na·ïve
naivetay : na·ive·te
na·ive·te or na·ive·té
naivety (*Brit.*) : na·ive·te
naivity : na·ive·te
na·ked
nakid : na·ked
nakked : na·ked
na·palm
napken : nap·kin
nap·kin
napom : na·palm
napsack : knap·sack
narate : nar·rate
naration : nar·ra·tion
narator : nar·ra·tor
narcisism : nar·cis·sism
nar·cis·sism
nar·cot·ic
narcotick : nar·cot·ic
narcottic : nar·cot·ic
narled : gnarled
nar·rate
narrater : nar·ra·tor
nar·ra·tion

nar·ra·tor
narrled : gnarled
narsisism : nar·cis·sism
na·sal
nasall : na·sal
na·scent
nascint : na·scent
nasea : nau·sea
nasel : na·sal
nasell : na·sal
nasent : na·scent
nash : gnash
nat : gnat
natiral : nat·u·ral
nativety : na·tiv·i·ty
nativitty : na·tiv·i·ty
na·tiv·i·ty
nattural : nat·u·ral
nat·u·ral
naturel : nat·u·ral
naturral : nat·u·ral
nau·sea
nau·se·ate
nausha : nau·sea
nausheate : nau·se·ate
naushia : nau·sea
nausia : nau·sea
nausiate : nau·se·ate
naut : knot (rope; one nautical
    mile); not (negative); nought
    (zero)
nau·ti·cal
nauticle : nau·ti·cal
nautilis : nau·ti·lus
nautillus : nau·ti·lus
nau·ti·lus
navagator : nav·i·ga·tor
Nav·a·ho or Nav·a·jo
Nav·a·jo or Nav·a·ho

na•val (of the navy); na•vel
   (belly button)
navegator : nav•i•ga•tor
Naveho : Nav•a•ho
na•vel (belly button); na•val (of
   the navy)
navigater : nav•i•ga•tor
nav•i•ga•tor
Naviho : Nav•a•ho
navil : na•val (of the navy) *or*
   na•vel (belly button)
navvigator : nav•i•ga•tor
naw : gnaw
nawsea : nau•sea
nawseate : nau•se•ate
nawsia : nau•sea
nawtical : nau•ti•cal
nawtilus : nau•ti•lus
naybob : na•bob
nay (no); neigh (whinny)
naypalm : na•palm
naypam : na•palm
naypom : na•palm
nealithic : neo•lith•ic
neap
neaphyte : neo•phyte
near
nearvous : ner•vous
neat
Nebbraska : Ne•bras•ka
nebbula : neb•u•la (*sing.*)
nebbulous : neb•u•lous
Ne•bras•ka
Nebrasska : Ne•bras•ka
neb•u•la (*sing.*)
neb•u•lae *or* neb•u•las (*plur.*)
neb•u•las *or* neb•u•lae (*plur.*)
nebulla : neb•u•la (*sing.*)
nebullous : neb•u•lous
neb•u•lous
nebulus : neb•u•lous
necesary : ne•ces•sary

necesity : ne•ces•si•ty
nec•es•sary
necessery : nec•es•sary
necessety : ne•ces•si•ty
necessitty : ne•ces•si•ty
ne•ces•si•ty
necissary : nec•es•sary
neck•lace
necklase : neck•lace
necklise : neck•lace
neckliss : neck•lace
necktar : nec•tar
necktarine : nec•tar•ine
nec•tar
nectarean : nec•tar•ine
nectareen : nec•tar•ine
nectarene : nec•tar•ine
nec•tar•ine
necter : nec•tar
necterine : nec•tar•ine
nectir : nec•tar
nectirine : nec•tar•ine
neece : niece
needal : nee•dle
needel : nee•dle
nee•dle
neep : neap
neer : near
neese : niece
neet : neat
nefew : neph•ew
neffew : neph•ew
neg•a•tive
negetive : neg•a•tive
neggative : neg•a•tive
neghbor : neigh•bor
negitive : neg•a•tive
neglagee : neg•li•gee
neglagence : neg•li•gence
neglegee : neg•li•gee
neglegence : neg•li•gence
neglegible : neg•li•gi•ble

negligeble : **neg·li·gi·ble**
negligibal : **neg·li·gi·ble**
neg·li·gee
neg·li·gence
negligense : **neg·li·gence**
negligibel : **neg·li·gi·ble**
neg·li·gi·ble
negligince : **neg·li·gence**
neglishay : **neg·li·gee**
neglishee : **neg·li·gee**
negociate : **ne·go·ti·ate**
negoshiate : **ne·go·ti·ate**
negoteate : **ne·go·ti·ate**
ne·go·ti·ate
neice : **niece**
neigh (whinny); **nay** (no)
neighber : **neigh·bor**
neigh·bor
neise : **niece**
nei·ther
nemesees : **nem·e·ses** (*plur.*)
nem·e·ses (*plur.*)
nem·e·sis (*sing.*)
nemesus : **nem·e·sis** (*sing.*)
nemises : **nem·e·ses** (*plur.*)
nemisis : **nem·e·sis** (*sing.*)
nemmises : **nem·e·ses** (*plur.*)
nemmisis : **nem·e·sis** (*sing.*)
nemonic : **mne·mon·ic**
nemonnic : **mne·mon·ic**
neofite : **neo·phyte**
neofyte : **neo·phyte**
neo·lith·ic
neolithick : **neo·lith·ic**
neolythic : **neo·lith·ic**
neo·phyte
neph·ew
nephiw : **neph·ew**
nephue : **neph·ew**
nervana : **nir·va·na**
nerviss : **ner·vous**
ner·vous

nervus : **ner·vous**
nesessary : **nec·es·sary**
nesessity : **ne·ces·si·ty**
nesissary : **nec·es·sary**
neugat : **nou·gat** (candy) *or*
  nug·get (lump)
neu·ral
neuralogy : **neu·rol·o·gy**
neurel : **neu·ral**
neuroligy : **neu·rol·o·gy**
neurollogy : **neu·rol·o·gy**
neu·rol·o·gy
neu·ron
neurosees : **neu·ro·ses** (*plur.*)
neu·ro·ses (*plur.*)
neu·ro·sis (*sing.*)
neurosus : **neu·ro·sis** (*sing.*)
neu·ter
neuteral : **neu·tral**
neu·tral
neutrel : **neu·tral**
neu·tron
Nev·a·da
Nevadda : **Nev·a·da**
new (not old); **gnu** (antelope);
  knew (was aware)
New·found·land
Newfundland : **New·found·land**
newget : **nou·gat** (candy) *or*
  nug·get (lump)
New Hampshir : **New**
  Hamp·shire
New Hamp·shire
New Hampsure : **New**
  Hamp·shire
New Hamshire : **New**
  Hamp·shire
New Jer·sey
New Jersy : **New Jer·sey**
New Mex·i·co
New Or·leans
New Orlines : **New Or·leans**

newrosis : **neu·ro·sis** (*sing.*)

newsreal : **news·reel**

news·reel

news·stand

newstand : **news·stand**

newter : **neu·ter**

newtron : **neu·tron**

New York

Newyork : **New York**

New Zea·land

New Zealund : **New Zea·land**

New Zeeland : **New Zea·land**

New Zeland : **New Zea·land**

Ni·ag·a·ra

Niagera : **Ni·ag·a·ra**

Niaggara : **Ni·ag·a·ra**

Niagra : **Ni·ag·a·ra**

nialism : **ni·hil·ism**

Niarobi : **Nai·ro·bi**

niave : **na·ive**

niavete : **na·ive·te**

Nibraska : **Ne·bras·ka**

nicatine : **nic·o·tine**

niccotine : **nic·o·tine**

nice·ty

nich : **niche**

niche

nicitty : **nice·ty**

nicity : **nice·ty**

nickal : **nick·el**

nickalodeon : **nick·el·ode·on**

nick·el

nick·el·ode·on

nickelodion : **nick·el·ode·on**

nickle : **nick·el**

nickleodeon : **nick·el·ode·on**

nicknack : **knick·knack**

nickotine : **nic·o·tine**

nicoteen : **nic·o·tine**

nicotene : **nic·o·tine**

nic·o·tine

niece

nieghbor : **neigh·bor**

niese : **niece**

niether : **nei·ther**

nieve : **na·ive**

nievete : **na·ive·te**

nife : **knife**

nifes : **knifes** (stabs) *or* **knives** (*plur.*)

nigardly : **nig·gard·ly**

Nigeeria : **Ni·ge·ria**

Nigerea : **Ni·ge·ria**

Ni·ge·ria

nig·gard·ly

niggerdly : **nig·gard·ly**

night (not day); **knight** (medieval soldier)

nihalism : **ni·hil·ism**

nihelism : **ni·hil·ism**

ni·hil·ism

Nijeria : **Ni·ge·ria**

nilism : **ni·hil·ism**

nilon : **ny·lon**

nimf : **nymph**

nimises : **nem·e·ses** (*plur.*)

nimisis : **nem·e·sis** (*sing.*)

nimmises : **nem·e·ses** (*plur.*)

nimmisis : **nem·e·sis** (*sing.*)

nimmonic : **mne·mon·ic**

nimonic : **mne·mon·ic**

nimph : **nymph**

ninetean : **nine·teen**

nine·teen

ninetene : **nine·teen**

nineth : **ninth**

nine·ti·eth

nine·ty

ninetyeth : **nine·ti·eth**

ninetyith : **nine·ti·eth**

ninteen : **nine·teen**

ninth

nintieth : **nine·ti·eth**

ninty : **nine·ty**

niophyte : **neo•phyte**
Nirobi : **Nai•ro•bi**
nir•va•na
nirvanna : **nir•va•na**
nitch : **niche**
nite : **knight** (medieval soldier)
   or **night** (not day)
nitragen : **ni•tro•gen**
nitregen : **ni•tro•gen**
ni•tro•gen
nitrogin : **ni•tro•gen**
nives : **knives**
no (negative); **know** (to be
   aware of); **now** (at this time)
noam : **gnome** (dwarf) *or*
   Nome (city)
nobilety : **no•bil•i•ty**
no•bil•i•ty
nobillity : **no•bil•i•ty**
noboddy : **no•body**
no•body
nockturnal : **noc•tur•nal**
nocternal : **noc•tur•nal**
noc•tur•nal
nocturnall : **noc•tur•nal**
nocturnel : **noc•tur•nal**
noddule : **nod•ule**
noduel : **nod•ule**
nod•ule
noledge : **knowl•edge**
noll : **knoll**
no•mad
Nome (city); **gnome** (dwarf)
nomenal : **nom•i•nal**
nomenate : **nom•i•nate**
nomenee : **nom•i•nee**
nom•i•nal
nom•i•nate
nom•i•nee
nominy : **nom•i•nee**
nommad : **no•mad**
nomminal : **nom•i•nal**

nomminate : **nom•i•nate**
nomminee : **nom•i•nee**
non•cha•lant
nonchalont : **non•cha•lant**
nonchelant : **non•cha•lant**
nonchilant : **non•cha•lant**
non•de•script
nondiscript : **non•de•script**
nonsence : **non•sense**
non•sense
nonshalant : **non•cha•lant**
nonshillant : **non•cha•lant**
nonsince : **non•sense**
nor•mal
nor•mal•cy
normalsy : **nor•mal•cy**
Normandee : **Nor•man•dy**
Nor•man•dy
normel : **nor•mal**
normelcy : **nor•mal•cy**
Normendy : **Nor•man•dy**
Normindy : **Nor•man•dy**
North Caralina : **North**
   Car•o•li•na
North Carlina : **North**
   Car•o•li•na
North Car•o•li•na
North Carrolina : **North**
   Car•o•li•na
North Dahkota : **North**
   Da•ko•ta
North Da•ko•ta
North Dakotah : **North**
   Da•ko•ta
Norwaygian : **Nor•we•gian**
Norweegian : **Nor•we•gian**
Norwegean : **Nor•we•gian**
Nor•we•gian
Norwejian : **Nor•we•gian**
nosetril : **nos•tril**
nostalgea : **nos•tal•gia**
nos•tal•gia

nostallgia : **nos•tal•gia**
nos•tril
nostrill : **nos•tril**
not (negative); **knot** (rope; one
  nautical mile); **nought** (zero)
not•a•ble
notafy : **not•i•fy**
notariety : **no•to•ri•ety**
noteble : **no•ta•ble**
notefy : **no•ti•fy**
noteriety : **no•to•ri•ety**
nothole : **knot•hole**
notible : **no•ta•ble**
noticable : **no•tice•able**
no•tice
no•tice•able
noticible : **no•tice•able**
notiffy : **no•ti•fy**
no•ti•fy
notiriety : **no•to•ri•ety**
notise : **no•tice**
notiseable : **no•tice•able**
notiss : **no•tice**
notoreous : **no•to•ri•ous**
notorietty : **no•to•ri•ety**
no•to•ri•ety
no•to•ri•ous
notorrious : **no•to•ri•ous**
notoryity : **no•to•ri•ety**
nottice : **no•tice**
nou•gat (candy); **nug•get**
  (lump)
nought (zero); **knot** (rope; one
  nautical mile); **not** (negative)
nour•ish
Nova Scocia : **No•va Sco•tia**
Nova Scosha : **No•va Sco•tia**
No•va Sco•tia
Nova Scotshia : **No•va Sco•tia**
novacaine : **no•vo•caine**
novacane : **no•vo•caine**
nov•ice

novise : **nov•ice**
noviss : **nov•ice**
no•vo•caine
novocane : **no•vo•caine**
novvice : **nov•ice**
now (at this time); **know** (to be
  aware of); **no** (negative)
now•a•days
nowdays : **now•a•days**
nowledge : **knowl•edge**
nozal : **noz•zle**
nozle : **noz•zle**
nozzal : **noz•zle**
noz•zle
nu : **gnu**
nu•ance
nuanse : **nu•ance**
nuckle : **knuck•le**
nu•cle•ar
nucleer : **nu•cle•ar**
nuclere : **nu•cle•ar**
nu•cle•us
nuclius : **nu•cle•us**
nucular : **nu•cle•ar**
nuculer : **nu•cle•ar**
nuculis : **nu•cle•us**
nuculus : **nu•cle•us**
nudaty : **nu•di•ty**
nudety : **nu•di•ty**
nuditty : **nu•di•ty**
nu•di•ty
nuematic : **pneu•mat•ic**
nuemonia : **pneu•mo•nia**
nueral : **neu•ral**
nuerology : **neu•rol•o•gy**
nueron : **neu•ron**
nueroses : **neu•ro•ses** (*plur.*)
nuerosis : **neu•ro•sis** (*sing.*)
nueter : **neu•ter**
nuetral : **neu•tral**
nuetron : **neu•tron**

nuget : **nougat** (candy) *or*
  nug•get (lump)
nugget (lump); **nou•gat** (candy)
nuggit : **nougat** (candy) *or*
  nug•get (lump)
nui•sance
nuisanse : **nui•sance**
nuisence : **nui•sance**
nuisense : **nui•sance**
nulify : **nul•li•fy**
nullafy : **nul•li•fy**
nullefy : **nul•li•fy**
nul•li•fy
num : **numb**
numaral : **nu•mer•al**
numarical : **nu•mer•i•cal**
numatic : **pneu•mat•ic**
numb
numb•ly
numbskull : **num•skull**
nu•mer•al
numerel : **nu•mer•al**
nu•mer•i•cal
numericle : **nu•mer•i•cal**
numiral : **nu•mer•al**
numly : **numb•ly**
numonia : **pneu•mo•nia**
num•skull
nunery : **nun•nery**
nunnary : **nun•nery**
nun•nery
nup•tial
nuptual : **nup•tial**
nuptuel : **nup•tial**
nuptule : **nup•tial**

nural : **neu•ral**
nurcery : **nurs•ery**
nurish : **nour•ish**
nurology : **neu•rol•o•gy**
nuron : **neu•ron**
nuroses : **neu•ro•ses** (*plur.*)
nurosis : **neu•ro•sis** (*sing.*)
nurral : **neu•ral**
nurralolgy : **neu•rol•o•gy**
nurrish : **nour•ish**
nurron : **neu•ron**
nursary : **nurs•ery**
nurserry : **nurs•ery**
nurs•ery
nursury : **nurs•ery**
nusance : **nui•sance**
nutral : **neu•tral**
nutrative : **nu•tri•tive**
nutreant : **nu•tri•ent**
nutretive : **nu•tri•tive**
nutriant : **nu•tri•ent**
nu•tri•ent
nu•tri•tion
nu•tri•tive
nutrittion : **nu•tri•tion**
nutron : **neu•tron**
nuzle : **nuz•zle**
nuzzal : **nuz•zle**
nuz•zle
nyeve : **na•ive**
nyevete : **na•ive•te**
ny•lon
nymf : **nymph**
nymph
Nyrobi : **Nai•ro•bi**

O

Oahoo : **Oa·hu**
Oa·hu
Oaklahoma : **Okla·ho·ma**
oa·ses (*plur.*)
oa·sis (*sing.*)
obaisance : **obei·sance**
obalisk : **obe·lisk**
obbelisk : **obe·lisk**
obcess : **ab·scess**
 (inflammation) *or* **ob·sess** (to
 preoccupy)
obcession : **ob·ses·sion**
obderate : **ob·du·rate**
ob·du·rate
obdurrate : **ob·du·rate**
obeadience : **obe·di·ence**
obeadient : **obe·di·ent**
obease : **obese**
obeasity : **obe·si·ty**
obecity : **obe·si·ty**
obedeance : **obe·di·ence**
obedianse : **obe·di·ence**
obediant : **obe·di·ent**
obe·di·ence
obediense : **obe·di·ence**
obe·di·ent
obeedience : **obe·di·ence**
obeedient : **obe·di·ent**
obeesity : **obe·si·ty**
obei·sance
obeisence : **obei·sance**
obeisense : **obei·sance**
obelesk : **obe·lisk**
obe·lisk
obellisk : **obe·lisk**
obese
obesety : **obe·si·ty**
obesitty : **obe·si·ty**
obe·si·ty
obeysance : **obei·sance**

obeysense : **obei·sance**
obittuary : **obit·u·ary**
obit·u·ary
obituery : **obit·u·ary**
objectafy : **ob·jec·ti·fy**
objectefy : **ob·jec·ti·fy**
objectiffy : **ob·jec·ti·fy**
ob·jec·ti·fy
obleek : **oblique**
obleeque : **oblique**
oblique
oblivian : **obliv·i·on**
oblivien : **obliv·i·on**
obliv·i·on
obnocksious : **ob·nox·ious**
ob·nox·ious
obo : **oboe**
oboe
obsalescent : **ob·so·les·cent**
ob·scene
obscerity : **ob·scu·ri·ty**
obscurety : **ob·scu·ri·ty**
ob·scu·ri·ty
obsean : **ob·scene**
obsene : **ob·scene**
obsequeous : **ob·se·qui·ous**
ob·se·qui·ous
ob·ser·vance
observanse : **ob·ser·vance**
observence : **ob·ser·vance**
observince : **ob·ser·vance**
obsesion : **ob·ses·sion**
ob·sess (to preoccupy);
 ab·scess (inflammation)
ob·ses·sion
obsiquious : **ob·se·qui·ous**
obsoleat : **ob·so·lete**
obsoleet : **ob·so·lete**
ob·so·les·cent
obsolessant : **ob·so·les·cent**

obsolessent : **ob•so•les•cent**
ob•so•lete
obstacal : **ob•sta•cle**
ob•sta•cle
obstecle : **ob•sta•cle**
obsticle : **ob•sta•cle**
ob•sti•nate
obstinet : **ob•sti•nate**
ob•tain
obtane : **ob•tain**
obthamalogy :
  oph•thal•mol•o•gy
obtical : **op•ti•cal**
obtimal : **op•ti•mal**
obtimism : **op•ti•mism**
obtimist : **op•ti•mist**
obtometrist : **op•tom•e•trist**
obtuce : **ob•tuse**
ob•tuse
obveate : **ob•vi•ate**
ob•vi•ate
obviaus : **ob•vi•ous**
ocaen : **ocean**
ocasion : **oc•ca•sion**
oc•ca•sion
occassion : **oc•ca•sion**
oc•cult
oc•cu•pant
occupent : **oc•cu•pant**
occupint : **oc•cu•pant**
oc•cur
occured : **oc•curred**
occurence : **oc•cur•rence**
occurrance : **oc•cur•rence**
occurranse : **oc•cur•rence**
oc•curred
oc•cur•rence
ocean
ocien : **ocean**
oc•ta•gon
octain : **oc•tane**
oc•tane

octapus : **oc•to•pus**
octegon : **oc•ta•gon**
octigon : **oc•ta•gon**
oc•to•pus
octopuss : **oc•to•pus**
ocult : **oc•cult**
ocupant : **oc•cu•pant**
ocupent : **oc•cu•pant**
ocupint : **oc•cu•pant**
ocur : **oc•cur**
ocured : **oc•curred**
ocurence : **oc•cur•rence**
ocurrance : **oc•cur•rence**
ocurrence : **oc•cur•rence**
oddety : **odd•i•ty**
oddissey : **od•ys•sey**
odd•i•ty
oddysey : **od•ys•sey**
oder : **odor**
odissey : **od•ys•sey**
odor
odysey : **od•ys•sey**
od•ys•sey
odyssie : **od•ys•sey**
ofense : **of•fense**
offacer : **of•fi•cer**
offecer : **of•fi•cer**
offen : **of•ten**
of•fence *or* **of•fense**
of•fense *or* **of•fence**
offeratory : **of•fer•to•ry**
offeritory : **of•fer•to•ry**
of•fer•to•ry
of•fi•cer
of•ten
oftin : **of•ten**
oger : **ogre**
ogre
Ohio
Okla•ho•ma
Oklihoma : **Okla•ho•ma**
ole•an•der

olfactary : **ol•fac•to•ry**
olfactery : **ol•fac•to•ry**
ol•fac•to•ry
oliander : **ole•an•der**
Olimpic : **Olym•pic**
Olym•pic
Olympick : **Olym•pic**
omaga : **ome•ga**
omage : **hom•age**
ome•ga
om•elet *or* **om•elette**
om•elette *or* **om•elet**
omen
omenous : **om•i•nous**
omilet : **om•elet**
omin : **omen**
om•i•nous
omision : **omis•sion**
omis•sion
omit
omlet : **om•elet**
omlette : **om•elet**
ommage : **hom•age**
ommelet : **om•elet**
ommit : **omit**
ommlet : **om•elet**
omnipotance : **om•nip•o•tence**
om•nip•o•tence
omnipotense : **om•nip•o•tence**
onamatopoeia :
    on•o•mato•poe•ia
onarous : **oner•ous**
oner•ous
one•self
onesself : **one•self**
onest : **hon•est**
onix : **on•yx**
onnest : **hon•est**
onnist : **hon•est**
onnix : **on•yx**
onnomatopoeia :
    on•o•mato•poe•ia

onnor : **hon•or**
onnorable : **hon•or•able**
onnorible : **hon•or•able**
onnui : **en•nui**
onnyx : **on•yx**
onomatopia : **on•o•mato•poe•ia**
on•o•mato•poe•ia
onomotapoeia :
    on•o•mato•poe•ia
onor : **hon•or**
onorable : **hon•or•able**
onorarium : **hon•o•rar•i•um**
onoreble : **hon•or•able**
onorible : **hon•or•able**
Ontareo : **On•tar•io**
On•tar•io
Ontarrio : **On•tar•io**
Onterio : **On•tar•io**
ontourage : **en•tou•rage**
ontrepreneur : **en•tre•pre•neur**
on•ward
onwerd : **on•ward**
onword : **on•ward**
on•yx
opacety : **opac•i•ty**
opacitty : **opac•i•ty**
opac•i•ty
opal
opassity : **opac•i•ty**
opel : **opal**
openess : **open•ness**
open•ness
op•era
op•er•a•ble
operible : **op•er•a•ble**
opeum : **opi•um**
oph•thal•mol•o•gy
ophthemalogy :
    oph•thal•mol•o•gy
ophthmalligy :
    oph•thal•mol•o•gy

ophthmallogy :
  oph·thal·mol·o·gy
ophthmollogy :
  oph·thal·mol·o·gy
opiem : **opi·um**
opi·um
oponant : **op·po·nent**
oponent : **op·po·nent**
oportunity : **op·por·tu·ni·ty**
oposite : **op·po·site**
oppal : **opal**
oppasite : **op·po·site**
oppera : **op·era**
opperable : **op·er·a·ble**
oppertunity : **op·por·tu·ni·ty**
oppiset : **op·po·site**
oppisite : **op·po·site**
opponant : **op·po·nent**
op·po·nent
opponint : **op·po·nent**
opportunety : **op·por·tu·ni·ty**
opportunitty : **op·por·tu·ni·ty**
op·por·tu·ni·ty
opposate : **op·po·site**
opposet : **op·po·site**
op·po·site
oppresion : **op·pres·sion**
oppresor : **op·pres·sor**
op·press
oppresser : **op·pres·sor**
op·pres·sion
op·pres·sor
oppulence : **op·u·lence**
opress : **op·press**
opression : **op·pres·sion**
opressor : **op·pres·sor**
optamism : **op·ti·mism**
optemal : **op·ti·mal**
optemism : **op·ti·mism**
opthalmology :
  oph·thal·mol·o·gy

opthamology :
  oph·thal·mol·o·gy
opthemology :
  oph·thal·mol·o·gy
op·tic
optick : **op·tic**
optickal : **op·ti·cal**
opticle : **op·ti·cal**
op·ti·mal
optimel : **op·ti·mal**
optimest : **op·ti·mist**
op·ti·mism
op·ti·mist
optimizm : **op·ti·mism**
optimmism : **op·ti·mism**
optimmist : **op·ti·mist**
optomatrist : **op·tom·e·trist**
op·tom·e·trist
optomitrist : **op·tom·e·trist**
optommetrist : **op·tom·e·trist**
opulance : **op·u·lence**
opulanse : **op·u·lence**
op·u·lence
opulense : **op·u·lence**
opullence : **op·u·lence**
oracion : **ora·tion**
or·a·cle
orafice : **or·i·fice**
oragin : **or·i·gin**
Oragon : **Or·e·gon**
oral
orangatang : **orang·utan**
or·ange
orangootan : **orang·utan**
orang·utan
orashion : **ora·tion**
orater : **or·a·tor**
ora·tion
or·a·tor
orbet : **or·bit**
or·bit
orcestra : **or·ches·tra**

or•chard
orched : **or•chid**
orcherd : **or•chard**
or•ches•tra
or•chid
orchird : **or•chard**
orchistra : **or•ches•tra**
or•dain
ordanary : **or•di•nary**
ordane : **or•dain**
or•deal
ordeel : **or•deal**
ordenance : **or•di•nance** (rule,
    law) *or* **ord•nance**
    (weaponry)
ordenary : **or•di•nary**
ordenince : **or•di•nance** (rule,
    law) *or* **ord•nance**
    (weaponry)
or•di•nance (rule, law);
    ord•nance (weaponry)
ordinarry : **or•di•nary**
or•di•nary
ordinense : **or•di•nance** (rule,
    law) *or* **ord•nance**
    (weaponry)
ordinerry : **or•di•nary**
ordinery : **or•di•nary**
ordnance (weaponry);
    ordinance (rule, law)
ordnanse : **or•di•nance** (rule,
    law) *or* **ord•nance**
    (weaponry)
orecle : **or•a•cle**
orefice : **or•i•fice**
Or•e•gon (state); **or•i•gin**
    (beginning)
Oregone : **Or•e•gon**
orel : **oral**
orenge : **or•ange**
oreole : **ori•ole**
oretor : **or•a•tor**

orfan : **or•phan**
orfanage : **or•phan•age**
orfin : **or•phan**
orfinage : **or•phan•age**
orfun : **or•phan**
orfunage : **or•phan•age**
or•gan•dy
organesm : **or•gan•ism**
or•gan•ic
organick : **or•gan•ic**
or•gan•ism
organnic : **or•gan•ic**
orgendy : **or•gan•dy**
orgenism : **or•gan•ism**
orgindy : **or•gan•dy**
oriant : **ori•ent**
orical : **or•a•cle**
oricle : **or•a•cle**
ori•ent
ori•en•tal
orientall : **ori•en•tal**
orientel : **ori•en•tal**
or•i•fice
orifise : **or•i•fice**
orifiss : **or•i•fice**
orifrice : **or•i•fice**
origen : **Or•e•gon** (state) *or*
    or•i•gin (beginning)
origenal : **orig•i•nal**
origenate : **orig•i•nate**
or•i•gin (beginning); **Or•e•gon**
    (state)
originait : **orig•i•nate**
orig•i•nal
orig•i•nate
originel : **orig•i•nal**
originnate : **orig•i•nate**
Origon : **Or•e•gon**
orijen : **or•i•gin**
oringe : **or•ange**
oriol : **ori•ole**
ori•ole

orioll : **ori•ole**
oritor : **or•a•tor**
orkestra : **or•ches•tra**
orkid : **or•chid**
orkistra : **or•ches•tra**
ornait : **or•nate**
ornameant : **or•na•ment**
or•na•ment
ornamint : **or•na•ment**
ornamment : **or•na•ment**
ornary : **or•nery**
or•nate
ornathology : **or•ni•thol•o•gy**
ornement : **or•na•ment**
ornerry : **or•nery**
or•nery
ornethology : **or•ni•thol•o•gy**
orniment : **or•na•ment**
ornithalogy : **or•ni•thol•o•gy**
ornitholigy : **or•ni•thol•o•gy**
ornithollogy : **or•ni•thol•o•gy**
or•ni•thol•o•gy
ornory : **or•nery**
or•phan
or•phan•age
orphanege : **or•phan•age**
orphanige : **or•phan•age**
orphen : **or•phan**
orphenage : **or•phan•age**
orphin : **or•phan**
orphinage : **or•phan•age**
orphun : **or•phan**
orphunage : **or•phan•age**
orral : **oral**
orrange : **or•ange**
orrangutang : **orang•utan**
orrator : **or•a•tor**
orrattion : **ora•tion**
Orregon : **Or•e•gon**
orrient : **ori•ent**
orrifice : **or•i•fice**
orrigin : **or•i•gin**

orriginal : **orig•i•nal**
orringe : **or•ange**
orriole : **ori•ole**
orthadontist : **or•tho•don•tist**
orthadox : **or•tho•dox**
orthedontist : **or•tho•don•tist**
orthedox : **or•tho•dox**
orthodontest : **or•tho•don•tist**
or•tho•don•tist
or•tho•dox
oscellate : **os•cil•late**
oscilate : **os•cil•late**
os•cil•late
osify : **os•si•fy**
osillate : **os•cil•late**
osmoasis : **os•mo•sis**
os•mo•sis
osmossis : **os•mo•sis**
ospray : **os•prey**
ospree : **os•prey**
os•prey
osprie : **os•prey**
ospry : **os•prey**
ossafy : **os•si•fy**
ossefy : **os•si•fy**
ossiffy : **os•si•fy**
os•si•fy
ossillate : **os•cil•late**
ostencible : **os•ten•si•ble**
ostensable : **os•ten•si•ble**
ostensibal : **os•ten•si•ble**
os•ten•si•ble
ostentacious : **os•ten•ta•tious**
ostentashious : **os•ten•ta•tious**
os•ten•ta•tious
os•teo•path
ostinsible : **os•ten•si•ble**
ostintatious : **os•ten•ta•tious**
ostiopath : **os•teo•path**
ostracesm : **os•tra•cism**
ostracise : **os•tra•cize**
os•tra•cism

os•tra•cize
ostrage : os•trich
ostrasism : os•tra•cism
ostrasize : os•tra•cize
ostrech : os•trich
ostrecism : os•tra•cism
ostrecize : os•tra•cize
ostrege : os•trich
ostretch : os•trich
os•trich
ostricism : os•tra•cism
ostricize : os•tra•cize
ostrige : os•trich
ostritch : os•trich
Otawa : Ot•ta•wa
otoman : ot•to•man
Ot•ta•wa
Ottiwa : Ot•ta•wa
Ottoa : Ot•ta•wa
ot•to•man
ottomin : ot•to•man
Ottowa : Ot•ta•wa
ounce
ounse : ounce
our (belonging to us); hour (60
    minutes)
outrageious : out•ra•geous
out•ra•geous
outrageus : out•ra•geous
outragious : out•ra•geous
ova (*plur.*); ovum (*sing.*)
ovar•i•an
ovarrian : ovar•i•an

ova•ry
ovaryan : ovar•i•an
overian : ovar•i•an
overrian : ovar•i•an
overry : ova•ry
overwelm : over•whelm
over•whelm
overy : ova•ry
overyan : ovar•i•an
ovum (*sing.*); ova (*plur.*)
ovvary : ova•ry
Owahu : Oa•hu
ownce : ounce
ownerous : on•er•ous
oxadation : ox•i•da•tion
oxagen : ox•y•gen
oxedation : ox•i•da•tion
oxegen : ox•y•gen
oxegin : ox•y•gen
Oxferd : Ox•ford
Ox•ford
ox•i•da•tion
oxigen : ox•y•gen
oxigin : ox•y•gen
oxsidation : ox•i•da•tion
ox•y•gen
oys•ter
oystir : oys•ter
Ozark
ozmosis : os•mo•sis
ozoan : ozone
ozone
Ozzark : Ozark
ozzone : ozone

P

pablem : **pab·u·lum**
pablum : **pab·u·lum**
pabulem : **pab·u·lum**
pab·u·lum
pacefy : **pac·i·fy**
pacifec : **pa·cif·ic**
paciffy : **pac·i·fy**
pa·cif·ic
pac·i·fi·er
pac·i·fist
pac·i·fy
pacivist : **pac·i·fist**
pac·ket
Packistan : **Pa·ki·stan**
packit : **pack·et**
pagamas : **pa·ja·mas**
pa·gan
pag·eant
pagen : **pa·gan**
pagent : **pag·eant**
paggan : **pa·gan**
pagiant : **pag·eant**
pagin : **pa·gan**
pagint : **pag·eant**
pa·go·da
pagota : **pa·go·da**
paid
pain (ache); **pane** (glass)
pain·ful
painfull : **pain·ful**
pair (two things); **pare** (to cut
    away); **pear** (fruit)
pais·ley
paizley : **pais·ley**
pa·ja·mas
pajammas : **pa·ja·mas**
Pakastan : **Pa·ki·stan**
paket : **pack·et**
Pa·ki·stan
palacade : **pal·i·sade**

pal·ace
palacial : **pa·la·tial**
palasade : **pal·i·sade**
palasaid : **pal·i·sade**
palase : **pal·ace**
palashial : **pa·la·tial**
pal·at·able
pa·la·tial
palatible : **pal·at·able**
Pal·es·tine
palice : **pal·ace**
palid : **pal·lid**
pal·i·sade
paliss : **pal·ace**
Palistine : **Pal·es·tine**
pallace : **pal·ace**
pallatable : **pal·at·able**
Pallestine : **Pal·es·tine**
pal·lid
pallisade : **pal·i·sade**
pal·lor
palm (tree; hand); **Pam** (name)
palor : **pal·lor**
pal·pa·ble
palpibal : **pal·pa·ble**
palpible : **pal·pa·ble**
Pam (name); **palm** (tree; hand)
pamflet : **pam·phlet**
pam·phlet
pamphlit : **pam·phlet**
pamplet : **pam·phlet**
pan·a·cea
panacia : **pan·a·cea**
Pa·na·ma
Panamma : **Pa·na·ma**
panaply : **pan·o·ply**
panarama : **pan·ora·ma**
panasia : **pan·a·cea**
pan·cre·as
pancreus : **pan·cre·as**

pandamonium :
   pan•de•mo•ni•um
pandemoniem :
   pan•de•mo•ni•um
pan•de•mo•ni•um
pandimonium :
   pan•de•mo•ni•um
pane (glass); **pain** (ache)
paneful : **pain•ful**
pan•el
pan•eled *or* **pan•elled**
panell : **pan•el**
pan•elled *or* **pan•eled**
panerama : **pan•ora•ma**
pan•ic
paniced : **pan•icked**
panick : **pan•ic**
pan•icked
pan•icky
panicy : **pan•icky**
paniked : **pan•icked**
panil : **pan•el**
paniled : **pan•eled**
panisea : **pan•a•cea**
pankreas : **pan•cre•as**
pankrius : **pan•cre•as**
pannacea : **pan•a•cea**
Pannama : **Pa•na•ma**
pannel : **pan•el**
panneled : **pan•eled**
panneply : **pan•o•ply**
pannic : **pan•ic**
panniply : **pan•o•ply**
pannoply : **pan•o•ply**
pan•o•ply
pan•ora•ma
panoramma : **pan•ora•ma**
panphlet : **pam•phlet**
pan•sy
panzy : **pan•sy**
pa•pa•cy
papasy : **pa•pa•cy**

paper mache : **pa•pier-mâ•ché**
papicy : **pa•pa•cy**
pa•pier-mâ•ché
papirus : **pa•py•rus**
papisy : **pa•pa•cy**
pappyrus : **pa•py•rus**
papreeka : **pa•pri•ka**
pa•pri•ka
papyris : **pa•py•rus**
pa•py•rus
paraboala: **pa•rab•o•la**
pa•rab•o•la
parabula : **pa•rab•o•la**
para•chute
paracite : **par•a•site**
pa•rade
paradice : **par•a•dise**
par•a•digm
paradime : **par•a•digm**
par•a•dise
par•a•dox
parafenalia : **par•a•pher•na•lia**
par•af•fin
par•a•gon
para•graph
paraid : **pa•rade**
par•a•keet
paralel : **par•al•lel**
paralesis : **pa•ral•y•sis**
paralisis : **pa•ral•y•sis**
par•al•lel
pa•ral•y•sis
para•noia
paranoya : **para•noia**
paraphenalia :
   par•a•pher•na•lia
par•a•pher•na•lia
paraphinalia : **par•a•pher•na•lia**
paraphrenalia :
   par•a•pher•na•lia
parashute : **para•chute**
par•a•site

para•sol
par•cel
parcell : par•cel
parcely : pars•ley
parden : par•don
pardin : par•don
par•don
pare (to cut away); pair (two
  things); pear (fruit)
paredigm : par•a•digm
paredime : par•a•digm
paredise : par•a•dise
paregon : par•a•gon
paret : par•rot
parety : par•i•ty
parichute : para•chute
paridigm : par•a•digm
paridise : par•a•dise
paridox : par•a•dox
paridy : par•o•dy
pariffin : par•af•fin
parifin : par•af•fin
parigraph : para•graph
parikeet : par•a•keet
par•ish (church community);
  per•ish (to cease to exist)
parisite : par•a•site
parisol : para•sol
paritty : par•i•ty
par•i•ty
parlament : par•lia•ment
par•lance
parlanse : par•lance
parlence : par•lance
parlense : par•lance
parler : par•lor
parleyment : par•lia•ment
par•lia•ment
parliment : par•lia•ment
par•lor
pa•ro•chi•al
par•o•dy

parot : par•rot
parrabola : pa•rab•o•la
parrade : pa•rade
parradise : par•a•dise
parradox : par•a•dox
parrafin : par•af•fin
parralel : par•al•lel
parralysis : pa•ral•y•sis
parret : par•rot
parridy : par•o•dy
parrifin : par•af•fin
parriket : par•a•keet
parrish : par•ish (church
  community) or per•ish (to
  cease to exist)
parrit : par•rot
parrity : par•i•ty
parrochial : pa•ro•chi•al
parrody : par•o•dy
parrokeet : par•a•keet
par•rot
parsel : par•cel
parsell : par•cel
pars•ley
parsly : pars•ley
partacle : par•ti•cle
partasan : par•ti•san
partesan : par•ti•san
partical : par•ti•cle
particepant : par•tic•i•pant
par•tic•i•pant
particlar : par•tic•u•lar
par•ti•cle
particlear : par•tic•u•lar
par•tic•u•lar
partikle : par•ti•cle
par•ti•san
partisen : par•ti•san
partisipant : par•tic•i•pant
partredge : par•tridge
partrege : par•tridge
par•tridge

partrige : **par•tridge**
Pas•a•de•na
Pasadina : **Pas•a•de•na**
pasafier : **pac•i•fi•er**
pasage : **pas•sage**
pashion : **pas•sion**
pasific : **pa•cif•ic**
pasifier : **pac•i•fi•er**
pasifist : **pac•i•fist**
pasify : **pac•i•fy**
pasion : **pas•sion**
pasley : **pais•ley**
Passadena : **Pas•a•de•na**
pas•sage
passege : **pas•sage**
passifier : **pac•i•fi•er**
passige : **pas•sage**
pas•sion
passtime : **pas•time**
pastary : **past•ry**
pas•tel
pastell : **pas•tel**
past•er (one that pastes);
    pas•tor (clergy)
pastery : **past•ry**
pasterize : **pas•teur•ize**
pas•teur•ize
pas•time
pas•tor (clergy); **past•er** (one
    that pastes)
pastorize : **pas•teur•ize**
past•ry
pasttime : **pas•time**
pasturize : **pas•teur•ize**
patchy
pateo : **pa•tio**
paternety : **pa•ter•ni•ty**
paternitty : **pa•ter•ni•ty**
pa•ter•ni•ty
pathalogy : **path•ol•o•gy**
pa•thet•ic
pathetick : **pa•thet•ic**

pathettic : **pa•thet•ic**
patholigy : **path•ol•o•gy**
pathollogy : **path•ol•o•gy**
path•ol•o•gy
pa•tio
patreot : **pa•tri•ot**
pa•tri•ot
pa•trol
patroll : **pa•trol**
pa•tron•age
patronige : **pa•tron•age**
pattio : **pa•tio**
paturnity : **pa•ter•ni•ty**
paucety : **pau•ci•ty**
pau•ci•ty
pause (to hesitate); **paws**
    (animal feet)
pausity : **pau•ci•ty**
pavilian : **pa•vil•ion**
pa•vil•ion
pavillion : **pa•vil•ion**
pawm : **palm**
paws (animal feet); **pause** (to
    hesitate)
payed : **paid**
peace (absence of conflict);
    piece (portion)
peace•ful
peacefull : **peace•ful**
peachy
peal (to ring); **peel** (to strip)
pea•nut
peany : **pe•o•ny**
pear (fruit); **pair** (two things);
    pare (to cut away)
pearl (gem); **purl** (knitting
    stitch)
peas•ant
peaseful : **peace•ful**
peasent : **peas•ant**
peasint : **peas•ant**
peavish : **pee•vish**

pebbal : **peb·ble**
pebbel : **peb·ble**
peb·ble
peble : **peb·ble**
pe·can
peccan : **pe·can**
pe·cu·liar
peculier : **pe·cu·liar**
pedagree : **ped·i·gree**
ped·al (foot lever); **ped·dle** (to
   sell); **pet·al** (flower part)
ped·ant
peddant : **ped·ant**
peddestal : **ped·es·tal**
peddigree : **ped·i·gree**
ped·dle (to sell); **ped·al** (foot
   lever); **pet·al** (flower part)
pedent : **ped·ant**
ped·es·tal
pedestill : **ped·es·tal**
ped·i·gree
pedistal : **ped·es·tal**
peeceful : **peace·ful**
peechy : **peachy**
peel (to strip); **peal** (to ring)
peenut : **pea·nut**
peeple : **peo·ple**
peeriod : **pe·ri·od**
pee·vish
peice : **peace** (absence of
   conflict) *or* **piece** (portion)
peirce : **pierce**
peise : **peace** (absence of
   conflict) *or* **piece** (portion)
pekan : **pe·can**
pelecan : **pel·i·can**
pelet : **pel·let**
pel·i·can
pelikan : **pel·i·can**
pel·let
pellican : **pel·i·can**
pellit : **pel·let**

pelvice : **pel·vis**
pel·vis
pelviss : **pel·vis**
penacillin : **pen·i·cil·lin**
pe·nal
pen·al·ty
pen·ance
penanse : **pen·ance**
penatrate : **pen·e·trate**
pencel : **pen·cil**
pen·chant
penchent : **pen·chant**
penchint : **pen·chant**
pen·cil
pen·dant (*noun or adj.*);
   pen·dent (*adj. only*)
pen·dent (*adj. only*); **pen·dant**
   (*noun or adj.*)
pendulam : **pen·du·lum**
pendulem : **pen·du·lum**
pen·du·lum
pen·e·trate
pen·guin
penicilin : **pen·i·cil·lin**
penicillan : **pen·i·cil·lin**
pen·i·cil·lin
penil : **pe·nal**
penilty : **pen·al·ty**
penince : **pen·ance**
penisillin : **pen·i·cil·lin**
pennacle : **pin·na·cle**
pennal : **pe·nal**
pennalty : **pen·al·ty**
pennance : **pen·ance**
pennetrate : **pen·e·trate**
pennicillin : **pen·i·cil·lin**
Pennsilvania : **Penn·syl·va·nia**
Pennsylvanea : **Penn·syl·va·nia**
Penn·syl·va·nia
pensil : **pen·cil**
pentaggon : **pen·ta·gon**
pen·ta·gon

pentegon : **pen·ta·gon**
penulty : **pen·al·ty**
penut : **pea·nut**
peonny : **pe·o·ny**
pe·o·ny
peo·ple
percarious : **pre·car·i·ous**
per·ceive
per·cent·age
percentege : **per·cent·age**
percentige : **per·cent·age**
perceve : **per·ceive**
percieve : **per·ceive**
percintage : **per·cent·age**
percipitation : **pre·cip·i·ta·tion**
peremptary : **pe·remp·to·ry**
peremptery : **pe·remp·to·ry**
pe·remp·to·ry
perfarate : **per·fo·rate**
perfectable : **per·fect·ible**
perfectibal : **per·fect·ible**
per·fect·ible
perfirate : **per·fo·rate**
per·fo·rate
per·for·mance
performanse : **per·for·mance**
performence : **per·for·mance**
performince : **per·for·mance**
perfunctary : **per·func·to·ry**
per·func·to·ry
perfunctry : **per·func·to·ry**
perfunktory : **per·func·to·ry**
perichute : **para·chute**
periferal : **pe·riph·er·al**
perigon : **par·a·gon**
per·il
pe·ri·od
peripharel : **pe·riph·er·al**
pe·riph·er·al
peri·scope
per·ish (to cease to exist);
 par·ish (church community)

perity : **par·i·ty**
perjery : **per·ju·ry**
per·ju·ry
perl : **pearl** (gem) *or* **purl**
 (knitting stitch)
per·ma·nent
per·me·able
per·me·ate
permeible : **per·me·able**
permenant : **per·ma·nent**
permiabel : **per·me·able**
permiable : **per·me·able**
permiate : **per·me·ate**
perminent : **per·ma·nent**
permisible : **per·mis·si·ble**
permissable : **per·mis·si·ble**
per·mis·si·ble
peroose : **pe·ruse**
perouette : **pir·ou·ette**
per·pe·trate
perpettual : **per·pet·u·al**
per·pet·u·al
perpetuel : **per·pet·u·al**
perpitrate : **per·pe·trate**
perril : **per·il**
perriod : **pe·ri·od**
perriscope : **peri·scope**
perruse : **pe·ruse**
persacute : **per·se·cute**
perscription : **pre·scrip·tion**
perseccute : **per·se·cute**
per·se·cute
persentage : **per·cent·age**
perserve : **pre·serve**
perserverance : **per·se·ver·ance**
perseveirance : **per·se·ver·ance**
per·se·ver·ance
perseveranse : **per·se·ver·ance**
perseverence : **per·se·ver·ance**
persicute : **per·se·cute**
per·son·age

per·son·al (private);
  per·son·nel (employees)
personege : **per·son·age**
personige : **per·son·age**
per·son·nel (employees);
  per·son·al (private)
per·suade
persuaid : **per·suade**
persue : **pur·sue**
persume : **pre·sume**
perswade : **per·suade**
pertanent : **per·ti·nent**
pertenant : **per·ti·nent**
perterb : **per·turb**
pertinant : **per·ti·nent**
per·ti·nent
pertinnent : **per·ti·nent**
per·turb
pe·ruse
peruze : **pe·ruse**
pervacive : **per·va·sive**
pervaseve : **per·va·sive**
per·va·sive
pervassive : **per·va·sive**
per·vert
pesimism : **pes·si·mism**
pesimist : **pes·si·mist**
pessamism : **pes·si·mism**
pessamist : **pes·si·mist**
pessant : **peas·ant**
pessemism : **pes·si·mism**
pessemist : **pes·si·mist**
pessent : **peas·ant**
pessimest : **pes·si·mist**
pes·si·mism
pes·si·mist
pessimizm : **pes·si·mism**
pessint : **peas·ant**
pestalence : **pes·ti·lence**
pestelence : **pes·ti·lence**
pestilance : **pes·ti·lence**
pes·ti·lence

pestilense : **pes·ti·lence**
pet·al (flower part); **ped·al**
  (foot lever); **ped·dle** (to sell)
peteet : **pe·tite**
petete : **pe·tite**
pe·tite
petoonia : **pe·tu·nia**
petrafy : **pet·ri·fy**
petrefy : **pet·ri·fy**
petriffy : **pet·ri·fy**
pet·ri·fy
pe·tro·leum
petroliam : **pe·tro·leum**
petrolium : **pe·tro·leum**
petrollium : **pe·tro·leum**
pettete : **pe·tite**
pettite : **pe·tite**
pettrify : **pet·ri·fy**
pettroleum : **pe·tro·leum**
pettulant : **pet·u·lant**
pettunia : **pe·tu·nia**
pet·u·lant
petulent : **pet·u·lant**
pe·tu·nia
petunya : **pe·tu·nia**
peuter : **pew·ter**
pew·ter
phalic : **phal·lic**
phal·lic
phantastic : **fan·tas·tic**
phan·ta·sy *or* **fan·ta·sy**
phan·tom
phar·ma·cy
pharmicy : **phar·ma·cy**
pharmissy : **phar·ma·cy**
pheas·ant
pheasco : **fi·as·co**
pheasent : **pheas·ant**
pheasint : **pheas·ant**
pheeble : **fee·ble**
Phenix : **Phoe·nix**
phe·nom·e·nal

phe·nom·e·non
phenominal : **phe·nom·e·nal**
phenominnal : **phe·nom·e·nal**
phenominnon : **phe·nom·e·non**
phenominon : **phe·nom·e·non**
phenommenal : **phe·nom·e·nal**
phenommenon :
 phe·nom·e·non
Pheonix : **Phoe·nix**
phesant : **pheas·ant**
phesible : **fea·si·ble**
phessant : **pheas·ant**
Philapino : **Fil·i·pi·no**
philibuster : **fi·li·bus·ter**
Philipino : **Fil·i·pi·no**
Phil·ip·pines
phillabuster : **fi·li·bus·ter**
Phillipines : **Phil·ip·pines**
Phillipino : **Fil·i·pi·no**
Phillippines : **Phil·ip·pines**
philoligy : **phi·lol·o·gy**
philollogy : **phi·lol·o·gy**
phi·lol·o·gy
philosiphy : **phi·los·o·phy**
phi·los·o·phy
philossophy : **phi·los·o·phy**
phinomenal : **phe·nom·e·nal**
phinomenon : **phe·nom·e·non**
phisical : **phys·i·cal**
phisician : **phy·si·cian**
phisics : **phys·ics**
phission : **fis·sion**
phobea : **pho·bia**
pho·bia
Phoe·nix
pho·net·ic
phonetick : **pho·net·ic**
phonettic : **pho·net·ic**
phosel : **fos·sil**
phosferris : **phos·pho·rous**
 (*adj.*) *or* **phos·pho·rus**
 (*noun*)

phosforus : **phos·pho·rous**
 (*adj.*) *or* **phos·phor·us**
 (*noun*)
phos·pho·rous (*adj.*);
 phos·pho·rus (*noun*)
phos·pho·rus (*noun*);
 phos·pho·rous (*adj.*)
phossil : **fos·sil**
photografy : **pho·tog·ra·phy**
pho·tog·ra·phy
physecal : **phys·i·cal**
phys·i·cal
phy·si·cian
physicion : **phy·si·cian**
physicks : **phys·ics**
physicle : **phys·i·cal**
phys·ics
physikal : **phys·i·cal**
physission : **phy·si·cian**
pianeer : **pi·o·neer**
piatza : **pi·az·za** (veranda) *or*
 piz·za (pie)
piaza : **pi·az·za** (veranda) *or*
 piz·za (pie)
pi·az·za (veranda); **piz·za** (pie)
piccalo : **pic·co·lo**
piccilo : **pic·co·lo**
pic·co·lo
pickal : **pick·le**
pickel : **pick·le**
pick·et
pickilo : **pic·co·lo**
pickit : **pick·et**
pick·le
picknic : **pic·nic**
picknick : **pic·nic**
picknicked : **pic·nicked**
pic·nic
picniced : **pic·nicked**
picnick : **pic·nic**
pic·nicked
picolo : **pic·co·lo**

pictoreal : **pic·to·ri·al**
pic·to·ri·al
picturial : **pic·to·ri·al**
pid·gin (language); **pi·geon** (bird)
piece (portion); **peace** (absence of conflict)
pierce
pierouette : **pir·ou·ette**
pietty : **pi·ety**
pi·ety
pi·geon (bird); **pid·gin** (language)
piggin : **pid·gin** (language) or **pi·geon** (bird)
pigion : **pid·gin** (language) or **pi·geon** (bird)
pigmy : **pyg·my**
pijamas : **pa·ja·mas**
pilar : **pil·lar**
pilet : **pi·lot**
pilgrem : **pil·grim**
pil·grim
pilgrum : **pil·grim**
pil·lar
pillary : **pil·lo·ry**
piller : **pil·lar**
pillery : **pil·lo·ry**
pillgrim : **pil·grim**
pil·lo·ry
pilory : **pil·lo·ry**
pi·lot
pinacle : **pin·na·cle**
pinchant : **pen·chant**
pindulem : **pen·du·lum**
pineer : **pi·o·neer**
pinguin : **pen·guin**
pin·na·cle
pinnecal : **pin·na·cle**
pinnical : **pin·na·cle**
pintagon : **pen·ta·gon**
pi·o·neer

pioneir : **pi·o·neer**
pionere : **pi·o·neer**
pi·ra·cy
pirassy : **pi·ra·cy**
pi·rate
pirce : **pierce**
piret : **pi·rate**
pirete : **pi·rate**
piricy : **pi·ra·cy**
pirissy : **pi·ra·cy**
pirl : **pearl** (gem) or **purl** (knitting stitch)
pirmeate : **per·me·ate**
piroette : **pir·ou·ette**
piromaniac : **py·ro·ma·ni·ac**
pir·ou·ette
pisston : **pis·ton**
pistal : **pis·til** (flower part) or **pis·tol** (handgun)
pistan : **pis·ton**
pisten : **pis·ton**
pis·til (flower part); **pis·tol** (handgun)
pis·tol (handgun); **pis·til** (flower part)
pis·ton
pitaful : **piti·ful**
pit·e·ous
pithon : **py·thon**
piti·able
piti·ful
pitious : **pit·e·ous**
Pitsburg : **Pitts·burgh**
pittiful : **piti·ful**
Pittsberg : **Pitts·burgh**
Pittsburg : **Pitts·burgh**
Pitts·burgh
pittuitary : **pit·u·itary**
pituetary : **pit·u·itary**
pit·u·itary
pituitery : **pit·u·itary**
pitunia : **pe·tu·nia**

pityable : **piti•able**
pityful : **piti•ful**
pityous : **pit•e•ous**
pivat : **piv•ot**
pivet : **piv•ot**
piv•ot
pivvot : **piv•ot**
piz•za (pie); **pi•az•za** (veranda)
plac•ard
placcid : **plac•id**
placed : **plac•id**
plac•id
plackard : **plac•ard**
plackerd : **plac•ard**
plagerism : **pla•gia•rism**
pla•gia•rism
plagierism : **pla•gia•rism**
plaguerism : **pla•gia•rism**
planed (leveled); **planned**
　(organized)
plan•et
planetariem : **plan•e•tar•i•um**
plan•e•tar•i•um
planetarrium : **plan•e•tar•i•um**
planeterium : **plan•e•tar•i•um**
planit : **plan•et**
planitarium : **plan•e•tar•i•um**
planned (organized); **planed**
　(leveled)
plannet : **plan•et**
plannetarium : **plan•e•tar•i•um**
plasstic : **plas•tic**
plastec : **plas•tic**
plas•tic
plastick : **plas•tic**
platanum : **plat•i•num**
platatude : **plat•i•tude**
pla•teau
platenum : **plat•i•num**
plat•i•num
plat•i•tude
pla•toon

platteau : **pla•teau**
plattinum : **plat•i•num**
plattitude : **plat•i•tude**
plattoon : **pla•toon**
plattow : **pla•teau**
platune : **pla•toon**
plausable : **plau•si•ble**
plauseble : **plau•si•ble**
plau•si•ble
playright : **play•wright**
play•wright
playwrite : **play•wright**
plead
pleas•ant
please
pleasent : **pleas•ant**
pleasint : **pleas•ant**
plea•sure
pleat
plebbisite : **pleb•i•scite**
pleb•i•scite
pledge
pleebiscite : **pleb•i•scite**
pleed : **plead**
pleese : **please**
pleet : **pleat**
pleez : **please**
plege : **pledge**
plenatude : **plen•i•tude**
plen•i•tude *or* **plen•ti•tude**
plentatude : **plen•i•tude**
plen•ti•tude *or* **plen•i•tude**
plentytude : **plen•i•tude**
pleshure : **plea•sure**
plessant : **plea•sant**
plessure : **plea•sure**
plesure : **plea•sure**
pli•able
pli•ant
plibiscite : **pleb•i•scite**
plible : **pli•able**
plient : **pli•ant**

Plimouth : **Plym•outh**
plum•age
plumb•er
plumb•ing
plumeage : **plum•age**
plumer : **plumb•er**
plumige : **plum•age**
plummer : **plumb•er**
plumming : **plumb•ing**
plu•ral
plurel : **plu•ral**
plurral : **plu•ral**
plurrel : **plu•ral**
plyable : **pli•able**
Plymath : **Plym•outh**
Plymeth : **Plym•outh**
Plym•outh
pneu•mat•ic
pneumattic : **pneu•mat•ic**
pneumoania : **pneu•mo•nia**
pneu•mo•nia
pnuematic : **pneu•mat•ic**
pnuemonia : **pneu•mo•nia**
pnumatic : **pneu•mat•ic**
pnumonia : **pneu•mo•nia**
poadium : **po•di•um**
poddium : **po•di•um**
po•di•um
po•em
pogoda : **pa•go•da**
poi•gnant
poignent : **poi•gnant**
poiniant : **poi•gnant**
poinsetta : **poin•set•tia**
poin•set•tia
poisen : **poi•son**
poi•son
poisson : **poi•son**
po•lar
polaritty : **po•lar•i•ty**
po•lar•i•ty
polarrity : **po•lar•i•ty**

polatics : **pol•i•tics**
polece : **po•lice**
po•lem•ic
polemick : **po•lem•ic**
polemmic : **po•lem•ic**
poleo : **po•lio**
poler : **po•lar**
polerity : **po•lar•i•ty**
po•lice
pol•i•cy
polimic : **po•lem•ic**
po•lio
polise : **po•lice**
polissy : **pol•i•cy**
polisy : **pol•i•cy**
politicks : **pol•i•tics**
pol•i•tics
pollanate : **pol•li•nate**
pollarity : **po•lar•i•ty**
pol•len
pollenate : **pol•li•nate**
pollice : **po•lice**
pollicy : **pol•i•cy**
pollin : **pol•len**
pol•li•nate
pollitics : **pol•i•tics**
pome : **po•em**
pomp•ous
pompus : **pomp•ous**
ponteff : **pon•tiff**
pon•tiff
pontive : **pon•tiff**
poodel : **poo•dle**
poo•dle
poperrie : **pot•pour•ri**
pop•lar (tree); **pop•u•lar**
  (accepted)
popler : **pop•lar** (tree) *or*
  pop•u•lar (accepted)
poporry : **pot•pour•ri**
poppulace : **pop•u•lace** (*noun*)
  or **pop•u•lous** (*adj.*)

poppulous : **pop•u•lace** (*noun*) *or* **pop•u•lous** (*adj.*)

populace (*noun*); **pop•u•lous** (*adj.*)

pop•u•lar (*accepted*); **pop•lar** (*tree*)

populise : **pop•u•lace** (*noun*) *or* **pop•u•lous** (*adj.*)

pop•u•lous (*adj.*); **pop•u•lace** (*noun*)

popurrie : **pot•pour•ri**

por•ce•lain

porcelin : **por•ce•lain**

porcilain : **por•ce•lain**

poreous : **po•rous**

poridge : **por•ridge**

po•rous

porrage : **por•ridge**

porrege : **por•ridge**

por•ridge

porrige : **por•ridge**

porrous : **po•rous**

porselin : **por•ce•lain**

por•ta•ble

portaco : **por•ti•co**

por•tal

portel : **por•tal**

portfoleo : **port•fo•lio**

port•fo•lio

portfollio : **port•fo•lio**

portible : **por•ta•ble**

porticko : **por•ti•co**

por•ti•co

Porto Rico : **Puer•to Ri•co**

por•trait

portrate : **por•trait**

portrayt : **por•trait**

portret : **por•trait**

Portugeese : **Por•tu•guese**

Portugese : **Por•tu•guese**

Portugeze : **Por•tu•guese**

Por•tu•guese

posative : **pos•i•tive**

posess : **pos•sess**

posible : **pos•si•ble**

pos•i•tive

possable : **pos•si•ble**

pos•se

pos•sess

pos•si•ble

possitive : **pos•i•tive**

possy : **pos•se**

post•age

post•al

postarity : **pos•ter•i•ty**

postege : **post•age**

postel : **post•al**

posteritty : **pos•ter•i•ty**

pos•ter•i•ty

posterrity : **pos•ter•i•ty**

postige : **post•age**

po•ta•ble

po•ta•to

potatoe : **po•ta•to**

po•ta•toes

potatos : **po•ta•toes**

potible : **po•ta•ble**

potperrie : **pot•pour•ri**

pot•pour•ri

potpurrie : **pot•pour•ri**

pottable : **po•ta•ble**

povarty : **pov•er•ty**

pov•er•ty

povirty : **pov•er•ty**

poyson : **poi•son**

pracktical : **prac•ti•cal**

practacal : **prac•ti•cal**

prac•ti•cal

practicle : **prac•ti•cal**

prafer : **pre•fer**

prai•rie

prarie : **prai•rie**

preach

precareous : **pre·car·i·ous**
pre·car·i·ous
pre·cede (to go before);
   pro·ceed (to continue)
prec·e·dent (that which comes
   before); **pres·i·dent** (one who
   presides)
precepice : **prec·i·pice**
pre·cious
precipace : **prec·i·pice**
precipatation : **pre·cip·i·ta·tion**
prec·i·pice
pre·cip·i·ta·tion
precippation : **pre·cip·i·ta·tion**
predater : **pred·a·tor**
pred·a·tor
preditor : **pred·a·tor**
predjudice : **prej·u·dice**
preech : **preach**
pre-empt
preemptory : **pe·remp·to·ry**
preest : **priest**
pref·ace
pre·fer
prefface : **pref·ace**
preffer : **pre·fer**
prefice : **pref·ace**
prefiss : **pref·ace**
prefundity : **pro·fun·di·ty**
preg·nant
pregnent : **preg·nant**
pregnint : **preg·nant**
preimpt : **pre-empt**
preist : **priest**
prejewdice : **prej·u·dice**
prejudace : **prej·u·dice**
prej·u·dice
prejudiss : **prej·u·dice**
premeer : **pre·mier** (prime
   minister) *or* **pre·miere** (first
   performance)

premeir : **pre·mier** (prime
   minister) *or* **pre·miere** (first
   performance)
premere : **pre·mier** (prime
   minister) *or* **pre·miere** (first
   performance)
pre·mier (prime minister);
   pre·miere (first performance)
pre·miere (first performance);
   pre·mier (prime minister)
prepair : **pre·pare**
pre·pare
prescious : **pre·cious**
pre·scrip·tion
pres·ence (*noun,* being
   present); **pre·sents** (*verb,*
   introduces); **pres·ents** (*noun,*
   gifts)
pre·serve
pres·i·dent (one who presides);
   pre·ce·dent (that which
   comes before)
presious : **pre·cious**
presipice : **prec·i·pice**
presipitation : **pre·cip·i·ta·tion**
pressipice : **prec·i·pice**
presstige : **pres·tige**
prestege : **pres·tige**
presteze : **pres·tige**
pres·tige
pre·sume
presumetuous :
   pre·sump·tu·ous
pre·sump·tu·ous
presumtuous : **pre·sump·tu·ous**
pretence : **pre·tense**
pre·tense
pretsel : **pret·zel**
pret·zel
pretzell : **pret·zel**
pretzil : **pret·zel**
pre·vail

prevailent : **prev·a·lent**
prevale : **pre·vail**
prev·a·lent
prevelant : **prev·a·lent**
prevert : **per·vert**
previlent : **prev·a·lent**
priempt : **pre-empt**
prier : **pri·or**
priest
primative : **prim·i·tive**
prim·i·tive
primmitive : **prim·i·tive**
principal (*noun,* one in charge;
    adj., most important);
    prin·ci·ple (rule, standard)
principle (rule, standard);
    prin·ci·pal (*noun,* one in
    charge; *adj.,* most important)
pri·or
priorety : **pri·or·i·ty**
pri·or·i·ty
priorrity : **pri·or·i·ty**
prisen : **pris·on**
prism
pris·on
prisson : **pris·on**
pri·va·cy
privalege : **priv·i·lege**
pri·vate
privelege : **priv·i·lege**
privet (bush); **pri·vate** (personal)
privicy : **pri·va·cy**
priviledge : **priv·i·lege**
priv·i·lege
privilige : **priv·i·lege**
privissy : **pri·va·cy**
prizm : **prism**
prizzen : **pris·on**
prob·a·ble
probible : **prob·a·ble**
prob·lem
problim : **prob·lem**

problum : **prob·lem**
pro·ce·dure
pro·ceed (to continue);
    pre·cede (to go before)
proceedure : **pro·ce·dure**
procidure : **pro·ce·dure**
procktor : **proc·tor**
pro·claim
proclaimation : **proc·la·ma·tion**
proc·la·ma·tion
proclame : **pro·claim**
proclemation : **proc·la·ma·tion**
proclimation : **proc·la·ma·tion**
procrasstinate : **pro·cras·ti·nate**
procrastentate : **pro·cras·ti·nate**
pro·cras·ti·nate
procter : **proc·tor**
proc·tor
proddigal : **prod·i·gal**
prodegy : **prod·i·gy**
prodicle : **prod·i·gal**
prod·i·gal
prodigle : **prod·i·gal**
prod·i·gy
prodogy : **prod·i·gy**
pro·duce
produse : **pro·duce**
profacy : **proph·e·cy** (*noun*) *or*
    proph·e·sy (*verb*)
profain : **pro·fane**
pro·fane
profanety : **pro·fan·i·ty**
pro·fan·i·ty
profannity : **pro·fan·i·ty**
profesor : **pro·fes·sor**
professer : **pro·fes·sor**
pro·fes·sor
profet : **prof·it**
proffit : **prof·it**
prof·it
profoundity : **pro·fun·di·ty**
profundety : **pro·fun·di·ty**

pro•fun•di•ty
prohibbit : **pro•hib•it**
prohibet : **pro•hib•it**
pro•hib•it
proliffic : **pro•lif•ic**
pro•lif•ic
promanent : **prom•i•nent**
prom•e•nade
promice : **prom•ise**
prominade : **prom•e•nade**
prominant : **prom•i•nent**
prom•i•nent
prom•ise
promisory : **prom•is•so•ry**
promiss : **prom•ise**
prom•is•so•ry
prommenade : **prom•e•nade**
promminent : **prom•i•nent**
prommise : **prom•ise**
pronounciation :
  pro•nun•ci•a•tion
pro•nun•ci•a•tion
pro•pa•gan•da
propeganda : **pro•pa•gan•da**
propencity : **pro•pen•si•ty**
pro•pen•si•ty
prophacy : **proph•e•cy** (*noun*)
  or **proph•e•sy** (verb)
proph•e•cy (*noun*); **proph•e•sy**
  (*verb*)
proph•e•sy (*verb*); **proph•e•cy**
  (*noun*)
prophissy : **proph•e•cy** (*noun*)
  or **proph•e•sy** (*verb*)
propiganda : **pro•pa•gan•da**
propinsity : **pro•pen•si•ty**
proppaganda : **pro•pa•gan•da**
pros•e•cute
prosicute : **pros•e•cute**
pros•per•ous
prospirous : **pros•per•ous**
prossicute : **pros•e•cute**

protacol : **pro•to•col**
Prot•es•tant
Protestint : **Prot•es•tant**
Protistant : **Prot•es•tant**
protocall : **pro•to•col**
pro•to•col
prowace : **prow•ess**
prow•ess
prowice : **prow•ess**
prowiss : **prow•ess**
proximety : **prox•im•i•ty**
prox•im•i•ty
proximmity : **prox•im•i•ty**
psalm
psam : **psalm**
pseudanym : **pseu•do•nym**
pseudonim : **pseu•do•nym**
pseu•do•nym
psiche : **psy•che**
psichiatrist : **psy•chi•a•trist**
psichic : **psy•chic**
psichologist : **psy•chol•o•gist**
psichology : **psy•chol•o•gy**
psudonym : **pseu•do•nym**
psuedonym : **pseu•do•nym**
psychalogist : **psy•chol•o•gist**
psychalogy : **psy•chol•o•gy**
psy•che
psy•chi•a•trist
psy•chic
psycholagist : **psy•chol•o•gist**
psycholagy : **psy•chol•o•gy**
psychollogist : **psy•chol•o•gist**
psychollogy : **psy•chol•o•gy**
psy•chol•o•gist
psy•chol•o•gy
psychyatrist : **psy•chi•a•trist**
psycologist : **psy•chol•o•gist**
psycology : **psy•chol•o•gy**
ptarodactyl : **ptero•dac•tyl**
pteradactyl : **ptero•dac•tyl**
pteridactyl : **ptero•dac•tyl**

pterodactile : **ptero•dac•tyl**
pterodactill : **ptero•dac•tyl**
ptero•dac•tyl
ptomain : **pto•maine**
pto•maine
ptomane : **pto•maine**
Puarto Rico : **Puer•to Ri•co**
publacize : **pub•li•cize**
publicety : **pub•lic•i•ty**
publicise : **pub•li•cize**
pub•li•cist
publicitty : **pub•lic•i•ty**
pub•lic•i•ty
pub•li•cize
publisist : **pub•li•cist**
publisity : **pub•lic•i•ty**
puddel : **pud•dle**
pud•dle
pudle : **poo•dle** (dog) *or*
   pud•dle (water)
Puer•to Ri•co
pueter : **pew•ter**
pullmonary : **pul•mo•nary**
pulmanary : **pul•mo•nary**
pul•mo•nary
pulmonery : **pul•mo•nary**
pulpet : **pul•pit**
pul•pit
pumace : **pum•ice**
pum•ice
pumiss : **pum•ice**
pumkin : **pump•kin**
pummice : **pum•ice**
pumpken : **pump•kin**
pump•kin
pundet : **pun•dit**
pun•dit
punesh : **pun•ish**
pun•gent

pungint : **pun•gent**
pun•ish
punken : **pump•kin**
punkin : **pump•kin**
punnish : **pun•ish**
pupel : **pu•pil**
pu•pil
pup•pet
puppil : **pu•pil**
puppit : **pup•pet**
purety : **pu•ri•ty**
puriffy : **pu•ri•fy**
pu•ri•fy
pu•ri•tan
puriten : **pu•ri•tan**
puritty : **pu•ri•ty**
pu•ri•ty
purjury : **per•ju•ry**
purl (knitting stitch); **pearl**
   (gem)
purpetrate : **per•pe•trate**
purrify : **pu•ri•fy**
purritan : **pu•ri•tan**
purrity : **pu•ri•ty**
pursacute : **per•se•cute**
pursuade : **per•suade**
pur•sue
purterb : **per•turb**
putrafy : **pu•tre•fy**
pu•tre•fy
putriffy : **pu•tre•fy**
putrify : **pu•tre•fy**
puzle : **puz•zle**
puzzal : **puz•zle**
puzzel : **puz•zle**
puz•zle
pyg•my
py•ro•ma•ni•ac
py•thon

Q

Quabec : **Que•bec**
quack
quackary : **quack•ery**
quack•ery
quackry : **quack•ery**
quadrain : **qua•train**
quadrangel : **quad•ran•gle**
quad•ran•gle
quad•rant
quadrill : **qua•drille**
qua•drille
quadruble : **qua•dru•ple**
quadrublet : **qua•dru•plet**
qua•dru•ple
quaf : **quaff**
quafe : **quaff**
quaff
quaggmire : **quag•mire**
quagmier : **quag•mire**
quag•mire
quagmyre : **quag•mire**
quaik : **quake**
quail
quaint
quaisar : **qua•sar**
quaiver : **qua•ver**
quak : **quack**
quake
qualafication : **qual•i•fi•ca•tion**
qualafied : **qual•i•fied**
qualafy : **qual•i•fy**
qualaty : **qual•i•ty**
quale : **quail**
qualefy : **qual•i•fy**
qualifacation : **qual•i•fi•ca•tion**
qual•i•fi•ca•tion
qual•i•fied
qual•i•fy
qual•i•ty
quallification : **qual•i•fi•ca•tion**

quallified : **qual•i•fied**
quallify : **qual•i•fy**
quallity : **qual•i•ty**
qualm
quam : **qualm**
quan•da•ry
quandery : **quan•da•ry**
quandrent : **quad•rant**
quandry : **quan•da•ry**
quanity : **quan•ti•ty**
quantafy : **quan•ti•fy**
quante : **quaint**
quantety : **quan•ti•ty**
quan•ti•fy
quan•ti•ty
quantom : **quan•tum**
quan•tum
quaranteen : **quar•an•tine**
quar•an•tine
quarel : **quar•rel**
quareled : **quar•reled**
quareling : **quar•rel•ing**
quarentine : **quar•an•tine**
quarintine : **quar•an•tine**
quarl : **quar•rel**
quar•rel
quar•reled or **quar•relled**
quar•rel•ing or **quar•rel•ling**
quar•relled or **quar•reled**
quar•rel•ling or **quar•rel•ing**
quarrey : **quar•ry**
quar•ry
quart
quar•ter
quarts (*plur.*); **quartz** (mineral)
quartz (mineral); **quarts** (*plur.*)
quary : **quar•ry**
qua•sar
quasarre : **qua•sar**
quaser : **qua•sar**

237

quater : **quar•ter**
qua•train
quatrane : **qua•train**
quatrangle : **quad•ran•gle**
qua•ver
quawlified : **qual•i•fied**
quawlify : **qual•i•fy**
quay (wharf); **key** (for a lock)
quazar : **qua•sar**
Qubec : **Que•bec**
que : **queue** (pigtail; line) *or*
  cue (signal; poolstick)
quean : **queen**
quear : **queer**
queary : **que•ry**
queasaly : **quea•si•ly**
quea•si•ly
queasly : **quea•si•ly**
quea•sy
queazy : **quea•sy**
Que•bec
Quebeck : **Que•bec**
queeche : **quiche**
queen
queer
queery : **que•ry**
queesh : **quiche**
queesly : **quea•si•ly**
queesy : **quea•sy**
queezy : **quea•sy**
queishe : **quiche**
quene : **queen**
quere : **queer**
querie : **que•ry**
querry : **que•ry**
que•ry
questin : **ques•tion**
ques•tion
questionaire : **ques•tion•naire**
questionnair : **ques•tion•naire**
ques•tion•naire

queue (pigtail; line); **cue**
  (signal; poolstick)
quey : **quay**
quiche
quick
quicksotic : **quix•o•tic**
quiescant : **qui•es•cent**
qui•es•cent
quiesent : **qui•es•cent**
quiessent : **qui•es•cent**
qui•et (silent); **quite** (entirely)
quik : **quick**
quillt : **quilt**
quilt
quinntet : **quin•tet**
quintecence : **quin•tes•sence**
quintescence : **quin•tes•sence**
quintesence : **quin•tes•sence**
quin•tes•sence
quintessense : **quin•tes•sence**
quin•tet
quintette : **quin•tet**
quior : **choir**
quire : **choir**
quiseen : **cui•sine**
quisine : **cui•sine**
quis•ling
quite (entirely); **qui•et** (silent)
quivver : **quiv•er**
quix•ot•ic
quixottic : **quix•ot•ic**
quizacal : **quiz•zi•cal**
quizes : **quiz•zes**
quizical : **quiz•zi•cal**
quizine : **cui•sine**
quizling : **quis•ling**
quizotic : **quix•ot•ic**
quizzacal : **quiz•zi•cal**
quiz•zi•cal
quoat : **quote**
quoatable : **quot•able**
quoatient : **quo•tient**

quoff : **quaff**
quoram : **quo•rum**
quorom : **quo•rum**
quorrey : **quar•ry**
quorrum : **quo•rum**
quort : **quart**
quo•rum
quoshent : **quo•tient**
quotabile : **quot•able**
quot•able
quoteable : **quot•able**
quotent : **quo•tient**
quo•tient
qwack : **quack**
qwackery : **quack•ery**
qwadrangle : **quad•ran•gle**
qwadrant : **quad•rant**
qwadruple : **qua•dru•ple**
qwadruplet : **qua•dru•plet**
qwaff : **quaff**
qwagmire : **quag•mire**

qwaint : **quaint**
qwake : **quake**
qwalified : **qual•i•fied**
qwalify : **qual•i•fy**
qwality : **qual•i•ty**
qwandary : **quan•da•ry**
qwantify : **quan•ti•fy**
qwantity : **quan•ti•ty**
qwarantine : **quar•an•tine**
qwarrel : **quar•rel**
qwarreling : **quar•rel•ing**
qwarry : **quar•ry**
qwart : **quart**
qwarter : **quar•ter**
qwartz : **quartz**
qwasar : **qua•sar**
qwaver : **qua•ver**
qweasily : **quea•si•ly**
qweasy : **quea•sy**
Qwebec : **Que•bec**
qwote : **quote**

R

rabbed : **ra•bid**
rab•bi
rabbid : **ra•bid**
rabi : **rab•bi**
ra•bid
rac•coon
raccune : **rac•coon**
rac•ism
rack•et
rackit : **rack•et**
rackonteur : **ra•con•teur**
ra•con•teur
racontoor : **ra•con•teur**
racontuer : **ra•con•teur**
racoon : **rac•coon**
racunteur : **ra•con•teur**
raddish : **rad•ish**
radeator : **ra•di•a•tor**
radesh : **rad•ish**
radiam : **ra•di•um**
ra•di•ance
radianse : **ra•di•ance**
radiater : **ra•di•a•tor**
ra•di•a•tor
radience : **ra•di•ance**
radiense : **ra•di•ance**
rad•ish
ra•di•um
rag•ged
raggid : **rag•ged**
raign : **reign**
rai•ment
raindeer : **rein•deer**
rainment : **rai•ment**
raisen : **rai•sin**
rai•sin
rament : **rai•ment**
ram•pant
rampent : **ram•pant**
rampint : **ram•pant**

ranced : **ran•cid**
rancer : **ran•cor**
ran•cid
ran•cor
rancore : **ran•cor**
randam : **ran•dom**
randem : **ran•dom**
randim : **ran•dom**
ran•dom
randum : **ran•dom**
rangler : **wran•gler**
rankor : **ran•cor**
ransid : **ran•cid**
raon : **ray•on**
rap•id
raport : **rap•port**
rappid : **rap•id**
rappore : **rap•port**
rap•port
rappsody : **rhap•so•dy**
rapsady : **rhap•so•dy**
rapsody : **rhap•so•dy**
rarafied : **rar•efied**
rar•efied
rarety : **rar•i•ty**
rarified : **rar•efied**
raritty : **rar•i•ty**
rar•i•ty
rarrity : **rar•i•ty**
rasberry : **rasp•ber•ry**
ras•cal
rasen : **rai•sin**
rasin : **rai•sin**
rasism : **rac•ism**
raskal : **ras•cal**
raskel : **ras•cal**
rasor : **ra•zor**
raspbarry : **rasp•ber•ry**
rasp•ber•ry
raspbery : **rasp•ber•ry**

rasscal : **ras•cal**
rassel : **wres•tle**
rassle : **wres•tle**
ratafy : **rat•i•fy**
ratefy : **rat•i•fy**
ratiffy : **rat•i•fy**
rat•i•fy
ratler : **rat•tler**
rattify : **rat•i•fy**
rattlar : **rat•tler**
rat•tler
raught : **wrought**
rav•age
raveen : **ra•vine**
ravege : **rav•age**
ravene : **ra•vine**
raveoli : **rav•i•o•li**
ravesh : **rav•ish**
ravige : **rav•age**
ra•vine
raviole : **rav•i•o•li**
rav•i•o•li
ravioly : **rav•i•o•li**
rav•ish
ravvage : **rav•age**
ravvish : **rav•ish**
ray•on
razer : **ra•zor**
ra•zor
razzberry : **rasp•ber•ry**
razzor : **ra•zor**
reacter : **re•ac•tor**
re•ac•tor
read (book); **red** (color); **reed** (grass)
read•able
readible : **read•able**
readolent : **red•o•lent**
ready
reak : **reek** (to stink) *or* **wreak** (to inflict)
realise (*Brit.*) : **re•al•ize**

re•al•ize
realm
realter : **re•al•tor**
re•al•tor
reap
reasin : **rea•son**
rea•son
reath : **wreath** (*noun*) *or* **wreathe** (*verb*)
reathe : **wreath** (*noun*) *or* **wreathe** (*verb*)
rebelion : **re•bel•lion**
rebellian : **re•bel•lion**
re•bel•lion
re•but•tal
rebuttel : **re•but•tal**
rebuttle : **re•but•tal**
recalcetrant : **re•cal•ci•trant**
re•cal•ci•trant
recalcitrent : **re•cal•ci•trant**
recalsitrant : **re•cal•ci•trant**
reccognize : **re•cog•nize**
reccommend : **rec•om•mend**
recead : **re•cede**
re•cede
receed : **re•cede**
re•ceipt
receit : **re•ceipt**
re•ceive
recepe : **rec•i•pe**
re•cep•ta•cle
receptecle : **re•cep•ta•cle**
receptical : **re•cep•ta•cle**
recepticle : **re•cep•ta•cle**
recete : **re•ceipt**
receve : **re•ceive**
rech : **retch** (to vomit) *or* **wretch** (miserable one)
reciept : **re•ceipt**
recieve : **re•ceive**
rec•i•pe
recipiant : **re•cip•i•ent**

re•cip•i•ent
recippy : rec•i•pe
reciprical : re•cip•ro•cal
re•cip•ro•cal
reciprocitty : re•ci•proc•i•ty
re•ci•proc•i•ty
reciproety : re•ci•proc•i•ty
reciprosity : re•ci•proc•i•ty
reciprossity : re•ci•proc•i•ty
re•cit•al
re•cite
recitel : re•cit•al
recitle : re•cit•al
reck : wreak (to inflict) or
   wreck (to destroy)
reckage : wreck•age
reckondite : re•con•dite
reckonize : rec•og•nize
recognise (Brit.) : rec•og•nize
rec•og•nize
recomend : rec•om•mend
rec•om•mend
recompence : rec•om•pense
rec•om•pense
recompince : rec•om•pense
recompinse : rec•om•pense
rec•on•cile
recondight : re•con•dite
re•con•dite
reconsile : re•con•cile
recorse : re•course
recource : re•course
re•course
recovary : re•cov•ery
re•cov•ery
re•cruit
recrut : re•cruit
recrute : re•cruit
rectafy : rec•ti•fy
rectatude : rec•ti•tude
rectefy : rec•ti•fy
rectetude : rec•ti•tude

rectiffy : rec•ti•fy
rec•ti•fy
rectitood : rec•ti•tude
rec•ti•tude
recumpense : rec•om•pense
recurence : re•cur•rence
recurrance : re•cur•rence
re•cur•rence
red (color); read (book)
redalent : red•o•lent
reddolent : red•o•lent
reddress : re•dress
redduce : re•duce
reddy : ready
redeam : re•deem
re•deem
redeme : re•deem
rediculous : ri•dic•u•lous
red•o•lent
redolint : red•o•lent
re•dress
re•duce
re•dun•dant
redundent : re•dun•dant
reduse : re•duce
reed (grass); read (book)
reek (to stink); wreak (to
   inflict)
reelize : re•al•ize
reeltor : re•al•tor
reep : reap
reeson : rea•son
referance : ref•er•ence
ref•er•ee
ref•er•ence
referense : ref•er•ence
ref•er•ent
referie : ref•er•ee
referint : ref•er•ent
referrence : ref•er•ence
referrent : ref•er•ent
refery : ref•er•ee

refferee : **ref·er·ee**
refference : **ref·er·ence**
refirent : **ref·er·ent**
refrigarator : **re·frig·er·a·tor**
refrigerater : **re·frig·er·a·tor**
re·frig·er·a·tor
refriggerator : **re·frig·er·a·tor**
refrijerator : **re·frig·er·a·tor**
re·fus·al
re·fuse (*verb*); **ref·use** (*noun*)
refusel : **re·fus·al**
refussal : **re·fus·al**
regada : **re·gat·ta**
regadda : **re·gat·ta**
regail : **re·gale**
re·gal
re·gale
regamen : **reg·i·men**
re·gard
re·gat·ta
regaurd : **re·gard**
regeme : **re·gime**
regemen : **reg·i·men**
re·gen·cy
regensy : **re·gen·cy**
regergitate : **re·gur·gi·tate**
regester : **reg·is·ter**
reggale : **re·gale**
reggimen : **reg·i·men**
reggister : **reg·is·ter**
reggular : **reg·u·lar**
regiman : **reg·i·men**
re·gime
reg·i·men
regirgitate : **re·gur·gi·tate**
reg·is·ter
regle : **re·gal**
regotta : **re·gat·ta**
reguard : **re·gard**
reg·u·lar
reguler : **reg·u·lar**
regulir : **reg·u·lar**

regurgetate : **re·gur·gi·tate**
re·gur·gi·tate
regurjitate : **re·gur·gi·tate**
rehabilatate : **re·ha·bil·i·tate**
re·ha·bil·i·tate
rehabillitate : **re·ha·bil·i·tate**
rehearcel : **re·hears·al**
re·hears·al
re·hearse
rehearsel : **re·hears·al**
reherce : **re·hearse**
rehercil : **re·hears·al**
rehersal : **re·hears·al**
reherse : **re·hearse**
reign
reimberse : **re·im·burse**
reimburce : **re·im·burse**
re·im·burse
rein·deer
reitarate : **re·it·er·ate**
re·it·er·ate
reiterrate : **re·it·er·ate**
re·joice
rejoise : **re·joice**
rejoyce : **re·joice**
rejuvanate : **re·ju·ve·nate**
re·ju·ve·nate
rejuvinate : **re·ju·ve·nate**
reknown : **re·nown**
relagate : **rel·e·gate**
rel·a·tive
relavent : **rel·e·vant**
releace : **re·lease**
re·lease
releave : **re·lieve**
rel·e·gate
releive : **re·lieve**
relenquish : **re·lin·quish**
relese : **re·lease**
relesh : **rel·ish**
rel·e·vant
releve : **re·lieve**

relevent : **rel•e•vant**
reliabal : **re•li•able**
re•li•able
re•li•ance
relianse : **re•li•ance**
re•li•ant
relible : **re•li•able**
rel•ic
relick : **rel•ic**
relieble : **re•li•able**
relience : **re•li•ance**
reliense : **re•li•ance**
relient : **re•li•ant**
re•lieve
religate : **rel•e•gate**
relinquesh : **re•lin•quish**
re•lin•quish
rel•ish
relitive : **rel•a•tive**
relize : **re•al•ize**
rellative : **rel•a•tive**
rellavent : **rel•e•vant**
rellegate : **rel•e•gate**
rellevant : **rel•e•vant**
relliable : **re•li•able**
rellic : **rel•ic**
relligate : **rel•e•gate**
rellish : **rel•ish**
relm : **realm**
re•luc•tance
reluctanse : **re•luc•tance**
re•luc•tant
reluctense : **re•luc•tance**
reluctent : **re•luc•tant**
reluctince : **re•luc•tance**
reluctint : **re•luc•tant**
relyance : **re•li•ance**
remady : **rem•e•dy**
re•main
remane : **re•main**
remanisce : **rem•i•nisce**
re•mark•able

remarkible : **re•mark•able**
remeadial : **re•me•di•al**
remeddy : **rem•e•dy**
remedeal : **re•me•di•al**
re•me•di•al
rem•e•dy
remedyal : **re•me•di•al**
remeedial : **re•me•di•al**
remeidial : **re•me•di•al**
re•mem•brance
remembranse : **re•mem•brance**
remembrence : **re•mem•brance**
remembrense : **re•mem•brance**
remembrince : **re•mem•brance**
remiddy : **rem•e•dy**
remidy : **rem•e•dy**
reminice : **rem•i•nisce**
rem•i•nisce
reminiss : **rem•i•nisce**
remitance : **re•mit•tance**
re•mit•tance
remittanse : **re•mit•tance**
remittence : **re•mit•tance**
remittense : **re•mit•tance**
remittince : **re•mit•tance**
remminisce : **rem•i•nisce**
remmittance : **re•mit•tance**
remmoval : **re•mov•al**
rem•nant
remnent : **rem•nant**
remnint : **rem•nant**
re•mov•al
removel : **re•mov•al**
remunarate : **re•mu•ner•ate**
re•mu•ner•ate
remunnerate : **re•mu•ner•ate**
renagade : **ren•e•gade**
renavate : **ren•o•vate**
rench : **wrench**
rendavous : **ren•dez•vous**
rendevoo : **ren•dez•vous**
ren•dez•vous

ren•e•gade
re•new•al
renewel : re•new•al
renigade : ren•e•gade
rennagade : ren•e•gade
rennovate : ren•o•vate
renoun : re•nown
re•nounce
renounse : re•nounce
ren•o•vate
re•nown
renownce : re•nounce
renumerate : re•mu•ner•ate
reoccurrence : re•cur•rence
Reo de Janeiro : **Rio de Ja•nei•ro**
reostat : rheo•stat
re•pair
repare : re•pair
re•peal
re•peat
repeel : re•peal
repeet : re•peat
repele : re•peal
repelent : re•pel•lent
repellant : re•pel•lent
re•pel•lent
re•pen•tance
repentanse : re•pen•tance
repentence : re•pen•tance
rep•e•ti•tion
repintance : re•pen•tance
repitition : rep•e•ti•tion
repleat : re•plete
repleca : rep•li•ca
repleet : re•plete
re•plen•ish
replennish : re•plen•ish
re•plete
rep•li•ca
replicka : rep•li•ca
replinish : re•plen•ish

repplica : rep•li•ca
repprobate : rep•ro•bate
repramand : rep•ri•mand
repreave : re•prieve
reprehencible : rep•re•hen•si•ble
reprehensable : rep•re•hen•si•ble
rep•re•hen•si•ble
repreive : re•prieve
repremand : rep•ri•mand
repreve : re•prieve
repribate : rep•ro•bate
re•prieve
reprihensible : rep•re•hen•si•ble
rep•ri•mand
re•pri•sal
reprisel : re•pri•sal
reprissal : re•pri•sal
reprizal : re•pri•sal
re•proach
rep•ro•bate
reproch : re•proach
re•proof (*noun*); re•prove (*verb*)
reproove : re•proof (*noun*) *or* re•prove (*verb*)
re•prove (*verb*); re•proof (*noun*)
reptial : rep•tile
rep•tile
republec : re•pub•lic
re•pub•lic
republick : re•pub•lic
repudeate : re•pu•di•ate
re•pu•di•ate
rep•u•ta•ble
reputible : rep•u•ta•ble
requiam : re•qui•em
re•qui•em
requiset : req•ui•site
req•ui•site
requissite : req•ui•site
requium : re•qui•em
requizite : req•ui•site

resarrect : **res•ur•rect**
resavoir : **res•er•voir**
rescend : **re•scind**
re•scind
re•search
reseptacle : **re•cep•ta•cle**
reserch : **re•search**
resergence : **re•sur•gence**
res•er•voir
residdence : **res•i•dence**
res•i•dence
residense : **res•i•dence**
re•sign
resiliant : **re•sil•ient**
re•sil•ient
resillient : **re•sil•ient**
res•in
resine : **re•sign**
resipe : **rec•i•pe**
resipient : **re•cip•i•ent**
resiprocal : **re•cip•ro•cal**
resiprocity : **rec•i•proc•i•ty**
resipy : **rec•i•pe**
resirgence : **re•sur•gence**
re•sis•tance
resistence : **re•sis•tance**
resistense : **re•sis•tance**
resital : **re•cit•al**
resite : **re•cite**
resivoir : **res•er•voir**
reson : **rea•son**
resorce : **re•source**
resorse : **re•source**
re•source
resourse : **re•source**
re•spect•able
respectible : **re•spect•able**
resperator : **res•pi•ra•tor**
respirater : **res•pi•ra•tor**
res•pi•ra•tor
respit : **res•pite**
res•pite

responcible : **re•spon•si•ble**
responsable : **re•spon•si•ble**
responseble : **re•spon•si•ble**
re•spon•si•ble
ressel : **wres•tle**
ressend : **re•scind**
ressidence : **res•i•dence**
ressin : **res•in**
ressind : **re•scind**
ressle : **wres•tle**
restarant : **res•tau•rant**
restatution : **res•ti•tu•tion**
res•tau•rant
restetution : **res•ti•tu•tion**
res•ti•tu•tion
restle : **wres•tle**
restorant : **res•tau•rant**
resurect : **res•ur•rect**
re•sur•gence
resurgince : **re•sur•gence**
res•ur•rect
retacence : **ret•i•cence**
re•tail
retale : **re•tail**
retaleate : **re•tal•i•ate**
re•tal•i•ate
retalliate : **re•tal•i•ate**
retch (to vomit); wretch
   (miserable one)
ret•i•cence
reticense : **ret•i•cence**
ret•i•na
ret•i•nue
retisense : **ret•i•cence**
retreave : **re•trieve**
retreive : **re•trieve**
retreve : **re•trieve**
re•trieve
rettail : **re•tail**
retticence : **ret•i•cence**
rettina : **ret•i•na**
rettinue : **ret•i•nue**

revalation : **rev•e•la•tion**
revalry : **rev•el•ry**
revanue : **rev•e•nue**
revarence : **rev•er•ence**
revarent : **rev•er•ent**
revarie : **rev•er•ie**
re•veal
revecable : **re•vo•ca•ble**
reveel : **re•veal**
rev•eil•le
reveilly : **rev•eil•le**
rev•el
rev•e•la•tion
revele : **re•veal**
revell : **rev•el**
revellie : **rev•eil•le**
rev•el•ry
revennue : **rev•e•nue**
rev•e•nue
reverance : **rev•er•ence**
revercil : **re•ver•sal**
reveree : **rev•er•ie**
rev•er•ence
reverense : **rev•er•ence**
rev•e•rent
rev•er•ie
re•ver•sal
reversel : **re•ver•sal**
revery : **rev•er•ie**
revil : **rev•el**
revilation : **rev•e•la•tion**
reville : **rev•eil•le**
revinue : **rev•e•nue**
revirence : **rev•er•ence**
revirie : **rev•er•ie**
revirsal : **re•ver•sal**
re•vise
re•vi•sion
revission : **re•vi•sion**
re•viv•al
revivel : **re•viv•al**
revize : **re•vise**

revizion : **re•vi•sion**
re•vo•ca•ble
revoceble : **re•vo•ca•ble**
revocibal : **re•vo•ca•ble**
revokable : **re•vo•ca•ble**
revokeble : **re•vo•ca•ble**
rezervoir : **res•er•voir**
rezin : **res•in**
rhapsady : **rhap•so•dy**
rhapsiddy : **rhap•so•dy**
rhapsidy : **rhap•so•dy**
rhap•so•dy
rheo•stat
rhetaric : **rhet•o•ric**
rhet•o•ric
rhetorick : **rhet•o•ric**
rhettoric : **rhet•o•ric**
rhine•stone
rhi•noc•er•os
rhinocirus : **rhi•noc•er•os**
rhinoseros : **rhi•noc•er•os**
rhinosserus : **rhi•noc•er•os**
rhithm : **rhythm**
Rhode Is•land
rhu•barb
rhyme (poetry); **rime** (frost)
rhythem : **rhythm**
rhythm
rhythum : **rhythm**
rib•ald
ribbald : **rib•ald**
ribben : **rib•bon**
ribbin : **rib•bon**
rib•bon
ribon : **rib•bon**
ricachay : **ric•o•chet**
rickachet : **ric•o•chet**
rickashay : **ric•o•chet**
rick•ety
rickitty : **rick•ety**
rickity : **rick•ety**
ric•o•chet

ricoshay : **ric·o·chet**
ridacule : **rid·i·cule**
riddecule : **rid·i·cule**
riddicule : **rid·i·cule**
riddiculous : **ri·dic·u·lous**
rid·i·cule
ri·dic·u·lous
ridiculus : **ri·dic·u·lous**
rie : **rye** (grain) *or* **wry** (ironic)
riegn : **reign**
riendeer : **rein·deer**
rifal : **rif·fle** (to thumb
   through) *or* **ri·fle** (gun)
rifel : **rif·fle** (to thumb
   through) *or* **ri·fle** (gun)
rif·fle (to thumb through);
   ri·fle (gun)
ri·fle (gun); **rif·fle** (to thumb
   through)
rig·a·ma·role *or* **rig·ma·role**
riged : **rig·id**
riger : **rig·or**
riggamarole : **rig·ma·role**
riggid : **rig·id**
riggle : **wrig·gle**
riggor : **rig·or**
righ·teous
rightious : **righ·teous**
rightius : **righ·teous**
rig·id
rig·ma·role *or* **rig·a·ma·role**
rigmaroll : **rig·ma·role**
rigmerole : **rig·ma·role**
rig·or
rijid : **rig·id**
rime (frost); **rhyme** (poetry)
rimedial : **re·me·di·al**
rinagade : **ren·e·gade**
rinestone : **rhine·stone**
rinkle : **wrin·kle**
rinoceros : **rhi·noc·er·os**
rinovate : **ren·o·vate**

Rio de Ja·nei·ro
Rio de Janerro : **Rio de
   Ja·nei·ro**
Rio de Janiero : **Rio de
   Ja·nei·ro**
riostat : **rheo·stat**
riskay : **ris·qué**
risquay : **ris·qué**
ris·qué
rist : **wrist**
riter : **writ·er**
rithe : **writhe**
rithm : **rhythm**
rithum : **rhythm**
riting : **writ·ing**
rittual : **rit·u·al**
rit·u·al
rituel : **rit·u·al**
ri·val
rivel : **ri·val**
roadeo : **ro·deo**
Road Island : **Rhode Is·land**
robbot : **ro·bot**
ro·bot
robott : **ro·bot**
rock·et
rocketery : **rock·et·ry**
rock·et·ry
rockit : **rock·et**
rockitry : **rock·et·ry**
rodant : **ro·dent**
roddent : **ro·dent**
Rode Island : **Rhode Is·land**
ro·dent
ro·deo
rodio : **ro·deo**
roial : **roy·al**
roiel : **roy·al**
rollette : **rou·lette**
ro·mance
romanntic : **ro·man·tic**
romanse : **ro·mance**

ro•man•tic
romantick : **ro•man•tic**
rondavoo : **ren•dez•vous**
rondezvous : **ren•dez•vous**
roomate : **room•mate**
room•mate
rootabaga : **ru•ta•ba•ga**
rosarry : **ro•sa•ry**
ro•sa•ry
roserry : **ro•sa•ry**
rosery : **ro•sa•ry**
rotarry : **ro•ta•ry**
ro•ta•ry
roterry : **ro•ta•ry**
rotery : **ro•ta•ry**
rotory : **ro•ta•ry**
rough•age
roughege : **rough•age**
roughian : **ruf•fi•an**
roughige : **rough•age**
rought : **wrought**
rou•lette
routean : **rou•tine**
routeen : **rou•tine**
routene : **rou•tine**
rou•tine
roy•al
royel : **roy•al**
rubarb : **rhu•barb**
rubrec : **ru•bric**
ru•bric
rubrick : **ru•bric**
ruckas : **ruck•us**
ruckis : **ruck•us**

ruck•us
rudament : **ru•di•ment**
rudement : **ru•di•ment**
ru•di•ment
ruff : **rough**
ruffein : **ruf•fi•an**
ruf•fi•an
ruffien : **ruf•fi•an**
rufian : **ruf•fi•an**
rulette : **rou•lette**
rumage : **rum•mage**
rumanante : **ru•mi•nate**
rumer : **ru•mor**
ru•mi•nate
rum•mage
rummege : **rum•mage**
rummige : **rum•mage**
rumminnate : **ru•mi•nate**
rummor : **ru•mor**
ru•mor
rumpace : **rum•pus**
rumpis : **rum•pus**
rum•pus
Rushia : **Rus•sia**
Rusia : **Rus•sia**
Rus•sia
rus•tic
rustick : **rus•tic**
ru•ta•ba•ga
rutabaiga : **ru•ta•ba•ga**
rutabega : **ru•ta•ba•ga**
rutebaga : **ru•ta•ba•ga**
rutine : **rou•tine**
rye (grain); **wry** (ironic)
ryly : **wry•ly**

S

sabateur : **sab•o•teur**
Sabath : **Sab•bath**
sabatical : **sab•bat•i•cal**
sabatoor : **sab•o•teur**
Sab•bath
sab•bat•i•cal
sabbaticle : **sab•bat•i•cal**
Sabbeth : **Sab•bath**
Sabbith : **Sab•bath**
sabbotage : **sab•o•tage**
sabboteur : **sab•o•teur**
sa•ber *or* **sa•bre**
sabitage : **sab•o•tage**
sab•o•tage
sab•o•teur
saboture : **sab•o•teur**
sa•bre *or* **sa•ber**
sachel : **satch•el**
sacksiphone : **sax•o•phone**
sacrafice : **sac•ri•fice**
sac•ra•ment
sa•cred
sacrefice : **sac•ri•fice**
sacrement : **sac•ra•ment**
sacrid : **sa•cred**
sac•ri•fice
sacriment : **sac•ra•ment**
saddal : **sad•dle**
saddel : **sad•dle**
sad•dle
sa•fa•ri
safarri : **sa•fa•ri**
safe•ty
saffari : **sa•fa•ri**
saffire : **sap•phire**
safire : **sap•phire**
safty : **safe•ty**
Sahaira : **Sa•ha•ra**
Sa•ha•ra
Saharra : **Sa•ha•ra**

sail•er (ship); **sail•or** (one who sails)
sail•or (one who sails); **sail•er** (ship)
sal•able *or* **sale•able**
sal•ad
sal•a•man•der
sal•a•ry (wages); **cel•ery** (vegetable)
sale•able *or* **sal•able**
saleble : **sal•able**
salery : **cel•ery** (vegetable) *or* **sal•a•ry** (wages)
saliant : **sa•lient**
salible : **sal•able**
salid : **sal•ad**
sa•lient
salimander : **sal•a•man•der**
saliry : **cel•ery** (vegetable) *or* **sal•a•ry** (wages)
sa•li•va
sallable : **sal•able**
sallad : **sal•ad**
sallamander : **sal•a•man•der**
sallary : **cel•ery** (vegetable) *or* **sal•a•ry** (wages)
salled : **sal•ad**
sallid : **sal•ad**
sallient : **sa•lient**
salliva : **sa•li•va**
sallmon : **salm•on**
sallon : **sa•lon**
salloon : **sa•loon**
sallune : **sa•loon**
sallute : **sa•lute**
sallvage : **sal•vage**
salman : **salm•on**
salmin : **salm•on**
salm•on
sa•lon

sa•loon
salor : **sail•or**
sa•lute
sal•vage
salve (ointment); save (to rescue); solve (to find a solution)
salvege : **sal•vage**
salvige : **sal•vage**
Sambeezi : **Zam•be•zi**
Sambezi : **Zam•be•zi**
sammon : **salm•on**
sammurai : **sam•u•rai**
samon : **salm•on**
samouri : **sam•u•rai**
sampel : **sam•ple**
sam•ple
sampul : **sam•ple**
sam•u•rai
samuri : **sam•u•rai**
sanatarium : **san•a•to•ri•um**
sanatary : **san•i•tary**
san•a•to•ri•um *or* san•i•tar•i•um
san•dal
sandel : **san•dal**
sandle : **san•dal**
sandwhich : **sand•wich**
sand•wich
sandwitch : **sand•wich**
sanety : **san•i•ty**
San Fran•cis•co
San Francisko : **San Fran•cis•co**
San Fransiso : **San Fran•cis•co**
san•i•tar•i•um *or* san•a•to•ri•um
san•i•tary
saniterium : **san•a•to•ri•um**
sanitery : **san•i•tary**
sanitty : **san•i•ty**
san•i•ty
sannatarium : **san•a•to•ri•um**
sannatary : **san•i•tary**
sannity : **san•i•ty**

Sansibar : **Zan•zi•bar**
santer : **saun•ter**
Sanzibar : **Zan•zi•bar**
saphire : **sap•phire**
sap•phire
sarcasem : **sar•casm**
sarcasim : **sar•casm**
sar•casm
sarcasstic : **sar•cas•tic**
sar•cas•tic
sarcazm : **sar•casm**
sardeen : **sar•dine**
sardene : **sar•dine**
sar•dine
sarene : **se•rene**
sargent : **ser•geant**
sargient : **ser•geant**
sarrate : **ser•rate**
sassage : **sau•sage**
satalite : **sat•el•lite**
sa•tan•ic
satanick : **sa•tan•ic**
satannic : **sa•tan•ic**
satarize : **sat•i•rize**
satasfy : **sat•is•fy**
satch•el
satelite : **sat•el•lite**
sat•el•lite
Saterday : **Sat•ur•day**
saterize : **sat•i•rize**
Satern : **Sat•urn**
satesfactory : **sat•is•fac•to•ry**
satesfy : **sat•is•fy**
sat•in
sat•i•rize
satisfactery : **sat•is•fac•to•ry**
sat•is•fac•to•ry
sat•is•fy
sattelite : **sat•el•lite**
sattellite : **sat•el•lite**
satten : **sat•in**
sattin : **sat•in**

sattirize : **sat•i•rize**
sattisfactory : **sat•is•fac•to•ry**
sattisfy : **sat•is•fy**
Satturday : **Sat•ur•day**
Satturn : **Sat•urn**
Sat•ur•day
Sat•urn
saucege : **sau•sage**
sau•cer
saun•ter
sau•sage
sausege : **sau•sage**
sauser : **sau•cer**
sausige : **sau•sage**
sav : **salve** (ointment) *or* **save**
   (to rescue)
sav•age
save (to rescue); **salve**
   (ointment)
savege : **sav•age**
saveor : **sav•ior**
sav•ior *or* **sav•iour**
sav•iour *or* **sav•ior**
sa•vor
savour (*Brit.*) : **sa•vor**
sawcer : **sau•cer**
saxaphone : **sax•o•phone**
saxiphone : **sax•o•phone**
sax•o•phone
Saylon : **Cey•lon**
scabard : **scab•bard**
scab•bard
scabboard : **scab•bard**
scabbord : **scab•bard**
scaf•fold
scafold : **scaf•fold**
scairy : **scary**
scald
scalpal : **scal•pel**
scal•pel
scalple : **scal•pel**
scan•dal

scandel : **scan•dal**
Scandenavia : **Scan•di•na•via**
Scandinavea : **Scan•di•na•via**
Scan•di•na•via
Scandinnavia : **Scan•di•na•via**
scandle : **scan•dal**
scar•ab
scareb : **scar•ab**
scared (frightened); **scarred**
   (having a scar)
scarey : **scary**
scarib : **scar•ab**
scar•let
scarlit : **scar•let**
scarred (having a scar); **scared**
   (frightened)
scary
scauld : **scald**
scedule : **sched•ule**
sceme : **scheme**
sce•nar•io
scenarrio : **sce•nar•io**
scenary : **scen•ery**
sceneario : **sce•nar•io**
scenec : **sce•nic**
scenerry : **scen•ery**
scen•ery
sce•nic
scenick : **sce•nic**
scent•ed
sceptacism : **skep•ti•cism**
sceptecism : **skep•ti•cism**
scep•ter
scep•tic *or* **skep•tic**
scep•ti•cism *or* **skep•ti•cism**
sceptick : **skep•tic**
sceptisism : **skep•ti•cism**
sceptor : **scep•ter**
sceptre (*Brit.*) : **scep•ter**
scervy : **scur•vy**
scheam : **scheme**
scheddule : **sched•ule**

scheduel : **sched•ule**
sched•ule
scheme
schism
schissors : **scis•sors**
schisum : **schism**
schitxophrenia : **schizo•phre•nia**
schizm : **schism**
schizofrenai : **schizo•phre•nia**
schizophreania :
    schizo•phre•nia
schizo•phre•nia
schizzophrenia :
    schizo•phre•nia
scho•lar
scholasstic : **scho•las•tic**
scho•las•tic
scholer : **scho•lar**
schollar : **scho•lar**
schollastic : **scho•las•tic**
school
schoon•er
schuner : **schoon•er**
sciance : **sci•ence**
sci•ence
sciense : **sci•ence**
scientiffic : **sci•en•tif•ic**
sci•en•tif•ic
scimatar : **scim•i•tar**
scim•i•tar
scinted : **scent•ed**
scirry : **scur•ry**
scism : **schism**
scisors : **scis•sors**
scissers : **scis•sors**
scissophrania : **schizo•phre•nia**
scis•sors
scithe : **scythe**
scizzors : **scis•sors**
scolar : **scho•lar**
scolastic : **scho•las•tic**
scooner : **schoon•er**

scorpian : **scor•pi•on**
scorpien : **scor•pi•on**
scor•pi•on
scoundral : **scoun•drel**
scoun•drel
scoundril : **scoun•drel**
scourge
scrach : **scratch**
scral : **scroll**
scraped (rubbed); **scrapped**
    (discarded)
scrapped (discarded); **scraped**
    (rubbed)
scratch
screach : **screech**
scream
screan : **screen**
screech
screem : **scream**
screen
screne : **screen**
scrimage : **scrim•mage**
scrim•mage
scrimmege : **scrim•mage**
scroll
scrutanize : **scru•ti•nize**
scru•ti•nize
sculpter : **sculp•tor** (artist) *or*
    sculp•ture (work of art)
sculp•tor (artist); **sculp•ture**
    (work of art)
sculp•ture (work of art);
    sculp•tor (artist)
scurge : **scourge**
scur•ry
scur•vy
scythe (blade); **sigh** (deep
    breath)
seafairer : **sea•far•er**
sea•far•er
seafaror : **sea•far•er**
seamy

sé•ance
seap : **seep**
search
seasen : **sea•son**
seasin : **sea•son**
sea•son
seathe : **seethe**
Seattal : **Se•at•tle**
Seattel : **Se•at•tle**
Se•at•tle
secand : **sec•ond**
se•cede
seceed : **se•cede**
seceshion : **se•ces•sion**
se•ces•sion
secide : **se•cede**
seckular : **sec•u•lar**
sec•ond
secracy : **se•cre•cy**
secratary : **sec•re•tary**
se•cre•cy
secresy : **se•cre•cy**
se•cret
sec•re•tary
secretery : **sec•re•tary**
secrisy : **se•cre•cy**
secrit : **se•cret**
secritary : **sec•re•tary**
secter : **sec•tor**
sec•tor
sec•u•lar
seculer : **sec•u•lar**
secund : **sec•ond**
securety : **se•cu•ri•ty**
securitty : **se•cu•ri•ty**
se•cu•ri•ty
securrity : **se•cu•ri•ty**
sedament : **sed•i•ment**
se•dan
sedar : **ce•dar** (tree) *or* **se•der**
  (Passover meal)
sed•a•tive

seddan : **se•dan**
seddative : **sed•a•tive**
seddiment : **sed•i•ment**
seddition : **se•di•tion**
se•der (Passover meal); **ce•dar**
  (tree)
sedetive : **sed•a•tive**
sed•i•ment
se•di•tion
seditive : **sed•a•tive**
seefarer : **sea•far•er**
seege : **siege**
seemy : **seamy**
seep
seeson : **sea•son**
seethe
seeze : **seize**
segragate : **seg•re•gate**
seg•re•gate
segrigate : **seg•re•gate**
seige : **siege**
seis•mic
seismollogy : **seis•mol•o•gy**
seis•mol•o•gy
seive : **sieve**
seize
seizh : **siege**
seizmic : **seis•mic**
seizmology : **seis•mol•o•gy**
selary : **cel•ery** (vegetable) *or*
  sal•a•ry (wages)
seldem : **sel•dom**
sel•dom
selebrate : **cel•e•brate**
selebrity : **ce•leb•ri•ty**
se•lect
selery : **cel•ery** (vegetable) *or*
  sal•a•ry (wages)
selestial : **ce•les•tial**
selldom : **sel•dom**
sellect : **se•lect**
sellestial : **ce•les•tial**

selluloid : **cel•lu•loid**
Seltic : **Cel•tic**
sematary : **cem•e•tery**
sematery : **cem•e•tery**
sem•blance
semblanse : **sem•blance**
semblence : **sem•blance**
semenar : **sem•i•nar**
semenary : **sem•i•nary**
semesster : **se•mes•ter**
se•mes•ter
semeterry : **cem•e•tery**
semetery : **cem•e•tery**
sem•i•nar
sem•i•nary
seminerry : **sem•i•nary**
seminery : **sem•i•nary**
semmester : **se•mes•ter**
semminar : **sem•i•nar**
semminary : **sem•i•nary**
senario : **sce•nar•io**
sen•ate
senater : **sen•a•tor**
sen•a•tor
sence : **sense** (intelligence) *or*
  since (from that time)
sencery : **sen•so•ry**
sencible : **sen•si•ble**
senery : **scen•ery**
senet : **sen•ate**
senic : **sce•nic**
se•nile
senilety : **se•nil•i•ty**
se•nil•i•ty
senillity : **se•nil•i•ty**
senitor : **sen•a•tor**
sennate : **sen•ate**
sennator : **sen•a•tor**
sennile : **se•nile**
sensable : **sen•si•ble**
sensary : **sen•so•ry**
sensative : **sen•si•tive**

sense (intelligence); **cents**
  (money); **since** (from that
  time)
senseble : **sen•si•ble**
senser : **cen•ser** (incense
  container) *or* **cen•sor** (to
  remove objectionable
  material) *or* **cen•sure** (to
  condemn) *or* **sen•sor** (that
  which senses)
sensery : **sen•so•ry**
sensetive : **sen•si•tive**
sensibal : **sen•si•ble**
sen•si•ble
sensis : **cen•sus**
sen•si•tive
sen•sor (that which senses);
  cen•ser (incense container);
  cen•sor (to remove
  objectionable material);
  cen•sure (to condemn)
sen•so•ry
sen•su•al
sensuel : **sen•su•al**
sensus : **cen•sus**
sentament : **sen•ti•ment**
sentaur : **cen•taur**
sented : **scent•ed**
sentenal : **sen•ti•nel**
sen•ti•ment
sentimeter : **cen•ti•me•ter**
sentinal : **sen•ti•nel**
sen•ti•nel
sentinle : **sen•ti•nel**
sentrifugal : **cen•trif•u•gal**
sentripetal : **cen•trip•e•tal**
sentury : **cen•tu•ry**
sep•a•rate
sepea : **se•pia**
seperate : **sep•a•rate**
se•pia
sepirate : **sep•a•rate**

seppalcre : **sep•ul•cher**
seppalker : **sep•ul•cher**
sepparate : **sep•a•rate**
sepperate : **sep•a•rate**
seppia : **se•pia**
seppulchre : **sep•ul•cher**
Sep•tem•ber
Septembre : **Sep•tem•ber**
septer : **scep•ter**
Septimber : **Sep•tem•ber**
septor : **scep•ter**
sep•ul•cher *or* **sep•ul•chre**
sepulcre : **sep•ul•cher**
se•quence
sequense : **se•quence**
sequince : **se•quence**
sequinse : **se•quence**
Seracuse : **Syr•a•cuse**
seram : **se•rum**
seramic : **ce•ram•ic**
serate : **ser•rate**
serch : **search**
serean : **se•rene**
serebellum : **cer•e•bel•lum**
serebral : **cer•e•bral**
sereen : **se•rene**
seremony : **cer•e•mo•ny**
se•rene
serf (peasant); **surf** (waves)
serge (cloth); **surge** (to rise up)
ser•geant
sergent : **ser•geant**
sergeon : **sur•geon**
sergery : **sur•gery**
sergient : **ser•geant**
se•ri•al (in a series); **ce•re•al** (grain)
serine : **se•rene**
serman : **ser•mon**
sermin : **ser•mon**
ser•mon
ser•pent

serpint : **ser•pent**
serplus : **sur•plice** (vestment) *or* **sur•plus** (excess)
ser•rate
sertain : **cer•tain**
sertificate : **cer•tif•i•cate**
se•rum
servace : **ser•vice**
servaceable : **ser•vice•able**
ser•vant
servent : **ser•vant**
ser•vice
ser•vice•able
serviceble : **ser•vice•able**
servicible : **ser•vice•able**
servint : **ser•vant**
servise : **ser•vice**
servisible : **ser•vice•able**
serviss : **ser•vice**
servissible : **ser•vice•able**
ses•a•me
sesede : **se•cede**
seseed : **se•cede**
sesession : **se•ces•sion**
sesime : **ses•a•me**
sessame : **ses•a•me**
sessimy : **ses•a•me**
sesspool : **cess•pool**
sevarity : **se•ver•i•ty**
seveer : **se•vere**
sev•er•al
se•vere
severel : **sev•er•al**
severety : **se•ver•i•ty**
severitty : **se•ver•i•ty**
se•ver•i•ty
sevier : **se•vere**
seviral : **sev•er•al**
sevveral : **sev•er•al**
sew•age
sewige : **sew•age**
sex•tant

sextent : **sex•tant**
sextint : **sex•tant**
sex•u•al
sexuel : **sex•u•al**
seyance : **sé•ance**
Seylon : **Cey•lon**
shaddoe : **shad•ow**
shaddow : **shad•ow**
shadoe : **shad•ow**
shad•ow
shaffeur : **chauf•feur**
shaffure : **chauf•feur**
shampagne : **cham•pagne**
shampaign : **cham•pagne**
shampaine : **cham•pagne**
shampane : **cham•pagne**
sham•poo
shampu : **sham•poo**
shantie : **shan•ty**
shan•ty
shaparon : **chap•er•on**
shaperone : **chap•er•on**
sharade : **cha•rade**
shareff : **sher•iff**
shariff : **sher•iff**
sharlatan : **char•la•tan**
sharlaten : **char•la•tan**
sharletan : **char•la•tan**
shartreuse : **char•treuse**
shartroose : **char•treuse**
shartruese : **char•treuse**
shartruse : **char•treuse**
shateau : **cha•teau**
shatieu : **cha•teau**
shatoe : **cha•teau**
shatoue : **cha•teau**
shauffer : **chauf•feur**
shauvenism : **chau•vin•ism**
shauvinism : **chau•vin•ism**
sheaf
sheafs : **sheaves**
sheald : **shield**

shealf : **shelf**
sheaves
shedule : **sched•ule**
sheef : **sheaf**
sheeld : **shield**
sheepherd : **shep•herd**
sheeves : **sheaves**
sheif : **sheaf**
sheild : **shield**
shelac : **shel•lac**
shelf (*noun*); **shelve** (*verb*)
shel•lac
shellaced : **shel•lacked**
shellack : **shel•lac**
shel•lacked
shellter : **shel•ter**
shel•ter
sheltor : **shel•ter**
shelve (*verb*); **shelf** (*sing.*)
shelves (*plur.*)
shemise : **che•mise**
shepard : **shep•herd**
shephard : **shep•herd**
shep•herd
sher•bet
sherbit : **sher•bet**
shereff : **sher•iff**
sher•iff
Sheyenne : **Chey•enne**
shield
shillac : **shel•lac**
shillacked : **shel•lacked**
shingal : **shin•gle**
shingel : **shin•gle**
shin•gle
shirbet : **sher•bet**
shism : **schism**
shivalry : **chiv•al•ry**
shivelry : **chiv•al•ry**
shoalder : **shoul•der**
shoartage : **short•age**
shoffeur : **chauf•feur**

sholder : **shoul•der**
short•age
shortege : **short•age**
shortige : **short•age**
should•er
shov•el
shov•eled
shovelled : **shov•eled**
shovil : **shov•el**
shovilled : **shov•eled**
shovinism : **chau•vin•ism**
shrapnal : **shrap•nel**
shrap•nel
shrapnle : **shrap•nel**
shread : **shred**
shreak : **shriek**
shred
shreek : **shriek**
shreik : **shriek**
shrewd
shriek
shrival : **shriv•el**
shrivaled : **shriv•eled**
shriv•el
shriv•eled *or* **shriv•elled**
shriv•elled *or* **shriv•eled**
shrivil : **shriv•el**
shrivle : **shriv•el**
shrude : **shrewd**
shugar : **sug•ar**
shuger : **sug•ar**
shurbet : **sher•bet**
shute : **chute**
shutle : **shut•tle**
shuttal : **shut•tle**
shuttel : **shut•tle**
shut•tle
Siameese : **Si•a•mese**
Si•a•mese
Siameze : **Si•a•mese**
sianide : **cy•a•nide**
Siattle : **Se•at•tle**

Sibeeria : **Si•be•ria**
Si•be•ria
sibernetics : **cy•ber•net•ics**
Sibirea : **Si•be•ria**
Sicaly : **Sic•i•ly**
sicamore : **syc•a•more**
Sicely : **Sic•i•ly**
Sicili : **Sic•i•ly**
Sicilly : **Sic•i•ly**
Sic•i•ly
sickal : **cy•cle** (rotation) *or*
  sick•le (knife)
sickel : **cy•cle** (rotation) *or*
  sick•le (knife)
sick•le (knife); **cy•cle** (rotation)
siclone : **cy•clone**
sicomore : **syc•a•more**
sicophant : **sy•co•phant**
sidal : **si•dle**
sidan : **se•dan**
sid•le
siege
sience : **sci•ence**
siesmic : **seis•mic**
siesmology : **seis•mol•o•gy**
sieve
sieze : **seize**
sigar : **ci•gar**
sigh (deep breath); **scythe**
  (blade)
signafy : **sig•ni•fy**
sig•nal
signall : **sig•nal**
sig•na•ture
signefy : **sig•ni•fy**
signel : **sig•nal**
sig•net (ring); **cyg•net** (swan)
signeture : **sig•na•ture**
signifacant : **sig•nif•i•cant**
signifficant : **sig•nif•i•cant**
signiffy : **sig•ni•fy**
sig•nif•i•cant

sig•ni•fy
signiture : **sig•na•ture**
silacon : **sil•i•con**
silance : **si•lence**
si•lence
silense : **si•lence**
sil•hou•ette
sil•i•con
silince : **si•lence**
silinder : **cyl•in•der**
siliva : **sa•li•va**
sillable : **syl•la•ble**
sillabus : **syl•la•bus**
sillence : **si•lence**
sillhoette : **sil•hou•ette**
sillicon : **sil•i•con**
silloette : **sil•hou•ette**
silute : **sa•lute**
simalar : **sim•i•lar**
simblance : **sem•blance**
simbol : **cym•bal** (brass plate)
   or **sym•bol** (meaningful
   image)
Simese : **Si•a•mese**
simester : **se•mes•ter**
sim•i•lar
sim•i•le
similer : **sim•i•lar**
similiar : **sim•i•lar**
similie : **sim•i•le**
simitar : **scim•i•tar**
simmetry : **sym•me•try**
simmilar : **sim•i•lar**
simmulate : **sim•u•late**
simpathize : **sym•pa•thize**
simphony : **sym•pho•ny**
simplafy : **sim•pli•fy**
simplefy : **sim•pli•fy**
simpliffy : **sim•pli•fy**
sim•pli•fy
simposium : **sym•po•sium**
simptem : **symp•tom**

simptom : **symp•tom**
simtem : **symp•tom**
simtom : **symp•tom**
sim•u•late
sinagogue : **syn•a•gogue**
sinario : **sce•nar•io**
since (from that time); **sense**
   (intelligence)
sinceer : **sin•cere**
sinceir : **sin•cere**
sin•cere
sincerety : **sin•cer•i•ty**
sin•cer•i•ty
sinchronize : **syn•chro•nize**
Sincinnati : **Cin•cin•nati**
sindicate : **syn•di•cate**
sinema : **cin•e•ma**
sinemon : **cin•na•mon**
Singapoor : **Sin•ga•pore**
Sin•ga•pore
Singapour : **Sin•ga•pore**
singe•ing (burning); **sing•ing**
   (music)
sing•ing (music); singe•ing
   (burning)
Singopore : **Sin•ga•pore**
sing•u•lar
singuler : **sing•u•lar**
sinicism : **cyn•i•cism**
sinile : **se•nile**
sinility : **se•nil•i•ty**
sin•is•ter
sinnamon : **cin•na•mon**
sinnister : **sin•is•ter**
sinonym : **syn•o•nym**
sinphony : **sym•pho•ny**
sinsere : **sin•cere**
sinserity : **sin•cer•i•ty**
sinsual : **sen•su•al**
sinted : **scent•ed**
sintenal : **sen•ti•nel**
sinthesize : **syn•the•size**

sipher : **ci•pher**
sipress : **cy•press**
Siracuse : **Syr•a•cuse**
sirca : **cir•ca**
sircus : **cir•cus**
sirfeit : **sur•feit**
sirfiet : **sur•feit**
sirgeon : **sur•geon**
sirgery : **sur•gery**
sirgion : **sur•geon**
sir•loin
sirmount : **sur•mount**
sirname : **sur•name**
sirpent : **ser•pent**
sirplus : **sur•plice** (vestment) *or*
   sur•plus (excess)
sirrhosis : **cir•rho•sis**
sirum : **se•rum**
sirup *or* **syr•up**
Sisily : **Sic•i•ly**
sism : **schism**
sissors : **scis•sors**
sistem : **sys•tem**
sistern : **cis•tern**
sithe : **scythe**
sitrus : **cit•rus**
siv : **sieve**
sive : **sieve**
siz•able *or* **size•able**
size•able *or* **siz•able**
sizeble : **siz•able**
sizible : **siz•able**
sizmic : **seis•mic**
sizzel : **siz•zle**
siz•zle
skaffold : **scaf•fold**
skalpel : **scal•pel**
Skandinavia : **Scan•di•na•via**
skarlet : **scar•let**
skech : **sketch**
skedule : **sched•ule**
skelaton : **skel•e•ton**

skeletan : **skel•e•ton**
skeletin : **skel•e•ton**
skel•e•ton
skeliton : **skel•e•ton**
skelleton : **skel•e•ton**
skeme : **scheme**
skep•tic *or* **scep•tic**
skep•ti•cism *or* **scep•ti•cism**
skepticizm : **skep•ti•cism**
skermish : **skir•mish**
sketch
ski
skie : **ski**
skied
skiied : **skied**
ski•ing
skiis : **skis**
skilet : **skil•let**
skil•let
skillit : **skil•let**
sking : **ski•ing**
skirmesh : **skir•mish**
skir•mish
skirmush : **skir•mish**
skis
skolar : **schol•ar**
skool : **school**
skorpion : **scor•pi•on**
skulptor : **sculp•tor** (artist)
skulpture : **sculp•ture** (work of
   art)
skurmish : **skir•mish**
skurry : **scur•ry**
slagh : **sleigh**
slaghter : **slaugh•ter**
slaigh : **sleigh**
slaugh•ter
slauter : **slaugh•ter**
slavary : **slav•ery**
Slavec : **Slav•ic**
slaverry : **slav•ery**
slav•ery

Slav•ic
Slavick : **Slav•ic**
Slavvic : **Slav•ic**
slawter : **slaugh•ter**
slay (to kill); **sleigh** (sled)
sleak : **sleek**
sleap : **sleep**
sleapily : **sleep•i•ly**
sleasy : **slea•zy**
sleat : **sleet**
sleave : **sleeve**
slea•zy
sledge
sleek
sleep
sleep•i•ly
sleepyly : **sleep•i•ly**
sleesy : **slea•zy**
sleet
sleeve
slege : **sledge**
sleigh (sled); **slay** (to kill)
sleih : **sleigh**
sleive : **sleeve**
sleizy : **slea•zy**
slepe : **sleep**
slete : **sleet**
sleuth
slewth : **sleuth**
slice
sliceing : **slic•ing**
slic•ing
sliegh : **sleigh**
slimey : **slimy**
slimmy : **slimy**
slimy
slipery : **slip•pery**
slippary : **slip•pery**
slip•pery
slise : **slice**
slive : **sleeve**
slobenly : **slov•en•ly**

slo•gan
slogen : **slo•gan**
slogin : **slo•gan**
sloped (at an angle); **slopped**
(spilled)
slopped (spilled); **sloped** (at an
angle)
slouch
slov•en•ly
slovinly : **slov•en•ly**
slowch : **slouch**
sluce : **sluice**
slueth : **sleuth**
slugard : **slug•gard**
slug•gard
sluggerd : **slug•gard**
sluggird : **slug•gard**
sluice
sluise : **sluice**
sluth : **sleuth**
smear
smeer : **smear**
smithareens : **smith•er•eens**
smith•er•eens
smitherenes : **smith•er•eens**
smitherines : **smith•er•eens**
smoak : **smoke**
smoalder : **smol•der**
smoke
Smo•key (the Bear); **smoky**
(filled with smoke)
smoky (filled with smoke);
Smo•key (the Bear)
smol•der *or* **smoul•der**
smorgasboard : **smor•gas•bord**
smor•gas•bord
smorgesbord : **smor•gas•bord**
smorgisbord : **smor•gas•bord**
smoul•der *or* **smol•der**
smudge
smuge : **smudge**
smuggel : **smug•gle**

smugglar : **smug•gler**
smug•gle
smug•gler
smugle : **smug•gle**
snach : **snatch**
snatch
sneak
sneak•er
sneaky
snease : **sneeze**
sneaze : **sneeze**
sneek : **sneak**
sneeker : **sneak•er**
sneeky : **sneaky**
sneeze
sneke : **sneak**
snipet : **snip•pet**
snip•pet
snippit : **snip•pet**
sniv•el
sniv•el•ing *or* **sniv•el•ling**
sniv•el•ling *or* **sniv•el•ing**
snivil : **sniv•el**
snoarkel : **snor•kel**
snobbary : **snob•bery**
snob•bery
snobery : **snob•bery**
snobry : **snob•bery**
snorkal : **snor•kel**
snor•kel
snorkle : **snor•kel**
snuggal : **snug•gle**
snuggel : **snug•gle**
snug•gle
soak•ing
soap
soap•i•er
soapyer : **soap•i•er**
soarcerer : **sor•cer•er**
soarcery : **sor•cery**
soard : **sword**
soberiety : **so•bri•ety**

sobrietty : **so•bri•ety**
so•bri•ety
soccar : **soc•cer**
soc•cer
socciology : **so•ci•ol•o•gy**
soceable : **so•cia•ble**
soceology : **so•ci•ol•o•gy**
sociabal : **so•cia•ble**
sociabilety : **so•cia•bil•i•ty**
so•cia•bil•i•ty
so•cia•ble
socialibility : **so•cia•bil•i•ty**
socible : **so•cia•ble**
societty : **so•ci•ety**
so•ci•ety
sociollogy : **so•ci•ol•o•gy**
so•ci•ol•o•gy
sodder : **sol•der**
soddium : **so•di•um**
sodeum : **so•di•um**
sodiem : **so•di•um**
so•di•um
soffen : **soft•en**
sofisticated : **so•phis•ti•cat•ed**
sofmore : **soph•o•more**
sofomore : **soph•o•more**
soft•en
sojern : **so•journ**
sojorn : **so•journ**
so•journ
sojurn : **so•journ**
soking : **soak•ing**
so•lace
so•lar
solataire : **sol•i•taire**
solatary : **sol•i•tary**
solatude : **sol•i•tude**
sol•der (metal); **sol•dier**
   (fighter)
soldiar : **sol•dier**
sol•dier (fighter); **sol•der**
   (metal)

sole (only; fish; part of foot or shoe); **soul** (inner essence)
soled (having a sole); **sol·id** (not gas or liquid)
soledarity : **sol·i·dar·i·ty**
sole·ly
solem : **sol·emn**
sol·emn
soler : **so·lar**
solice : **so·lace**
solicet : **so·lic·it**
solicetor : **so·lic·i·tor**
solicetous : **so·lic·i·tous**
so·lic·it
so·lic·i·tor
so·lic·i·tous
solicitus : **so·lic·i·tous**
sol·id (not gas or liquid); **soled** (having a sole)
solidarety : **sol·i·dar·i·ty**
sol·i·dar·i·ty
solidefy : **so·lid·i·fy**
soliderity : **sol·i·dar·i·ty**
so·lid·i·fy
solilaquy : **so·lil·o·quy**
solilloquy : **so·lil·o·quy**
so·lil·o·quy
soliloqy : **so·lil·o·quy**
solise : **so·lace**
soliset : **so·lic·it**
solisetor : **so·lic·i·tor**
solisetous : **so·lic·i·tous**
soliss : **so·lace**
solissit : **so·lic·it**
solissitor : **so·lic·i·tor**
solissitous : **so·lic·i·tous**
sol·i·taire
solitare : **sol·i·taire**
sol·i·tary
solitery : **sol·i·tary**
sol·i·tude
sollace : **so·lace**

sollatude : **sol·i·tude**
sollemn : **sol·emn**
sollicit : **so·lic·it**
sollicitor : **so·lic·i·tor**
sollicitous : **so·lic·i·tous**
sollid : **sol·id**
sollidarity : **sol·i·dar·i·ty**
sollidify : **so·lid·i·fy**
solliloquy : **so·lil·o·quy**
sollitaire : **sol·i·taire**
sollitary : **sol·i·tary**
sollitude : **sol·i·tude**
solluble : **sol·u·ble**
sollvency : **sol·ven·cy**
sollvent : **sol·vent**
solstace : **sol·stice**
sol·stice
solstiss : **sol·stice**
soluable : **sol·u·ble**
sol·u·ble
soluible : **sol·u·ble**
solumn : **sol·emn**
solv·able
solve (to find a solution); **salve** (ointment)
sol·ven·cy
solvensy : **sol·ven·cy**
sol·vent
solvible : **solv·able**
solvincy : **sol·ven·cy**
solvint : **sol·vent**
soly : **sole·ly**
som·er·sault or **sum·mer·sault**
sommersault : **som·er·sault**
sonada : **so·na·ta**
so·na·ta
sonatta : **so·na·ta**
sonet : **son·net**
son·ic
son·net
sonnic : **son·ic**
sonnick : **son·ic**

sonnit : **son·net**
sonter : **saun·ter**
soparific : **so·po·rif·ic**
sope : **soap**
sophistacated : **so·phis·ti·cat·ed**
sophistecated : **so·phis·ti·cat·ed**
so·phis·ti·cat·ed
sophmoar : **soph·o·more**
sophmore : **soph·o·more**
soph·o·more
sopier : **soap·i·er**
soporiffic : **so·po·rif·ic**
so·po·rif·ic
sopranno : **so·pra·no**
so·pra·no
sor·cer·er
sorceror : **sor·cer·er**
sor·cery
sord : **sword**
sorded : **sor·did**
sor·did
soroarity : **so·ror·i·ty**
sororety : **so·ror·i·ty**
sororitty : **so·ror·i·ty**
so·ror·i·ty
sororrity : **so·ror·i·ty**
sorrority : **so·ror·i·ty**
sosiety : **so·ci·e·ty**
sosiology : **so·ci·ol·o·gy**
sosser : **sau·cer**
sossialibility : **so·cia·bil·i·ty**
sothern : **south·ern**
soufflay : **souf·flé**
souf·flé
souffley : **souf·flé**
soufle : **souf·flé**
soul (inner essence); **sole** (only; fish; part of foot or shoe)
sourcerer : **sor·cer·er**
sourcery : **sor·cery**

South Caralina : **South Car·o·li·na**
South Carlina : **South Car·o·li·na**
South Car·o·li·na
South Carrolina : **South Car·o·li·na**
South Dahkota : **South Da·ko·ta**
South Da·ko·ta
South Dakotah : **South Da·ko·ta**
south·ern
souveneer : **sou·ve·nir**
sou·ve·nir
souvineer : **sou·ve·nir**
souvineir : **sou·ve·nir**
soveregn : **sov·er·eign**
sov·er·eign
soveriegn : **sov·er·eign**
soviat : **so·vi·et**
so·vi·et
sovrin : **sov·er·eign**
spaceious : **spa·cious**
spacial : **spa·tial**
spa·cious
spacius : **spa·cious**
spagetti : **spa·ghet·ti**
spa·ghet·ti
spaghetty : **spa·ghet·ti**
Span·iard
span·iel
Spanierd : **Span·iard**
Span·ish
Spanniard : **Span·iard**
spanniel : **span·iel**
Spannish : **Span·ish**
sparce : **sparse**
sparcety : **spar·si·ty**
sparcity : **spar·si·ty**
sparow : **spar·row**
spar·row

sparse
sparsety : **spar·si·ty**
sparsitty : **spar·si·ty**
spar·si·ty
spasial : **spa·tial**
spasim : **spasm**
spasm
spatela : **spat·u·la**
spa·tial
spatiel : **spa·tial**
spattula : **spat·u·la**
spat·u·la
spatulla : **spat·u·la**
spaun : **spawn**
spawn
spazm : **spasm**
speach : **speech**
speak
spear
specafy : **spec·i·fy**
specamen : **spec·i·men**
specamin : **spec·i·men**
spechial : **spe·cial**
spe·cial
specifec : **spe·cif·ic**
speciffic : **spe·cif·ic**
speciffy : **spec·i·fy**
spe·cif·ic
specifick : **spe·cif·ic**
spec·i·fy
spec·i·men
specimin : **spec·i·men**
speckter : **spec·ter**
spectackular : **spec·tac·u·lar**
spec·ta·cle
spec·tac·u·lar
spectaculer : **spec·tac·u·lar**
spectater : **spec·ta·tor**
spec·ta·tor
spectecle : **spec·ta·cle**
spec·ter
spectical : **spec·ta·cle**

specticle : **spec·ta·cle**
spector : **spec·ter**
spectre (*Brit.*) : **spec·ter**
spedometer : **speed·om·e·ter**
speech
speedameter : **speed·om·e·ter**
speed·om·e·ter
speedomiter : **speed·om·e·ter**
speek : **speak**
speer : **spear**
speghetti : **spa·ghet·ti**
speir : **spear**
sperit : **spir·it**
speritual : **spir·i·tu·al**
spern : **spurn**
sperrow : **spar·row**
spert : **spurt**
spesafy : **spec·i·fy**
spesamen : **spec·i·men**
spesial : **spe·cial**
spesific : **spe·cif·ic**
spesify : **spec·i·fy**
spesimin : **spec·i·men**
spessify : **spec·i·fy**
spheer : **sphere**
spheir : **sphere**
sphenx : **sphinx**
sphere
sphinks : **sphinx**
sphinx
spicket : **spig·ot**
spicy
spigget : **spig·ot**
spiggit : **spig·ot**
spiggot : **spig·ot**
spighetti : **spa·ghet·ti**
spig·ot
spilled
spilt : **spilled**
spin·ach
spinaker : **spin·na·ker**
spi·nal

spindal : **spin•dle**
spindel : **spin•dle**
spin•dle
spinel : **spi•nal**
spinich : **spin•ach**
spinnacer : **spin•na•ker**
spinnach : **spin•ach**
spin•na•ker
spinnal : **spi•nal**
spinneker : **spin•na•ker**
spinnet : **spin•et**
spinnich : **spin•ach**
spinx : **sphinx**
spi•ral
spirel : **spi•ral**
spiret : **spir•it**
spiretual : **spir•i•tu•al**
spir•it
spir•i•tu•al
spirituel : **spir•i•tu•al**
spirrit : **spir•it**
spirritual : **spir•i•tu•al**
spirt : **spurt**
spisy : **spicy**
splean : **spleen**
spleen
splended : **splen•did**
splender : **splen•dor**
splen•did
splen•dor
splerge : **splurge**
splindid : **splen•did**
splindor : **splen•dor**
splirge : **splurge**
splurge
spoiled *or* **spoilt**
spoilt *or* **spoiled**
Spokan : **Spo•kane**
Spo•kane
sponser : **spon•sor**
spon•sor
spontaineous : **spon•ta•ne•ous**

spontainious : **spon•ta•ne•ous**
spon•ta•ne•ous
spread
spred : **spread**
spright•ly
sprily : **spry•ly**
spritely : **spright•ly**
sprock•et
sprockit : **sprock•et**
sproose : **spruce**
spruce
spruse : **spruce**
spry•ly
spu•mo•ne *or* **spu•mo•ni**
spu•mo•ni *or* **spu•mo•ne**
spumonie : **spu•mo•ni**
spureous : **spu•ri•ous**
spu•ri•ous
spurn
spurrious : **spu•ri•ous**
spurt
squadren : **squad•ron**
squadrin : **squad•ron**
squad•ron
squak : **squawk**
squaled : **squal•id** (filthy) *or*
   squalled (cried)
squal•id (filthy); **squalled**
   (cried)
squalled (cried); **squal•id**
   (filthy)
squall•er (one that cries);
   squal•or (filthiness)
squallid : **squal•id** (filthy) *or*
   squalled (cried)
squallor : **squall•er** (one that
   cries) *or* **squal•or** (filthiness)
squal•or (filthiness); **squall•er**
   (one that cries)
squawk
squeak
squeal

squeam·ish
squeaze : **squeeze**
squeek : **squeak**
squeel : **squeal**
squeemesh : **squeam·ish**
squeemish : **squeam·ish**
squeese : **squeeze**
squeeze
squerrel : **squir·rel**
squiar : **squire**
squier : **squire**
squire
squirl : **squir·rel**
squirral : **squir·rel**
squir·rel
squirrl : **squir·rel**
squirt
squize : **squeeze**
stabelize : **sta·bi·lize**
stabilety : **sta·bil·i·ty**
sta·bil·i·ty
sta·bi·lize
stabillity : **sta·bil·i·ty**
stableize : **sta·bi·lize**
stablize : **sta·bi·lize**
stacado : **stac·ca·to**
stacato : **stac·ca·to**
stacatto : **stac·ca·to**
stac·ca·to
stackato : **stac·ca·to**
stacotto : **stac·ca·to**
staddium : **sta·di·um**
stadiem : **sta·di·um**
sta·di·um
stag·nant
stagnent : **stag·nant**
stagnint : **stag·nant**
staid (set in one's ways);
    stayed (remained)
stair (step); **stare** (look)
stake (pointed piece of wood;
    to bet); **steak** (meat)

sta·lac·tite
sta·lag·mite
stalion : **stal·lion**
stallactite : **sta·lac·tite**
stallagmite : **sta·lag·mite**
stallian : **stal·lion**
stal·lion
stallwart : **stal·wart**
stal·wart
stalwert : **stal·wart**
stalwirt : **stal·wart**
sta·men
stamena : **stam·i·na**
stamin : **sta·men**
stam·i·na
staminna : **stam·i·na**
stammina : **stam·i·na**
stam·pede
stampeed : **stam·pede**
stampide : **stam·pede**
stan·dard
standerd : **stan·dard**
stapel : **sta·ple**
sta·ple
stapple : **sta·ple**
stare (look); **stair** (step)
stareotype : **ste·reo·type**
starile : **ster·ile**
statec : **stat·ic**
stat·ic
sta·tion·ary (fixed);
    sta·tion·ery (paper)
sta·tion·ery (paper);
    sta·tion·ary (fixed)
statisstic : **sta·tis·tic**
sta·tis·tic
statium : **sta·di·um**
stattic : **stat·ic**
stattistic : **sta·tis·tic**
stattue : **stat·ue**
statture : **stat·ure**
stattus : **sta·tus**

stattute : **sta·tute**
stat·ue
stat·ure
sta·tus
stat·ute
stayed (remained); **staid** (set in one's ways)
stead·fast
steady
steak (meat); **stake** (pointed piece of wood; to bet)
steal (to rob); **steel** (metal)
steaple : **stee·ple**
stear : **steer**
steddy : **steady**
stedfast : **stead·fast**
stedy : **steady**
steel (metal); **steal** (to rob)
steepal : **stee·ple**
steepel : **stee·ple**
stee·ple
steer
stelactite : **sta·lac·tite**
stel·lar
steller : **stel·lar**
stencel : **sten·cil**
sten·cil
stensel : **sten·cil**
stensil : **sten·cil**
steralize : **ster·il·ize**
ste·reo·type
stergeon : **stur·geon**
steril : **ster·ile**
ster·ile
sterilety : **ste·ril·i·ty**
sterilise (*Brit.*) : **ster·il·ize**
ste·ril·i·ty
ster·il·ize
sterillity : **ste·ril·i·ty**
sterillize : **ster·il·ize**
sternam : **ster·num**
ster·num

sterrile : **ster·ile**
stethascope : **steth·o·scope**
steth·o·scope
stew·ard
stew·ard·ess
stewardiss : **stew·ard·ess**
stewerd : **stew·ard**
stewerdess : **stew·ard·ess**
stewird : **stew·ard**
stifel : **sti·fle**
stiffle : **sti·fle**
sti·fle
stilactite : **sta·lac·tite**
stilagmite : **sta·lag·mite**
stileto : **sti·let·to**
sti·let·to
stilleto : **sti·let·to**
stimied : **sty·mied**
stimmulate : **stim·u·late**
stimmulus : **stim·u·lus**
stim·u·late
stimulis : **stim·u·lus**
stimulous : **stim·u·lus**
stim·u·lus
stincil : **sten·cil**
stipand : **sti·pend**
sti·pend
stippulate : **stip·u·late**
stip·u·late
stirep : **stir·rup**
stirrep : **stir·rup**
stir·rup
stirup : **stir·rup**
stoalen : **sto·len**
Stock·holm
Stockhome : **Stock·holm**
sto·len
stol·id
stollid : **stol·id**
stom·ach
stomache : **stom·ach**
stomack : **stom·ach**

stomich : **stom•ach**

stomick : **stom•ach**

stopige : **stop•page**

stop•page

stoppige : **stop•page**

straddel : **strad•dle**

strad•dle

straight (not crooked); **strait** (isthmus)

straight•laced or **strait•laced**

strait (isthmus); **straight** (not crooked)

strait•laced or **straight•laced**

straitlased : **strait•laced**

stratafy : **strat•i•fy**

strat•a•gem

stratajem : **strat•a•gem**

stratajy : **strat•e•gy**

stratasphere : **strat•o•sphere**

stratefy : **strat•i•fy**

strategem : **strat•a•gem**

strat•e•gy

strategy : **strat•e•gy**

stratiffy : **strat•i•fy**

strat•i•fy

stratosfere : **strat•o•sphere**

stratospheer : **strat•o•sphere**

strat•o•sphere

strattify : **strat•i•fy**

strattigem : **strat•a•gem**

strattigy : **strat•e•gy**

strattle : **strad•dle**

strattosphere : **strat•o•sphere**

streak

stream

streat : **street**

strech : **stretch**

streek : **streak**

streem : **stream**

street

strenghthen : **strength•en**

strength•en

stretch

strichnine : **strych•nine**

stricknine : **strych•nine**

stridant : **stri•dent**

stri•dent

strin•gent

stringient : **strin•gent**

stringint : **strin•gent**

striped (with stripes); **stripped** (pealed)

stripped (pealed); **striped** (with stripes)

stroake : **stroke**

stroaler : **stroll•er**

stroke

stroler : **stroll•er**

stroll•er

struggel : **strug•gle**

strug•gle

strugle : **strug•gle**

strych•nine

stubbern : **stub•born**

stub•born

stuborn : **stub•born**

stuc•co

stucko : **stuc•co**

stuco : **stuc•co**

studant : **stu•dent**

studdio : **stu•dio**

stu•dent

studeo : **stu•dio**

studeous : **stu•di•ous**

stu•dio

stu•di•ous

stultafy : **stul•ti•fy**

stultefy : **stul•ti•fy**

stul•ti•fy

stupafy : **stu•pe•fy**

stuped : **stu•pid**

stupeffy : **stu•pe•fy**

stu•pe•fy

stuper : **stu•por**

stu•pid

stupify : **stu•pe•fy**

stu•por

stuppid : **stu•pid**

stur•geon

sturgion : **stur•geon**

sturgon : **stur•geon**

sty•mied

suacidal : **sui•cid•al**

suade : **suede**

suami : **swa•mi**

suarthy : **swar•thy**

suave

suavety : **sua•vi•ty**

sua•vi•ty

subblety : **sub•tle•ty**

subbtle : **sub•tle**

subcidize : **sub•si•dize**

suberb : **sub•urb**

suberban : **sub•ur•ban**

subgigate : **sub•ju•gate**

subjagate : **sub•ju•gate**

subjigate : **sub•ju•gate**

sub•ju•gate

sublamate : **sub•li•mate**

sub•li•mate

sub•merge

sub•merse

submirge : **sub•merge**

submirse : **sub•merse**

submishion : **sub•mis•sion**

submissian : **sub•mis•sion**

sub•mis•sion

submurge : **sub•merge**

submurse : **sub•merse**

subpena : **sub•poe•na**

subpina : **sub•poe•na**

sub•poe•na

subsadize : **sub•si•dize**

subsedize : **sub•si•dize**

sub•se•quent

subsequint : **sub•se•quent**

subservant : **sub•ser•vi•ent**

subservent : **sub•ser•vi•ent**

subserviant : **sub•ser•vi•ent**

sub•ser•vi•ent

subsiddy : **sub•sid•iary**
(auxilliary) *or* **sub•si•dy**
(assistance)

sub•side

sub•sid•iary (auxilliary);
sub•si•dy (assistance)

sub•si•dize

sub•si•dy (assistance);
sub•sid•iary (auxilliary)

subsiquent : **sub•se•quent**

sub•stance

substanse : **sub•stance**

substatute : **sub•sti•tute**

substence : **sub•stance**

substetute : **sub•sti•tute**

substince : **sub•stance**

sub•sti•tute

subtel : **sub•tle**

subteranean : **sub•ter•ra•nean**

sub•ter•ra•nean

sub•tle

sub•tle•ty (*noun*); **sub•tly** (*adv.*)

subturrainian : **sub•ter•ra•nean**

sub•urb (city outskirts);
su•perb (superior)

sub•ur•ban

suburben : **sub•ur•ban**

succede : **suc•ceed**

suc•ceed

succeptible : **sus•cep•ti•ble**

suc•cess

suc•cinct

succulant : **suc•cu•lent**

suc•cu•lent

succulint : **suc•cu•lent**

suc•cumb

sucede : **suc•ceed**

sucess : **suc•cess**

sucidal : **sui·cid·al**
sucint : **suc·cinct**
suckulent : **suc·cu·lent**
sucsede : **suc·ceed**
sucum : **suc·cumb**
sucumb : **suc·cumb**
suecidal : **sui·cid·al**
suede
suffacate : **suf·fo·cate**
sufficate : **suf·fo·cate**
suf·fice
suffise : **suf·fice**
suffle : **souf·flé**
suf·fo·cate
sufice : **suf·fice**
sug·ar
suger : **sug·ar**
sugest : **sug·gest**
sug·gest
suggestable : **sug·gest·ible**
sug·gest·ible
sui·cid·al
sui·cide
suisidal : **sui·cid·al**
suiside : **sui·cide**
suit·able
suiter : **suit·or**
suitible : **suit·a·ble**
suit·or
sulfer : **sul·phur**
sullphur : **sul·phur**
sulltan : **sul·tan**
sulpher : **sul·phur**
sul·phur
sul·tan
sulten : **sul·tan**
sultin : **sul·tan**
su·mac
sumack : **su·mac**
sumary : **sum·ma·ry**
sumersalt : **som·er·sault**
sumit : **sum·mit**

sumlemate : **sub·li·mate**
summac : **su·mac**
sum·ma·ry
summen : **sum·mon**
summersalt : **som·er·sault**
summersault : **som·er·sault**
sum·mer·y (like summer);
    sum·ma·ry (synopsis)
summet : **sum·mit**
sum·mit
sum·mon
sumon : **sum·mon**
sun·dae (confection); **Sun·day**
    (day of week)
Sun·day (day of week);
    sun·dae (confection)
supeerior : **su·pe·ri·or**
supeeriority : **su·pe·ri·or·i·ty**
supeirior : **su·pe·ri·or**
supeiriority : **su·pe·ri·or·i·ty**
su·perb (superior); **sub·urb**
    (city outskirts)
su·per·cede *or* **su·per·sede**
superceed : **su·per·sede**
supercileous : **su·per·cil·ious**
su·per·cil·ious
supercillious : **su·per·cil·ious**
superentendent :
    su·per·in·ten·dent
su·per·fi·cial
superfishial : **su·per·fi·cial**
superfisial : **su·per·fi·cial**
superfissial : **su·per·fi·cial**
superier : **su·pe·ri·or**
superierity : **su·pe·ri·or·i·ty**
superintendant :
    su·per·in·ten·dent
su·per·in·ten·dent
su·pe·ri·or
superiorety : **su·pe·ri·or·i·ty**
su·pe·ri·or·i·ty
superiorrity : **su·pe·ri·or·i·ty**

su•per•sede
superseed : **su•per•sede**
supersilious : **su•per•cil•ious**
supersillious : **su•per•cil•ious**
su•per•vise
superviser : **su•per•vi•sor**
su•per•vi•sor
supervize : **su•per•vise**
supervizor : **su•per•vi•sor**
supirior : **su•pe•ri•or**
supiriority : **su•pe•ri•or•i•ty**
suplament : **sup•ple•ment**
suplant : **sup•plant**
suplement : **sup•ple•ment**
suplicate : **sup•pli•cate**
suply : **sup•ply**
suport : **sup•port**
suppena : **sub•poe•na**
suppina : **sub•poe•na**
supplacate : **sup•pli•cate**
supplament : **sup•ple•ment**
sup•plant
supplecate : **sup•pli•cate**
sup•ple•ment
sup•pli•cate
suppliment : **sup•ple•ment**
sup•ply
sup•port
sup•press
supreem : **su•preme**
su•prem•a•cy
supremasy : **su•prem•a•cy**
su•preme
supremicy : **su•prem•a•cy**
supremissy : **su•prem•a•cy**
supress : **sup•press**
suprimacy : **su•prem•a•cy**
suprime : **su•preme**
suprise : **sur•prise**
suprize : **sur•prise**
surch : **search**

sure•ly (with certainty); **sur•ly** (sullen)
surf (waves); **serf** (peasant)
sur•face
sur•feit
surfet : **sur•feit**
surfice : **sur•face**
surfiet : **sur•feit**
surfise : **sur•face**
surfiss : **sur•face**
surfit : **sur•feit**
surge (to rise up); **serge** (cloth)
sur•geon
sur•gery
surgion : **sur•geon**
surgirgy : **sur•gery**
surloin : **sir•loin**
sur•ly (sullen); **sure•ly** (with certainty)
sur•mise
surmize : **sur•mise**
sur•mount
sur•name
surogate : **sur•ro•gate**
surpent : **ser•pent**
sur•plice (vestment); **sur•plus** (excess)
sur•plus (excess); **sur•plice** (vestment)
surpreme : **su•preme**
surpress : **sup•press**
sur•prise
surprize : **sur•prise**
surragate : **sur•ro•gate**
surregate : **sur•ro•gate**
sur•ro•gate
surroget : **sur•ro•gate**
survaillance : **sur•veil•lance**
survallence : **sur•veil•lance**
survay : **sur•vey**
survayer : **sur•vey•or**
survayor : **sur•vey•or**

surveilance : **sur•veil•lance**
sur•veil•lance
survellance : **sur•veil•lance**
sur•vey
surveyer : **sur•vey•or**
sur•vey•or
surviellance : **sur•veil•lance**
sur•viv•al
survivel : **sur•viv•al**
surviver : **sur•viv•or**
survivil : **sur•viv•al**
sur•viv•or
susceptable : **sus•cep•ti•ble**
sus•cep•ti•ble
suscinct : **suc•cinct**
suspence : **sus•pense**
sus•pense
suspician : **sus•pi•cion**
sus•pi•cion
sus•pi•cious
suspince : **sus•pense**
suspinse : **sus•pense**
suspishious : **sus•pi•cious**
suspission : **sus•pi•cion**
suspissious : **sus•pi•cious**
suspition : **sus•pi•cion**
suspitious : **sus•pi•cious**
susseptible : **sus•cep•ti•ble**
sussinct : **suc•cinct**
sustainance : **sus•te•nance**
sustanence : **sus•te•nance**
sus•te•nance
sustenanse : **sus•te•nance**
sustinance : **sus•te•nance**
sutable : **suit•able**
suthern : **south•ern**
suttle : **sub•tle**
suvenir : **sou•ve•nir**
swade : **suede**
swammi : **swa•mi**
swamy : **swa•mi**
swar•thy

swasstika : **swas•ti•ka**
swastica : **swas•ti•ka**
swasticka : **swas•ti•ka**
swas•ti•ka
swave : **suave**
swealter : **swel•ter**
sweap : **sweep**
sweapstakes : **sweep•stakes**
sweat•er
Swedan : **Swe•den**
Swe•den
Swed•ish
Sweeden : **Swe•den**
Sweedish : **Swed•ish**
sweep
sweep•stakes
sweepsteaks : **sweep•stakes**
swel•ter
swerve
sweter : **sweat•er**
swetter : **sweat•er**
swindlar : **swin•dler**
swin•dler
Swisserland : **Switz•er•land**
Switzarland : **Switz•er•land**
Switz•er•land
swival : **swiv•el**
swiv•el
swiv•eled
swivelled : **swiv•eled**
Switzzerland : **Switz•er•land**
swoallem : **swol•len**
swolen : **swol•len**
swol•len
sword
sworthy : **swarthy**
swove : **suave**
swurve : **swerve**
syanide : **cy•a•nide**
sybernetics : **cy•ber•net•ics**
sycamoor : **syc•a•more**
syc•a•more

sycaphant : **sy•co•phant**
sycaphent : **sy•co•phant**
syckle : **cy•cle** (rotation) *or*
  sick•le (knife)
sycle : **cy•cle** (rotation) *or*
  sick•le (knife)
sycofant : **sy•co•phant**
sycomore : **syc•a•more**
sy•co•phant
sykamore : **syc•a•more**
sykophant : **sy•co•phant**
sylabus : **syl•la•bus**
sylalble : **syl•la•ble**
sylinder : **cyl•in•der**
syl•la•ble
syl•la•bus
sylleble : **syl•la•ble**
syllebus : **syl•la•bus**
symbal : **cym•bal** (brass plate)
  or **sym•bol** (meaningful
  image)
sym•bol (meaningful image);
  cym•bal (brass plate)
symetry : **sym•me•try**
symmatry : **sym•me•try**
sym•me•try
sym•pa•thize
sympethize : **sym•pa•thize**
sym•pho•ny
symposiem : **sym•po•sium**
sym•po•sium

symptam : **symp•tom**
symptem : **symp•tom**
symp•tom
symtom : **symp•tom**
syn•a•gogue
synanym : **syn•o•nym**
synchrinize : **syn•chro•nize**
syn•chro•nize
syncronize : **syn•chro•nize**
syndacate : **syn•di•cate**
syndecate : **syn•di•cate**
syndicat : **syn•di•cate**
syn•di•cate
synegogue : **syn•a•gogue**
synicism : **cyn•i•cism**
synonim : **syn•o•nym**
syn•o•nym
synpathize : **sym•pa•thize**
synphony : **sym•pho•ny**
synthasize : **syn•the•size**
synthesise : **syn•the•size**
syn•the•size
sypress : **cy•press**
Syr•a•cuse
syrep : **syr•up**
syrrup : **syr•up**
syr•up *or* **sirup**
systam : **sys•tem**
sys•tem
systum : **sys•tem**
sythe : **scythe**

T

tabarnacle : **tab·er·na·cle**
tabbernacle : **tab·er·na·cle**
tabbleau : **tab·leau**
tabblet : **tab·let**
tabbloe : **tab·leau**
tabboo : **ta·boo**
tabelware : **ta·ble·ware**
tabernacal : **tab·er·na·cle**
tabernackle : **tab·er·na·cle**
tab·er·na·cle
tab·leau
tab·let
ta·ble·ware
tablewear : **ta·ble·ware**
tablieu : **tab·leau**
tablit : **tab·let**
ta·boo
tabu : **ta·boo**
tacet : **tac·it**
taceturn : **tac·i·turn**
tac·it
tacitern : **tac·i·turn**
tac·i·turn
tackal : **tack·le**
tackel : **tack·le**
tack·le
tacktics : **tac·tics**
tactecs : **tac·tics**
tact·ful
tactfull : **tact·ful**
tac·ti·cal
tacticks : **tac·tics**
tacticle : **tac·ti·cal**
tac·tics
tactikal : **tac·ti·cal**
tafeta : **taf·fe·ta**
taf·fe·ta
taffita : **taf·fe·ta**
tafita : **taf·fe·ta**
Taheti : **Ta·hi·ti**

Ta·hi·ti
Tahitti : **Ta·hi·ti**
Tahity : **Ta·hi·ti**
Tailand : **Thai·land**
tailer : **tai·lor**
tai·lor
Talahassee : **Tal·la·has·see**
talant : **tal·ent**
talcem : **tal·cum**
tal·cum
talen : **tal·on**
tal·ent
tal·is·man
talissman : **tal·is·man**
talk·ative
talkitive : **talk·ative**
Tallahasee : **Tal·la·has·see**
Tal·la·has·see
tallant : **tal·ent**
tallcum : **tal·cum**
tallent : **tal·ent**
tallisman : **tal·is·man**
tallon : **tal·on**
Talmed : **Tal·mud**
Talmid : **Tal·mud**
Tal·mud
tal·on
talor : **tai·lor**
ta·ma·le
tamaly : **ta·ma·le**
tamborine : **tam·bou·rine**
tambourene : **tam·bou·rine**
tam·bou·rine
tamburine : **tam·bou·rine**
tamole : **ta·ma·le**
tamolle : **ta·ma·le**
tan·dem
tandim : **tan·dem**
tandum : **tan·dem**
tangarine : **tan·ger·ine**

tangeble : **tan•gi•ble**
tan•gent
tangerene : **tan•ger•ine**
tan•ger•ine
tangibal : **tan•gi•ble**
tan•gi•ble
tangient : **tan•gent**
tangierine : **tan•ger•ine**
tangint : **tan•gent**
tangirine : **tan•ger•ine**
tanjerine : **tan•ger•ine**
tannary : **tan•nery**
tan•nery
tantalise (*Brit.*) : **tan•ta•lize**
tan•ta•lize
tantallize : **tan•ta•lize**
tantelize : **tan•ta•lize**
tantilize : **tan•ta•lize**
tantrem : **tan•trum**
tantrim : **tan•trum**
tan•trum
tapeoca : **tap•i•o•ca**
tapestery : **tap•es•try**
tap•es•try
tap•i•o•ca
tapioka : **tap•i•o•ca**
tapistry : **tap•es•try**
tappestry : **tap•es•try**
tappioca : **tap•i•o•ca**
tappistry : **tap•es•try**
taranchula : **ta•ran•tu•la**
tarantoola : **ta•ran•tu•la**
ta•ran•tu•la
tareff : **tar•iff**
tar•get
targit : **tar•get**
tar•iff
tarnesh : **tar•nish**
tar•nish
tarpalin : **tar•pau•lin**
tarpaulen : **tar•pau•lin**
tar•pau•lin

tarpolin : **tar•pau•lin**
tarriff : **tar•iff**
tar•tan
tar•tar
tarten : **tar•tan**
tarter : **tar•tar**
tasel : **tas•sel**
taseturn : **tac•i•turn**
tasit : **tac•it**
tasiturn : **tac•i•turn**
tas•sel
tassit : **tac•it**
tassiturn : **tac•i•turn**
tassle : **tas•sel**
tatle : **tat•tle**
tatoo : **tat•too**
tattel : **tat•tle**
tat•tle
tat•too
tav•ern
tavurn : **tav•ern**
tavvern : **tav•ern**
tax•able
taxadermy : **taxi•der•my**
taxedermy : **taxi•der•my**
taxible : **tax•able**
taxi•der•my
taxidurmy : **taxi•der•my**
tea (drink); **tee** (golf)
teach
teadious : **te•dious**
tear•ful
tearfull : **tear•ful**
tease
technecal : **tech•ni•cal**
tech•ni•cal
technicle : **tech•ni•cal**
tech•nique
tecnical : **tech•ni•cal**
tecnique : **tech•nique**
tedeum : **te•di•um**
te•dious

te•di•um
tedius : te•dious
tee (golf); tea (drink)
teech : teach
teerful : tear•ful
teese : tease
teeth (*noun*); teethe (*verb*)
teethe (*verb*); teeth (*noun*)
Te•he•ran *or* Teh•ran
Teh•ran *or* Te•he•ran
telacast : tele•cast
telagram : tele•gram
telaphone : tele•phone
telascope : tele•scope
telavise : tele•vise
telavision : tele•vi•sion
tele•cast
tele•gram
tele•phone
tele•scope
tele•vise
tele•vi•sion
televize : tele•vise
tellecast : tele•cast
tellegram : tele•gram
tellephone : tele•phone
tellescope : tele•scope
tellevise : tele•vise
tellevision : tele•vi•sion
temblar : tem•blor
tembler : tem•blor
tem•blor
te•mer•i•ty
temmeritty : te•mer•i•ty
temmerity : te•mer•i•ty
tempachure : tem•per•a•ture
temparary : tem•po•rary
tempature : tem•per•a•ture
tem•per•ance
temperanse : tem•per•ance
tem•per•a•ture
temperence : tem•per•ance

temperince : tem•per•ance
temperment : tem•per•a•ment
temperture : tem•per•a•ture
tem•pest
tempirary : tem•po•rary
tempist : tem•pest
tem•po•rary
temporery : tem•po•rary
temprature : tem•per•a•ture
ten•a•ble
te•na•cious
tenacle : ten•ta•cle
tenament : ten•e•ment
tenamint : ten•e•ment
ten•ant
Tenasee : Ten•nes•see
tenat : te•net
tenatious : ten•a•ble
tenative : ten•ta•tive
tendan : ten•don
tendancy : ten•den•cy
tendansy : ten•den•cy
ten•den•cy
tendensy : ten•den•cy
tenderhook : ten•ter•hook
tendin : ten•don
tendincy : ten•den•cy
ten•don
tendrel : ten•dril
ten•dril
tendrill : ten•dril
ten•e•ment
tenent : ten•ant
tener : ten•or
Tenesee : Ten•nes•see
te•net
tenint : ten•ant
tenir : ten•or
tenis : ten•nis
Tenisee : Ten•nes•see
tenit : te•net
tennable : ten•a•ble

tennacious : **te•na•cious**
tennament : **ten•e•ment**
tennant : **ten•ant**
tennement : **ten•e•ment**
tennent : **ten•ant**
tennes : **ten•nis**
Tennesee : **Ten•nes•see**
Ten•nes•see
tennet : **te•net**
ten•nis
tennor : **ten•or**
tennuous : **ten•u•ous**
tennure : **ten•ure**
ten•or
ten•ta•cle
ten•ta•tive
ten•ter•hook
tentetive : **ten•ta•tive**
tentical : **ten•ta•cle**
tenticle : **ten•ta•cle**
tentitive : **ten•ta•tive**
ten•u•ous
ten•ure
teped : **tep•id**
tep•id
teppid : **tep•id**
terace : **ter•race**
teradactyl : **ptero•dac•tyl**
terain : **ter•rain**
terantula : **ta•ran•tu•la**
terban : **tur•ban** (headdress) *or*
    tur•bine (engine)
terbine : **tur•ban** (headdress) *or*
    tur•bine (engine)
terestrial : **ter•res•tri•al**
terible : **ter•ri•ble**
teridactyl : **ptero•dac•tyl**
terier : **ter•ri•er**
teriffy : **ter•ri•fy**
terific : **ter•rif•ic**
terify : **ter•ri•fy**
teritory : **ter•ri•to•ry**

terkey : **tur•key**
termenal : **ter•mi•nal**
ter•mi•nal
terminel : **ter•mi•nal**
terminnal : **ter•mi•nal**
ter•mite
termmite : **ter•mite**
ternip : **tur•nip**
terodactile : **ptero•dac•tyl**
terodactill : **ptero•dac•tyl**
terpentine : **tur•pen•tine**
terquoise : **tur•quoise**
terrable : **ter•ri•ble**
ter•race
terrafy : **ter•ri•fy**
ter•rain
terrane : **ter•rain**
terratory : **ter•ri•to•ry**
terrestial : **ter•res•tri•al**
ter•res•tri•al
terretory : **ter•ri•to•ry**
terribal : **ter•ri•ble**
ter•ri•ble
terrice : **ter•race**
ter•ri•er
terriffic : **ter•rif•ic**
ter•rif•ic
ter•ri•fy
terriss : **ter•race**
territorey : **ter•ri•to•ry**
ter•ri•to•ry
tesstify : **tes•ti•fy**
testafy : **tes•ti•fy**
tes•ta•ment
testamony : **tes•ti•mo•ny**
testement : **tes•ta•ment**
testemony : **tes•ti•mo•ny**
testiffy : **tes•ti•fy**
tes•ti•fy
testiment : **tes•ta•ment**
tes•ti•mo•ny
tetanis : **tet•a•nus**

tet•a•nus
tetnis : tet•a•nus
tetnus : tet•a•nus
tettanus : tet•a•nus
Teusday : Tues•day
Tex•as
textil : tex•tile
tex•tile
textill : tex•tile
Texus : Tex•as
thach : thatch
Thai•land
than (rather than); then (not
  now)
thatch
theaf : thief
thealogy : the•ol•o•gy
thearem : the•o•rem
theary : the•o•ry
theasaurus : the•sau•rus
the•a•ter or the•a•tre
the•a•tre or the•a•ter
theavery : thiev•ery
theaves : thieves
theef : thief
theevery : thiev•ery
theeves : thieves
theif : thief
their (belonging to them);
  there (not here); they're (they
  are)
theirem : the•o•rem
theirfore : there•fore
theirs (belonging to them);
  there's (there is)
theiry : the•o•ry
theiter : the•a•ter
theivery : thiev•ery
theives : thieves
then (not now); than (rather
  than)
theoligy : the•ol•o•gy

theollogy : the•ol•o•gy
the•ol•o•gy
the•o•rem
theorum : the•o•rem
the•o•ry
ther•a•peu•tic
therapuetic : ther•a•peu•tic
theraputic : ther•a•peu•tic
ther•a•py
there (not here); their
  (belonging to them); they're
  (they are)
therefor : there•fore
there•fore
therem : the•o•rem
therepeutic : ther•a•peu•tic
there's (there is); theirs
  (belonging to them)
theripy : ther•a•py
ther•mal
thermel : ther•mal
thermiss : ther•mos
ther•mos
thermus : ther•mos
therrapy : ther•a•py
Thersday : Thurs•day
thery : the•o•ry
the•sau•rus
thesoris : the•sau•rus
thesorrus : the•sau•rus
thesorus : the•sau•rus
theter : the•a•ter
thevery : thiev•ery
theves : thieves
they're (they are); their
  (belonging to them); there
  (not here)
Thialand : Thai•land
thief
thiefery : thiev•ery
thiefs : thieves
thievary : thiev•ery

thiev·ery
thieves
thievry : **thiev·ery**
thirmos : **ther·mos**
thiroid : **thy·roid**
Thirsday : **Thurs·day**
thirtean : **thir·teen**
thir·teen
thir·ti·eth
thirtine : **thir·teen**
thirtyeth : **thir·ti·eth**
thisel : **this·tle**
thissle : **this·tle**
this·tle
thoarax : **tho·rax**
tho·rax
thorogh : **thor·ough**
   (painstaking) *or* **through**
   (into and out of)
thor·ough (painstaking);
   through (into and out of)
thorow : **thor·ough**
   (painstaking) *or* **through**
   (into and out of)
thou·sand
thousend : **thou·sand**
thousind : **thou·sand**
thowsand : **thou·sand**
thread
thread·bare
thred : **thread**
thredbare : **thread·bare**
threshhold : **thresh·old**
thresh·old
through (into and out of);
   thor·ough (painstaking)
thru : **through**
thrugh : **thor·ough**
   (painstaking) *or* **through**
   (into and out of)
thum : **thumb**
thumb

thurmal : **ther·mal**
thurmos : **ther·mos**
Thurs·day
thy·roid
ti·ara
tiarra : **ti·ara**
tibbia : **tib·ia**
tibea : **tib·ia**
tib·ia
tickal : **tick·le**
tickel : **tick·le**
tick·le
tiera : **ti·ara**
tigar : **ti·ger**
ti·ger
tigeress : **ti·gress**
tigger : **ti·ger**
ti·gress
tigriss : **ti·gress**
tim·ber (wood); **tim·bre**
   (quality of sound)
tim·bre (quality of sound);
   tim·ber (wood)
Timbucktu : **Tim·buk·tu**
Timbuktoo : **Tim·buk·tu**
Tim·buk·tu
timerity : **te·mer·i·ty**
tim·id
timmid : **tim·id**
timpature : **tem·per·a·ture**
timperament : **tem·per·a·ment**
timperature : **tem·per·a·ture**
timperment : **tem·per·a·ment**
timperture : **tem·per·a·ture**
tinant : **ten·ant**
tinc·ture
Tinnessee : **Ten·nes·see**
tin·sel
tinsell : **tin·sel**
tinsill : **tin·sel**
tinsle : **tin·sel**
tinture : **tinc·ture**

tinuous : **ten·u·ous**
tipest : **typ·ist**
tipewriter : **type·writ·er**
tiphoid : **ty·phoid**
tiphoon : **ty·phoon**
tipical : **typ·i·cal**
ti·rade
tiraid : **ti·rade**
tiranny : **tyr·an·ny**
tirban : **tur·ban** (headdress) *or* **tur·bine** (engine)
tirmite : **ter·mite**
tirnip : **tur·nip**
tirrade : **ti·rade**
ti·tan
ti·tan·ic
titannic : **ti·tan·ic**
titen : **ti·tan**
tittan : **ti·tan**
toaken : **to·ken**
toast
to·bac·co
tobacko : **to·bac·co**
tobaco : **to·bac·co**
tobbacco : **to·bac·co**
tobogan : **to·bog·gan**
to·bog·gan
toboggen : **to·bog·gan**
toboggin : **to·bog·gan**
tobogin : **to·bog·gan**
tocan : **tou·can**
tocksic : **tox·ic**
tofee : **tof·fee**
tof·fee
toffy : **tof·fee**
toi·let
toilit : **toi·let**
to·ken
tokin : **to·ken**
tol·er·a·ble
tol·er·ance
toleranse : **tol·er·ance**

tol·er·ate
tolerence : **tol·er·ance**
tolerent : **tol·er·ance**
tolerible : **tol·er·a·ble**
tolirable : **tol·er·a·ble**
tollarance : **tol·er·ance**
tollerable : **tol·er·a·ble**
tollerance : **tol·er·ance**
tollerate : **tol·er·ate**
tollerense : **tol·er·ance**
tollerent : **tol·er·ant**
tollerint : **tol·er·ant**
tom·a·hawk
tomain : **pto·maine**
tomane : **pto·maine**
to·ma·to
tomatoe : **to·ma·to**
to·ma·toes
tomatos : **to·ma·toes**
tomb·stone
tommahawk : **tom·a·hawk**
tommorow : **to·mor·row**
tommorrow : **to·mor·row**
tomohawk : **tom·a·hawk**
tomorow : **to·mor·row**
to·mor·row
tonage : **ton·nage**
tonge : **tongue**
tongue
ton·ic
tonick : **ton·ic**
to·night
tonite : **to·night**
ton·nage
tonnege : **ton·nage**
tonnic : **ton·ic**
tonnige : **ton·nage**
tonsal : **ton·sil**
tonsel : **ton·sil**
tonsell : **ton·sil**
ton·sil
top·ic

topick : **top·ic**
toppic : **top·ic**
Toranto : **To·ron·to**
torchure : **tor·ture**
torent : **tor·rent**
torid : **tor·rid**
tornaddo : **tor·na·do**
tor·na·do
tornaido : **tor·na·do**
tornato : **tor·na·do**
To·ron·to
torpeado : **tor·pe·do**
tor·pe·do
torpeto : **tor·pe·do**
torpido : **tor·pe·do**
torrant : **tor·rent**
torrea : **tor·ti·lla**
torred : **tor·rid**
tor·rent
tor·rid
Torronto : **To·ron·to**
tort (civil wrong); **torte** (pastry)
torte (pastry); **tort** (civil wrong)
tortia : **tor·ti·lla**
tortice : **tor·toise**
tortila : **tor·ti·lla**
tor·ti·lla
tortise : **tor·toise**
tortiss : **tor·toise**
tor·toise
tor·tu·ous
tor·ture
torturous : **tor·tu·ous**
tost : **toast**
toste : **toast**
to·tal
totam : **to·tem**
totel : **to·tal**
to·tem
totil : **to·tal**
totim : **to·tem**
tottal : **to·tal**

totum : **to·tem**
tou·can
tough
tounge : **tongue**
toupay : **tou·pee**
tou·pee
toupey : **tou·pee**
tour·ist
tournakette : **tour·ni·quet**
tour·na·ment
tournamint : **tour·na·ment**
tournaquet : **tour·ni·quet**
tournement : **tour·na·ment**
tournequet : **tour·ni·quet**
tour·ney
tourniment : **tour·na·ment**
tour·ni·quet
tousalled : **tou·sled**
touselled : **tou·sled**
tou·sled
towal : **tow·el**
to·ward
tow·el
towerd : **to·ward**
towl : **tow·el**
towselled : **tou·sled**
toxec : **tox·ic**
tox·ic
toxick : **tox·ic**
tra·chea
trachia : **tra·chea**
trackia : **tra·chea**
trackter : **trac·tor**
tracktor : **trac·tor**
tracter : **trac·tor**
trac·tor
trad·er (one who trades);
　　trai·tor (one who betrays)
traffec : **traf·fic**
traffecked : **traf·ficked**
traf·fic
trafficed : **traf·ficked**

traffick : **traf·fic**
traf·ficked
trafic : **traf·fic**
traficked : **traf·ficked**
tragectory : **tra·jec·to·ry**
trageddy : **trag·e·dy**
trag·e·dy
tragety : **trag·e·dy**
tragidy : **trag·e·dy**
traichea : **tra·chea**
traitor (one who betrays);
  trad·er (one who trades)
trajactary : **tra·jec·to·ry**
trajectery : **tra·jec·to·ry**
tra·jec·to·ry
trama : **trau·ma**
tramel : **tram·mel**
trammal : **tram·mel**
tram·mel
trancend : **tran·scend**
trancient : **tran·sient**
trancit : **tran·sit**
tranquel : **tran·quil**
tran·quil
tranquill : **tran·quil**
transam : **tran·som**
tran·scend
transcet : **tran·sit**
transcind : **tran·scend**
transem : **tran·som**
transferance : **trans·fer·ence**
trans·fer·ence
transferense : **trans·fer·ence**
transferrence : **trans·fer·ence**
transiant : **tran·sient**
tran·sient
tran·sit
tran·som
transsend : **tran·scend**
transum : **tran·som**
trapazoid : **trap·e·zoid**
trapeeze : **tra·peze**

trapese : **tra·peze**
tra·peze
trap·e·zoid
trappeze : **tra·peze**
trappezoid : **trap·e·zoid**
trau·ma
travasty : **trav·es·ty**
trav·el
travessty : **trav·es·ty**
trav·es·ty
travil : **trav·el**
travisty : **trav·es·ty**
travvel : **trav·el**
treacal : **trea·cle**
treachary : **treach·ery**
treacherry : **treach·ery**
treach·ery
trea·cle
tread
treakle : **trea·cle**
treashure : **trea·sure**
trea·son
trea·sure
treat
treatace : **trea·tise**
treatase : **trea·tise**
treatice : **trea·tise**
trea·tise
trebal : **tre·ble**
trebble : **tre·ble**
trebel : **tre·ble**
trebile : **tre·ble**
tre·ble
trechery : **treach·ery**
treck : **trek**
tred : **tread**
treecle : **trea·cle**
treeson : **trea·son**
treet : **treat**
treetise : **trea·tise**
trek
trekea : **tra·chea**

tremer : **trem•or**
trem•or
trenket : **trin•ket**
tres•pass
tresspass : **tres•pass**
tressure : **trea•sure**
tresure : **trea•sure**
trib•al
tribbutary : **trib•u•tary**
tribel : **trib•al**
tributarry : **trib•u•tary**
trib•u•tary
tributery : **trib•u•tary**
trilegy : **tril•o•gy**
triligy : **tril•o•gy**
trilligy : **tril•o•gy**
trillogy : **tril•o•gy**
tril•o•gy
trimor : **trem•or**
Trinadad : **Trin•i•dad**
Trin•i•dad
trin•ket
trinkit : **trin•ket**
Trinnidad : **Trin•i•dad**
tripal : **tri•ple**
tripel : **tri•ple**
tri•ple
trip•let
triplit : **trip•let**
tripple : **tri•ple**
tripplet : **trip•let**
triumf : **tri•umph**
tri•umph
trivea : **triv•ia**
triv•ia
trivvia : **triv•ia**
troley : **trol•ley**
trol•ley
trolly : **trol•ley**
troma : **trau•ma**
troop (organized group);
    troupe (group of actors)

tropec : **trop•ic**
trop•ic
trop•i•cal
tropicle : **trop•i•cal**
troppic : **trop•ic**
troppical : **trop•i•cal**
troubador : **trou•ba•dour**
trou•ba•dour
troubidor : **trou•ba•dour**
trou•ble
troul : **trow•el**
troupe (group of actors);
    troop (organized group)
trou•sers
trouzers : **trou•sers**
trow•el
trowl : **trow•el**
trowsers : **trou•sers**
tru•ant
trubadour : **trou•ba•dour**
trubble : **trou•ble**
truely : **tru•ly**
truent : **tru•ant**
trully : **tru•ly**
tru•ly
trum•pet
trumpit : **trum•pet**
trust•ee (*noun*); **trusty** (*adj.*)
trusty (*adj.*); **trust•ee** (*noun*)
tsar *or* **czar**
tucan : **tou•can**
Tues•day
tuff : **tough**
tulep : **tu•lip**
tu•lip
tullip : **tu•lip**
tumbstone : **tomb•stone**
tumer : **tu•mor**
tumestone : **tomb•stone**
tummor : **tu•mor**
tummult : **tu•mult**
tu•mor

tu·mult
tunec : **tu·nic**
tungue : **tongue**
tu·nic
tunnal : **tun·nel**
tun·nel
tunnic : **tu·nic**
tunnle : **tun·nel**
tupee : **tou·pee**
tur·ban (headdress); **tur·bine**
  (engine)
turbelant : **tur·bu·lent**
turben : **tur·ban** (headdress) *or*
  tur·bine (engine)
turbin : **tur·ban** (headdress) *or*
  tur·bine (engine)
tur·bine (engine); **tur·ban**
  (headdress)
tur·bu·lent
turet : **tur·ret**
turist : **tour·ist**
tur·key
turkoise : **tur·quoise**
turky : **tur·key**
turmite : **ter·mite**
turnament : **tour·na·ment**
turnep : **tur·nip**
turney : **tour·ney**
tur·nip
turniquet : **tour·ni·quet**
tur·pen·tine
turpintine : **tur·pen·tine**
turquoice : **tur·quoise**
turquois : **tur·quoise**

tur·quoise
tur·ret
turrit : **tur·ret**
Tusday : **Tues·day**
tuter : **tu·tor**
tu·tor
tux·e·do
tuxeto : **tux·e·do**
tuxido : **tux·e·do**
tweazers : **twee·zers**
tweesers : **twee·zers**
twee·zers
twelfth
twelth : **twelfth**
twelvth : **twelfth**
twen·ti·eth
twentyith : **twen·ti·eth**
tyfoid : **ty·phoid**
tyfoon : **ty·phoon**
typeriter : **type·writ·er**
type·writ·er
ty·phoid
ty·phoon
typhune : **ty·phoon**
typ·i·cal
typicle : **typ·i·cal**
typ·ist
typpical : **typ·i·cal**
typpist : **typ·ist**
tyr·an·ny
ty·rant
tyrenny : **tyr·an·ny**
tyrent : **ty·rant**
tzar : **czar**

U

ubiguitous : **ubiq·ui·tous**
ubiquitiss : **ubiq·ui·tous**
ubiq·ui·tous
ubiquitus : **ubiq·ui·tous**
Ucharist : **Eu·cha·rist**
ufemism : **eu·phe·mism**
Ugan·da
Ugganda : **Ugan·da**
ug·li·ness
uglyness : **ug·li·ness**
Ugonda : **Ugan·da**
ukalele : **uku·le·le**
ukelale : **uku·le·le**
ukelayle : **uku·le·le**
ukelele : **uku·le·le**
ukeley : **uku·le·le**
ukilele : **uku·le·le**
Ukrain : **Ukraine**
Ukraine
Ukrane : **Ukraine**
uku·le·le
ul·cer
ulogy : **eu·lo·gy**
ulser : **ul·cer**
ultearior : **ul·te·ri·or**
ulteerior : **ul·te·ri·or**
ultereor : **ul·te·ri·or**
ulterier : **ul·te·ri·or**
ul·te·ri·or
ul·ti·mate
ultimet : **ul·ti·mate**
ultimite : **ul·ti·mate**
ultirior : **ul·te·ri·or**
ultravilet : **ul·tra·vi·o·let**
ultravilot : **ul·tra·vi·o·let**
ul·tra·vi·o·let
ultraviolit : **ul·tra·vi·o·let**
ultreviolet : **ul·tra·vi·o·let**
umbrela : **um·brel·la**
um·brel·la

umpior : **um·pire**
um·pire
unabal : **un·able**
unabel : **un·able**
un·able
unacorn : **uni·corn**
unafy : **uni·fy**
unalatiral : **uni·lat·er·al**
unanamous : **unan·i·mous**
unanemous : **unan·i·mous**
unan·i·mous
unanimus : **unan·i·mous**
unannimous : **unan·i·mous**
unarring : **un·er·ring**
unason : **uni·son**
unatural : **un·nat·u·ral**
unaverse : **uni·verse**
unaversity : **uni·ver·si·ty**
unbeleavable : **un·be·liev·able**
unbeleevable : **un·be·liev·able**
unbeleivable : **un·be·liev·able**
unbelievabel : **un·be·liev·able**
un·be·liev·able
unbelieveble : **un·be·liev·able**
uncal : **un·cle**
un·can·ny
uncany : **un·can·ny**
un·cle
uncooth : **un·couth**
un·couth
uncuth : **un·couth**
undalate : **un·du·late**
undelate : **un·du·late**
un·de·ni·able
undenyable : **un·de·ni·able**
un·der·neath
underneeth : **un·der·neath**
underneith : **un·der·neath**
undertoe : **un·der·tow**
un·der·tow

underware : **un•der•wear**
un•der•wear
undulait : **un•du•late**
un•du•late
undully : **un•du•ly**
un•du•ly
unecorn : **uni•corn**
uneeke : **unique**
uneeque : **unique**
unefy : **uni•fy**
uneqivocal : **un•equiv•o•cal**
unequivacal : **un•equiv•o•cal**
unequivecal : **un•equiv•o•cal**
un•equiv•o•cal
unering : **un•err•ing**
un•err•ing
uneson : **uni•son**
unet : **unit**
unety : **uni•ty**
uneversal : **uni•ver•sal**
unfaigned : **un•feigned**
unfained : **un•feigned**
un•feigned
unfeined : **un•feigned**
unferl : **un•furl**
un•furl
unholesome : **un•whole•some**
uni•corn
uniffy : **uni•fy**
uni•fy
unike : **unique**
uni•lat•er•al
unilaterel : **uni•lat•er•al**
unilatiral : **uni•lat•er•al**
unilatteral : **uni•lat•er•al**
unint : **unite**
unique
unisen : **uni•son**
uni•son
unit (*noun*); unite (*verb*)
unite (*verb*); **unit** (*noun*)
uni•ty

univercity : **uni•ver•si•ty**
uni•ver•sal
universel : **uni•ver•sal**
universety : **uni•ver•si•ty**
universitty : **uni•ver•si•ty**
uni•ver•si•ty
univursal : **uni•ver•sal**
univurse : **uni•verse**
univursity : **uni•ver•si•ty**
unkanny : **un•can•ny**
un•kempt
unkimpt : **un•kempt**
unkle : **un•cle**
unkouth : **un•couth**
unkuth : **un•couth**
un•law•ful
unlawfull : **un•law•ful**
un•leav•ened
unlevened : **un•leav•ened**
un•mer•ci•ful
unmercifull : **un•mer•ci•ful**
unmersiful : **un•mer•ci•ful**
unmurciful : **un•mer•ci•ful**
unnateral : **un•nat•u•ral**
un•nat•u•ral
unnaturel : **un•nat•u•ral**
unnicorn : **uni•corn**
unnify : **uni•fy**
unnit : **unit**
unnite : **unite**
unnity : **uni•ty**
unniversal : **uni•ver•sal**
unniverse : **uni•verse**
unniversity : **uni•ver•si•ty**
un•pal•at•able
unpaletable : **un•pal•at•able**
unpalitable : **un•pal•at•able**
unpallatable : **un•pal•at•able**
un•prec•e•dent•ed
unprecidented :
  un•prec•e•dent•ed

unpresedented :
  un•prec•e•dent•ed
unpressidented :
  un•prec•e•dent•ed
unraval : **un•rav•el**
un•rav•el
unravil : **un•rav•el**
unravvel : **un•rav•el**
un•ready
unreddy : **un•ready**
un•re•li•able
unrelible : **un•re•li•able**
unrelieble : **un•re•li•able**
unrelyable : **un•re•li•able**
un•ri•valed or **un•ri•valled**
un•ri•valled or **un•ri•valed**
unriveled : **un•ri•valed**
unrivelled : **un•ri•valed**
unrivilled : **un•ri•valed**
unruley : **un•ruly**
unrully : **un•ruly**
un•ruly
unsanatary : **un•san•i•tary**
unsanetary : **un•san•i•tary**
unsanitarry : **un•san•i•tary**
un•san•i•tary
unsaniterry : **un•san•i•tary**
unsanitery : **un•san•i•tary**
unsavarry : **un•sa•vory**
unsaverry : **un•sa•vory**
unsavery : **un•sa•vory**
unsavorry : **un•sa•vory**
un•sa•vory
unscaithed : **un•scathed**
un•scathed
unseamly : **un•seem•ly**
unseemely : **un•seem•ly**
unseemily : **un•seem•ly**
un•seem•ly
unsheath : **un•sheathe**
un•sheathe
unsheeth : **un•sheathe**

unsheethe : **un•sheathe**
unsheith : **un•sheathe**
unsheithe : **un•sheathe**
unsoceable : **un•so•cia•ble**
unsochable : **un•so•cia•ble**
un•so•cia•ble
unspeakabel : **un•speak•able**
un•speak•able
unspeakible : **un•speak•able**
unspeekable : **un•speak•able**
un•steady
unsteddy : **un•steady**
un•til
untill : **un•til**
un•time•ly
untimly : **un•time•ly**
untootered : **un•tu•tored**
untudored : **un•tu•tored**
untutered : **un•tu•tored**
un•tu•tored
unuch : **eu•nuch**
unussual : **un•usu•al**
un•usu•al
unusuel : **un•usu•al**
unuzual : **un•usu•al**
unvail : **un•veil**
unvale : **un•veil**
un•veil
unviel : **un•veil**
unwealdy : **un•wieldy**
unweeldy : **un•wieldy**
unweildy : **un•wieldy**
un•whole•some
unwholesum : **un•whole•some**
unwhollsome : **un•whole•some**
unwholsome : **un•whole•some**
un•wieldy
upbrade : **up•braid**
up•braid
up•heav•al
upheavel : **up•heav•al**
upheeval : **up•heav•al**

upheevel : **up‧heav‧al**
upheival : **up‧heav‧al**
uphemism : **eu‧phem‧ism**
uphevel : **up‧heav‧al**
upholstary : **up‧hol‧stery**
upholsterry : **up‧hol‧stery**
up‧hol‧stery
upholstry : **up‧hol‧stery**
uphoria : **eu‧pho‧ria**
uppraid : **up‧braid**
uproareous : **up‧roar‧i‧ous**
up‧roar‧i‧ous
uprorious : **up‧roar‧i‧ous**
up‧stream
upstreem : **up‧stream**
Uraguay : **Uru‧guay**
urainium : **ura‧ni‧um**
Urainus : **Ura‧nus**
uraneum : **ura‧ni‧um**
uraniem : **ura‧ni‧um**
Uranis : **Ura‧nus**
ura‧ni‧um
Ura‧nus
urbain : **ur‧ban**
ur‧ban (of a city); **ur‧bane** (witty)
ur‧bane (witty); **ur‧ban** (of a city)
urbanitty : **ur‧ban‧i‧ty**
ur‧ban‧i‧ty
urbannety : **ur‧ban‧i‧ty**
urbannity : **ur‧ban‧i‧ty**
urben : **ur‧ban**
urchen : **ur‧chin**
ur‧chin
Ureguay : **Uru‧guay**
urene : **urine**
ur‧gen‧cy
urgensy : **ur‧gen‧cy**
urgincy : **ur‧gen‧cy**
urginsy : **ur‧gen‧cy**
urine

urinn : **urine**
urn (vase); **earn** (work for gain)
Uroguay : **Uru‧guay**
Urope : **Eu‧rope**
urranium : **ura‧ni‧um**
Urranus : **Ura‧nus**
Uru‧guay
Urugway : **Uru‧guay**
usabal : **us‧able**
usabel : **us‧able**
us‧able *or* **us‧eble**
usadge : **us‧age**
us‧age
usally : **usu‧al‧ly**
useable : **us‧able**
us‧eble *or* **us‧able**
use‧ful
usefull : **use‧ful**
usege : **us‧age**
useing : **us‧ing**
userp : **usurp**
usery : **usu‧ry**
usful : **use‧ful**
usible : **us‧able**
usidge : **us‧age**
usige : **us‧age**
us‧ing
usirp : **usurp**
usserp : **usurp**
ussurp : **usurp**
ussury : **usu‧ry**
usuage : **us‧age**
usu‧al‧ly
usully : **usu‧al‧ly**
usuly : **usu‧al‧ly**
usurp
usury
Uta : **Utah**
Utah
utalize : **uti‧lize**
utelize : **uti‧lize**
utencil : **uten‧sil**

utensel : **uten·sil**
uten·sil
uterice : **uter·us**
uteris : **uter·us**
uteriss : **uter·us**
uter·us
uthanasia : **eu·tha·na·sia**
utilatarian : **util·i·tar·i·an**
utiletarian : **util·i·tar·i·an**
utilety : **util·i·ty**
utilise (*Brit.*) : **uti·lize**
util·i·tar·i·an
utiliterian : **util·i·tar·i·an**
utilitty : **util·i·ty**
util·i·ty
uti·lize
utillety : **util·i·ty**
utillitarian : **util·i·tar·i·an**

utillity : **util·i·ty**
utillize : **uti·lize**
utilyze : **uti·lize**
utincil : **uten·sil**
utinsel : **uten·sil**
utinsil : **uten·sil**
utirus : **uter·us**
utopea : **uto·pia**
uto·pia
utoppia : **uto·pia**
Utta : **Utah**
ut·ter·ance
utteranse : **ut·ter·ance**
utterence : **ut·ter·ance**
utterense : **ut·ter·ance**
uttopia : **uto·pia**
utturance : **ut·ter·ance**
uturus : **uter·us**

V

vacacion : **va•ca•tion**
va•can•cy
vacansy : **va•can•cy**
vacasion : **va•ca•tion**
va•ca•tion
vaccancy : **va•can•cy**
vaccant : **va•cant**
vaccate : **va•cate**
vaccation : **va•ca•tion**
vaccene : **vac•cine**
vac•cine
vaccume : **vac•u•um**
vaccuous : **vac•u•ous**
vaccuum : **vac•u•um**
vacellate : **vac•il•late**
vacency : **va•can•cy**
vacilate : **vac•il•late**
vacillait : **vac•il•late**
vac•il•late
vacine : **vac•cine**
vacissitude : **vi•cis•si•tude**
vacseen : **vac•cine**
vacsene : **vac•cine**
vacsillate : **vac•il•late**
vacsine : **vac•cine**
vacuim : **vac•u•um**
vacuiss : **vac•u•ous**
vacume : **vac•u•um**
vac•u•ous
vac•u•um
vacuus : **vac•u•ous**
vadeville : **vaude•ville**
vag•a•bond
vagarry : **va•ga•ry**
va•ga•ry
vagebond : **vag•a•bond**
vagery : **va•ga•ry**
vaggabond : **vag•a•bond**
vaggery : **va•ga•ry**
va•grant

vagrent : **va•grant**
vagrint : **va•grant**
vagury : **va•ga•ry**
vaiporize : **va•por•ize**
vakcume : **vac•u•um**
valadictorian : **val•e•dic•to•ri•an**
va•lance (drapery); **va•lence** (in atoms)
valantine : **val•en•tine**
valece : **va•lise**
valed : **val•id**
valedictorean :
   val•e•dic•to•ri•an
val•e•dic•to•ri•an
valeece : **va•lise**
va•lence (in atoms); **va•lance** (drapery)
val•en•tine
valese : **va•lise**
valey : **val•ley**
val•iant
valice : **va•lise**
val•id
validdity : **va•lid•i•ty**
validety : **va•lid•i•ty**
validitty : **va•lid•i•ty**
va•lid•i•ty
valient : **val•iant**
va•lise
valladictorian :
   val•e•dic•to•ri•an
vallant : **val•iant**
vallantine : **val•en•tine**
valled : **val•id**
valledictorian :
   val•e•dic•to•ri•an
vallentine : **val•en•tine**
valler : **val•or**
val•ley
vallid : **val•id**

vallidity : **va•lid•i•ty**
vallient : **val•iant**
vallise : **va•lise**
vallor : **val•or**
valluable : **valu•able**
vally : **val•ley**
val•or
valour (*Brit.*) : **val•or**
valting : **vault•ing**
valuabel : **valu•able**
valu•able
valubel : **valu•able**
valuble : **valu•able**
valueble : **valu•able**
valuible : **valu•able**
valure : **val•or**
vampiar : **vam•pire**
vam•pire
vampyre : **vam•pire**
Vancoover : **Van•cou•ver**
Van•cou•ver
Vancuover : **Van•cou•ver**
Vancuver : **Van•cou•ver**
van•dal
vandel : **van•dal**
vandle : **van•dal**
vanella : **va•nil•la**
vanety : **van•i•ty**
vangard : **van•guard**
vangarde : **van•guard**
vangaurd : **van•guard**
van•guard
vanguish : **van•quish**
vanila : **va•nil•la**
va•nil•la
van•ish
vanitty : **van•i•ty**
van•i•ty
vannilla : **va•nil•la**
vannish : **van•ish**
vannity : **van•i•ty**
vanqish : **van•quish**

vanquesh : **van•quish**
van•quish
vantadge : **van•tage**
van•tage
vantege : **van•tage**
vantige : **van•tage**
vaperize : **va•por•ize**
va•pid
vaporise (*Brit.*) : **va•por•ize**
va•por•ize
vappid : **va•pid**
vapporize : **va•por•ize**
vaquous : **vac•u•ous**
varafy : **ver•i•fy**
varanda : **ve•ran•da**
varatious : **ve•ra•cious**
varcety : **var•si•ty**
varcitty : **var•si•ty**
varcity : **var•si•ty**
vareable : **vari•able**
vareance : **vari•ance**
vareation : **vari•a•tion**
varecose : **var•i•cose**
vareous : **var•i•ous**
variabal : **vari•able**
variabel : **vari•able**
vari•able
vari•ance
varianse : **vari•ance**
variasion : **vari•a•tion**
variatian : **vari•a•tion**
vari•a•tion
variatty : **va•ri•ety**
variaty : **va•ri•ety**
varible : **vari•able**
var•i•cose
varience : **vari•ance**
variense : **vari•ance**
varietty : **va•ri•ety**
va•ri•ety
varify : **ver•i•fy**
varily : **ver•i•ly**

var•i•ous
varnesh : **var•nish**
var•nish
varrecose : **var•i•cose**
varriable : **vari•able**
varriance : **vari•ance**
varriation : **vari•a•tion**
varricose : **var•i•cose**
varriety : **va•ri•ety**
varrious : **var•i•ous**
varsetty : **var•si•ty**
varsety : **var•si•ty**
varsitty : **var•si•ty**
var•si•ty
varyable : **vari•able**
varyation : **vari•a•tion**
varyis : **var•i•ous**
varyous : **var•i•ous**
vasal : **vas•sal**
vasel : **vas•sal**
vasillate : **vac•il•late**
vas•sal
vassel : **vas•sal**
Vatecan : **Vat•i•can**
Vat•i•can
Vatikan : **Vat•i•can**
Vattican : **Vat•i•can**
vaudaville : **vaude•ville**
vaudevile : **vaude•ville**
vaude•ville
vaudville : **vaude•ville**
vault•ing
vecinity : **vi•cin•i•ty**
veehicle : **ve•hi•cle**
Veetnam : **Viet•nam**
vegatable : **veg•e•ta•ble**
vegetabal : **veg•e•ta•ble**
veg•e•ta•ble
vegeteble : **veg•e•ta•ble**
vegetible : **veg•e•ta•ble**
veggetable : **veg•e•ta•ble**
vegitable : **veg•e•ta•ble**

vegtable : **veg•e•ta•ble**
vehamence : **ve•he•mence**
vehemance : **ve•he•mence**
vehemanse : **ve•he•mence**
ve•he•mence
vehemense : **ve•he•mence**
vehical : **ve•hi•cle**
vehicel : **ve•hi•cle**
vehickal : **ve•hi•cle**
vehickel : **ve•hi•cle**
ve•hi•cle
vehimence : **ve•he•mence**
Veinna : **Vi•en•na**
veinous : **ve•nous**
Veitnam : **Viet•nam**
veiw : **view**
vejetable : **veg•e•ta•ble**
veksatious : **vex•a•tious**
vellocity : **ve•loc•i•ty**
vellosity : **ve•loc•i•ty**
vellvet : **vel•vet**
velocety : **ve•loc•i•ty**
velocitty : **ve•loc•i•ty**
ve•loc•i•ty
velosity : **ve•loc•i•ty**
velvat : **vel•vet**
vel•vet
velvette : **vel•vet**
velvit : **vel•vet**
vemence : **ve•he•mence**
Venace : **Ven•ice**
venareal : **ve•ne•re•al**
venarial : **ve•ne•re•al**
venason : **ven•i•son**
Venazuela : **Ven•e•zu•e•la**
vendebta : **ven•det•ta**
vend•er *or* **vend•or**
vendeta : **ven•det•ta**
ven•det•ta
vendette : **ven•det•ta**
ven•dor *or* **vend•er**
venear : **ve•neer**

Venece : **Ven•ice**
ve•neer
veneir : **ve•neer**
ven•er•a•ble
ve•ne•re•al
venerial : **ve•ne•re•al**
venerible : **ven•er•a•ble**
veneson : **ven•i•son**
Venesuela : **Ven•e•zu•e•la**
Venezeula : **Ven•e•zu•e•la**
Venezuala : **Ven•e•zu•e•la**
Ven•e•zu•e•la
vengance : **ven•geance**
ven•geance
vengeanse : **ven•geance**
venge•ful
vengefull : **venge•ful**
vengence : **ven•geance**
vengense : **ven•geance**
vengful : **venge•ful**
vengiance : **ven•geance**
vengince : **ven•geance**
Ven•ice (city); **Ve•nus** (planet)
venicen : **ven•i•son**
venier : **ve•neer**
venigar : **vin•e•gar**
venim : **ven•om**
venimous : **ven•om•ous**
venirable : **ven•er•a•ble**
Venis : **Ven•ice** (city) *or* **Ve•nus**
(planet)
Venise : **Ven•ice**
ven•i•son
Veniss : **Ven•ice** (city) *or*
Ve•nus (planet)
Venizuela : **Ven•e•zu•e•la**
vennareal : **ve•ne•re•al**
Vennazuela : **Ven•e•zu•e•la**
venndetta : **ven•det•ta**
vennerable : **ven•er•a•ble**
vennereal : **ve•ne•re•al**
Vennezuela : **Ven•e•zu•e•la**

Vennice : **Ven•ice**
Vennis : **Ven•ice** (city) *or*
Ve•nus (planet)
vennison : **ven•i•son**
vennom : **ven•om**
vennomous : **ven•om•ous**
vennum : **ven•om**
vennumous : **ven•om•ous**
Vennus : **Ven•ice** (city) *or*
Ve•nus (planet)
ven•om
venomiss : **ven•om•ous**
ven•om•ous
venomus : **ven•om•ous**
venoo : **ven•ue**
ve•nous (having veins); **Ve•nus**
(planet)
ventalate : **ven•ti•late**
ventelate : **ven•ti•late**
ven•ti•late
ventrilloquist : **ven•tril•o•quist**
ventriloquest : **ven•tril•o•quist**
ven•tril•o•quist
venue
venum : **ven•om**
venumous : **ven•om•ous**
Ve•nus (planet); **Ven•ice** (city);
ve•nous (having veins)
veracety : **ve•rac•i•ty**
ve•ra•cious (truthful);
vo•ra•cious (hungry)
veracitty : **ve•rac•i•ty**
ve•rac•i•ty
veracose : **var•i•cose**
verafiable : **ver•i•fi•able**
veraly : **ver•i•ly**
ve•ran•da *or* **ve•ran•dah**
ve•ran•dah *or* **ve•ran•da**
veranduh : **ve•ran•da**
verashious : **ve•ra•cious**
verasious : **ve•ra•cious**
verasitty : **ve•rac•i•ty**

verasity : **ve·rac·i·ty**
veratious : **ve·ra·cious**
verbage : **ver·biage**
verbaitim : **ver·ba·tim**
verbatem : **ver·ba·tim**
ver·ba·tim
verbatum : **ver·ba·tim**
verbeage : **ver·biage**
verbege : **ver·biage**
ver·biage
verbige : **ver·biage**
verboce : **ver·bose**
verbocity : **ver·bos·i·ty**
ver·bose
verbosety : **ver·bos·i·ty**
verbositty : **ver·bos·i·ty**
ver·bos·i·ty
verbossity : **ver·bos·i·ty**
verces : **ver·sus**
vercify : **ver·si·fy**
vercis : **ver·sus**
ver·dant
verdect : **ver·dict**
verdent : **ver·dant**
verdick : **ver·dict**
ver·dict
verdint : **ver·dant**
verefiable : **ver·i·fi·able**
verefy : **ver·i·fy**
verely : **ver·i·ly**
vergen : **vir·gin**
vergin : **vir·gin**
Verginia : **Vir·gin·ia**
vericose : **var·i·cose**
ver·i·fi·able
ver·i·fy
verifyable : **ver·i·fi·able**
verile : **vir·ile**
verillity : **vi·ril·i·ty**
ver·i·ly
verious : **var·i·ous**
verman : **ver·min**

vermen : **ver·min**
vermilian : **ver·mil·ion**
ver·mil·ion
vermillion : **ver·mil·ion**
ver·min
Ver·mont
vermooth : **ver·mouth**
Vermount : **Ver·mont**
ver·mouth
vermuth : **ver·mouth**
vernackular : **ver·nac·u·lar**
ver·nac·u·lar
vernaculer : **ver·nac·u·lar**
vernakular : **ver·nac·u·lar**
ver·nal
vernel : **ver·nal**
verracious : **ve·ra·cious**
verracity : **ve·rac·i·ty**
verraly : **ver·i·ly**
verranda : **ve·ran·da**
verrifiable : **ver·i·fi·able**
verrify : **ver·i·fy**
verrily : **ver·i·ly**
versafy : **ver·si·fy**
Ver·sailles
Versalles : **Ver·sailles**
ver·sa·tile
versatle : **ver·sa·tile**
versefy : **ver·si·fy**
versetile : **ver·sa·tile**
ver·si·fy
Versigh : **Ver·sailles**
Versilles : **Ver·sailles**
versis : **ver·sus**
versitile : **ver·sa·tile**
versitle : **ver·sa·tile**
versittle : **ver·sa·tile**
ver·sus
Versye : **Ver·sailles**
vertabra : **ver·te·bra** (*sing.*)
vertabrae : **ver·te·brae** (*plur.*)
vertacle : **ver·ti·cal**

vertago : **ver•ti•go**

ver•te•bra (*sing.*); **ver•te•brae**
  (*plur.*)

ver•te•brae (*plur.*); **ver•te•bra**
  (*sing.*)

vertebray : **ver•te•brae** (*plur.*)

vertecle : **ver•ti•cal**

vertego : **ver•ti•go**

vertibra : **ver•te•bra** (*sing.*)

vertibrae : **ver•te•brae** (*plur.*)

ver•ti•cal

verticel : **ver•ti•cal**

verticle : **ver•ti•cal**

vertiggo : **ver•ti•go**

ver•ti•go

vertikal : **ver•ti•cal**

vertue : **vir•tue**

vesel : **ves•sel**

vessal : **ves•sel**

ves•sel

vessle : **ves•sel**

vestabule : **ves•ti•bule**

vestage : **ves•tige**

vestebule : **ves•ti•bule**

vestege : **ves•tige**

vestiboole : **ves•ti•bule**

ves•ti•bule

vestidge : **ves•tige**

ves•tige

vestigeal : **ves•ti•gial**

ves•ti•gial

vetaran : **vet•er•an**

vetarinarian : **vet•er•i•nar•i•an**

vet•er•an

veteren : **vet•er•an**

veterenarian : **vet•er•i•nar•i•an**

veterin : **vet•er•an**

veterinarean : **vet•er•i•nar•i•an**

vet•er•i•nar•i•an

veterinerian : **vet•er•i•nar•i•an**

veternarian : **vet•er•i•nar•i•an**

veterran : **vet•er•an**

veterrinarian : **vet•er•i•nar•i•an**

vetiran : **vet•er•an**

ve•to

vetoe : **ve•to**

ve•toes

vetos : **ve•toes**

vettaran : **vet•er•an**

vetteran : **vet•er•an**

vetterinarian : **vet•er•i•nar•i•an**

vexacious : **vex•a•tious**

vexasious : **vex•a•tious**

vex•a•tious

vexatius : **vex•a•tious**

viabal : **vi•a•ble**

viabel : **vi•a•ble**

viabilety : **vi•a•bil•i•ty**

viabilitty : **vi•a•bil•i•ty**

vi•a•bil•i•ty

viabillity : **vi•a•bil•i•ty**

vi•a•ble

viablety : **vi•a•bil•i•ty**

viaduck : **via•duct**

via•duct

vi•al (container); **vile** (filthy)

vibility : **vi•a•bil•i•ty**

vible : **vi•a•ble**

vi•brant

vibrater : **vi•bra•tor**

vi•bra•tor

vibrent : **vi•brant**

vic•ar

vicareous : **vi•car•i•ous**

vi•car•i•ous

vicarrious : **vi•car•i•ous**

vicenity : **vi•cin•i•ty**

vicerious : **vi•car•i•ous**

vicinetty : **vi•cin•i•ty**

vicinety : **vi•cin•i•ty**

vicinitty : **vi•cin•i•ty**

vi•cin•i•ty

vicinnity : **vi•cin•i•ty**

vi•cious (immoral); vis•cous
(thick liquid)
vicisitude : vi•cis•si•tude
vicissatude : vi•cis•si•tude
vi•cis•si•tude
vicker : vic•ar
victary : vic•to•ry
victem : vic•tim
victer : vic•tor
victery : vic•to•ry
vic•tim
vic•tor
victorry : vic•to•ry
vic•to•ry
victum : vic•tim
viddeo : vid•eo
viddio : vid•eo
vid•eo
vidio : vid•eo
viduct : via•duct
viel : vi•al (container) or vile
(filthy)
Viena : Vi•en•na
Vienese : Vi•en•nese
Vi•en•na
Viennease : Vi•en•nese
Vi•en•nese
Vienneze : Vi•en•nese
Viet•nam
Vietnom : Viet•nam
view
vigalant : vig•i•lant
vigel : vig•il
vigelant : vig•i•lant
viger : vig•or
vigger : vig•or
vig•il
vig•i•lant
vigilent : vig•i•lant
vigill : vig•il
vignet : vi•gnette
vi•gnette

vig•or
vijil : vig•il
viker : vic•ar
vilafication : vil•i•fi•ca•tion
vilafy : vil•i•fy
vilage : vil•lage
vilain : vil•lain
vilan : vil•lain
vilate : vi•o•late
vile (filthy); vi•al (container)
vilefy : vil•i•fy
vile•ly
vilent : vi•o•lent
vilet : vi•o•let
vilifacation : vil•i•fi•ca•tion
vil•i•fi•ca•tion
vil•i•fy
vilin : vi•o•lin
villadge : vil•lage
vil•lage
vil•lain (evil one); vil•lein
(peasant)
villan : vil•lain (evil one) or
vil•lein (peasant)
villege : vil•lage
vil•lein (peasant); vil•lain (evil
one)
villen : vil•lain (evil one) or
vil•lein (peasant)
villidge : vil•lage
villification : vil•i•fi•ca•tion
villify : vil•i•fy
villige : vil•lage
villin : vil•lain (evil one) or
vil•lein (peasant)
vily : vile•ly
vinagar : vin•e•gar
vinager : vin•e•gar
vindacate : vin•di•cate
vindecate : vin•di•cate
vineer : ve•neer
vin•e•gar

vineger : **vin•e•gar**
vineir : **ve•neer**
vinel : **vi•nyl**
vinell : **vi•nyl**
vinette : **vi•gnette**
vine•yard
viniette : **vi•gnette**
vinigar : **vin•e•gar**
vinil : **vi•nyl**
vinill : **vi•nyl**
vin•tage
vintedge : **vin•tage**
vintege : **vin•tage**
vintelate : **ven•ti•late**
vintidge : **vin•tage**
vintige : **vin•tage**
vintilate : **ven•ti•late**
Vinus : **Ven•ice** (city) *or*
  Ve•nus (planet)
vinyard : **vine•yard**
vinyette : **vi•gnette**
vi•nyl
violant : **vi•o•lent**
vi•o•late
violen : **vi•o•lin**
vi•o•lent
vi•o•let
vi•o•lin
violint : **vi•o•lent**
virgen : **vir•gin**
Virgenia : **Vir•gin•ia**
vir•gin
Vir•gin•ia
Virginnia : **Vir•gin•ia**
vir•ile
virilitty : **vi•ril•i•ty**
vi•ril•i•ty
virill : **vir•ile**
virillity : **vi•ril•i•ty**
viris : **vi•rus**
virmooth : **ver•mouth**
virmouth : **ver•mouth**

virmuth : **ver•mouth**
virrus : **vi•rus**
vir•tue
vi•rus
visability : **vis•i•bil•i•ty**
visable : **vis•i•ble**
vis•age
viscious : **vi•cious** (immoral) *or*
  vis•cous (thick liquid)
viscositty : **vis•cos•i•ty**
vis•cos•i•ty
viscossity : **vis•cos•i•ty**
vis•cous (thick liquid); **vi•cious**
  (immoral)
viseble : **vis•i•ble**
visege : **vis•age**
viser : **vi•sor**
visibal : **vis•i•ble**
visibel : **vis•i•ble**
visibilety : **vis•i•bil•i•ty**
visibilitty : **vis•i•bil•i•ty**
vis•i•bil•i•ty
visibillity : **vis•i•bil•i•ty**
vis•i•ble
visige : **vis•age**
visinity : **vi•cin•i•ty**
visious : **vi•cious**
visissitude : **vi•cis•si•tude**
visiter : **vis•i•tor**
vis•i•tor
vi•sor
vissage : **vis•age**
vissitor : **vis•i•tor**
vis•u•al
visualise : **vis•u•al•ize**
vis•u•al•ize
visuel : **vis•u•al**
visule : **vis•u•al**
visulize : **vis•u•al•ize**
vi•tal
vitalitty : **vi•tal•i•ty**
vi•tal•i•ty

vitallity : **vi•tal•i•ty**
vitamen : **vi•ta•min**
vi•ta•min
vitel : **vi•tal**
vitemin : **vi•ta•min**
vit•re•ous
vitrious : **vit•re•ous**
vivacety : **vi•vac•i•ty**
vi•va•cious
vivacitty : **vi•vac•i•ty**
vi•vac•i•ty
vivasity : **vi•vac•i•ty**
vivassity : **vi•vac•i•ty**
vivatious : **vi•va•cious**
vix•en
vixin : **vix•en**
vizage : **vis•age**
vizer : **vi•sor**
vizitor : **vis•i•tor**
vocabularry : **vo•cab•u•lary**
vo•cab•u•lary
vocabulerry : **vo•cab•u•lary**
vocabulery : **vo•cab•u•lary**
vocal chords : **vo•cal cords**
vo•cal cords
vodca : **vod•ka**
voddville : **vaude•ville**
vod•ka
voiage : **voy•age**
vol•a•tile
volatle : **vol•a•tile**
volcanno : **vol•ca•no**
vol•ca•no
volentary : **vol•un•tary**
volenteer : **vol•un•teer**
voletile : **vol•a•tile**
voletle : **vol•a•tile**
volkano : **vol•ca•no**
vollatile : **vol•a•tile**

vol•ley•ball
vollume : **vol•ume**
vollyball : **vol•ley•ball**
volt•age
voltege : **volt•age**
voltige : **volt•age**
vol•ume
voluntarry : **vol•un•tary**
vol•un•tary
vol•un•teer
volunteir : **vol•un•teer**
voluntery : **vol•un•tary**
voluntier : **vol•un•teer**
vom•it
vommit : **vom•it**
vo•ra•cious (hungry);
  ve•ra•cious (truthful)
votarry : **vo•ta•ry**
vo•ta•ry
votery : **vo•ta•ry**
voudeville : **vaude•ville**
vow•el
vowl : **vow•el**
voy•age
voyege : **voy•age**
voyige : **voy•age**
vulcano : **vol•ca•no**
vul•gar
vulger : **vul•gar**
vulnerabal : **vul•ner•a•ble**
vul•ner•a•ble
vulnerble : **vul•ner•a•ble**
vulnerible : **vul•ner•a•ble**
vurbatim : **ver•ba•tim**
vurbose : **ver•bose**
vurbosity : **ver•bos•i•ty**
vurnacular : **ver•nac•u•lar**
vynel : **vi•nyl**
vynil : **vi•nyl**

W

wachful : **watch·ful**

wad (small mass); **wade** (to walk in water)

waddel : **wad·dle** (to move clumsily) *or* **wat·tle** (hut)

wad·dle (to move clumsily); **wat·tle** (hut)

wade (to walk in water); **wad** (small mass)

wadle : **wad·dle** (to move clumsily) *or* **wat·tle** (hut)

wafe : **waif**

waf·er (disk); **waiv·er** (relinquishment); **wav·er** (to hesitate)

waffer : **wa·fer** (disk) *or* **waiv·er** (relinquishment) *or* **wav·er** (to hesitate)

waf·fle

wafle : **waf·fle**

wagen : **wag·on**

wa·ger

waggon (*Brit.*) : **wag·on**

waght : **weight**

wag·on

wagur : **wa·ger**

waif

waifer : **wa·fer** (disk) *or* **waiv·er** (relinquishment) *or* **wav·er** (to hesitate)

Wai·ki·ki

wail (to cry); **whale** (mammal)

wain (cart); **wane** (to diminish)

wainscoat : **wain·scot**

wain·scot

wainscote : **wain·scot**

wairily : **wari·ly**

waist (part of body); **waste** (unused)

waistbasket : **waste·bas·ket**

waistbassket : **waste·bas·ket**

waistful : **waste·ful**

waistrel : **wast·rel**

wait (to stay for); **weight** (heaviness)

waiteress : **wait·ress**

wait·ress

waive (to forgo); **wave** (ridge of water; gesture)

waiv·er (relinquishment); **waf·er** (disk); **wav·er** (to hesitate)

wake·ful

wakefull : **wake·ful**

walet : **wal·let**

walit : **wal·let**

wallep : **wal·lop**

wal·let

wallip : **wal·lop**

wallit : **wal·let**

wallnut : **wal·nut**

walloe : **wal·low**

wal·lop

wal·low

wallris : **wal·rus**

wallrus : **wal·rus**

wal·nut

walow : **wal·low**

walris : **wal·rus**

walriss : **wal·rus**

wal·rus

walts : **waltz**

waltz

wane (to diminish); **wain** (cart)

wanescot : **wain·scot**

want (desire); **wont** (custom); **won't** (will not)

wanten : **wan·ton**

wan·ton

warant : **war·rant**

warbal : **war·ble**
war·ble
war·den
wardon : **war·den**
ware·house
warely : **wari·ly**
warent : **war·rant**
warf : **wharf**
wari·ly
warior : **war·rior**
war·rant
war·ran·tee (one who receives warranty); **war·ran·ty** (guarantee)
war·ran·ty (guarantee); **war·ran·tee** (one who receives warranty)
warrent : **war·rant**
warrentee : **war·ran·tee** (one who receives warranty) *or* **war·ran·ty** (guarantee)
warrier : **war·rior**
warrint : **war·rant**
warrintee : **war·ran·tee** (one who receives warranty) *or* **war·ran·ty** (guarantee)
war·rior
warsh : **wash**
Warshington : **Wash·ing·ton**
wash
washabel : **wash·able**
wash·able
washeble : **wash·able**
washible : **wash·able**
Washingten : **Wash·ing·ton**
Washingtin : **Wash·ing·ton**
Wash·ing·ton
Washinton : **Wash·ing·ton**
was·sail
wassal : **was·sail**
wassel : **was·sail**
wassell : **was·sail**

wasstrel : **wast·rel**
wastbasket : **waste·bas·ket**
waste (loss of use); **waist** (part of body)
waste·bas·ket
wastebaskit : **waste·bas·ket**
waste·ful
wastefull : **waste·ful**
wastful : **waste·ful**
wastral : **wast·rel**
wast·rel
wastrell : **wast·rel**
wastrill : **wast·rel**
watch·ful
watchfull : **watch·ful**
wa·ter
wateress : **wait·ress**
watermelan : **wa·ter·mel·on**
watermelin : **wa·ter·mel·on**
watermellin : **wa·ter·mel·on**
watermellon : **wa·ter·mel·on**
wa·ter·mel·on
waterry : **wa·tery**
watershead : **wa·ter·shed**
wa·ter·shed
wa·tery
watter : **wa·ter**
wattermelon : **wa·ter·mel·on**
wattershed : **wa·ter·shed**
wattery : **wa·tery**
wave (ridge of water; gesture); **waive** (to forgo)
wav·er (to hesitate); **waf·er** (disk); **waiv·er** (relinquishment)
wayfairer : **way·far·er**
way·far·er
waylade : **way·laid**
way·laid
waylayed : **way·laid**
way·ward
waywerd : **way·ward**

wayword : **way·ward**
weadle : **whee·dle**
weak·en
weakleng : **weak·ling**
weak·ling
weald : **wield**
wealp : **whelp**
wealterweight : **wel·ter·weight**
wealthy
weapen : **weap·on**
weap·on
wearas : **where·as**
wearhouse : **ware·house**
wearisom : **wea·ri·some**
wea·ri·some
weary
wearysome : **wea·ri·some**
wearysum : **wea·ri·some**
weasal : **wea·sel**
wea·sel
weasil : **wea·sel**
weath·er (atmospheric
  condition); **weth·er** (sheep);
  wheth·er (if)
weave
weavel : **wee·vil**
weavil : **wee·vil**
Weddnesday : **Wednes·day**
Wednes·day
weedal : **whee·dle**
weedle : **whee·dle**
weeken : **weak·en**
weekling : **weak·ling**
weel : **wheel**
weeld : **wield**
weerd : **weird**
weerisome : **wea·ri·some**
weerwolf : **were·wolf**
weerwulf : **were·wolf**
weery : **weary**
weerysome : **wea·ri·some**
weesel : **wea·sel**

weeval : **wee·vil**
weeve : **weave**
weevel : **wee·vil**
wee·vil
weght : **weight**
weight (heaviness); **wait** (to stay
  for)
weiken : **weak·en**
weild : **wield**
weird
weirwolf : **were·wolf**
weiry : **weary**
weirysome : **wea·ri·some**
weisel : **wea·sel**
weive : **weave**
weivil : **wee·vil**
welch (to cheat); **Welsh** (from
  Wales)
wel·come
welcume : **wel·come**
welfair : **wel·fare**
wel·fare
wellcome : **wel·come**
wellfair : **wel·fare**
wellfare : **wel·fare**
wellterweight : **wel·ter·weight**
wellthy : **wealthy**
welp : **whelp**
Welsh (from Wales); **welch** (to
  cheat)
wel·ter·weight
welterwieght : **wel·ter·weight**
welthy : **wealthy**
weman : **wom·en**
wemman : **wom·en**
wence : **whence** (from where)
  or **wince** (to flinch)
wendlass : **wind·lass**
Wendnisday : **Wednes·day**
Wendsday : **Wednes·day**
wendward : **wind·ward**
Wensday : **Wednes·day**

wepen : **weap·on**

wepon : **weap·on**

weppen : **weap·on**

weppin : **weap·on**

weppon : **weap·on**

were (*past of* to be); **we're** (we are)

we're (we are); **were** (*past of* to be)

were·wolf

werewulf : **were·wolf**

werl : **whirl**

wership : **wor·ship**

wersted : **wor·sted**

werthy : **wor·thy**

werwolf : **were·wolf**

Wesconsin : **Wis·con·sin**

West Verginia : **West Vir·gin·ia**

West Vir·gin·ia

west·ward

westwerd : **west·ward**

westword : **west·ward**

wet (moist); **whet** (to sharpen)

weth·er (sheep); **weath·er** (atmospheric condition); **wheth·er** (if)

wetstone : **whet·stone**

whale (mammal); **wail** (to cry)

wharf

wharfs : **wharves**

wharves

wheadle : **whee·dle**

wheal : **wheel**

whealp : **whelp**

wheaze : **wheeze**

whee·dle

wheel

wheeze : **wheeze**

wheil : **wheel**

whelp

whemsical : **whim·si·cal**

whence (from where); **wince** (to flinch)

wheras : **where·as**

where as : **where·as**

where·as

wherehouse : **ware·house**

wherewolf : **were·wolf**

whet (to sharpen); **wet** (moist)

wheth·er (if); **weath·er** (atmospheric condition); **weth·er** (sheep)

whetstoan : **whet·stone**

whet·stone

which (what one); **witch** (sorceress)

whicked : **wick·ed** (evil) *or* **wick·et** (gate)

whicket : **wick·ed** (evil) *or* **wick·et** (gate)

whickit : **wick·ed** (evil) *or* **wick·et** (gate)

whim·per

whimsecal : **whim·si·cal**

whim·si·cal

whimsickal : **whim·si·cal**

whim·sy

whimzy : **whim·sy**

whince : **whence** (from where) *or* **wince** (to flinch)

whine (sound); **wine** (beverage)

whin·ny (neigh); **whiny** (given to whining)

whiny (given to whining); **whin·ny** (neigh)

whip

whipet : **whip·pet**

whipit : **whip·pet**

whipoorwill : **whip·poor·will**

whipperwill : **whip·poor·will**

whip·pet

whippit : **whip·pet**

whip·poor·will

whipporwill : **whip·poor·will**
whirl
whis·ker
whis·key *or* **whis·ky**
whis·ky *or* **whis·key**
whis·per
whissle : **whis·tle**
whisstel : **whis·tle**
whisteria : **wis·te·ria**
whistful : **wist·ful**
whis·tle
whith·er (to where); **with·er** (to shrivel)
whittal : **whit·tle**
whittel : **whit·tle**
whit·tle
whol·ly (completely); **hol·ly** (tree); **ho·ly** (sacred)
wholy : **ho·ly** (sacred) *or* **whol·ly** (completely)
who's (who is); **whose** (belonging to whom)
whose (belonging to whom); **who's** (who is)
wich : **which** (what one) *or* **witch** (sorceress)
wick·ed (evil); **wick·et** (gate)
wick·et (gate); **wick·ed** (evil)
wickit : **wick·ed** (evil) *or* **wick·et** (gate)
wieght : **weight**
wield
wierd : **weird**
wierwolf : **were·wolf**
wiery : **weary**
wiesel : **wea·sel**
wieve : **weave**
wievil : **wee·vil**
Wikeekee : **Wai·ki·ki**
wikked : **wick·ed** (evil) *or* **wick·et** (gate)
wildernes : **wil·der·ness**

wil·der·ness
wilderniss : **wil·der·ness**
wildurness : **wil·der·ness**
wil·ful *or* **will·ful**
wilfull : **will·ful**
wil·i·ness
willderness : **wil·der·ness**
will·ful *or* **wil·ful**
willfull : **will·ful**
wilyness : **wil·i·ness**
wiman : **wom·en**
wimen : **wom·en**
wimman : **wom·en**
wimmen : **wom·en**
wimper : **whim·per**
wimsical : **whim·si·cal**
wimsy : **whim·sy**
winary : **win·ery**
wince (to flinch); **whence** (from where)
windlas : **wind·lass**
wind·lass
windles : **wind·lass**
Windsday : **Wednes·day**
windsheald : **wind·shield**
windsheeld : **wind·shield**
windsheild : **wind·shield**
wind·shield
wind·ward
windwerd : **wind·ward**
windword : **wind·ward**
wine (beverage); **whine** (sound)
winerry : **win·ery**
win·ery
wintery : **win·try**
win·try
Wioming : **Wy·o·ming**
wip : **whip**
wippet : **whip·pet**
wippoorwill : **whip·poor·will**
wird : **weird**
wirl : **whirl**

Wisconsen : **Wis•con•sin**
Wis•con•sin
wis•dom
wisdum : **wis•dom**
wish•ful
wishfull : **wish•ful**
wisker : **whis•ker**
wiskey : **whis•key**
Wiskonsin : **Wis•con•sin**
wisky : **whis•key**
wisper : **whis•per**
wissel : **whis•tle**
wis•ta•ria or **wis•te•ria**
wis•te•ria or **wis•ta•ria**
wistfull : **wist•ful**
wistle : **whis•tle**
witch (sorceress); **which** (what one)
with•al
withall : **with•al**
with•draw•al
withdrawel : **with•draw•al**
withdrawl : **with•draw•al**
with•er (to shrivel); **whith•er** (to where)
with•hold
withold : **with•hold**
wit•ness
witniss : **wit•ness**
wit•ti•cism
wittisism : **wit•ti•cism**
wittle : **whit•tle**
wittness : **wit•ness**
wittycism : **wit•ti•cism**
wiz•ard
wiz•ard•ry
wizerd : **wiz•ard**
wizerdry : **wiz•ard•ry**
wizzard : **wiz•ard**
wizzardry : **wiz•ard•ry**
wizzerd : **wiz•ard**
wizzerdry : **wiz•ard•ry**

wod : **wad**
woddle : **wad•dle** (to move clumsily) or **wat•tle** (hut)
wofel : **waf•fle**
woffle : **waf•fle**
wofle : **waf•fle**
wolf (animal); **woof** (weaving)
wolfs : **wolves**
wollow : **wal•low**
woltz : **waltz**
wolves
wom•an (*sing.*); **wom•en** (*plur.*)
wom•en (*plur.*); **wom•an** (*sing.*)
womman : **wom•an**
wommen : **wom•en**
won•der•ful
wonderfull : **won•der•ful**
wonderous : **won•drous**
won•drous
wont (custom); **want** (desire); **won't** (will not)
won't (will not); **want** (desire); **wont** (custom)
woof (weaving); **wolf** (animal)
wool•en or **wool•len**
wool•len or **wool•en**
wool•ly
wooly : **wool•ly**
worbal : **war•ble**
worble : **war•ble**
word•age
wordege : **word•age**
wordige : **word•age**
world•li•ness
worldlyness : **world•li•ness**
wor•ri•some
worrysome : **wor•ri•some**
worrysum : **wor•ri•some**
wor•ship
wor•ship•ing or **wor•ship•ping**
wor•ship•ping or **wor•ship•ing**
worstead : **wor•sted**

wor•sted

wor•thy

worysome : **wor•ri•some**

wranglar : **wran•gler**

wran•gler

wrastle : **wres•tle**

wraught : **wrought**

wreak (to inflict); **reek** (to stink); **wreck** (to destroy)

wreath (*noun*); **wreathe** (*verb*)

wreathe (*verb*); **wreath** (*noun*)

wrech : **wreak** (to inflict) *or* **wreck** (to destroy) *or* **wretch** (miserable one)

wreck (to destroy); **weak** (to inflict)

wreck•age

wreckege : **wreck•age**

wreckige : **wreck•age**

wreek : **wreak** (to inflict) *or* **wreck** (to destroy)

wreeth : **wreath** (*noun*)

wreethe : **wreathe** (*verb*)

wreith : **wreath** (*noun*)

wreithe : **wreathe** (*verb*)

wrekage : **wreck•age**

wrench

wressel : **wres•tle**

wrestal : **wres•tle**

wrestel : **wres•tle**

wres•tle

wretch (miserable one); **retch** (to vomit)

wriggal : **wrig•gle**

wriggel : **wrig•gle**

wrig•gle

wrigle : **wrig•gle**

wrily : **wry•ly**

wrinch : **wrench**

wrinkal : **wrin•kle**

wrinkel : **wrin•kle**

wrin•kle

wrist

writen : **writ•ten**

writ•er

writh : **writhe**

writhe

writ•ing

writ•ten

writter : **writ•er**

writting : **writ•ing**

wrought

wry (ironic); **rye** (grain)

wry•ly

wrythe : **writhe**

wufe : **wolf** (animal) *or* **woof** (weaving)

wulf : **wolf** (animal) *or* **woof** (weaving)

wunderful : **won•der•ful**

wundrous : **won•drous**

wursted : **wor•sted**

wurthy : **wor•thy**

wyerd : **weird**

Wykiki : **Wai•ki•ki**

Wy•o•ming

wyrd : **weird**

X

xe•non

xe•no•pho•bia

Xe•rox

xilophone : **xy•lo•phone**

xylaphone : **xy•lo•phone**

xylephone : **xy•lo•phone**

xy•lo•phone

Y

yacht

yack : **yak**

yaht : **yacht**

yak

yall : **yawl** (sailboat) *or* **yowl** (howl)

yamaka : **yar·mul·ke**

Yanckee : **Yan·kee**

Yan·kee

Yankey : **Yan·kee**

Yankie : **Yan·kee**

Yanky : **Yan·kee**

yard·age

yardege : **yard·age**

yardidge : **yard·age**

yardige : **yard·age**

yar·mul·ke

yat : **yacht**

yaught : **yacht**

yaun : **yawn**

yawl (sailboat); **yowl** (howl)

yawn

yeald : **yield**

year

yearn·ing

yeast

yeer : **year**

yeest : **yeast**

yeild : **yield**

yello : **yel·low**

yelloe : **yel·low**

yel·low

yelow : **yel·low**

Yeman : **Ye·men**

Ye·men

yeo·man

yerning : **yearn·ing**

yerself : **your·self**

yestday : **yes·ter·day**

yes·ter·day

yestoday : **yes·ter·day**

yesturday : **yes·ter·day**

yew (tree); **ewe** (female sheep); **you** (*pron.*)

Yid·dish

Yidish : **Yid·dish**

yield

yo·del

yodell : **yo·del**

yo·ga (Hindu philosophy); **yo·gi** (follower of yoga)

yogah : **yo·ga**

yogart : **yo·gurt**

yogert : **yo·gurt**

yogha : **yo·ga**

yoghi : **yo·gi**

yoghourt : **yo·gurt**

yoghurt : **yo·gurt**

yo·gi (follower of yoga); **yo·ga** (Hindu philosophy)

yo·gurt

yoke (harness); **yolk** (egg yellow)

yo·kel

yokle : **yo·kel**

yolk (egg yellow); **yoke** (harness)

yoman : **yeo·man**

Yoming : **Wy·o·ming**

yondur : **yon·der**

yool : **yule**

yor : **yore** (time past) *or* **your** (belonging to you) *or* **you're** (you are)

yore (time past); **your** (belonging to you); **you're** (you are)

Yosemety : **Yo·sem·i·te**

Yo·sem·i·te

Yosemitty : **Yo·sem·i·te**

Yosimete : **Yo•sem•i•te**
yot : **yacht**
you (*pron.*); **ewe** (female sheep); **yew** (tree)
young
youngstor : **young•ster**
your (belonging to you); **yore** (time past); **you're** (you are)
you're (you are); **yore** (time past); **your** (belonging to you)
yours
your's : **yours**
your•self
yoursself : **your•self**
youth
Yu•ca•tán
yuc•ca

Yuccatan : **Yu•ca•tán**
yucka : **yuc•ca**
Yucon : **Yu•kon**
yuel : **yule**
Yugaslavia : **Yu•go•sla•via**
Yu•go•sla•via *or* **Ju•go•sla•via**
Yugoslovia : **Yu•go•sla•via**
Yu•kon
yule
yull : **yule**
yung : **young**
yur : **yore** (time past) *or* **your** (*pron.*) *or* **you're** (you are)
yurning : **yearn•ing**
yurself : **your•self**
Yutah : **Utah**
yuth : **youth**

Z

Zambeezi : **Zam•be•zi**
Zam•be•si *or* **Zam•be•zi**
Zam•be•zi *or* **Zam•be•si**
Zambezy : **Zam•be•zi**
zaney : **za•ny**
Zansibar : **Zan•zi•bar**
za•ny
Zan•zi•bar
zar : **czar**
zeabra : **ze•bra**
zeal
zeal•ot
zeal•ous
zealus : **zeal•ous**
zearo : **ze•ro**
ze•bra
zeel : **zeal**
zeenith : **ze•nith**
zefer : **zeph•yr**
zeffer : **zeph•yr**
zefir : **zeph•yr**
zellot : **zeal•ot**
zellous : **zeal•ous**
zelot : **zeal•ot**
zeneth : **ze•nith**
zenia : **zin•nia**
ze•nith
zennith : **ze•nith**
zenon : **xe•non**
zenophobia : **xe•no•pho•bia**
zepelin : **zep•pe•lin**
zepher : **zeph•yr**
zephir : **zeph•yr**
zeph•yr
zep•pe•lin
zeppilen : **zep•pe•lin**
zercon : **zir•con**
ze•ro

Zerox : **Xe•rox**
zigote : **zy•gote**
zinc
zinck : **zinc**
zin•fan•del
zinfendel : **zin•fan•del**
zinfundel : **zin•fan•del**
zinia : **zin•nia**
zink : **zinc**
zin•nia
zinya : **zin•nia**
zippur : **zip•per**
zir•con
zirkon : **zir•con**
ziro : **ze•ro**
zoan : **zone**
zodeac : **zo•di•ac**
zo•di•ac
zodiac : **zo•di•ac**
zodiack : **zo•di•ac**
zodiak : **zo•di•ac**
zology : **zo•ol•o•gy**
zom•bie
zomby : **zom•bie**
zoolegy : **zo•ol•o•gy**
zo•ol•o•gy
Zooloo : **Zu•lu**
zuc•chi•ni
zuccini : **zuc•chi•ni**
zucheni : **zuc•chi•ni**
zukeeni : **zuc•chi•ni**
Zu•lu
zuology : **zo•ol•o•gy**
Zu•rich
Zurick : **Zu•rich**
zurkon : **zir•con**
Zurrich : **Zu•rich**
zy•gote
zylophone : **xy•lo•phone**

Guidelines for American English Spelling

1. *I* BEFORE *E*...

The most well-known spelling rule is

> *i* before *e*
> except after *c*
> or when sounded like *ay*
> as in *neighbor* and *weigh*.

This one works for many common words like *field, niece, receive*, and *ceiling*. The rule even works for some more unusual words like *sleigh* and *chow mein*. But there are a number of qualifications and exceptions.

    a. The rule applies only when the *c* is sounded like *see*. *Science* is spelled *ie*, because the *c* is not sounded *see*. When the *c* is sounded as *sh*, the spelling also remains "*i* before *e*," as in *efficient, proficient*, and *ancient*.

    b. The "*i* before *e*" rule applies after a *see* sound, even when the letter *c* is not actually present, as in *seize* and *seizure*.

    c. The following words are spelled *ei* even though they do not come after a *see* sound and are not sounded *ay*:

caffeine	*height*
codeine	*leisure*
counterfeit	*neither*
either	*protein*
forfeit	*sovereign*
heifer	*weird*

d. The following words follow a *see* sound, yet are spelled *ie*:

fancier   *financier*   *siege*

2. *-CEDE/-CEED/-SEDE*

There are scores of verbs that end with the sound *-seed*. All of these are spelled *-cede* except for four:

succeed   *exceed*   *proceed*

Only one *-seed* verb ends *-sede*:

supersede

3. *-IFY/-EFY*

There are likewise a great number of verbs ending *-ify*. Only five end *-efy*:

liquefy   *stupefy*
putrefy   *tumefy*
rarefy

4. *-ND* BECOMES *-NSE*

When a verb ends *-nd*, some of the words derived from it will substitute *s* for *d*:

defend   →   *defense*
expand   →   *expansive*
offend   →   *offense*
pretend   →   *pretense*
suspend   →   *suspenseful*

5. *-DGE* ENDINGS

Words ending *-dge* drop the *e* before adding *-ment*:

abridge   →   *abridgment*
acknowledge   →   *acknowledgment*
judge   →   *judgment*

6. -ABLE/-IBLE

There are more words ending -*able* than -*ible*, so if it comes to a coin toss, choose -*able*. Generally, -*able* is added to words that could stand alone without a suffix:

agree	→	*agreeable*
break	→	*breakable*
depend	→	*dependable*
predict	→	*predictable*

-*able* also follows word stems ending *i*: *appreciable, reliable, sociable*.

The ending -*ible* is usually added to word parts that could not stand alone without the suffix:

aud	+	*ible*	=	*audible*
cred	+	*ible*	=	*credible*
feas	+	*ible*	=	*feasible*
vis	+	*ible*	=	*visible*

7. HARD C/SOFT C

The letter *c* can be sounded like a *k* (as in *cash*) or like an *s* (as in *city*). These are called "hard *c*" and "soft *c*," respectively.

Normally, when adding -*able* to a word ending in -*e*, drop the *e*:

desire	→	*desirable*
pleasure	→	*pleasurable*
use	→	*usable*

However, if a word ends soft *c* + *e*, retain the *e* befor -*able* (to retain the soft *c* sound):

notice	→	*noticeable*
peace	→	*peaceable*
service	→	*serviceable*

Word stems ending with a hard *c* sound take the -*able* suffix:

applicable
despicable
implacable

8. HARD *G*/SOFT *G*

Like the letter *c, g* can be sounded as a "hard *g*" (as in *gate*) or "soft *g*" (as in *gentle*). The spelling rules regarding hard *g* and soft *g* are similar to those concerning hard *c* and soft *c*.

Words ending soft *g* + *e* retain the *e* before adding *-able* or *-ous* (to retain the soft *g* sound):

change	→	*changeable*
knowledge	→	*knowledgeable*
manage	→	*manageable*
advantage	→	*advantageous*
courage	→	*courageous*
outrage	→	*outrageous*

Word stems ending hard *g* add *-able*:

indefatigable   *navigable*

Soft *g* may also be followed by *-ible* endings (see Rule 6 above):

eligible	*negligible*
intelligible	*tangible*

9. *C* ENDINGS

Words ending in *c* add a *k* (to retain the hard *c* sound) before adding a suffix:

bivouac	→	*bivouacked*
frolic	→	*frolicking*
panic	→	*panicking*
shellac	→	*shellacked*

10. *-Y/-EY*

In forming plurals, a final *-y* preceded by a consonant is usually replaced by *ie* before adding *s*:

baby	→	*babies*
caddy	→	*caddies*
poppy	→	*poppies*

But if the word ends *-ey*, simply add *s*:

alley	→	*alleys*
attorney	→	*attorneys*
chimney	→	*chimneys*
valley	→	*valleys*

(One exception here is *money* → *monies.*)

11. *PRIZE/-PRISE*

Prize ends *-ze*. But when part of another word, the ending is spelled *-prise*:

comprise   *enterprise*   *surprise*

12. *-N + -NESS*

When adding *-ness* to a word already ending with an *n*, retain both *n*'s:

drunkenness	*greenness*
evenness	*thinness*

13. **ADDING** *-LY*

Most words ending in *e* retain the *e* when the ending *-ly* is added.

love	→	*lovely*
base	→	*basely*

There are three common exceptions, words in which the *e* is dropped when *-ly* is added:

true	→	*truly*
due	→	*duly*
whole	→	*wholly*

When adding *-ly* to words ending in *l*, retain the *l:*

brutal	→	*brutally*
cynical	→	*cynically*

14. WORDS ENDING IN SILENT *E*

Most words drop a silent final *e* before adding a suffix beginning with a vowel. The *e* is usually not dropped if the suffix begins with a consonant:

suffix begins with vowel		suffix begins with consonant	
forgive →	*forgiving*	*forgive* →	*forgiveness*
confine →	*confining*	*confine* →	*confinement*

15. DOUBLING CONSONANTS

When adding *-ed* or *-ing* to words ending in *t* or *l* preceded by a single vowel, double the *t* or *l* if the last syllable of the word is accented. Use only one *t* or *l* if the last syllable is not accented:

last syllable accented		last syllable unaccented	
commit →	*committed*	*limit* →	*limited*
control →	*controlling*	*cancel* →	*canceled*

Words ending in a single accented vowel and consonant usually double the consonant when a suffix that begins with a vowel is added. The consonant is usually not doubled if the suffix begins with a consonant:

suffix begins with vowel		suffix begins with consonant	
fit →	*fitting*	*fit* →	*fitful*
regret →	*regretting*	*regret* →	*regretful*

16. *-ISE/-IZE*

In American spelling, there are hundreds of verbs ending in *-ize*. There are only ten common verbs ending in *-ise*:

advertise	*exercise*
advise	*improvise*
chastise	*revise*
despise	*supervise*
devise	*surprise*

BONUS SECTION
OF
303 SILLY SPELLING GOOFS

Introduction

Absence makes the heart grow fonder. Or is it *absense*? Words like these separate good spellers from bad spellers. Or is it *seperate*? If you can't remember how to spell *absence* or *separate,* don't feel bad. You're not alone.

A great many words in American English deserve to be misspelled. We often spell *glamour* with a *u*, like the British, but we leave this *u* out of *glamorous.* The word *through* doesn't rhyme with *bough, cough, dough,* or *rough,* but it does rhyme with *to, two,* and *too.*

The dramatist George Bernard Shaw illustrated just how ludicrous spelling can become when he pointed out that the word *fish* can quite logically be spelled *ghoti: gh* as in *laugh, o* as in *women,* and *ti* as in *nation.*

If you're not thoroughly confused by now, you're not paying attention. In Spanish or German, words are generally spelled just as they sound. In English, one's only hope is a good memory. Some of America's most celebrated thinkers and writers have been notoriously bad spellers. F. Scott Fitzgerald, one of America's most distinguished novelists, was an atrocious speller. He used to address letters to his good friend "Earnest Hemmingway" misspelling both the first and last names of Ernest Hemingway.

The only spelling rule in English that is worth much is this:

> *i* before *e*
> except after *c*
> or when sounded like *ay*
> as in *neighbor* and *weigh*

That's well and good for *receive, deceive,* and their cousins, as well as for *neighbor* and *weigh.* But what about *weird* and *sovereign* and *counterfeit* and more than thirty other exceptions? What rule tells us when the rules apply and when they don't?

Spelling in English is not a matter of logic, sounding out words, or learning rules. It is simply a matter of remembering how a word looks on the page. Some people remember spelling without trying, just as some people remember phone numbers without trying. Most of us, however, have to rely on phone books and dictionaries.

Keep in mind that some phone numbers are easier to remember than others. You would want to write down *960-3182,* but you might not need a pencil if the number were *123-4567*. Likewise, a number is easy to recall if it spells out a word on the phone dial. Could you remember the number of a jeweler if I told you to call 1(800) 289-4367? How about if I gave it to you as 1(800) BUY-GEMS?

Like remembering phone numbers, good spelling is based on two principles:

PRINCIPLE NUMBER ONE: A pattern is easier to remember than a random assortment.

Below are two sets of 25 letters.

COLUMN A	COLUMN B
seven	fyquv
shorn	pxlza
sheep	rsdwt
stood	mydkj
still	cbguh

Which column would you prefer to memorize? Column A, of

course. It can be memorized in an instant. On the other hand, the letters in Column B would take a few minutes to learn, and even then you are likely to make mistakes. That's because the first column is full of patterns; the letters make up words, the words make up a sentence, and they all start with *s*. In the second column, however, you have to rely on painstaking memorization of individual letters.

PRINCIPLE NUMBER TWO: It is easier to remember something if you can visualize it.

People often say, "I can't recall the name, but I never forget a face." And it's true. Our imaginations can store mental pictures much more effectively and permanently than our intellects can store individual bits of information. If I asked you, "Who was our twenty-sixth President?" you probably couldn't answer, even if you have seen a list of U.S. Presidents sometime recently. But if I showed you his picture, chances are you'd recognize him at once as Theodore Roosevelt.

The secret of good spelling is to invent patterns and pictures to help you recall the hard parts of hard words. Rather than memorizing spelling rules or spelling lists, or trying to sound out difficult words, try enlisting the aid of your visual imagination.

When you come across a word you are likely to misspell, focus on the part of the word that gives you the most trouble. It may be an unaccented vowel. (Is it *correspondance* or *correspondence*?) Or it may be a question of doubling consonants (*satellite, sattelite,* or *satelite*?).

In the first example above, the correct spelling is *correspondence with an e.* You can remember the *e* by thinking of your correspond**e**nce going into an **e**nvelope. In the second example, it's one *t* and two *l*'s. Notice the word *tell* in the middle of sat**ell**ite. If you remember that satellites **tell** us more about our world, you will also remember how to spell the word correctly.

In my years of college teaching, I have corrected at least 50,000 misspellings. That number would be staggering if I had actually circled that many *different* misspelled words. But I haven't run across 50,000 misspelled words, or even

5,000. Rather, it is the same three or four hundred words that I see misspelled over and over and over again.

This book is a collection of some of those commonly misspelled words, along with mnemonic patterns and pictures. Some of these memory devices are logical and some are not. Some are humorous and some are not. But all of them should help you lock the correct spelling into your visual memory. I've had students laugh or groan when I drew one of these on the blackboard, but they have come back years later to tell me that they have never had trouble spelling the word after seeing my illustration.

Of course, the following list of entries is not exhaustive, but it shows you how to conjure up mental pictures or letter patterns to aid you in spelling. In addition to this list, you should start your own collection of words you have trouble spelling. As you add words to your list, underline the most troublesome letters in the word. Then think up a picture or look for a pattern to help you visualize the correct spelling in your own mind. Applying this technique consistently, you will eventually become a competent speller.

A

ABANDON is spelled just like the three words **a band on**. Think of *a band on* a desert island whose members have been abandoned.

A BANDON

ABDOMEN has the word **dome** in the middle of it. Picture a man with a dome in his middle.

ABSENCE ends in **-ce**, not **-se**. Remember that students with many absences end up with a grade of *C* (or worse!).

ABUNDANCE ends **-dance**. It is spelled just like the three words *a bun dance*.

ABUNDANCE

A BUN DANCE

ABYSS has a **y** in the middle. Picture the *y* as a deep abyss within the word.

An **ACCIDENT** leaves a **dent** in the end.

ACCOMMODATE begins with **a** and ends with **-date**. In between are three pairs of letters, *c*'s, *m*'s, and *o*'s. Think of those *c*'s, *m*'s, and *o*'s as couples out on a date—all three in pairs.

$$A^{CC}O_{MM}ODATE$$

ADDRESS has two **d**'s. The address is what you **add** to the letter before you mail it.

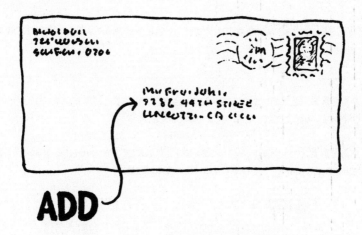

ADD

ADVERTISE ends in **-se**, not *-ze*. Remember that the purpose of advertising is to **se**ll, not to "**ze**ll."

ADVICE / ADVISE. *Advice* is a noun, *advise* is a verb. Compare these to **rice** and **rise**. *Rice* is a noun, a thing, while *rise* is a verb, an action. (The same holds true for *device* and *devise*.)

NOUNS	VERBS
R**ICE**	R**ISE**
ADV**ICE**	ADV**ISE**
DEV**ICE**	DEV**ISE**

THE CHEF WATCHED THE
RICE RISE

ALIEN begins with **a lie**. Watch out for *a lie* when you first meet an *ali*en.

ALTAR (a ceremonial table) ends **-ar**. Think of the *Arch*bishop who might stand before it.

ALTER (to change) ends **-er**. Think of the word *erase*. To al**ter** something, you **er**ase the original.

ALT**AR**	ALT**ER**
ARCHBISHOP	**ER**ASE

AMATEUR begins with the words **a mate**. Think of an amateur golfer who learns the game by practicing with his or her spouse, or mate.

An **AMBULANCE** has **Lance** hanging off the back!

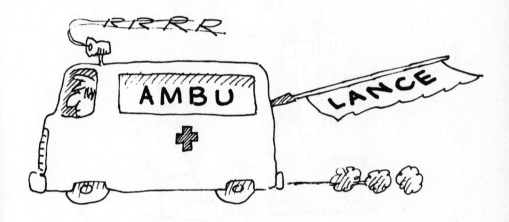

ANGEL ends **-el**. An ange*l* lives at a high *el*evation.

ANGLE, the bend formed by the meeting of two lines, ends in **-le**. Think of a *l*eg, which bends at the knee to form an an-g*le*.

ANOINT is spelled with one **n** after the **a**. To *anoint* someone is to pour *an oint*ment over his or her head.

AN **OINT** (MENT)

A Matter of Some **Ant**ics

Some of the most commonly misspelled words are those that sound as if they end with *-ent* but that actually end with **-ant**: *pregnant, fragrant, vagrant,* and *defendant.* When you run across such a word, try to imagine ants being or doing what the word describes.

VAGR**ANT**

FRAGR**ANT**

TRU**ANT**

OBSERV**ANT** SERGE**ANT**

DEFEND**ANT**

REPENT**ANT**

RELUCT**ANT**

RADI**ANT**

PREGN**ANT**

INF**ANT**

DEFEND**ANT**

Don't forget the first **c** in **ARCTIC**. The **arc**tic is the area north of the polar *arc.*

ARDUOUS has a **duo** in the middle. Think of some ar*duo*us task, such as mountain climbing, that is best undertaken by no less than two.

ARGUMENT drops the *e* in *argue* before adding *-ment*. Remember that argument has **gum** in the middle.

AR GUM ENT

ARTILLERY. One finds **tiller**, like a *tiller* of the soil, in the middle of ar*tille*ry.

ASCENT with a **c** is the act of **c**limbing.

ASSENT with an **ss** is to say *so*, to agree to or affirm.

```
              B     A S S E N T
          M         A O
      I             Y
    L
  A S C E N T
```

ASCERTAIN is spelled like the two words **as certain.** To *ascertain* something is to be *as certain* as possible about it.

ATTENDANCE ends -**DANCE.** Remember that most students like to *attend a dance.*

attend

atten**dance**

dance

ATTENDANCE

AUGER with an -**er** is a bor*er*, a tool for boring holes.

AUGUR with an -**ur** is one who tries to read the future, like a gu*ru*. An *augur* shows up in the middle of an in*augur*ation, because everyone hopes that new leadership *augurs* well for the future.

B

BADMINTON. In this game, a **bad** shot is one that goes **into** the net.

BALANCE ends **-ance**, not *-ence*. Think of a knight using his *lance* to keep his ba*lance*.

BA**LANCE**

BALLOON has two l's to go with its two **o's**. Think of the o's as balloons, each with its own string.

BALL OO N

A **BARGAIN** is something that ends in a **gain** for the buyer.

BARRAGE is spelled just like the two words **bar** and **rage**.

A **BATTALION** goes into **batt**le. And battalion has two t's and one l just like ba**ttl**e.

A **BEACH** with **ea** is by the *sea*.

A **BEECH** with **ee** is a tr*ee*.

BEECH   BEACH

TREE   SEA

A **BEGGAR** tries to **gar**ner loose change from passersby.

BEG**GAR**

GARNER

BELEAGUER contains the word **league**. When you are be-*league*red, it feels as if you have the whole *league* against you.

BE**LEAGUE**R

Be careful about your **BELIEFS** as well as those people you **BELIEVE** in. Both *believe* and *belief* have a **lie** in the middle!

A **BERG** is another name for an ice**berg**, a mountain of ice. Think of Ev**er**est.

A **BURG** is a city or town. Think of **ur**ban.

B**ER**G   **BUR**G

EV**ER**EST   **UR**BAN

BURG ON BERG

BESEECH has three **e**'s. It is an old word meaning "to seek help or favor."

BESEECH

SEEK

BLEAK ends *-eak*, not *-eek*. Notice that *bleak* has a **leak** in the end. Things are indeed b*leak* when there is a *leak* in the end.

BOUNDARY contains an **ar**. A *boundary* contains the *area* enclosed.

BOUND**AR**Y

AREA

BOUNDARY

BREACH with an **ea** refers to a break. Breach of promise means breaking one's promise.

BREECH with an **ee** refers to the back end or something to cover the back end, such as knee breeches.

BREADTH ends **-dth**, just like the other dimension—wi*dth*.

BREA**DTH**

WI**DTH**

BRIDAL with a **-dal** refers to a bride standing at the *al*tar to be married.

BRIDLE with a **-dle** is for riding a horse, as is a sad*dle*.

BRIDAL	**BRIDLE**
ALTAR	SAD**DLE**

BRIDAL's BRIDLE

BUDGET ends **-get**. Sometimes you have to bud*get* your funds to *get* what you really want.

BULLETIN is spelled just like the two words **bullet in**. You will certainly hear a news *bulletin* if someone fires a *bullet in* the vicinity of the White House.

BULLETIN

BULWARK. A *bulwark* is a big **bulk** with **war** in the middle of it.

BURGLAR ends -**lar**, not -*ler*. A burg*lar* is one who commits *lar*-ceny, or theft.

BUR**GLAR**

LARCENY

BUSINESS, with an **i**, is for making *i*ncome.

BUSYNESS with a **y** is just being bus**y**.

BUS **I** NESS	BUS**Y**
N	BUS**Y**NESS
C	
O	
M	
E	

BUTTE has two **t**'s.

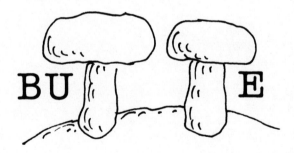

C

CABARET. Picture, if you will, a **cat** that is **bare** in the middle.

BARE

CA $\wedge$ T

CAFETERIA begins **cafe-**; just like *café*.

A **CALENDAR** ends **-dar**. Remember that a calen*dar* is for marking *days* and *dates*.

DAYS

CALEN**DA**R

DATES

CALORIE ends **-ie** as in d*ie*t. Beginning a low-calor*ie* d*ie*t means eating fewer calor*ie*s.

CALOR**IE**

D**IE**T

CALOR**IE**
D**IE**T

CAPITOL ends **-ol** when referring to that building called the statehouse. All other uses are spelled capital. Think of the *o* as the dome in the capit*o*l building.

CAPSIZE is spelled like the two words **cap** and **size**.

CARESS has one **r** and two **s**'s. Ca*ress* begins with *care*.

CASUALTIES is spelled like the two words **casual** and **ties**.

CATEGORY is in a category all by itself because it begins cate-, not cata-. Think of the word having a big **ego** in the middle because it is not like *catacomb, cataclysm,* and *catatonic*.

CEMETERY. Strangely enough, *cemetery* has a **meter** in the middle of it.

Ce**METER**y

CHASTISE ends -**se**, not -*ze*. Remember that *chasti**se*** is another word for *scold*.

CHASTISE
    C
    O
    L
    D

CHOOSE is present tense, when you select now.

CHOSE is past tense, when you have already selected.

A **CHORD** is a combination of notes played in harmony. Remember the *h* that begins *h*armony.

A **CORD,** with four letters, is a rope, another word with four letters.

CHORD   CORD
A   ROPE
R
M
O
N
Y

To **CITE** something with a **c** is to *c*all it to mind.

To **SIGHT** something refers to seeing it with one's eye**sight**.

A **SITE** is where something **sits**, where it is *si*tuated on the terrain.

CLIMATIC conditions, from the word clim**ate**, depend on where you are **at** on the globe.

CLIMACTIC moments are turning points, like the key **act** in a drama where the plot reaches its climax.

COLLAR ends -**ar**, not -*er*. In police jargon, a coll*ar* is an *arrest*.

COLL**AR**

ARREST

COMPARISON has **Paris** in the middle. Is there any com*paris*on to the beauty of *Paris*?

comP**ARIS**on

COMPETITION. The second vowel is an **e** as in comp**e**te. Visualize your **pet** turtle in the middle of comp*et*ition—the annual turtle race.

COMPLIMENT / COMPLEMENT. A compliment is a flattering remark. Think, "*I* like being in the middle of a compl*i*ment." A complement completes something (His tie complements his shirt.), and like *complete,* it is spelled with two *e*'s.

COMPL**I**MENT   **COMPLE**MENT

           L   **COMPLE**TE

           I

          K

          E

          I

          T

CONQUEROR ends -**or**, not -*er*. Conquerors may feel they must conquer *or* be conquered.

CONQUER**OR**

CONQUER **OR** BE CONQUERED

CONSCIENCE. Science comes from the Latin word *scientia,* which means "having knowledge." The word con*science* has *science* in it, which makes sense because con*science* is "the knowledge within."

CONSPIRACY ends -*acy*. It is spelled like two words, **cons** and **piracy**. Think of some *cons* (convicts) engaged in a *conspiracy* to commit *piracy*.

CONTEMPORARY has **tempo** in it. To be con*tempo*rary is to be in the swing of things, to be in touch with the *tempo* of the times.

$$\text{CON}\textbf{TEMPO}\text{RARY}$$

CONTROVERSY. Poor old **Rover** is always at the center of con*trover*sy.

CONVENIENT. On a see-saw, it is most conve**nient** when the weight is equal on each side. Picture *convenient* with those -*en*'s on each side of the *i*.

$$\text{conv} \quad \underline{\textbf{EN}} \quad \underline{\textbf{EN}} \quad \text{t}$$
$$\text{I}$$

CONVERTIBLE ends **-ible**, not *-able*. Think to yourself "I wish I were sitting in a convertible."

CORRESPONDENCE ends **-ence**. When you have finished writing your correspond*ence*, you put it in an *en*velope.

COWARD, like *backward*, ends with **-ward**. Cowards are those who run back*wards* when the battle begins.

CRATER ends **-ter**, not *-tor*. A crater is a bowl-shaped depression in the *ter*rain.

CRATER in the TERRAIN

CRITICISM ends *-cism*. Sometimes criticism arises because the **critic is m**ad at someone.

CRITIC IS MAD
CRITIC IS M

CROCODILE is spelled with an *o* in the middle. Picture a crocodile with a **cod** inside of it.

CRO**COD**ILE

CUPBOARD. Don't be misled by its pronunciation. A *cupboard* is simply a **board**, or cabinet, where **cup**s are stored.

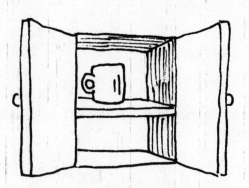

A **CURRANT** is a sweet, raisin-like fruit that might attract **ants**. Curr*ent* is the spelling of *every* other use.

```
CURRANT     CURRENT
   N            V
   T            E
   S            R
                Y
                T
                H
                I
                N
                G

                E
                L
                S
                E
```

CYMBALS are brass discs banged together to make a crashing sound during the **ban**d concert.

SYMBOLS are Significant images, or Signs, such as one finds in a *book*.

```
CYMBAL        SYMBOL
  R   BAND      I   BOOK
  A             G
  S             N
  H
```

D

DEFENSE is spelled with an **s**, not a *c*. Think of *defense* as keeping things *s*afe and *s*ound. (Actually, the British spell defense with a *c*, but they can write their own spelling books.)

DEFEN**S**E
　　　A
　　　F
　　　E

DELEGATE begins *dele-*, not *dela-*. The word **leg** appears in the center of de*leg*ate. Picture a convention of long-*leg*ged basketball players.

DEMAGOGUE begins *dema-*, not *demo-*. The word **agog** appears in the middle of dem*agog*ue. Think of a crowd all *agog* at some demagogue's spell-binding oration.

DEPENDENT ends *-dent*, not *-dant*. Children are called depen**dent**s because they put a major *dent* in the family budget.

DESCENDANT ends *-ant*. The opposite of descend**ant** is **an**cestor, both words containing *an*.

ANCESTOR
DESCEND**ANT**

DESCEND**ANT**

> **DISCREET** means "careful, discerning." *Discreet* people, those who are careful, are at ease together, so keep those *e*'s together in *discreet*.
>
> **DISCRETE** means "separate" or "distinct," so let's do what the word says and keep the **e**'s separate in discr**e**t**e**.

DISILLUSIONMENT. *Disillusion* originally meant to lose one's illusions. Remember that there is an **illusion** in the middle of dis*illusion*ment.

DISSECT has two **s**'s, as if the *s* itself were di*s*sected.

DISTURBANCE ends *-ance*. Notice there is a **turban** in the middle of dis*turban*ce.

DISTURBANCE

DIVIDE begins **di**- not *de*-. Think of a letter *i* that gets di*v*ided by a sharp edged *v*.

DUEL / DUAL. *Duel* with an **e** is a fight between two enemies. *Dual* with an **a** is used for all other references to two of something.

```
DUEL        DUAL
  N           L
  E           L
  M
  I           O
  E           T
  S           H
              E
              R
```

E

ELEGANT. The first vowel, the *e*, is easy, but the other two vowels are often switched around. Remember that *elegant* is another *-ant* word, this time an **ant** with its **leg** in front.

E LEG ANT

ELICIT / ILLICIT. To *elicit* is to draw out or **e**voke something; *illicit* is something **i**mproper or **i**llegal.

E L I C I T
V O K E

ILL I C I T
E G A L

EMIGRATE is to **ex**it from a country, to migrate out.

IMMIGRATE is to migrate **in**to a country.

*Em*igrate has one **m**; *imm*igrate has two. Think of the *m*'s as *m*igrants. In the U.S. there are at least twice as many people trying to get **in**to the country as there are trying to **ex**it, so the two *m*'s go with the immigrants.

EMPHASIZE ends in -**size**, a good way to empha*size* a point.

ENDORSE begins with an *e*, not an *i*. Remember that you en-dorse a check by writing your name on the back at one **end**.

ENTERPRISE also begins with an *e*, not an *i*, and ends *-se*, not *-ze*. An **enter**prise often involves *enter*ing into the business of *se*lling.

ENTER INTO **SE**LLING

ENTER PRI **SE**

ENTOURAGE has both an *o* and a *u*. Notice the word **tour** in the middle. A performer's en*tour*age consists of the people who go on *tour* with him or her.

ENVIRONMENT has the word **iron** in it, just as the mineral *iron* exists in our natural env*iron*ment.

EQUATOR ends **-tor**, not *-ter*. Mapmakers call the hot region around the equator the *Torr*id Zone.

EQUA**TOR**

TORRID ZONE

-ERY VS. **-ARY.** One way to tell whether a word ends *-ery* or *-ary* is to ask if the word is related to an occupation, naming a kind of work**er**.

A BAK**ER** bakes bread at a BAK**ERY**.

A BIND**ER** binds books at a BIND**ERY**.

A GROC**ER** sells food at a GROC**ERY**.

A HOSI**ER** sells hose (stockings) called HOSI**ERY**.

EVAPORATION is the process of a liquid turning to **vapor**, so it should come as no surprise that *vapor* is in the middle of e*vapor*ation.

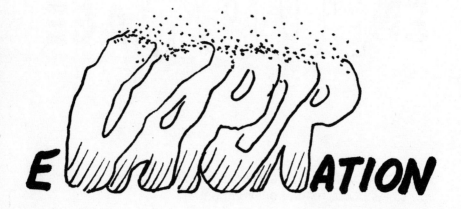

EXALT / EXULT. *Exalt* means elevating someone or something, holding them up for praise or esteem. The **-alt** ending comes from the same root as *alt*itude, or height. *Exult*, which ends **-ult**, means to rejoice in a lively way, as if you've experienced the *ult*imate thrill in life.

EX**ALT**   EX**ULT**

ALTITUDE   **ULT**IMATE THRILL

EXULT

EXCELLENT has two *l*'s followed by an *e*. The name **Ellen** appears in the middle of the word. Notice, however, that *Ellen* is also in the middle of rep*ellen*t! Think, "*Ellen* has invented an exc*ellen*t insect rep*ellen*t."

EXC**ELLEN**T   REP**ELLEN**T

EXERCISE ends *-se*, not *-ce*. Associate the **s** with the *sweat* that often goes with exercise.

EXERCI **S** E
W
E
A
T

EXPENSE ends -*se*, not -*ce*. Think of the *s* as a dollar sign (**$**) with which expenses are measured.

EXPEN$E

EXTRAORDINARY. Though the *a* gets lost in pronunciation, *extraordinary* is simply **extra ordinary**, out of the ordinary.

F

FAMILIAR. Don't forget that second *i*. *Familiar* ends with the word **liar**.

FAMI**LIAR**

FARCE has a **c**, not an **s**. A farce is a kind of *comedy*.

FAR**CE**
O
M
E
D
Y

FEBRUARY is sometimes pronounced without the first *r*, like *Febuary*. Remember to include both *r*'s, so that you can spell **brr** in the month of Fe*brr*uary.

FRIEND follows the "*i*- before -*e*" rule, and so ends with -*end*. A good fri**end** will stay with you to the very **end**.

FLUORESCENT does not begin like *flour*. (Would you want to eat bread that glows in the dark?) But it does have **ores** in the middle. Think of rock museums displaying mineral ores that glow in the dark.

FORTY is the age at which some people feel they have lost their youth. So lose the **U**th in *four* to make forty.

FOREWORD / FORWARD. A *foreword* is the preface in a book that comes be**fore** the **words** in the main text. *Forward* ends **-ward** like its opposite, back*ward*.

FORE	**WORD**	FOR**WARD**
BE**FORE** THE OTHER **WORDS**		BACK**WARD**

FORE- WORDS.   We use the word *before* in reference to time (She arrived *before* noon.) and in reference to space (He stood *before* the king.). If you are trying to figure out whether a word begins *for-* or *fore-*, first decide if either meaning of *before* is involved in the definition of the word you are trying to spell. If it is, begin the word with *fore-*.

BEFORE ("prior in time")

FORECAST	**FORE**SEEABLE
FOREFATHER	**FORE**SHADOW
FOREGONE	**FORE**THOUGHT
FORERUNNER	**FORE**WARN

BEFORE ("in front")

FOREARM	**FORE**HEAD
FOREHAND	**FORE**MAN

FOUL/FOWL. *Fowl* with a *w* refers to birds (such as an **owl**). *Foul* with a *u* refers to something **ou**t of **bou**nds, whether on the playing field or *out*side the *bou*nds of good taste.

FOWL FOUL

OWL OUT OF

BOUNDS

F OWL

FOUL
OUT OF
BOUNDS

FOUNTAIN ends **-ain**. The falling droplets of water from a fountain are almost like r*ain*.

FOUNT**AIN**

R**AIN**

"FUL" WORDS.   *Full* is a **full** word all by itself. But when attached, *full* is no longer **full**, since it loses an *l*.

art**ful**	**ful**fill
aw**ful**	**ful**some
beauti**ful**	help**ful**
cup**ful**	right**ful**
dread**ful**	wonder**ful**

G

GARBAGE is spelled with **bag** in it, like when the gar*bage* over-flows the *bag*.

GAR**BAG**E

GAUGE begins *ga-*, not *gu-*. One may find a **gauge** attached to a **ga**dget, and the spelling of the two starts out the same way.

GAUGE

GADGET

GENEALOGY. Though it's pronounced like all those other studies ending in *-ology,* genealogy has *al* in the middle, not *ol*. Think of researching your family tree, and don't forget to include Uncle **Al**.

GOVERNMENT. The *n* sometimes gets lost in pronunciation. Still, a government has a responsibility to gover*n*.

GOVER**N**MENT

GOVER**N**

GRAMMAR ends **-mar**. Remember that a *ram* bumps *ma* in the middle of g*ram*m*a*r.

G RAM MA R

GUARD begins **gu-**, not *ga-*. Remember that a *gu*ard sometimes carries a *gu*n, and the two words begin the same way.

GUARD

GUN

H

HAMBURGER is spelled *burg*, not *berg*. Notice the word **urge** in the middle of hamb*urge*r. People often have an *urge* for a hamb*urge*r.

HANGAR/HANGER. A hanger for clothes is spelled just the way it sounds. But a hangar for airplanes ends **-gar**. You can remember that by thinking of a han*gar* as a *gar*age for airplanes.

HAN**GAR**

GARAGE for AIRPLANES

HARBOR ends -*bor*, not -*ber*. Remember that a har**bo**r is for **bo**ats.

HAR**BOR**

BOATS

HEIGHT ends with the word **eight**. A person who is *eight* feet tall certainly has h*eight*.

I

IDLE / IDOL. Being id**le**, not engaged in any activity, may be associated with **le**thargy, lack of energy. An id**ol**, an image of a god, is associated with **ol**d deities and **ol**d religions.

ID**LE**   ID**OL**

    LETHARGY   **OL**D RELIGIONS

IMPLY / INFER. When an author or speaker **imp**lies something, a hidden meaning is *imp*lanted. When a reader or listener in**fer**s something, he or she *fer*rets out the meaning of what someone else has said.

IMPLY

IMPLANTED BY THE AUTHOR

IN**FER**

    FERRETED OUT BY THE READER

IMPRUDENT ends *-ent*, not *-ant*. Notice the word **rude** in imp*rude*nt. Being *rude* is usually imp*rude*nt.

INCENSE ends *-se*, not *-ce*. Incense is fragrant smoke.

E
K
O
M
INCENSE

INCUMBENT ends with the word **bent**. Think of politicians who have been in office so long that they are decrepit and *bent* over.

INCUM**BENT**

INCUM**BENT**

INDEBTED contains an unsounded *b*. One usually becomes indebted by **borrowing** something.

```
INDEBTED
       O
       R
       R
       O
       W
       I
       N
       G
```

INDISPENSABLE ends with **-sable**. Picture a wealthy couple who simply couldn't live without their *sable* furs.

INDULGENT ends **-gent**. Picture an aristocratic *gent* who is very indul*gent*.

INDUL**GENT**

INNOVATION is spelled just like the two words **inn** and **ovation**. Think of a fine hotel or *inn*, with all the latest innovations, which earns an *ovation* from its guests.

INTERRUPT has two *r*'s. Notice the word **err** in the middle. If you int*err*upt someone, you *err* in etiquette.

INTERVENE ends **-ene**. An *n* interv*en*es between the last two *e*'s.

INTIMATE ends *-mate*. A person you are inti**mate** with is your **mate**.

-IS / -ES ENDINGS.   We all know that **this** refers to something singular and **these** to something plural. In other words as well, *-is* endings are singular and *-es* endings are plural.

TH**IS**	TH**ES**E
THES**IS**	THES**ES**
ANALYS**IS**	ANALYS**ES**
HYPOTHES**IS**	HYPOTHES**ES**
NEUROS**IS**	NEUROS**ES**

ITS/IT'S. The confusion between these two words produces a common misspelling.

It's is the contraction of **it is**. The apostrophe stands for a missing letter, just as it does in *don't, shouldn't,* or *you're*.

Its is the possessive form of **it**. Just as *his* and *hers* do not have apostrophes, neither should *its*.

K

KNOWLEDGE is spelled like the two words **know** and **ledge**. *Knowledgeable* is spelled like the three words **know**, **ledge**, and **able**.

KNOWLEDGEABLE = **KNOW** THE **LEDGE**
IS AVOID**ABLE**

L

LABEL ends -*el*. Think of a la*bel* with **abe** in the middle.

LABOR ends in -**or**. Lab*or* is another word for w*ork*.

LAB**OR**

W**OR**K

LABORATORY has four vowels. Think of a **lab orator**, speaking to his fellow scientists. (And if you can't remember how to spell or*at*or, look for the *rat* inside.)

LAB**ORATOR**Y

LESSEN / LESSON. To make something less is to **lessen** it—*less* + *-en*. A **lesson** is something you might teach your **son**.

LETTUCE ends **-uce**. Lett*uce* is one kind of prod*uce*.

LETT**UCE**

PROD**UCE**

LIBRARY has two *r*'s. Think of a library with a **ra** in the middle.

LICENSE ends *-se*, not *-ce*. In most states, **s**ixteen is the age one can acquire a driver's license.

LICEN**S**E

I

X

T

E

E

N

LIEUTENANT. This word can be creatively misspelled in any number of ways. Visualize an ant lieutenant ordering ten young recruits to hit the dirt. He is barking to ten dazed ant privates, **"Lie, u ten ants!"**

LITERATURE. The preferred pronunciation of this word includes all four syllables: lit-er-a-ture. Note the **era** in the middle. Many classic works of lit*era*ture take us to another *era*.

$$LIT^{ERA}TURE$$

LONELINESS. Don't forget that first *e*. *Loneliness* begins with the word **lone**. A *lone* survivor might well experience *lone*liness.

LONELINESS

LONE SURVIVOR

LOOSE with two *o*'s is the opposite of *tight* or *bound*. *Lose* with one *o* is the opposite of *find* or *win*. **Loose** rhymes with m**oose** and ends with the same letters. Just remember, "The m*oose* is l*oose*!"

M

MANAGER is spelled like **man** and **ager**. Being a manager can be a job that makes one old before his time—that is, a real *man ager*.

MAN**AGER**

MANTEL / MANTLE. A *mantel*, ending **-el**, is a she*l*f over a fireplace. The *mantle* you wear ends with **e**, like the cape that it is.

```
MANTEL                    C
     SHELF                A
                          P
              MANTLE
```

MANUAL / MANUEL. *Manual*, ending **-al**, refers to the hand, either hand labor or a handbook. *Manuel*, ending **-el**, is the hispanic name, *el nombre hispanico*.

```
         H
MANUAL       MANUEL
         N       El nombre
         D
```

MARRIAGE. Don't forget the **i**. The *y* in *marry* turns to *i* in *marriage*. Remember, mar**ri**age should never end in *rage*!

MATERIAL / MATERIEL. *Materiel*, ending **-el**, refers to the *equipment* of an organization. It is most often used in reference to military weapons and supplies. *Material*, the more general word, is used for **all** other meanings.

```
MATERIEL        MATERIAL
        Q           ALL OTHER USES
        U
        I
        P
        M
        E
        N
        T
```

MAXIMUM / MINIMUM. Both words end with -**mum**.

MAXI**MUM**   MINI**MUM**

MEAGER includes **eager**. Think of store clerks whose m*eager* salaries make them *eager* for a raise.

MEDAL / METAL / MEDDLE. A *medal* with a **d** is a *d*isk to *d*ecorate *d*oers of *d*istinguished *d*eeds. *Metals* are mineral elements such as *t*in, copper, gold, and the like. *Meddle* is a verb—to intrude into the mi*dd*le of someone else's business.

```
MEDAL      METAL      MEDDLE = get into the
  E          I        MIDDLE
  C          N
  O
  R          E
  A          T
  T          C
  I
  V
  E

  D
  I
  S
  K
```

MEDALLION has one *d* and two *l*'s, like the two words **medal** and **lion**.

MEDIEVAL contains the word **die** in the middle. The plague and the crusades caused many people to *die* in the middle of the me*die*val era.

ME**DIE**VAL

DIE

MEMENTO begins **mem**-, not *mom*-. A *mem*ento helps you re-*mem*ber an important occasion.

MEMENTO

R**EMEMB**ER

MENACE is spelled like the two words **men** and **ace**. Think of the *menace* that would occur if all the *men* playing poker have *aces*.

MINER / MINOR. A miner is a digg*er* in a mi*ne*. A mi-nor is someone who is *not* very old.

```
        D
        I
        G
        G
MINER   ER      MINOR
        R               OL
                        TD
```

MINOR **MINER**

MISSPELL has two *s*'s. Don't mi*ss* that second *s* in misspell.

MOSQUITOES. The preferred spelling ends *-es*. Mosqui**toes** keep you on your *toes*.

MOSQUI**TOES**

MOTOR ends **-or**. A mo*tor* produces *torque*.

MO**TOR**

TORQUE

MOUNTAIN ends **-ain** just like its opposite, the pl*ain*.

MOUNT**AIN**

PL**AIN**

MUSCLE. You can remember the spelling of this word if you've ever seen a T-shirt worn by athletes at the University of Southern California (USC).

N

NAVAL / NAVEL. Nava*l*, ending **-al**, refers to ships and sailors, like nautica*l*. Nave*l* ending **-el**, refers to the be*l*ly button.

NAVAL	NAVEL
NAUTIC**AL**	B**E**LLY BUTTON

NAVAL'S NAVEL

NORMAL ends *-al*. It's spelled like the names **Norm** and **Al**.

NUCLEAR. Despite its common mispronunciation (NUKE-u-ler), *nuclear* is pronounced *NU-klee-er* and spelled like un**clear** with the first two letters reversed.

It is UN**CLEAR** to many whether or not

   NU**CLEAR** power is the energy of the future.

O

OBSCENE. Someone who is ob**scene** may end up creating quite a *scene*.

OFFENSE, like defense, ends *-se,* not *-ce*. In sports, the offense usually tries to **score** point**s**.

```
OFFENSE   P
      C   O
      O   I
      R   N
      ET  T
       S
```

OPPRESSION. Unlike *depress* and *repress*, *oppress* has two *p*'s, not one. Think of **oppression** as *persistent persecution*.

```
O P P R E S S I O N
  E E
  R R
  S S
  I E
  S C
  T U
  E T
  N I
  T O
      N
```

An **ORNAMENT** has a **name** inside.

P

A **PAGODA** has **a god** in the middle.

PARISH / PERISH. A **par**ish is a church community served by a *par*son or priest. To **per**ish, or be "wiped out," is to be *er*adicated.

PARISH   **PER**ISH

PARSON   **ER**ADICATED

PASSED / PAST. Passed is any action of passing which has already occurred. Past is a reference to *tense* or to *times* gone by. "In the pa*st* week Congress pa*ss*ed three bills."

PASSED =

ACT OF **PASS**ING WHICH ALREADY OCCURRED

PASTENSE
IME
GONEBY

IN THE **PAST** HE
PASSED THE BALL

PATIENCE / PATIENTS. Patience is the trait of *calm* endurance. Pati**ents** are the clie*nts* of a doctor or dentist. Patie*nts* at a clinic must often have patie*nce*.

```
P A T I E N C E        PATIENT
          A N          CLIENT
          L D
          M U
            R
            A
            N
            C
            E
```

PENALTY. Imagine a player named **Al** in the middle of the pena*l*ty box.

PERMANENT has an *a* in the middle and an *e* in the last syllable. Notice the **mane** in the middle of a per*mane*nt.

PERSONAL / PERSONNEL. *Personnel* refers to the people working for a particular company, or to their names on a list. *Personal* refers to *all* other uses relating to a person.

```
P E R S O N N E L   PERSONAL
          A M I           ALL OTHER USES
          M P S
          E L T
          S O
            Y
          O E
          N E
```

PHENOMENON ends with the three words **no men on**. A baseball pitcher is considered a phenomenon if there are *no men on* base during an entire game.

PHONY has no *e*. It is spelled like **pony** with an added **h**. Think of a *p*hony pony.

PIGEON is spelled like the words **pig** and **eon**. Visualize, if you must, a *pig* who after an *eon* evolves into a *pigeon*.

PILGRIM ends -*im*. Imagine a pil**grim** enduring a *grim* winter in a new land.

GRIM
PIL**GRIM**

PILLAR ends **-ar**. A pill*ar* is a component of *ar*chitecture.

> PILL**AR**
> **AR**CHITECTURE

PLAYWRIGHTS may *write* and their dramas may be all *right*. But they are named **wrights** because they shape and fashion their works as do wheel*wrights* and cart*wrights*. The same verb—*wright*—gives us *wrought*, something fashioned with effort into a particular shape.

> WHEEL**WRIGHT**   PLAY**WRIGHT**

POLAR ends *-ar*. Pol*ar* bears and other pol*ar* things are associated with the *ar*ctic.

> POL**AR**
> **AR**CTIC

POPULAR ends *-lar*, not *-ler*. To be popu*lar* means you have a *lar*ge fan club.

POPU**LAR**

LARGE FAN CLUB

POTATOES and **TOMATOES** both have **toes**!

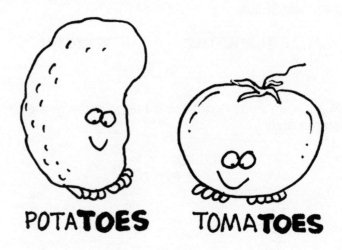

POTA**TOES**   TOMA**TOES**

PRAY / PREY. To pray involves *asking* God for something. Prey involves *hunting* and *killing* something to *eat*.

PRAY	PREY
S	A
K	T
I	I
N	N
G	G

PRECEDENT derives from precede, that which comes earlier.

PRESIDENT, the one who steers an institution, derives from preside.

```
P R E C E D E N T        P R E S I D E N T
      A A                      T N
      M R                      E S
      E L                      E T
        I                      R I
        E                      S T
        R                        U
                                 T
                                 I
                                 O
                                 N
```

PREPARATION is the act of preparing. It retains the middle a in prepare.

```
        PREPARATION
        PREPARE
```

PRETENSE ends -se, not -ce. A pretense is basically a sham.

```
        PRETENSE
             H
             A
             M
```

PRINCIPAL / PRINCIPLE.   *Principle* is a noun referring to some fundamental ru*le*, law, or standard of conduct such as moral princip*les*. **All** other uses, whether nouns or adjectives, are spelled *principal*, referring to someone or something of first importance: a school princip*al*; princip*al* parts; princip*als* in a business deal; the princip*al* on a loan.

PRINCIP**LE**   PRINCIP**AL**

RU**LE**   **AL**L OTHER USES

PRINCIPAL's PRINCIPLE

PROFESSOR has one **f** and two **s**'s. A professor should pro*fess* to know his or her field.

PURSUE is spelled like **purse** with an extra **u** added. *"U"* might *pursue* a *purse*-snatcher.

R

RASPBERRY is spelled as if each berry were a **rasp**.

RASPBERRY

RECOMMEND is simply *re-* + *commend*. If you have commended someone's work, you can *re*commend him or her to other employers.

REHEARSAL has *hear* in the middle. A conductor re**hear**ses a symphony orchestra so that he or she can **hear** how it sounds.

RE**HEAR**SAL

REINDEER is just the two words **rein** and *deer*. Santa puts *reins* on this kind of deer to have them pull his sl*ei*gh.

R**EI**NDEER

SL**EI**GH

REMINISCENT could be the title of an unusual memo—**re: mini scent**.

RE **MINI'SCENT**

RENOWN may be short-lived in today's world. Famous today, forgotten tomorrow, as the word *renown* reminds us with *now* in the middle.

RE**NOW**N

REPETITION does what it says. First there is a repetition of **e**'s, then a repetition of **i**'s.

R**E**P**E**T**I**T**I**ON

Your **RESIDENCE** is where you **reside**.

RESIDENCE

RESIDE

RESTAURANT has the word **aura** in the middle. A popular restaurant usually has a special atmosphere or *aura* about it.

The **REVEREND** is one whom the people of the church **revere**. But if the sermon goes on too long, the congregation may remember that *reverend* also rhymes with *never end*.

R**EVER**E

R**EVER**END

NEVER END

RIDICULOUS begins *ri-*, not *re-*. **Rid**iculous notions are ones you want to get *rid* of.

RODENT ends **-dent**. A ro*dent* can put a *dent* in the cheese.

ROTOR, like motor, ends **-tor**, not *-ter*. The ro*tor* in a mo*tor* produces *tor*que.

ROTOR

TORQUE

MOTOR

S

A **SACRILEGIOUS** person is "not religious," and *sacrilegious* is not spelled like *religious* either, because the *e* and *i* are reversed. Notice the word **rile** in the middle. A sac*rile*gious remark will *rile* the devout.

SAC**RILE**GIOUS

SANDAL ends -*al*. After wearing sand*al*s, you may find sand **all** over your feet.

SAND**AL**

SAND **ALL** OVER YOUR FEET

SATELLITE has one *t* and two *l*'s. Sate*ll*ite has the word **tell** in the middle. From its orbit high in space, a sa*tell*ite can *tell* us much more about the world.

SCARED / SCARRED. *Scared* (afraid) has one *r*. *Scarred* has two. After you've been scared once, you may be scarred for life.

SECRETARY begins with the word **secret**. A good secretary is discreet with confidential information and knows how to keep a *secret*.

Both **SEGREGATION** and **CONGREGATION** have a fellow named **Greg** in the middle.

SE**GREG**ATION   CON**GREG**ATION

In **SEPARATE,** the two *a*'s separate the two **e**'s. Remember, there's **a rat** in sep*arate*.

SHEPHERD ends **-herd**, which makes sense because a shep-*herd* looks after a *herd* of sheep.

SLAUGHTER. As strange as it is, s*laughter* is actually **laughter** with an **s** at the beginning.

SOLAR ends **-ar**. For no good reason, many adjectives referring to heavenly bodies end *-ar* (like st*ar*).

ST**AR**
SOL**AR**
LUN**AR**
STELL**AR**
PLANET**AR**Y

SOLDER. Don't forget the I, even though this word is pronounced *sodder*. Remember, *solder* is used to make a joint or connection *solider*.

SOL DER

SOLIDER

SOLDIER ends *-ier*. Notice the word **die** in the middle. A sol*dier* risks having to *die* in battle.

SOVEREIGN ends **-reign**. A sove*reign* is one who *reigns*.

SOVE**REIGN**

STAKE / STEAK.   A steak is to *eat*, while a **stake** is a stick to *stabilize* a tent or to *stab* a vampire.

STEAK   STAKE

EAT   STABILIZE

STAB

STALACTITE / STALAGMITE. These cave formations which look like petrified icicles may not come up in conversation everyday, but do you remember which is which? Every self-respecting person should know that *stalac*tites, spelled with *ct*, hang from the *c*eiling, or *t*op, while *stalag-m*ites, with *gm*, rise up from the *g*round in cone-like *m*ounds.

```
S T A L A C T I T E S     S T A L A G M I T E S
          E O                         R O
          I P                         O U
          L                           U N
          I                           N D
          N                           D S
          G
```

> **STATIONARY / STATIONERY.** *Stationary* means "anchored," moving **nary** an inch. *Stationery* is pap**er** purchased from a station**er**, a supplier of pap**er** and office supplies.
>
> STATIO**NARY**   STATION**ER**Y
>
> **NARY** AN INCH   PAP**ER**

THE **STATIONERY** WASN'T **STATIONARY**

SURGEON ends with the two words **urge** and **on**. Think of a weary surgeon who must *urge on* his or her medical team after performing surgery all through the night.

SUSPENSE ends *-se*, not *-ce*. When you think of suspense, think of a movie or book with a *scary ending.*

```
S U S P E N S E
        C N
        A D
        R I
        Y N
          G
```

T

TEMPERAMENT.   Don't forget the *a*. Note the word **ram** in the middle. Someone with a fiery temperament might actually *ram* those who get in the way.

TEMPE**RAM**ENT

THE SUMMER OF OUR DISCON**TENT.** You can remember the endings of some words by thinking of them happening to or near a **tent**.

INCOMPE**TENT**   INADVER**TENT**

PENI**TENT**   CO-EXIS**TENT**

DISC ON TENT

THERE / THEIR / THEY'RE. All three begin **the-**, so everyone should get the first three letters right. It's the endings that are commonly confused.

—*The**re*** ends just like he*re*, another pronoun of location.

—*Thei**r*** ends with an *r* just like other possessives, you*r*, he*r*, and ou*r*.

—*They**'re*** ends just like other contractions: yo*u're* = you are; we*'re* = we are.

THERE

THEIR

THEY'RE

THERE	THEIR	THEY**'RE** (they are)
HERE	YOUR	YOU**'RE** (you are)
	HER	WE**'RE** (we are)

TOURNAMENT begins with the words **tour** and **name**. Sponsors of a major tennis or golf *tournamen*t hope to attract every big *name* on the *tour*.

TOUR**NAME**NT

TRAGEDY.   In the middle of every **trage**dy, whether theatrical or real-life, there is always some *rage*.

TRAGEDY

U

UPHOLSTERY has a **holster** in the middle. Think of cowboy's chair decorated with guns and holsters.

UP**HOLSTER**Y

V

VICE / VISE. Vice with a *c* stands for two very different (we hope) concepts. One is for **vic**arious (in place of) representatives (*vice* president, *vice*roy). The other is for **c**orrupt practices.

Vise with an **s** describes a device for *squeezing* or holding something so it won't move.

VILLAIN ends *-ain*. A stereotypical vill**ain** loves to cause p**ain**.

VILL**AIN**

P**AIN**

W

WAGON is spelled like the two words **wag** and **on**. Think of a little girl in her wagon commanding her dog to *"wag on!"*

WAGON

WAILS / WALES / WHALES. All three sound alike and all start with a **w**. Drop the *w* and you can remember which is which.

- A child w**ails** when he or she *ails*.

- In W**ales** one can drink traditional British *ales*.

- W**hales** are an endangered species; we have to work to keep them *hale* and hearty.

WAILS   WALES   WHALES
  AILS   ALES   HALE & HEARTY

WARE / WEAR / WHERE. Here are three more words that sound alike and begin with **w**. Again, drop the *w* and find your clues.

- W**are**s are *ar*ticles for sale.

- W**ear** goes with t*ear* in the phrase *wear and tear*, and both end *-ear*.

- The question "w**here**?" can be answered "*here*."

WARES   **WEAR** &   **WHERE**
  ARTICLES   **TEAR**   **HERE**

WELFARE has only one *l*. Note that **elf** in the middle and think of a little fellow who has hit upon hard times.

Appendix: Patterns of Spelling in American English

It is difficult to learn spelling by the "rules," because there are so many rules and so many exceptions. What is offered here is an overview of the more reliable rules, some of the more predictable spelling regularities of American English.

1. *I* before *E*...

The great and famous spelling rule is

> *i* before *e*
> except after *c*
> or when sounded like *ay*
> as in *neighbor* and *weigh*

This one works for many common words like f*ie*ld, n*ie*ce, rece*i*ve, and ce*i*ling. The rule even works for some more unusual words like sl*ei*gh and chow m*ei*n. But there are a number of qualifications and exceptions.

    a. The rule applies only when the *c* is sounded like *see*. When the *c* is sounded as *sh*, the letters that follow are *ie*, not *ei*. Note, for example, effic*ie*nt, profic*ie*nt, and anc*ie*nt. Sc*ie*nce is also spelled *ie*, because again the *c* is not sounded *see*.

    b. The "*i* before *e*..." rule applies after a *see* sound, even when the letter *c* is not actually present: s*ei*ze, s*ei*zure.

c. These words are spelled *ei* even though they do not come after a *see* sound and are not sounded *ay*.

caff*ei*ne	h*ei*ght
cod*ei*ne	l*ei*sure
counterf*ei*t	n*ei*ther
*ei*ther	prot*ei*n
forf*ei*t	sover*ei*gn
h*ei*fer	w*ei*rd

d. These words follow a *see*-sound, yet are spelled *ie*.

fanc*ie*r   financ*ie*r   s*ie*ge

2. -CEDE/-CEED/-SEDE

There are scores of verbs that end with the sound *seed*. All of these are spelled *-cede* except for these four:

Three *-seed* verbs end *-ceed*.

suc*ceed*   ex*ceed*   pro*ceed*

Only one *-seed* verb ends *-sede*.

super*sede*.

3. -IFY/-EFY

There are likewise a great number of verbs ending *-ify*. Only four end *-efy*.

lique*fy*	rare*fy*
putre*fy*	stupe*fy*

4. -ND becomes -NSE

When a verb ends *-nd*, some of the words derived from it will substitute *s* for *d*:

defe*nd*	→	defe*nse*
expa*nd*	→	expa*nsive*
offe*nd*	→	offe*nse*
prete*nd*	→	prete*nse*
suspe*nd*	→	suspe*nse*ful

5. -DGE ENDINGS

Words ending *-dge* drop the *e* before adding *-ment*.

abri*dge*	→	abri*dgment*
acknowle*dge*	→	acknowle*dgment*
ju*dge*	→	ju*dgment*

6. -ABLE/-IBLE

There are more words ending *-able* than *-ible*, so if it comes to a coin toss, choose *-able*. Generally, *-able* is added to words that could stand alone without a suffix.

agree	→	agree*able*
break	→	break*able*
depend	→	depend*able*
predict	→	predict*able*

-able also follows word stems ending *i*: appreci-*able*, reli-*able*, soci-*able*.

The ending *-ible* is usually added to word parts that could not stand alone without the suffix.

aud	+	ible	=	aud*ible*
cred	+	ible	=	cred*ible*
feas	+	ible	=	feas*ible*
vis	+	ible	=	vis*ible*

Normally, when adding *-able* to a word ending in *-e*, one drops the *e*:

desire	+	*able*	=	desir*able*
pleasure	+	*able*	=	pleasur*able*
use	+	*able*	=	us*able*

7. HARD *C*/SOFT *C*

The letter *c* can be sounded like a *k* (*cash*) or like an *s* (*city*). These are called "hard *c*" and "soft *c*," respectively.

However, if a word ends "soft *c* + *e*," retain the *e* before *-able* (to retain the "soft *c*" sound).

noti*ce*	noti*ceable*
pea*ce*	pea*ceable*
servi*ce*	servi*ceable*

Word stems ending with a "hard *c*" sound take the *-able* suffix.

appli*cable*

despi*cable*

impla*cable*

8. HARD G/SOFT G

Like the letter *c*, *g* can be sounded as a "hard *g*" (*gate*) or "soft *g*" (*gentleman*). The spelling rules regarding hard *g*/soft *g* are similar to those concerning hard *c*/soft *c*.

Words ending "soft *g* + *e*" retain the *e* before adding *-able* or *-ous* (to retain the "soft *g*" sound).

change	→ chan*geable*	advantage	→ advanta*geous*
knowledge	→ knowled*geable*	courage	→ coura*geous*
manage	→ mana*geable*	outrage	→ outra*geous*

Word stems ending "hard *g*" add *-able*:

indefati*gable*   navi*gable*

Soft *g* may also be followed by *-ible* endings:

eli*gible*	negli*gible*
intelli*gible*	tan*gible*

9. *C ENDINGS*

Words ending in *c* add a *k* (to retain the "hard *c*" sound) before adding a suffix.

bivouac	→ bivoua*cked*
frolic	→ froli*cking*
panic	→ pani*cking*
shellac	→ shella*cked*

10. *Y/EY*

In forming plurals, a final *y* preceded by a consonant is usually re-placed by *ie* before adding *s*.

baby → bab*ies*
caddy → cadd*ies*
poppy → popp*ies*

But if the word ends -*ey*, simply add *s*.

alley → alle*ys*
attorney → attorne*ys*
chimney → chimne*ys*
valley → valle*ys*

(One exception here is money → mon*ies*.)

11. **PRIZE/-PRISE**

Prize ends -*ze*. But when part of another word, the ending is spelled -*prise*.

com*prise*   enter*prise*   sur*prise*

12. *N+NESS*

When adding -*ness* to a word already ending with an *n*, retain both *n*'s.

drunke*nness*   gree*nness*
eve*nness*   thi*nness*

Other books of similar interest from Random House Value Publishing:

GOOD GRAMMAR MADE EASY

DOS, DON'TS & MAYBES OF ENGLISH USAGE